MW00512287

Praise for the Previous Edition

"Crisply written, comprehensive and packed with examples, Mark Risjord's new *Philosophy of Social Science: A Contemporary Introduction* is a wonderful achievement. What is most remarkable is how deeply the philosophical account is embedded in and informed by contemporary empirical work in behavioral economics, evolutionary psychology, and cognitive science; to pull this off without sacrificing accessibility is something of a miracle. This is just what philosophy of social science should be and both teacher and student will benefit accordingly."

Lee McIntyre, *Boston University*

"This book is a rare accomplishment—it is comprehensive, judicious, and clear. It is comprehensive in its coverage of the central issues in the philosophy of social science and thorough in its treatment of the central responses to each of these issues. It is judicious in that it provides a careful and sympathetic exposition of the various positions and gives motivated ways of thinking about the relevant debate. It is clear, so that the reader is not unnecessarily tired by the dialectic. It reflects both traditional issues in the philosophy of social science and recent developments in the field. Both initiates and veteran investigators in the philosophy of science can benefit from reading it. It will provide a standard against which general texts in the philosophy of social science will be judged. I must say that I am very happy with the result, and I plan to use this book in my classes and recommend it to others."

David Henderson, *University of Nebraska, Lincoln*

Philosophy of Social Science

Philosophy of Social Science: A Contemporary Introduction examines perennial questions of philosophy through engaging the empirical study of society. Questions of normativity concern the place of values in social scientific inquiry. Questions of naturalism concern the relationship between the natural and the social sciences. And questions of reductionism ask how social institutions relate to the people who constitute them.

This accessible text offers a comprehensive overview of debates in the field, with special attention to new research programs. Topics include the relationship of social policy to social science, interpretive research, cognitive and evolutionary explanations, intentional action explanation, rational choice theory, conventions and social norms, joint intentionality, causal inference, and experimentation.

Detailed examples of social scientific research motivate the philosophical questions and illustrate the important concepts. Treating philosophical commitments as implicit in social science, students of the social sciences will benefit from its application of philosophical argument to methodological and theoretical problems. The text argues that social science transforms philosophical questions, and students of philosophy will benefit from its direct engagement with contemporary debates.

The Second Edition provides updates with the most recent literature and adds two new chapters: one on modeling and one on the role of race and gender in the social sciences.

Key Updates to the *Second Edition*:

- A new chapter on "Modeling and Explaining," which explores how models represent social systems and whether highly idealized models explain
- A new chapter on "Race and Other Social Constructions," capturing much of the recent empirical research and philosophical interest in the social construction of categories like race and gender
- Revised and updated chapters throughout, clarifying earlier presentations and bringing discussions from the *First Edition* into line with new research
- Updated annotated Further Reading lists, which now include relevant publications from 2013 to 2022.

Mark Risjord is Professor of Philosophy at Emory University in Atlanta, Georgia, USA, where he was awarded the Emory Williams Distinguished Teaching Award and the Excellence in Teaching Award, and he has served as the Masse-Martin/NEH Distinguished Teaching Chair.

ROUTLEDGE CONTEMPORARY INTRODUCTIONS TO PHILOSOPHY

Series editor:
Paul K. Moser
Loyola University of Chicago

This innovative, well-structured series is for students who have already done an introductory course in philosophy. Each book introduces a core general subject in contemporary philosophy and offers students an accessible but substantial transition from introductory to higher-level college work in that subject. The series is accessible to non-specialists and each book clearly motivates and expounds the problems and positions introduced. An orientating chapter briefly introduces its topic and reminds readers of any crucial material they need to have retained from a typical introductory course. Considerable attention is given to explaining the central philosophical problems of a subject and the main competing solutions and arguments for those solutions. The primary aim is to educate students in the main problems, positions and arguments of contemporary philosophy rather than to convince students of a single position.

Recently Published Volumes:

For a full list of published *Routledge Contemporary Introductions to Philosophy*, please visit www.routledge.com/Routledge-Contemporary-Introductions-to-Philosophy/book-series/SE0111

Philosophy of Social Science

A Contemporary Introduction

Second Edition

Mark Risjord

Routledge
Taylor & Francis Group

NEW YORK AND LONDON

Cover image: © Shutterstock

Second edition published 2023
by Routledge
605 Third Avenue, New York, NY 10158

and by Routledge
4 Park Square, Milton Park, Abingdon, Oxon, OX14 4RN

Routledge is an imprint of the Taylor & Francis Group, an informa business

© 2023 Taylor & Francis

First edition published by Routledge 2014

Library of Congress Cataloging-in-Publication Data
A catalog record for this book has been requested

ISBN: 978-1-032-07587-7 (hbk)
ISBN: 978-1-032-07586-0 (pbk)
ISBN: 978-1-003-20779-5 (ebk)

DOI: 10.4324/9781003207795

Typeset in Times New Roman
by Apex CoVantage, LLC

Contents

Figures

Acknowledgments

The philosophy of social science has changed significantly in recent decades, and meetings of the *Philosophy of Social Science Roundtable* have been midwife to many of those trends. Both this book and the field it represents are in debt to the original co-organizers of that annual event: James Bohman, Paul Roth, and Alison Wylie. They have also been mentors to many young scholars, and I hope this text reflects at least some of what they have taught me.

David Henderson, Kareem Khalifa, Harold Kincaid, Frank Lechner, Robert McCauley, Mark Ravina, Martin Paleček, Dan Reiter, Julian Reiss, Norman Risjord, Daniel Steel, Karsten Stueber, David Teira, and Stephen Turner provided invaluable feedback throughout the process. David Henderson was particularly helpful, working through several versions of the manuscript. A wonderful group of colleagues at Emory University have also been influential on my thinking; thank you to Sandra Dunbar, Nicholas Fotion, Ivan Karp, Cory Kratz, Jeffery Lesser, and Devin Stewart. Students in my classes at Emory University and the University of Hradec Králové also helped shape my presentation of the issues.

Research and writing were supported in part by the Fulbright Scholars Program. Special thanks to Hana Rambouskova, the staff at the Czech Fulbright Commission, and to the faculty and staff of the University of Hradec Králové for their generous welcome.

From its initial conceptualization, I intended this text to draw on a rich set of social scientific examples. This aspect of the project received a huge boost from Ian Kirby, who was able to work with me with the support of Emory College's SIRE Fellowship program. Many examples were fleshed out with Ian's research. Revision of the text was aided by Ian's excellent ear for the language. Thank you to Andrea Risjord for creating the illustrations.

A lesson of the philosophy of social science is that social structures are sometimes invisible to those who occupy them. Upon hearing that I was embarking on another book project, my daughter Hannah remarked, "So, will we be sliding food under your office door again?" I am confident that I don't fully comprehend the many ways in which my family has supported this work, but that doesn't prevent me from being deeply grateful for it. Thank you to Barbara, Andrea, Hannah, and the rest of the Risjord and Jacobsen clans.

Acknowledgments for the Second Edition. Over the last several years, I have had the pleasure of working closely on the philosophy of social science with a number of students and scholars. Discussions with them have shaped and updated my understanding, and those conversations are reflected in the changes and additions to the text. Kevin Cahill, David Henderson, Kareem Khalifa, Yuan Jihong, Jared Millson, Martin Palecek, Joe Rouse, Paul Roth, Preston Stovall, and Stephen Turner all deserve special mention and my deep thanks.

1 Introduction

1.1. What Is the Philosophy of Social Science?

Human nature is a social nature. Because the central questions of philosophy concern what it means to be human, philosophers have been thinking about the fundamental characteristics of society since antiquity. In the 19th century, anthropology, sociology, economics, and psychology broke away from philosophy. The central questions of the philosophy of social *science* arise with the birth of these empirical disciplines. While they distinguished themselves with new methods, their theories were continuous with those proposed by philosophers from Plato to Mill. The *philosophy* of social science examines some of the perennial questions of philosophy by engaging with the empirical study of human society.

The questions distinctive of the philosophy of the social sciences are encompassed within three broad themes: normativity, naturalism, and reductionism. The questions of normativity concern the place of values in social scientific inquiry. Social science is closely linked to social policy concerns, so can social science be objective? The social sciences also theorize about the origin and function of values, rules, and norms within human society. They thereby touch the foundation of ethics. The questions of naturalism concern the relationship between the natural and the social sciences. Must the social sciences emulate the successful methods of the natural sciences? Or are there dimensions of human society that require unique methods or kinds of theorizing? The questions of reductionism ask how social structures relate to the individuals who constitute them. Do churches have causal powers over and above those of their members? Or can all social-level correlations be explained in terms of individual beliefs, goals, and choices?

Ultimately, the questions of the philosophy of the social sciences are about our place in the universe. What is the source of value? How is human nature related to non-human nature? What can we know? Reflection on the social sciences therefore contributes to the fundamental inquiries of philosophy. The topics of this book are commonly discussed in theoretical and methodological writing in the social sciences. Therefore, reflection on these philosophical themes also contributes to the fundamental inquiries of the social sciences. The philosophy of the social sciences is an inherently interdisciplinary activity. When done well, it can advance both philosophy and the social sciences.

DOI: 10.4324/9781003207795-1

Throughout this book, we will tack back and forth between examples of social scientific research and philosophical argumentation. The examples will have two roles in our discussion. First, the examples illustrate how important philosophical questions are built into social scientific research. We will extract these questions and examine answers put forward by philosophers and social scientific theorists. Then—and this is the second role—we will use the examples as a testing ground for the philosophical views. Positions taken by philosophers ought to help us resolve the social scientific puzzles that gave rise to the questions in the first place. Let us begin, then, by looking at some examples of social scientific research. In the next section, we will elaborate on the issues of normativity, naturalism, and reductionism to which they give rise.

The Democratic Peace

Modern democracy emerged in the late 18th and early 19th century with increasing popular participation in voting and office-holding. The republics of France and the United States put decision-making power into the hands of elected representatives. Theorists postulated that the responsiveness of leaders to the will of the people would bring an end to war. Immanuel Kant, in an essay entitled "Perpetual Peace," argued this way:

> Now the republican constitution apart from the soundness of its origin, since it arose from the pure source of the concept of right, has also the prospect of attaining the desired result, namely, perpetual peace. And the reason is this. If, as must be so under this constitution, the consent of the subjects is required to determine whether there shall be war or not, nothing is more natural than that they should weigh the matter well, before undertaking such a bad business. For in decreeing war, they would of necessity be resolving to bring down the miseries of war upon their country.
>
> (Kant 1903 [1795], 121–2)

Kant's argument considers the rational course of action for a group of people who govern themselves. Since the costs of war are so high, it would be irrational for the citizens of a state to vote for war unless the situation was dire. Elected governments will, therefore, be reluctant to go war. As a philosophical argument, the reasoning seems sound. But we know from experience that people are not perfectly rational. So, it raises an interesting question: are democracies less likely to go to war? This question has been at the heart of an extensive social scientific literature. The evidence suggests that while democracies are not less warlike in general, they very rarely go to war against each other. Indeed, the correlation is so strong that some have proposed this "democratic peace" to be a law of the social sciences.

The democratic peace is one of many cases where philosophical positions and arguments have directly inspired social scientific research. You might think that this would permanently fix the philosophical assumptions of social scientific theories, but it doesn't. Kant's argument, for example, supposes that the free choices of the citizens determine whether a nation goes to war. If researchers hewed closely to Kant's presuppositions, they would look at why individuals voted or did not vote for war-mongering politicians. By contrast, many social scientists have examined whether particular kinds of government institutions cause or inhibit war. In other words, their philosophical assumption is the opposite of Kant's: the causes of war are found at the social level. Scientific research tends to be diverse in its assumptions, even when the question is as focused as the question of why democracies do not go to war with each other. Different answers appeal to distinct philosophical commitments. In this domain, the philosophical differences include disputes about whether human events can be explained by causal laws and whether communities exist over-and-above the individuals who compose them.

Azande Witchcraft

Anthropologists have long been fascinated with beliefs about supernatural agents. It is common for humans to see the world as populated by beings who can pass through solid walls or change from human to animal form. Very often, the beliefs seem to fly in the face of simple common sense. In a famous study of the Azande, an ethnic group of central Africa, E. E. Evans-Pritchard reported practices which seemed rather incoherent to him. Among the Azande, "witches" (Evans-Pritchard's translation) were people who had the power to cause misfortune. When someone suddenly fell ill and died, a witch might be responsible. When this happened, the family would demand retribution. To determine the identity of the responsible witch, the Azande had a practice of consulting oracles. Based on the oracles, they would perform "vengeance magic" to kill the witch. Incoherencies arise when there are multiple deaths and multiple oracles. Evans-Pritchard wrote:

> If it were known that the death of a man X had been avenged upon a witch Y then the whole procedure would be reduced to an absurdity because the death of Y is also avenged by his kinsmen upon a witch Z.
>
> (Evans-Pritchard 1937, 27)

Was Y a witch or not? According to X's kinsmen he was (because the oracle said so), and their vengeance magic killed him. According to Y's kinsmen he was an innocent man who was killed by witch Z, as proved by their oracle and vengeance magic. In practice, Evans-Pritchard notes, the oracles and vengeance magic are family secrets. This kept the contradiction from being exposed, but it hardly resolves the puzzle. We can see that the practice is self-contradictory in principle. Why didn't the Azande notice?

When Evans-Pritchard wrote about the Azande, anthropologists were in the midst of a debate about "primitive rationality." Some anthropologists of the 19th and early 20th century proposed that ways of thinking evolved. Groups like the Azande were still in an earlier stage of psychological evolution, where logic had not yet taken hold and magical thinking predominated. Others, including Evans-Pritchard, thought that the variety of human practices and beliefs now observable did not represent holdovers from an earlier period. All humans have the same intellectual abilities. Azande witchcraft looks puzzling to us only because we have not yet understood it. The problem is to properly understand the Azande. If the Azande understood their practice of vengeance magic as Evans-Pritchard did, they couldn't continue to practice it in good faith. If they practiced vengeance magic in good faith, Evans-Pritchard must have misunderstood it. How can we come to understand what "witchcraft" means to the Azande? These theoretical and methodological questions of anthropology can be asked in ways that are quite familiar to philosophers: how can I know the contents of another person's mind? Are all humans rational? And what does "rationality" amount to anyway?

Freedom Riders and Free Riders

Why did Rosa Parks refuse to give up her bus seat to a White passenger? When the bus driver ordered Rosa Parks and three other Black passengers to move, the others complied. No doubt they too were fed-up with the laws which humiliated them. But defying the driver's order carried a high risk of punishment. Everyone therefore had a strong motivation *not* to challenge the system of segregated seating on the busses of Montgomery, Alabama. Yet if all acted together, the laws would change. The Civil Rights Movement of the 1950s and 60s eventually succeeded only because enough people defied the punishments. Social movements and revolutions all face the same problem. From the point of view of everyone, there are substantial costs to participating. At the same time, everybody benefits if the system changes. The rational choice for everyone, then, is to sit on the side and let others pay the costs of participation. If the movement fails, the individual loses nothing; if it succeeds, those who gave up their seats benefit from it just as much as Rosa Parks did. Paradoxically, then, social movements and revolutions should never get started. Problems of the same form—what are sometimes called "free rider" problems—show up in several fields. In economics, it arises as the tragedy of the commons. In anthropology, it is the puzzle of how human cooperation could have evolved.

At least sometimes, revolutions and social moments succeed, people conserve public resources, and we cooperate altruistically. Free rider problems get solved, but how? Answers to this question encompass two deeply different conceptions of human nature. The classical liberal view treats humans as autonomous choosers, each person seeking their own best interest. Community is possible only when the incentives make actions beneficial to the group also beneficial to the individual. Systems of norms and laws can support social coordination, but they raise new questions. Why do people follow norms which are contrary to their self-interest? On the other side of the philosophical divide, communitarians see humans as fundamentally social and oriented toward each other. Identity with a group and its norms is integral to human life. On this side of the issue, questions of agency push to the fore. How can an individual decide that some social norms are *wrong* and act in ways that subvert the dominant cultural ethos? What force does a social norm have, and from where does it arise?

Philosophy in the Social Sciences

In each of these examples, concepts and questions of longstanding interest to philosophers are close to the surface. In pursuing their questions, social scientists take positions on matters which have deep roots: conceptions of human agency, rationality, epistemological justification, value, causation, and community. The philosophical task is to link the social scientific commitments to the larger literature in philosophy. After all, there have been some pretty smart people who have thought about these matters over the last 2,000 years or so. Awareness of the philosophical issues and the ability to critically evaluate the philosophical commitments of a theory or methodology can significantly sharpen social scientific inquiry. The flip side of the deep kinship of philosophy and the social sciences is that contemporary social scientists are developing answers to ancient philosophical problems. The thinkers who we now identify as philosophers drew on the social theories of their time. Today, we have a rich resource of empirical evidence and theory which bears directly on traditional philosophical questions. Just as there is philosophy in the social sciences, there is social theorizing in philosophy. The philosophy of social science tries to hold both up to critical scrutiny.

Before getting too far into our discussion, something needs to be said about the word *science*. As we will discuss presently, one of the big issues in the philosophy of the social sciences is whether inquiry into the social world is different from inquiry into the natural world. This issue is often framed as a debate over what counts as a "science." Many disciplines have seen fractious debates over whether the field should be thought of as "scientific." To some ears, speaking of "the philosophy of social *science*" is already to focus on a limited set of theories, methods, and questions. However, the question of how social inquiry is related to inquiry into the non-social world is not best approached by demarcating what is and is not science. Our questions are about the form and structure of inquiry into the social world, and it would beg the important questions to limit the possibilities at the outset. In this book, therefore, *social science* will be understood broadly as including all systematic empirical investigation into the activities of human beings, with a special interest in those things we do together, as parts of larger social groups. It explicitly includes methods like interviews and participant observation. And unless otherwise specified, *theory* is not restricted to talk of causes and laws. *Theory* includes all ways that social scientists formulate and express their results.

The question of what counts as a social science has a practical dimension too. What fields are included within the domain of the philosophy of the social sciences? These examples draw on anthropology, sociology, economics, and political science, but what about linguistics, psychology, and history? What about medicine, nursing, public health, criminology, educational studies, and business? Here again, we will take a broad and inclusive approach. There is a set of philosophical questions—to be outlined presently—which cut across theories and methodologies of all the disciplines we have mentioned and more. To be sure, there are also philosophical issues specific to disciplines. The fields of history, psychology, and economics support well-developed philosophical literatures. Indeed, the series of which this book is a part includes texts on the philosophy of economics (Reiss 2013b) and the philosophy of psychology (Bermudez 2005). This text will cleave to the issues common among all studies of human behavior and social interaction.

1.2. A Tour of the Philosophical Neighborhood

The discipline of philosophy is commonly divided into the domains of value theory, epistemology, and metaphysics. Value theory concerns issues about the source and justification of values, rules, and norms. What makes an act morally permissible or a painting good? Epistemology concerns human knowledge. What constitutes knowledge, and how is knowledge justified? Finally, metaphysics asks about the fundamental characteristics of the world. What are causes? Are humans free? What does it mean to be rational? It should be clear from the three examples introduced in Section 1.1 that the philosophy of social science draws on all three of these sub-fields. What, then, makes the philosophy of social science distinctive as a domain of inquiry within philosophy?

The answer provided so far is that the philosophical questions arise out of the practice of a collection of empirical disciplines called "the social sciences." So far so good, but is there anything that ties these questions together? I think not, at least, not in any strong sense. Any attempt to strictly demarcate the philosophy of social science is bound to be overwhelmed with counterexamples. More importantly, such strict discipline would stunt our inquiries. As you study philosophy you will find that one question leads to another, sometimes in unexpected ways. The field of philosophy is crisscrossed by intellectual lines of inquiry, and the boundaries among domains must remain fuzzy if we are to follow where our investigations lead. That said, there are some prominent, well-trodden paths to which we will find ourselves returning. Three themes which are distinctive of the philosophy of social science will run throughout this book: normativity, naturalism, and reductionism.

Normativity

Issues about norms, values, and rules enter the social sciences in two rather different ways. On one hand, the norms, values, and rules of specific societies are part of what the social sciences study. On the other, there are norms, values, and rules which the social scientists recognize and are part of *their own* society. Let us begin with the second.

The idea that democracies do not wage war on other democracies has figured in the rhetoric and practice of American foreign policy. That social science should support social policy in this way is not surprising. Indeed, one might argue that the only way to create effective social programs is to know how the social world works. This line of thought presupposes that social science and social policy are independent. Some critics have argued that the expediencies of American foreign policy influenced the social scientific investigation of the democratic peace hypothesis. As you might imagine, defining *democracy* and *peace* are crucial to the research. Critics argue that these concepts cannot be defined in ways that are completely independent of political values. So, commitments to how we ought to be conducting our foreign policy influence the data and theories on which policy is based. In this way social scientists become involved in disputes over social policy, and they must defend their results as the results of "objective" inquiry.

We will explore several issues surrounding values and objectivity. The primary question concerns *value-freedom*, and this will be the topic of Chapter 2. Must social scientific research be conducted without commitment to ethical or political values? Many philosophers of social science think that the answer is "no;" some kind of commitment is always present, even necessary. This answer opens new questions. There are a variety of ways in which moral and political values figure into social scientific research. Selecting data to fit a preconceived agenda obviously constitutes a bias and undermines objectivity. The consequences of other influences are not so obvious. We need to understand the variety of ways in which science can be value laden. Then we need to ask: if the social sciences are not value-free (in a particular way), can they be objective? This question links the epistemology of the social sciences to the question of value-freedom. Because of the epistemological dimension of the question of value-freedom, we will touch on it again in Chapter 8 and in Sections 4.1, 6.1, 7.3, and 12.4.

The question of value-freedom is made more complicated by the fact that many projects in the social sciences are explicitly political. Critical theory, feminist research, and various forms of participatory action research aim at social change. They seek to develop knowledge which will make societies more just and humans more free. Can these projects produce social scientific knowledge? One might be initially reluctant to say so, but if we exclude them, then what are we to think about research which aims to improve student learning or reduce crime? Social science is often used in "engineering" projects which are explicitly in the service of social policy. These projects challenge us to think more deeply about what constitutes objectivity in the social sciences.

Questions about the role of values in the social sciences ultimately ask about the ways in which we conceptualize "fact" and "value." In the social sciences, these issues arise when theorists try to develop accounts of the values, norms, and rules operative in human societies. In the earlier discussion of free riders, we saw some of the ways that the social sciences often invoke norms in their theories. Rosa Parks thought that racial segregation was *wrong*, and this was an important reason for her action. It has been suggested that one of the ways that social movements and revolutions overcome the free rider problem is that the norms and shared values of social groups obligate their members to act. (We will discuss this theory further in Section 7.1.) From this theoretical point of view, it is relevant that Rosa

Parks was secretary of the Montgomery NAACP, and that the NAACP quickly organized the bus boycott in response. Social scientific theorizing often makes appeal to norms, rules, and values when explaining both individual action and social-level events like social movements or revolutions. In so doing, they must make metaphysical commitments about what norms *are* and how they are related to individual and group action. These are fundamental questions of value theory. Chapter 9 is devoted to these issues, and they are also discussed in Sections 7.4 and 10.3.

Naturalism

Perhaps *the* distinctive question of the philosophy of social science is whether and how the social sciences differ from the natural sciences. The sciences are paradigms of empirical knowledge, both of what can be known and how it should be established. Not all sciences are equal. Alchemy and astrology were once proclaimed "sciences," but nobody now takes their theories as knowledge. On the other hand, physics, particularly Newtonian mechanics, is widely taken as a model for scientific knowledge. The question of whether social science is like natural science has therefore been central to the legitimacy of the social sciences since their inception. "Naturalism" is the name for a variety of views holding that the social sciences should be like the natural sciences in some important way. Those who think that the social sciences need a distinctive method, form of theorizing, or ontology, are—you guessed it—anti-naturalists. Unfortunately, the term is used in a variety of ways. It will therefore be useful to engage in a little bit of stipulative definition.

Since the issues debated cover a wide variety of topics, it will be useful at the outset to distinguish epistemological naturalism from metaphysical naturalism. Epistemological forms of naturalism concern issues about theory, explanation, and method. In literature on social scientific methodology, one often encounters a distinction between "qualitative" and "quantitative" research. Qualitative research uses interviews, participant observation, focus groups, and similar methods. It expresses its research results in narrative form, often relying on illustrative cases and analyzing long passages of text. Quantitative research relies on methods that measure in some way, perhaps through surveys or experiments. It aims to uncover correlations and causes, and it may rely on mathematically formulated models. When this distinction is introduced in the methodology literature, it is usually insisted that qualitative research is deeply different from quantitative research. Authors who take this position are therefore adopting some form of epistemological anti-naturalism.

Metaphysical naturalists hold that humans are part of the natural world, and therefore they must be understood in terms of the same causes and mechanisms that animate all other creatures. Those who oppose metaphysical naturalism argue that humans or human societies are distinctive in some deep way. The arch anti-naturalist of a metaphysical stripe would be Rene Descartes, since he held that human minds were a non-physical sort of substance. What makes us human is literally not part of the natural world. In contemporary social science, evolutionary and psychological approaches have recently taken on a new importance. These are typically naturalistic in the metaphysical sense. Evolutionary explanations of how cooperation could arise, for example, treat human beings as sharing most traits with other animals. The challenge is to explain how our specific traits, like altruistic cooperation, could arise through selection. At the deepest level, the dispute over metaphysical naturalism is about whether human nature is part of the natural world or outside of it.

Naturalism is best understood as a nexus of closely related philosophical debates. The real work of answering the question "Should social scientific theories/methods/ontologies be like the natural sciences?" is carried out at a much lower level of abstraction. Several issues to be discussed in later chapters thus fall within the theme of naturalism.

A pair of questions forms the core of the debate over epistemic naturalism. Does understanding human behavior require special *methods*? And does it require forms of *theory* different from those in the natural sciences? In the discussion of Rosa Parks and the Civil Rights Movement, the problem was framed in terms of "free riders." Given this perspective, the social scientist may use the resources of game theory to analyze and explain social movements. Formalizing the preferences of abstract actors in a social movement, the main claims of the theory can be mathematically expressed. Some people think that because it abstracts away from the historical individuals, this sort of theory misses important issues. The real question is how Rosa Parks and other civil rights leaders were thinking about the challenges they faced. This cannot be expressed in terms of correlations or game-theoretical analyses. This debate will be the main topic of Chapter 3, and it will arise again in Chapter 5. The "qualitative" methods mentioned earlier were developed to find out how historical agents like Rosa Parks were thinking about their situation. In Chapter 4, we will look closely at the epistemology of these methods.

Questions about causality are staples of both epistemology and metaphysics. They arise across the sciences, but in the social sciences they have particular resonance. The question of free will asks whether human action is causally determined. In the social sciences, this question turns into one about explanation: can human action be causally explained? Anti-naturalists argue that it cannot because humans act for reasons, and reasons are not causes. This issue will be explored in Section 5.1, and Section 9.3 will touch on it again. The empiricist analysis of causation, handed down from Hume, holds that causes require laws. Are there laws of the social world? The democratic peace is sometimes put forward as a law, but this is debated. Many have thought that the creativity and complexity of human behavior precludes the kind of lawfulness found in the natural sciences. In the last several decades, analyses of causation which do not tie causes to laws so tightly have become popular. In Chapter 11, we will examine these different analyses of causation and their consequences for social scientific theorizing.

Law or not, the democratic peace hypothesis asserts a causal relationship between democracy and peace. How could such a causal hypothesis be tested in the social sciences? The problem, as readers of Hume well know, is that the evidence for a hypothesis like the democratic peace is a correlation: no observed democracies have gone to war with each other. The theory asserts an unobserved cause. The social sciences have developed several methodologies which purport to solve this epistemological problem. Chapter 12 will evaluate formal techniques of causal modeling, case studies, and experimentation.

A final broad issue which invokes the theme of naturalism is the role of rationality and rules in social scientific understanding. This issue intersects with the theme of normativity; but here we are concerned with the place of rules in social scientific theory. Social scientists often appeal to rules, but one might wonder whether rules really explain anything. Does the fact that Hannah *ought* to do something explain why she does it? Naturalists of a metaphysical stripe often argue that it does not, but this depends to some extent on how norms, rules, and values are conceptualized. Chapter 9 will be primarily devoted to this issue, though it will arise in Chapter 4, Section 5.1, and Section 10.3 as well.

Reductionism

Philosophers have often envisioned the sciences as arranged in a hierarchy. Physics is the foundation on which chemistry is built, followed in turn by biology, psychology, and then the social sciences. Having built such a house of cards, one wonders how much it would take to flatten it. Can the social sciences be reduced to psychology, which in turn reduces to biology? Does everything ultimately reduce to physics? These are the questions of reductionism. Like naturalism, reductionism is a theme that encompasses several issues, and like naturalism it comes in both epistemological and metaphysical varieties. The difference between the varieties depends on how *reduce* is to be understood. Some have held that reduction is a relationship between theories. Epistemological reductionism holds that theories at one level can be replaced by theories at a lower level. Everything explicable by sociology, for example, is ultimately explicable in terms of psychology. (One need not continue, of course; there may be reasons why psychology does not reduce to biology.) Metaphysical claims about reduction, on the other hand, contend that entities, properties, processes, or events at one level are nothing but objects at another. Minds do not exist, the reductionist might say, only brains. Like the distinction between epistemological and metaphysical naturalism, it is possible to adopt (anti-)reductionism of both flavors. It is also possible to be one sort of reductionist without being the other. We will encounter several philosophers and social scientists who accept a metaphysical reductionism but do *not* think that theories of the social sciences could be replaced by psychology.

The themes of reductionism and naturalism overlap, but they are not coextensive. Many who argue for reductionism (either epistemological or metaphysical) are motivated by naturalistic commitments. That is, one might argue that because there is one, causally connected world and humans are part of it (metaphysical naturalism), social and psychological properties must reduce to physical properties. As a rough generalization, it is probably fair to say that all reductionists are naturalists. But the converse is not true: not all naturalists are reductionists. It could be that the natural world contains a variety of fundamental kinds of things which are not all reducible to some substrate, and at the same time the social and natural sciences need to use the same theory structures and methodologies. Once again, it is difficult to resolve the issues when they are considered at this abstract level. The broad theme of reductionism gets substance from several specific issues in the philosophy of social science.

Students of the social sciences are likely to encounter the phrase *methodological individualism* in the course of their studies. It is the requirement that social theories must explain social events in terms of the choices, beliefs, and attitudes of individual people. Expressed this way, it is an epistemologically reductionist thesis. However, arguments for methodological individualism are often a mix of metaphysical and epistemological considerations, and Chapter 7 will be devoted to sorting out these issues. The metaphysical question is whether churches, schools, armies, and so on are things that exist over and above the individuals. The reductionist regards a social movement or a democratic nation as nothing more than patterns of individual actions. Game theory has been a particularly powerful tool for analyzing the way that group properties could emerge from individual choices. Section 5.2 will present a very brief primer on decision theory and game theory, and we will examine these tools and their application throughout the sections which invoke reductionist themes.

Methodological individualism reduces social-level objects to individual choice and action. Most who advocate this sort of reductionism do not go on to explain individual choices in terms of psychological or biological properties. This raises the question of whether agency and individual action have a kind of explanatory priority. A number of recent research programs in the social sciences have added new dimensions to this question. Game theory is a paradigmatic form of individualism insofar as it assumes that individuals rationally pursue actions with the greatest utility. Recent work in behavioral economics has revealed striking ways in which humans fail to satisfy this assumption. We will consider how these results affect game theory in Section 5.3. These experiments are consonant with much work in cognitive psychology, which seems to explain large-scale features of human behavior in terms of sub-conscious, or better, sub-personal processes. (The mechanisms discovered by contemporary cognitive psychology and neuroscience would be examples of "sub-personal" processes or properties.) In Section 7.4 we will discuss theories of the evolution of human cooperation which appeal to cultural evolution by selective forces acting on human groups. This family of empirical theories suggests a picture where the level of agency (belief, intention, choice) is eliminated and replaced by sub-personal cognitive capacities and super-personal social patterns. Not exactly your father's reductionism, but spooky, nonetheless.

Anti-reductionists, or "holists" as they are often called, point to social phenomena which seem to be impossible to explain or analyze in individualistic terms. Normativity is one of those phenomena. It is a philosophical commonplace to say that "ought" cannot be reduced to "is;" a norm or rule cannot be identified with a pattern of behavior. In Chapter 9, we will examine some social scientific and philosophical attempts to do so.

Social ontology has become an active area of philosophical inquiry, and we will take a deep dive into two of its domains. First, social statuses and roles appear to have explanatory uses. There are things we can say about teachers, for example, that do not seem equivalent to facts about particular individuals. Social statuses and roles are "social constructions" in the literal sense that they exist (whatever that means) because of human action. Race, especially as it figures in the US, is a particularly interesting and troubling example, and we will explore this idea in Chapter 8. In the 19th century, race was conceived as a natural, biological fact about humans that explained human differences, including social and cultural differences. By the middle of the 20th century, the idea that race is biological had been rejected in the sciences. However, race remains an important topic of study—often an independent variable—in the social sciences. Reductions normally run from the higher level to the lower, with social properties being reduced to psychological and biological properties. Race seems to have been "reduced" by eliminating the biological but keeping the social. What does it mean to say that race is a social construction? Joint action is the second area of social ontology with which we will be concerned. Joint actions are things that a single person cannot do alone, such as sing a duet or defeat Napoleon's army. In the last several decades, there has been a flurry of work in philosophy on the question of whether joint actions can be explained or understood as an aggregate of individual intentional actions, or whether there is some sort of joint intentionality. This issue will be the topic of Chapter 10.

Excelsior!

This book is oriented toward both students of the social sciences and students of philosophy. When teaching courses to such diverse audiences, I have found that the course benefits from the knowledge that students can contribute. As you read this, I encourage you to use your philosophical or social scientific expertise. If you are a social science major, use examples from your field to test the views being presented. While it may not always be obvious to you, the philosophical issues discussed here are embedded in the theoretical and methodological literature of your discipline. Ask: what is at stake for my field when this question is answered one way or another? If you are a philosophy major, you will hear echoes from your other courses and readings. Use these arguments, concepts, and positions to critique, elaborate, and nuance the arguments in the text. Listen also for reverberations back from the social sciences. As argued earlier, the social sciences have something to contribute to philosophy's ancient questions about the human condition.

While this text is self-sufficient, I have assumed that you will read it along with some of the primary literature in the field. Writing a philosophy textbook is a bit like being a tour guide, and I want you to get off the bus and explore on your own. Wittgenstein once likened language to "an ancient city: a maze of little streets and squares, of old and new houses, and of houses with additions from various periods" (Wittgenstein 1953, Section 18). Intellectual domains are like cities too, and in giving you a tour I have tried to find a path that both explores the important monuments and makes the whole city plan intelligible. The text will outline some of the important arguments and debates, and thereby provide some context as you read contemporary contributions and historically important literature.

Each chapter will include some advice about further reading. In addition, there are several general collections on the philosophy of social sciences. The following collections include synoptic essays that go into more detail on the topics of this text: Turner and Roth, *The Blackwell Guide to the Philosophy of the Social Sciences* (2003); Turner and Risjord, *Philosophy of Anthropology and Sociology* (2006); Outhwaite and Turner, *The SAGE Handbook of Social Science Methodology* (2007); Jarvie and Zamora-Bonilla, *The SAGE Handbook of The Philosophy of the Social Sciences* (2011); Kincaid, *The Oxford Handbook of Philosophy of Social Science* (2012); Kaldis, *The Encyclopedia of Philosophy and the Social Sciences* (2013); Cartwright and Montuschi, *Philosophy of Social Science* (2016); and Valsiner, *Social Philosophy of Science for the Social Sciences* (2019).

2 Objectivity, Values, and the Possibility of a Social Science

When governments make decisions about social policy, they need to answer difficult questions. Does raising taxes hurt or help economic growth? Will providing a social safety net improve the lives of everyone, or will it decrease motivation to work? If we fix the broken windows and clear the trash from the streets of our neighborhoods, will it lower the crime rate? The *objectivity* of scientific evidence recommends it as a basis for policy decisions. "Objectivity" in the sense of freedom from pre-existing value commitments seems necessary for sound social policy making. At the same time, we know that governments support social scientific projects. Development of many statistical methods and concepts, for example, was prompted by needs of policy makers. When social policy drives social scientific research, one might become concerned that the interests of the politicians are influencing the results. Is it possible to separate politics from social science?

The question of whether the social sciences are *value-laden* or *value-free* has both practical and conceptual dimensions. Practically, value-laden research would presumably undermine the usefulness of social scientific results for social policy purposes. Value-freedom means that scientific results cannot be contested by those with different political interests. If the social sciences are value-laden, on the other hand, we need to rethink their relationship to social policy. Conceptually, the issue of value-freedom is about the character of science itself. If the sciences are value-laden, then how can we distinguish between good science and poor science? Can we give any sense to the notion of objectivity in science? And are the social and natural sciences different on this score? Perhaps the social sciences are deeply different from the natural sciences precisely because the social sciences cannot be value-free. Indeed, some philosophers have gone so far as to suggest that because they are value-laden, the social sciences should not be counted as "sciences" at all.

2.1. The Ideal of Value-Freedom

In thinking about cases where political or moral considerations figure in a scientific dispute, there are two questions to ask:

How are the values influencing the science?
What values are involved?

DOI: 10.4324/9781003207795-2

One way that values could influence scientific research, for instance, would be when they directly motivate the choice of conclusions. For example, suppose a journal editor refused to publish results which went against their political views. This sort of behavior is an obvious epistemic failure. Not all real-life examples look like this, however. How, for instance, should we think about social scientists who receive grants from governmental sources? In this sort of case, the values of the government influence whether the research gets done, but it might not influence the research practice or conclusions. Is this an epistemic failure too? We need, therefore, to ask what sort of values are in play and how they are influencing the research, and then examine the epistemic consequences. With this understanding, we might be able to find an appropriate ideal of value-freedom for the social sciences.

The United States Census

The United States has a constitutional mandate to count the population once every ten years. The census determines the number of Representatives each state sends to the House of Representatives, as well as the allocation of federal funding for education, law enforcement, and similar enterprises. A census has been conducted every decade since 1790. While it seems a straightforward enough problem, it turns out that counting people is a tricky business. There are several issues.

First, people do not simply line up to be counted. According to the Centers for Disease Control, in 2009 there were approximately 2,400,000 deaths in the US and more than 4,000,000 births. In the time it has taken you to read this paragraph, then, it is likely that more than seven babies have been born and four people have died. Because conducting the census takes time, we cannot think of it as capturing the exact number of people in the country at a particular time. It is more like measuring acceleration than counting the beans in a jar. Moreover, those who are alive keep moving about. The census relies on addresses, but people change addresses. College students typically have multiple addresses, and the homeless have no address at all.

Second, there is a problem of criteria: who is to be counted? Obviously, citizens should be counted, but since citizenship is a legal status, there are interesting borderline cases to be adjudicated. How do we count dual citizens, legal immigrants seeking citizenship status, non-citizens serving in the military? What about patients in persistent vegetative states, or third-trimester fetuses?

Third, how are they counted? Two methods have been used traditionally: either go door-to-door and count people or mail questionnaires to each household. Both methods have predictable inaccuracies. The door-to-door method requires that respondents are willing to talk to the government representative who has knocked on their door. An advantage of the door-to-door method is that the census agents can track down people who are hard to reach, like the homeless. However, with a population in the hundreds of millions, contacting every citizen is expensive. For this reason, mailed questionnaires have come to predominate. However, this method depends on respondents who will make the effort to fill out the form and send it back. Those with multiple addresses or without address at all are difficult to count by mail.

No census is perfectly accurate; a census may *undercount* or *overcount* the population. In the 1990 census, the undercount was approximately 4 million, or about 1.6% of the population (US Department of Commerce 2013). But this didn't break down evenly across social groups. The undercount rate for Whites was 0.9%, while the rate for Blacks was 4.4% and for Hispanics was 5%. How do we know that this many people were missed? Through a *second* survey sent to the same households. The method counts the difference between the first and second samples. Of those who receive the second questionnaire, some will have filled out the first census, some will not. The fraction of those in the second survey who answered the first census is then inferred to be the fraction of the whole population who filled out the survey. Note that this too is subject to both bias (someone reluctant to fill out the first will be reluctant to fill out the second) and random error.

As you might imagine, none of this is free from politics. In response to the 1990 undercount estimate, the US Census Bureau recommended supplementing the direct mail census with a sampling method to estimate the under (or over) count. Selected areas would be canvassed by door-to-door census takers, and these results would be combined with the mailed forms to generate the "true" number. This happened at a time when a Democrat (President Clinton) was in office, and some Republicans objected. Those opposed to the Census Bureau's plan argued that it was prone to new errors and bias, and that it didn't really count the population, it just made educated guesses about it. Those who supported it argued that sophisticated sampling techniques were likely to generate a more accurate number than either a simple mailing or an attempt to contact every individual in the US.

At first look, this seems like a simple issue of scientific methodology. Sampling methods and the associated statistics are quite sophisticated, and we rely on them for the safety of everything from automobiles to power plants. However, there are different biases and sources of error (both known and suspected) in each method that might be used. The debate over which method is the best turns partly on our willingness to tolerate particular risks of error. The politicians got interested because they saw that the different methods might generate different results. Since it was presumed that those groups who were undercounted were more likely to vote Democratic, Republicans tended to favor direct methods (which had a risk of undercounting minorities). Democrats tended to support the sampling methods, which might increase the estimate of the number of Black and Hispanic constituents in their districts.

The problem is tricky because choice of a census method requires deciding which kinds of errors are acceptable. Politics sneaks in because the possible errors have different political consequences, and thus the choice of method has political motivation. In light of all this, can we say that there is a scientifically best, or objective, way to take a census? Or is our estimate of the number of people in the

United States always going to be a function of the political party that happens to be in power during the census year?

The issues in census-taking make clear the motivations for seeking a value-free social science. If social science is tainted by politics, one might think, it could not provide the kind of neutral support that policy makers seek. One might conclude that the ideal of value-freedom requires that values must be eliminated from methodological decisions. An initial gloss on the ideal of value-freedom might be this:

> *Strong Thesis of Value-Freedom:* Science is objective insofar as values play no role in scientific research.

The Strong Thesis is an ideal for science, not a description of how it is actually conducted. Proponents of the Strong Thesis can recognize that much social science fails to live up to this standard. It is therefore no criticism of the Thesis that scientists are often influenced by moral or political concerns. To get a critical grip on the Strong Thesis, we need to decide whether it is truly necessary for scientific objectivity.

Dimensions of Value-Freedom

To evaluate the Strong Thesis of Value-Freedom, let us ask: what values are playing a role in the decisions about how to conduct the US census, and what role are they playing? Notice that the dispute about the best method for determining the number of citizens living in the United States. The politicians were not cherry-picking the results; their dispute was about the process. So, the considerations of what was best for each political party were influencing *methodology*. This is a point about the role of the values in this example. The character of the values in play is apparent. Since each party wants to increase its number of Representatives, it prefers an overcount of people likely to vote in their favor and an undercount of those likely to vote against them. This is a clear example of a political value influencing the decision about scientific methodology.

Political values are not the only kind of values to influence the census. Different methods for taking the census have different virtues. Both a house-to-house census and a mailed survey are prone to undercounting (though, as we have seen, the sources of these errors are slightly different). Sampling methodologies correct for these errors, but they raise the risk of overcounting. This is a particular example of a general problem in methodology. If you've taken a statistics class, this problem has probably been described in terms of "Type I" and "Type II" errors, or perhaps "false positive" and "false negative" results of a test. (We will discuss these a bit more in Section 2.2.) As a general matter, we cannot simultaneously reduce both the chances of undercounting and the chances of overcounting. This means that scientists are faced with a choice when determining the best method for their study. Which risk is more acceptable for the research, the risk of overcounting or the risk of undercounting? The decision about how to make trade-offs between types of error must be based on values. In the absence of any values, there would be no grounds for deciding that one method was *better* than another. One can easily imagine cases where this decision did not involve any political considerations. In the absence of a political context, the decision depends on what is best for the research at hand. Which sort of error would most diminish confidence in the results?

You might think that the values involved in the dispute about undercounting and overcounting seem to be of a different kind than disputes over ethics or politics. A dispute over the virtues of different methodologies is a matter of choosing among different ways to achieve the best science. For this reason, many philosophers have distinguished *epistemic values* from moral or political values. Something is an epistemic value when it contributes to good science. Epistemic values are part of the norms and standards of good scientific reasoning. A dispute over which method is best, then, must invoke values in the judgment that one method is better than another, but these values contribute to objectivity. When moral or political values enter the discussion, one might argue, they bias the results and detract from objectivity. The ideal of value-freedom, then, must not be understood as excluding all values from science. Rather, value-freedom requires the exclusion of moral and political values—what we will call *non-epistemic* values—from science. In the dispute over the census, we see both epistemic and non-epistemic values playing a role in choosing the census methodology.

The distinction between epistemic and non-epistemic values is a distinction in the kind or character of the values involved. As we have already seen, how the values influence the decision makes a difference as well. Choosing results which fit a preferred conclusion is an epistemically poor practice, no matter which values are motivating it. On the other hand, while choosing a methodology may require values, objectivity seems to be preserved if those values are internal to science. The problem with the census, one might then say, is that the political values got mixed up in decisions that should have been properly scientific. Generalizing this idea, some philosophers of science have distinguished a *constitutive* role for values from a *contextual* role (Longino 1990). Constitutive values are necessary for an activity. They shape the activity from the inside, so to speak, and the activity cannot go on without commitment on constitutive values. Contextual values are part of the environment. They may shape the activity, but they are not necessary to conducting it.

For a non-scientific example of the distinction between constitutive and contextual values, one might think of the different roles of aesthetic values and money in the performing arts. Judgments about aesthetic virtues are crucial to determining the genre of the performance. A distorted guitar might be a good sound for rock music but be awful for folk music. These values are thus constitutive of the performance. When the performance comes to serve other ends, such as making a living for the artists, other values come into play. The fact that audiences are more likely to come to performances when certain songs are played, for example, might influence the performer's choices. In this way, the values that are part of the context come to influence the activity, even though they are not necessary for it.

Whether non-epistemic values undermine the objectivity of social scientific research depends on whether they are contextual or constitutive. One might argue that contextual values do not always undermine the reliability of scientific results. Science, even social science, is expensive. Researchers must be paid salaries, surveys must be copied and distributed, subjects must be given incentives, and so on. Throughout the history of the social sciences, political interest in measurement, prediction, and control of people has led to funding for specific research projects. Political values determine which research projects get funded and which are not (or, in some cases, even forbidden). Does this fact undermine the objectivity of the social sciences? One might argue that it does not, if the political values remain contextual. Funding science is a little bit like shining a flashlight into the dark: interests determine the direction of the beam, but not what we see when we look. To preserve objectivity, once the decision has been made to investigate a particular topic, only scientific considerations (epistemic values) should govern the research.

These considerations show that the Strong Thesis of Value-Freedom is too demanding a requirement. If values played no role whatsoever in science, then scientists could not make decisions at all. There must be some norm that makes one method *better* than another. It does not seem to threaten objectivity if the values invoked are epistemic. A more moderate thesis of value-freedom, then, could admit that epistemic values play a role in scientific research and forbid non-epistemic values.

A Moderate Thesis of Value-Freedom

The distinction between the roles of epistemic and non-epistemic values and between constitutive and contextual values permits a more nuanced conception of value-freedom. We might formulate it this way:

> *Moderate Thesis of Value-Freedom:* Science is objective when only epistemic values are constitutive of scientific practice; moral and political considerations must always remain contextual.

The Moderate Thesis of Value-Freedom has not been universally accepted. An initial criticism might be aimed at the attempt to separate contextual and constitutive roles for values. In the example of the census, the political considerations were used to support methodological virtues. The Democrats preferred the risk of an overcount, while the Republicans preferred the risk of an undercount. It is therefore misleading to say that the tradeoff between false positives and false negatives is strictly a scientific matter. The politics was determining the relative importance of under- and overcounting citizens. Since all science occurs in some social context, one might argue, contextual values will always have some influence on the core workings of scientific decision making. In response, the defender of value-freedom might agree that, as a practical matter, moral and political values are always present. Value-freedom is an ideal toward which we should strive. Moral and political values are not necessary for science, and the goal of objectivity requires minimizing their influence.

Can moral and political values ever become constitutive of a kind of scientific practice? Philosophers have focused on two potential constitutive roles for values in scientific practice. First, moral and political values might influence the justification of theories or the confirmation of hypotheses. This is the role that political values apparently had in the arguments over US census methodology. Some philosophers have used the term *impartial* to describe science that is value-free in this sense. Science can fail to be impartial when moral or political values are used to directly support preference for one conclusion or another. Or again, politics might preclude consideration of alternative explanations, narrowing the field of possible hypotheses to be tested. In these cases, failures of impartiality would be grounds for criticizing the research. But do all failures of partiality lead to bad science? And is it really possible to eliminate moral or political values from decisions about which hypotheses are best supported by the data? These questions will be addressed in Section 2.2.

A second way in which moral and political values might appear in scientific practice is as part of the content of a theory. This is the form of value-freedom advocated by Max Weber: "It can never be the task of an empirical science to provide binding norms and ideals from which directives for immediate practical activity can be derived" (Weber 1949 [1904], 52). In the case of the US census, the *results* of the census were purely descriptive. They purported to say how many people lived in various parts of the US. The census says nothing about how many people *ought* to live in a certain region. "Oughts" are policy matters; they are Weber's "binding norms and ideals." The census is neutral with respect to them, and value-freedom in this second sense has been called value *neutrality*. Since scientific research can tell us something about how the world is, but not how it ought to be, one might think that science should be value-free in the sense of being value-neutral. However, philosophers have challenged this version of value-freedom too, and we will consider those arguments in Section 2.3.

2.2. Impartiality and Theory Choice

Risk and Error

In an essay provocatively titled "The Scientist Qua Scientist Makes Value Judgments," Richard Rudner argued that non-epistemic values are a necessary part of hypothesis testing and theory choice (Rudner 1953). Rudner begins by pointing out that hypotheses are never proven definitively by any kind of test; they are only more or less probable. It is always possible that the test was mistaken. A standard way to express such possibilities of error in statistics is the use of a "p-value." A p-value is a mathematical construct that expresses the probability that the result could have come about by chance. A p-value of 0.01 means that there is a 1 in 100 chance that that the result could have come about by luck or random variation. In other words, if the hypothesis is false, the test would mistakenly show that it was true 1 in 100 tries. A p-value of 0.05 means that there is a 5 in 100 (1 in 20) chance of the test showing that the hypothesis was true when it was not.

To decide whether to accept a hypothesis, the social scientist will have to choose a level for the p-value. This will be a threshold for acceptability: if the p-value is lower than the specified level, it will be accepted. Rudner points out that the choice of level for the p-value depends on the costs of being mistaken. Suppose a social scientist is asked to test the efficacy of training about how to identify songbirds. If students do not really learn how to correctly identify a sparrow, then very little is lost. In such a case, it might be OK that the hypothesis has a 1 in 20 chance of being unsupported. On the other hand, suppose the training was for medical personnel in the use of a piece of lifesaving equipment. Since lives are at stake, 1 in 20 might be too much of a risk. So, the "cost" of a mistake—whether in lives, pain, or cold, hard cash—influences (and ought to influence) the decision to demand higher levels of probability. If deciding whether a hypothesis should be accepted or rejected is a core activity of science, then the values which determine whether the hypothesis is acceptable are playing a constitutive role. If Rudner's argument is correct, then even the Moderate Thesis of Value-Freedom is an unattainable goal. Rudner's argument has been developed and elaborated (Douglas 2000, 2009), and it is now discussed as the problem of "inductive risk."

In response to challenge of inductive risk, one might contend that relaxing our standards when there is little at stake is just sloppy research. It may be true that we can never eliminate the possibility of error, but we can always minimize it. If we really want to get at the *truth*, we should always demand maximum probability before accepting a hypothesis. This response will not serve, because there is no simple "maximum probability." A hypothesis might be mistaken in more than one way. The hypothesis might be false, but confirmed by the test, or it may be true, yet not confirmed by the test. These two kinds of mistakes are often called "Type I" and "Type II" errors, or "false positives" and "false negatives." Figure 2.1 shows the relationship. Unfortunately, we cannot devise a test that will simultaneously reduce the probability of false positives and the probability of false negatives. They tend to be inversely related. An airport metal detector, for example, may be set to be very sensitive, sounding the alarm even if the person has a tiny piece of metal

	Hypothesis is **true**	Hypothesis is **false**
Test **confirms** the hypothesis	True Positive (No error)	False Positive (Type I error)
Test **disconfirms** the hypothesis	False Negative (Type II error)	True Negative (No error)

Figure 2.1 Type I and Type II Errors

on their shoe. This setting will ensure that no one carrying a firearm walks through the scanner. That is, it will have a low rate of false negatives. On the other hand, many who are not carrying weapons will trigger the alarm: there will be more false positives.

The Moderate Thesis of Value-Freedom tries to preserve scientific objectivity by isolating moral and political values outside the constitutive activities of science. The argument from inductive risk seems to show that they seep through anyway. We cannot (in general) reduce both Type I and Type II errors, so when devising a test, we must choose which kind of error is more dangerous, costly, politically contentious, or morally problematic. The dispute over the US census was precisely about the acceptability of false positives (overcounting) and false negatives (undercounting). Since choice of the kind of error to minimize determines whether the hypothesis will be judged true or false, and since moral and political considerations are relevant to such choices, it seems like considerations of moral and political values are necessary for the justification of scientific theories. If this is correct, then it would be impossible to be impartial in some scientific fields.

What About Objectivity?

Suppose that the earlier argument is sound, and science cannot be impartial. What should our attitude be toward the sciences? Should we conclude that science is just another battleground for political differences? Is there any way to distinguish between better and worse empirical research? Is there any sense in which the social sciences are objective? The foregoing arguments thus invite us to reconsider what "objectivity" might mean in the context of value-laden inquiry.

Objectivity is not a univocal idea. Like many heavily burdened philosophical ideas, it is used to defend against a number of different philosophical dangers, and each of these contrasts shows a different side to the idea. Following Sharon Crasnow's analysis (2006), we might distinguish three different senses of objectivity:

1. Objectivity as freedom from bias.
2. Objectivity as intersubjectivity.
3. Objectivity as reliability.

We use the first sense when we say that an advertising claim is not objective. An advertiser's interest in selling the goods makes us suspicious that their claims are biased. One of the primary concerns about the appearance of moral or political values in scientific practice is that these values seem to bias the results. That is, they make us suspicious about whether the scientific claims are true. Moral and political values can certainly have this effect. So, if social science cannot be impartial, the challenge is to control or limit the biasing effects of non-epistemic values.

In the second sense, objectivity is contrasted with subjectivity (which is itself a complex and multifaceted idea). My feeling of hunger is subjective, while the fact that I am eating a sandwich is objective. Hunger is a state that bears a special relationship to the hungry person (the *subject* of the hunger). It is subjective insofar as the subject of hunger is in a unique position to recognize it. The fact that I am eating a sandwich is objective insofar as it is easily available to anyone in a position to see, and in this sense, objectivity means "intersubjectivity." Something is intersubjective to the degree that it is open for critical scrutiny by more than one person. Science is taken to be objective because it cultivates methods that are public: reproducible experiments, survey data that can be counted and re-counted, or interview texts that can be re-read and re-interpreted. Objectivity in the intersubjectivity sense is thought to be desirable because it is the basis for reasoned engagement over scientific results and processes. Since the theories and the evidence are intersubjective, we can (it might be argued) reach agreement about them, at least in principle.

Finally, the third sense of scientific objectivity derives from the reliability of scientific methods. A method is reliable insofar as it provides results that are likely to be true. Notice that a method might be intersubjective, but unreliable. A defective recording device, for example, produces data that is available to anyone, but it may reproduce speech at some times and gibberish at others. In the reliability sense, objectivity has to do with how well we trust our methods to be free from error. In the social sciences, the use of methods that involve measurement, such as surveys, are often said to be more objective than, say, interviews. One grounds for this (but not the only grounds—this critique typically invokes the second sense of objectivity too) is that interview subjects are often chosen in non-random ways, and the number of interviews is typically small. The purported results from a set of interviews, then, might be an accident of the choice of interviewees and not be reflective of the larger population.

If social science cannot be impartial, must it fail to be objective in any of these three senses? The third sense seems the least threatened. One might argue that whether a method is reliable does not depend on the political or moral commitments of either the inquirers or the subjects. Judgments of reliability do not need to be politically or morally motivated. To preserve objectivity, we might demand that judgments of reliability should not be based on non-epistemic values. Intersubjectivity can also be preserved even if social science is not impartial. Decisions about acceptable types of error should be open to criticism and discussion, even if non-epistemic values are required. Arguably, then, social science can be objective in the reliability and intersubjectivity senses, even if it is value-laden.

Deeper concerns arise when moral and political values bias decisions about methodology or otherwise color the results. The problem is that biases can be difficult to detect. Background beliefs that encompass value commitments are often invisible to those who hold them. They can take the form of deep presuppositions and assumptions that are taken as obvious and rarely articulated.

In *Science as Social Knowledge*, Helen Longino argued that the social character of science can protect against bias (Longino 1990). Public criticism can enhance objectivity in the intersubjectivity sense, and by doing so, it could limit bias. Objectivity thus requires mechanisms for public critique from a diverse range of voices. Critiques from those who do not share the presuppositions can bring the value commitments to light. Peer review can have this kind of corrective function, but only if several conditions are met. The critical voices must be heard, and the community must be responsive to them. This requires that there be shared authority and that the community has ways to rationally debate about the different positions. In the end, even if some inquiries cannot be impartial, objectivity can be maintained by a properly organized scientific community.

National censuses and other kinds of government-sponsored data gathering can be intractably partisan. Decisions about acceptable kinds of error are inevitable, and different parties will invoke different political values. If the foregoing arguments are correct, then such value-laden science can still be unbiased. Public debate over the political values at stake makes the decisions intersubjectively evaluable, and the reliability of the methods can be determined in a value-free way. While it is hard to imagine in these partisan times, such arguments project optimism about the possibility of objective, yet value-laden, social scientific inquiry.

2.3. Essentially Contested Ideas

Value-Neutrality and Emancipatory Research

Value-neutrality is the thesis that social scientific theories should describe facts, not make policy recommendations. Where impartiality focuses on the *process* of justification and theory choice, neutrality concerns the *products* of scientific inquiry. Value-neutrality forbids scientific theories from including statements about what *ought* to be done or not done. For example, to say that "murder is wrong" is an evaluation, for it says that one ought not to commit murder. Value-neutrality would demand that "murder is wrong" not appear as a part of a social scientific theory. Social scientists could, of course, report a murder rate or that a certain percentage of the population agrees with the statement "murder is wrong." Value-neutrality seems to be supported by a simple argument. Evaluations—like "murder is wrong"—cannot be supported by empirical research. No number of opinion surveys will establish the moral correctness of murder. So, one might conclude, whenever a social scientific theory includes a statement about what ought to be done, it must be over-reaching its empirical support.

While value-neutrality might seem to be necessary, there have been important programs of research with explicit political goals. In the 19th century, August Comte, Karl Marx, and Herbert Spencer all understood themselves to be engaged in research that was simultaneously political and empirical. In the early 20th century, the Frankfurt School's analysis of modern capitalist social structures had the explicit goal of "emancipation from slavery" (Horkheimer 2002 [1968], 246). Modern students of the social sciences are likely to encounter a wide variety of approaches, including feminism, post-colonialism, Marxism, and a variety of "critical theories," such as critical pedagogy, critical race theory, critical realism, and so on. All these programs explicitly disavow value-freedom, typically rejecting both impartiality and neutrality. They are often criticized by social scientists (and philosophers) who are suspicious of the role those political commitments play in this sort of research. It is impractical to evaluate, here, all the specific research programs. Nonetheless, there are some widely shared general themes which can shed some light on the challenge that emancipatory research programs present to the ideal of value-freedom.

Many programs of emancipatory social science begin with a critique of ideology. *Ideology* here is understood as the relationship between knowledge, oppression, and systems of power and authority. In human societies, power and authority are unevenly distributed. In complex, modern societies, the distribution of power depends on various social groupings, typically combinations of gender (including sexual identities), race (including ethnicity or national identification), and socioeconomic status (including caste, class, or profession). These differences in power are associated with oppressive practices, including exploitation, marginalization, powerlessness, and violence (Young 1988). In addition, in what has come to be called epistemic injustice, oppression can manifest as a silencing or effacing of a group's experiences. These forms of oppression limit access by persons of a particular race/gender/class to education, economic resources, or participation in the political process. The first step of an ideology critique is to recognize that the social scientists participate in the very same material conditions that create oppression in the larger society. Western academics and researchers in the public or private sectors tend to be male, White, and have professional family backgrounds. Social scientists have the authority to set the research agenda, identify acceptable methodologies, and evaluate the results. Under some circumstances, the institutions that determine what counts as a legitimate question for social scientific inquiry and what counts as a good answer—what counts as social scientific knowledge at all—contributes to the oppression of various social groups.

Emancipatory social scientists often argue that members of groups who suffer forms of oppression do not all have the same understanding of their social world. When I (a well-heeled, White male) stay in a hotel, for example, there is a complex social and technological mechanism that makes that stay possible. It is largely invisible to me as a guest. I do not know (and do not need to know) how the bed sheets are kept clean, how the mini-bar is stocked, or how the duties of the front desk differ from those of the bell-captain. The exploitation of the workers (as well as their marginalization and powerlessness) is not only invisible, but its invisibility is also a crucial part of "the experience" of staying in the hotel. My position thus makes those parts of the social world that create and sustain the oppression invisible to me. Of course, they are not literally invisible; if we turn the social scientific gaze upon them, they could be studied. However, because of the social position of professional social scientists, the fact that certain parts of the social world are not easily accessible means that questions about those aspects of society will not be important. Some social phenomena will appear as problems to be solved, and whether a phenomenon is a "social problem" depends on the position of the inquirer. As the basis for policy, the identification of problems, and development of solutions, the knowledge of the dominant group thus helps maintain the different social positions within that social system.

The argument concludes that there is both an epistemological and a power asymmetry between the dominant and oppressed groups in a society. Those in the dominant group produce and maintain a particular view of social reality. As already noted, however, their privileged position means that they do not have to understand many of the social processes that make their position possible (e.g., the work of the hospital nurses or hotel maids). Their view is incomplete, but they are not likely to see the parts of the social world that it excludes. Those who are in the oppressed group have a different relationship both to the social arrangements and to the social theory that is taken for knowledge. To survive under conditions of oppression, they must understand the social world from both the dominant perspective and their own. They are able to simultaneously see why the dominant view of society is persuasive and why it fails to represent the full picture. Feminists and critical theorists argue that the social sciences are unable to recognize crucial aspects of social life and human experience that arise for particular social positions, particularly in the dimensions of gender, race, and class.

Emancipatory research programs thus argue that the assertion of the ideal of value-freedom serves to hide the ways that power and position shape the social sciences and their results. It is better to make the value-orientation of all social science explicit so that the values can be criticized. As a political stance, social scientists should seek to improve the human lot, to work for justice and freedom from oppression. From this perspective, a new set of questions become interesting, and a new set of issues become the social problems needing solutions. Value-neutrality, the emancipatory social scientist concludes, is therefore an inappropriate ideal for the social sciences.

Objection: Values and the Logic of Discovery

One might respond that, even if it were accepted, the argument for emancipatory research has only shown that people who occupy particular social locations are in a better position to discover certain aspects of society than others. It is analogous to different perspectives on a single landscape. Some features may be difficult or impossible to see from certain vantage points. It might be an argument for diversity within the social sciences, but it does not show that the social sciences should not be value-neutral. The emancipatory social scientist will say that this response underplays the way in which a proper understanding of the system of power and oppression requires recognizing its injustices. To say that a particular social arrangement is "oppressive" is to say that it creates conditions for the unjust treatment of members of a group (women, racial or ethnic minorities, etc.) based on their group membership. The knowledge that is available through the recognition of such oppression thus requires value-judgments. In the varieties of critical theory and feminism, the practitioner must recognize certain practices as unjust and be committed to changing them. The knowledge is generated to raise awareness, challenge the injustices, and eliminate oppression. Value-judgments are thus *constitutive* of the practice of critical theory and feminist social science.

One might still insist that while the recognition of injustices is an important motivation for some kinds of social scientific inquiry, it remains outside of the domain of the strictly scientific part of a social scientist's mandate. The practical goal of eliminating oppression and injustice is laudable, one might argue, but it is a mistake to suppose that it is part of the content of the social scientific knowledge produced by feminist or critical theoretic research. At most, the political commitments orient the inquirer toward specific phenomena, make certain kinds of problems salient, and perhaps guide the choice of method in the ways discussed in Section 2.2. To take this line about emancipatory research, however, would be to suppose that the statement of fact contained in their research results could be strictly separated from the political values motivating the inquiry. Proponents of this sort of research deny that a meaningful separation of fact and value could be maintained. It would require, for example, that their research reports contain no mention of oppression. After all, oppression requires injustice, and to say that a practice is unjust is clearly an evaluation, not just a description. We thus encounter a deep philosophical question: how are facts and values related, and can they be clearly separated?

Value Presuppositions and Implicatures

A strict fact-value distinction would require that descriptions (statements of fact) have no evaluative consequences on their own. One way to make the distinction between descriptions and evaluations clear is to say that evaluative statements include explicitly evaluative predicates like *ought, good*, and their cognates. To make science value-neutral, we would thus simply forbid sentences containing evaluative predicates from appearing in scientific theories. Then scientific theories would have no evaluative consequences, at least not without the addition of extra-scientific evaluations. Separating descriptions from evaluations, however, is a tricky business. Consider the sentence "Jones murdered Smith." This sentence seems like a description. It can be true or false, and it is made true or false by a state of affairs. But contrast it with the sentence "Jones killed Smith." There is much contained in the first that is not contained in the second. In particular, the first entails that Jones intended, or at the very least foresaw, Smith's death. More to the point, to say that Jones murdered Smith implies that Jones did something morally wrong.

When we think of moral statements, we tend to think of very abstract predicates like *good, right*, and *obligatory*, not about *bicycle theft, a rude gesture*, or *jumping the queue*. The latter are as much evaluations as the former, even though they are not so lofty. Notice that the latter examples have a substantial descriptive component to their meaning along with the evaluative. I cannot steal a bicycle unless (1) I took possession of the bicycle without permission, (2) I was aware of the lack of permission, and (3) by doing so, I open myself to appropriate moral sanction. Their correct application depends on both the facts (the bicycle, my behavior) and the values (permission, moral sanction). Concepts which have both descriptive and evaluative components have sometimes been called "thick moral concepts" (Williams 1985). If social science is to be value-neutral, then, it must exclude not only all explicit evaluations (which use words like *good*), but all that use thick moral concepts as well.

Some have argued that the social sciences must deploy concepts with moral or political presuppositions, on pain of being empty and pointless. The social sciences study phenomena like unemployment and poverty because these things are bad, and we want to prevent them. The interests are thus not just helping to point the flashlight, so to speak; they are coloring the character of what is studied. The emancipatory programs in the social sciences take this argument one step further. A social scientific study of rape that somehow managed to forget the violence and suffering would not be good science because it was objective; it would be morally abhorrent. The very aspiration to be value-neutral is therefore itself a political or moral commitment. There are value presuppositions in many social scientific statements because those statements employ thick moral concepts. To ignore these presuppositions or pretend that they do not exist is to implicitly affirm the values already implicit in contemporary social science. But, the argument goes, these values should be up for debate, and the debate is not just philosophical. Since the concepts involve a mixture of descriptive and evaluative commitments, the debate must be partly empirical. By making oppressive practices the object of study, critical social science is not really doing something different from ordinary social science; it is simply doing it in a more self-conscious and explicit way.

If value-neutrality is abandoned and values become part of the content of social scientific theories, then it may seem as if objectivity has just flown out of the window. Again, one might worry that social science would become nothing more than a battleground for political conflict. It is not difficult to find examples that support such concerns. Political parties of all ideologies seek to support their views with empirical evidence, and if science need not be value-neutral, then it legitimates the dubious practice of treating industry representatives or political activists as scientific experts. To make this objection, however, is to focus solely on the differences over values and assume that value conflicts will exclude evidential, conceptual, and other theoretical considerations. The link between descriptions with evaluative presuppositions or implications cuts both ways. One might say: "when theories are value-laden, values become theory-laden" (Risjord 2007, 20).

If thickly evaluative concepts are integrated into the claims of a theory—that is, when the values become theory-laden—then changes to the theory can motivate changes in the values. Value-laden theories have observable consequences and therefore they can be tested in ordinary ways. When theories and models are disconfirmed by evidence, scientists adjust the theory. If the adjustments to the theory involve the statements involving thickly evaluative concepts, then changing the theory entails changing the implicit values too. In other words, contrary to first appearances, a non-neutral social science might provide *objective* grounds for value change. As an example, consider the 18th- and 19th-century theories of physiognomy. According to these theorists, some people were "born criminals." Their natural tendencies toward crime were correlated with specific physical characteristics, such as a receding forehead or protruding bones. The theory has long been discredited, and with it has gone the evaluation of some facial types as being naturally wicked. The matter is complicated, of course, since biological theories of criminality have continued to emerge along with their own embedded values. At the same time, inquiry into the causes of crime is not purely political. A better understanding of how empirical evidence can serve to undermine non-neutral theory might go some way toward meeting the concern about the politization of the social sciences.

It has also been argued that the kind of non-neutrality found in emancipatory projects can make science *more* objective. By making the values explicit, critical theorists and feminists take on the project of identifying and criticizing the moral and political values that are implicit in existing theories. Alison Wylie and Lynn Hankinson Nelson, for example, surveyed a number of cases

> in which a standpoint of gender sensitivity—a commitment to ensure that gender (and women) are not disappeared—has provoked a reexamination of disciplinary conventions about what can or should be studied archaeologically. This, in turn, directs attention to new ranges of data and new possibilities for interpreting (or reinterpreting) archaeological data that shifts the evidential horizons of the discipline as a whole. Sometimes the result is a reassessment of androcentric models that inverts gender conventions, so that women are recognized to have played a central role in domains of cultural life, and in processes of cultural change, that had typically been attributed to men.
>
> (Wylie and Nelson 2007, 67)

In these kinds of critical projects, the critique of background assumptions shows how evaluative commitments have led scientists to ignore some kinds of data or possible interpretations. The search for new data then yields evidence that undermines the established theories. The theories which result from problematic value commitments are overturned on empirical grounds, and not only because of the values critique. This way of conceptualizing objectivity has been called "strong objectivity" by Sandra Harding (1993). On this view, epistemic and non-epistemic values work together to produce better science than epistemic values alone could produce. As Wylie and Nelson point out, "science is objective *because* of the values with which it is infused" (Wylie and Nelson 2007, 58).

2.4. Wrap Up

Chapter Summary

Without some sort of evaluative commitment, social science would be impossible. When thinking about the influence of values on scientific research, the key questions are: (1) *what* values are playing a role? and (2) *how* are they influencing scientific practice? To help sort out answers to these questions, Section 2.1 introduced a pair of distinctions. The distinction between epistemic and non-epistemic values helps answer question (1). The distinction identifies two kinds of values with different consequences for objectivity. Epistemic values are not threatening to objectivity, while moral and political (non-epistemic) values can be potentially troublesome. The distinction between contextual and constitutive values shows two different ways in which values can influence scientific research, thereby addressing question (2). This pair of distinctions is the basis for the moderate thesis of value-freedom, discussed in Section 2.1: science is objective when only epistemic values are constitutive of scientific practice; moral and political considerations must always remain contextual.

The main debate over values in science today concerns whether moral and political values can be constitutive of scientific research in a way that preserves objectivity. Moral and political values might figure in the justification of social scientific theories (partiality/impartiality), or they might figure in the content (neutrality/non-neutrality). Section 2.2 presented the argument that in a large variety of cases, non-epistemic values must play a role in deciding the evidential support of a hypothesis. In Section 2.3, we examined arguments which questioned the strict separation of facts and values. Social scientific theories are always partly political, and therefore the evaluation of theory should take the political dimensions of the theory into account.

If either neutrality or impartiality is rejected based on the arguments in this chapter, then we need to inquire into the possibility of social scientific *objectivity*. Is it possible for social scientific research to be value-laden in either of these ways without being biased or unreliable? Objectivity is a multi-faceted concept, and a research program may fail to be objective in one way while remaining objective in others. As we come to understand these different senses of objectivity, two interesting avenues of philosophical inquiry arise. First, are there ways to organize science as a social practice which helps preserve or enhance its objectivity? Second, are there ways in which non-epistemic values can make a scientific research project *more* objective? These are important, open questions in the philosophy of the social sciences.

Teasing apart the issues of objectivity requires understanding how values might play a role in theory construction, concept formation, and hypothesis testing. How do concepts of social scientific theories get their content? Why should we theorize social phenomena in one way rather than another? The problem of objectivity thus reaches to epistemological questions about social scientific theorizing. In the next chapter, we turn to those questions. But don't think that we are done discussing value-freedom and objectivity. As we move into other issues, we will discover more ways in which values are tangled up with social scientific research.

Discussion Questions

1. Think of some recent examples of controversial research into human behavior or social problems. What values appear in this research, and what roles are they playing? Do they undermine the objectivity of the research?

2. Is it possible for moral or political values to play *only* a contextual role in social science?
3. Evaluate Rudner's argument against value-freedom. Does it show that scientists must always make value judgments as part of their inquiry? How might a defender of the strong thesis of value-freedom respond?
4. What are some thickly evaluative concepts that show up in social scientific research? Can social science use these concepts in empirical study without introducing bias?
5. Consider the three senses of objectivity presented in Section 2.2. Can an inquiry which is not impartial be objective in any of these senses? What about an inquiry which is not neutral? If the inquiry fails to be objective in a particular sense, what are the consequences?
6. The idea of "evidence-based" social policy has been prominent recently. What problems arise if the evidence is either not neutral or not impartial? Could there be evidence-based social policy which was entirely value-free?

Further Reading

Tommy Wright was the Chief of the Statistical Research Division of the US Bureau of the Census during the late 1990s. His essay "Sampling and Census 2000: The Concepts" gives a non-technical articulation and defense of the Bureau's plan (Wright 1998, 1999). See also Wright (1999) for a brief overview of the history of estimation in the census. Kastenbaum, "Census 2000: Where Science and Politics Count Equally" (1998) shows what the political landscape looked like at the time. Freedman and Wachter (2007) provide an accessible discussion of the methodological complexities.

All forms of scientific inquiry face the question of value-ladenness. Important general discussions include Hempel's "Valuation and Objectivity in Science" (1983); Rudner's "The Scientist *Qua* Scientist Makes Value-Judgments" (1953); Kuhn's "Objectivity, Value Judgment, and Theory Choice" (1977); Longino's *Science as Social Knowledge* (1990); Lacy's *Is Science Value-Free?* (1999); Douglas's *Science, Policy, and the Value-Free Ideal* (2009); Elliott and Richards (eds.) *Exploring Inductive Risk* (2017); and DiMarco and Khalifa "Inquiry Tickets: Values, Pursuit, and Underdetermination" (2019).

Turning to the social sciences specifically, the early discussions tried to isolate the social sciences from moral or political values: see Weber's "Objectivity in Social Science and Social Policy" (1949 [1904]) and Nagel's "The Value-Oriented Bias of Social Inquiry" in *The Structure of Science (1961)*. Root's *Philosophy of Social Science* (1993) has a number of arguments against value-freedom in the social sciences. Works that look closely at social scientific research include Gouldner's "The Sociologist as Partisan: Sociology and the Welfare State" (1968), Taylor's "Neutrality in Political Science" (1973 [1967]), Smith's "Women's Perspective as a Radical Critique of Sociology" (1974), Harding's (ed) *Feminism and Methodology: Social Science Issues* (1987b), Wylie's "The Interplay of Evidential

Constraints and Political Interests" (1992), Anderson's "Uses of Value Judgments in Science: A General Argument, with Lessons from a Case Study of Feminist Research on Divorce" (2004), Porter's "Speaking Precision to Power" (2006), Risjord's "Scientific Change as Political Action: Franz Boas and the Anthropology of Race" (2007), and Schroeder's "Which Values Should be Built Into Economic Measures?" (2019).

The concept of objectivity relates questions of value-freedom to questions about the character of scientific theory. John's *Objectivity in Science* (2021) is an accessible general treatment. Also see Anderson's "Knowledge, Human Interests, and Objectivity in Feminist Epistemology" (1995) and Wylie's "Rethinking Objectivity: Nozick's Neglected Third Option" (2000).

Critical theory encompasses a broad range of social scientific projects that are neither neutral nor impartial. Bohman's entry on critical theory in the *Stanford Encyclopaedia of Philosophy* (2021) is a very clear overview. See also Bohman, "Theories, Practices, and Pluralism: A Pragmatic Interpretation of Critical Social Science" (1999) and Flyvbjerg, *Making Social Science Matter* (2001). Zuberi and Bonilla-Silva (eds.) *White Logic, White Methods: Racism and Methodology* (2008) take a critical race theory perspective. A wide-ranging exploration of recent debates is found in Van Bouwel (ed.) *The Social Sciences and Democracy* (2009). For a good overview of feminist contributions, see Crasnow (2006) and Wylie (2006). Fricker's *Epistemic Injustice* (2007) has been influential, and the *Routledge Handbook of Epistemic Injustice* (Kidd et al 2017) covers key concepts and developments.

3 Theories, Interpretations, and Concepts

The phrase *social science* sometimes seems like an oxymoron. The sciences are a model of knowledge because they have demonstrated striking power over the last three centuries. By postulating laws, imagining mechanisms too small to view with the unaided eye, and by ever more-precise measurement, the sciences have yielded a mass of detailed empirical knowledge. When we turn our attention to the social world, however, theories of this sort seem impossible. Are there laws that will explain love? Can democracy be measured? There seems to be something about humans which makes them impossible to measure, predict, or explain. The objects of a social science are not objects at all; they are *subjects*. Subjects have their own ideas, concepts, and perspectives. We can study the stars without asking what they care about; not so with humans. Human subjectivity, many have concluded, constitutes a barrier to scientific theorizing about the social world. In this chapter, we will examine the question of naturalism through the lens of social scientific *concepts*. Where do social scientific concepts get their content? And what is the relationship between the theorist's concepts and the ways that the subjects think about themselves?

Scientific concepts are different from everyday concepts because they are deliberately refined. Notions like "atom" or "gene" were developed to explain observed phenomena; in the social sciences we have "inflation" and "culture." All by itself, a concept does not explain anything, just as a single word does not say anything. Words must be combined into sentences, and it is the sentences which are true or false, believable or unbelievable, well or poorly justified. Similarly, concepts change in the light of new evidence only insofar as they are parts of theories. Think of the dramatic changes in the concepts of "atom" and "gene" in the 20th century as the theories of physics and biology changed. The distinctive characteristic of a social science—as opposed to informal thinking about our social world—is therefore the development of concepts as parts of empirically tested theories. This means that answering the question about how social scientific concepts get their content will require an examination of the characteristics of scientific theory.

There are two broad frameworks for understanding social scientific theories and concepts: naturalism and interpretivism. Both have venerable pedigrees which reach back to the social sciences of the 19th century. Naturalists have traditionally used a conception of theories which draws on empiricism. On this view, both

DOI: 10.4324/9781003207795-3

social and natural sciences postulate laws to systematize observations and provide the basis for explanation. This form of naturalism has consequences for the way in which social phenomena are conceptualized. Survey methods are a product of the search for law-like regularities. Surveys need concepts that are measurable or otherwise empirically identifiable. In Section 3.2 we will begin our discussion of the *empiricist view of theory* and consider the problem of "construct validity" in the development of social scientific concepts. The alternative to an empiricist view of theory is often called *interpretivism*. Proponents of this view have argued that searching for laws and causal explanations misses the unique character of the social world. The arguments for this position, discussed in Section 3.3, will turn on the relationship between the social scientists' concepts and the concepts of the people being studied. Proponents of interpretivism conclude that the concepts developed by the social scientist must be closely related to those employed by the subjects. This makes social scientific theorizing like the translation or interpretation of a text.

The capacity of humans to apply concepts to themselves is the basis for arguments that the entities postulated by the social sciences are very different from those postulated by the natural sciences. Natural science, one might argue, discovers natural kinds—the fundamental properties of the natural world. Natural kinds might be things like quarks or DNA molecules. The analogues in the social world might be institutions like schools or statuses like being married. One might argue that if a couple does not think of themselves as married and if they are not treated as being married by neighbors, churches, or courts, then they are not married at all. By contrast, the DNA molecule doesn't care how it gets treated; it doesn't conceptualize itself. This not only entails that there is a metaphysical difference between the social and natural sciences; it means that the relationship between social scientific concepts and the conceptualizations of the people studied is a two-way street. While the social scientists are trying to form concepts and theories about a group of people, the subjects are observing the social scientists and learning from them. Humans take social scientific concepts and make them their own.

3.1. Aggression, Violence, and Video Games

Do violent video games cause aggressive behavior? As video game technology has made violent interaction more vivid and personal, concerns about their effects have risen. A broad research program in social psychology has investigated this question with both experimental and correlational studies. Several decades of research have caught the attention of parents and politicians. In 2000, the American Academy of Pediatrics declared that "At this time, well over 1,000 studies . . . point overwhelmingly to a causal connection between media violence and aggressive behavior in some children" (American Academy of Pediatrics 2000). A more recent analysis of the literature concluded that "there is an extensive body of theoretically consistent empirical evidence showing that exposure to media violence is a causal risk factor for aggression" (Bushman and Anderson 2015, 1818). Some investigators have embraced such strong claims, but others have been more circumspect, arguing that violent video games (and other media) at most modulate underlying aggressive tendencies that have other causes.

Social learning theories are one prominent approach to aggression. According to this kind of view, children learn how to respond to social situations by observing and modeling the behavior of others. An individual's knowledge of how to act in a given kind of situation is encoded in memory. While the details of the encoding vary among social learning theories, the upshot is largely the same. Children learn patterns of response to social situations. As we mature, these responses get hardened into personality structures that resist change. An investigator with this theoretical standpoint would expect a direct causal link between the environment in which a child develops and aggressive behavior. Proponents of different social learning theories have different views about which elements of the environment provide the strongest models for emulation. It may be that greater exposure to violent video games, especially first-person shooting games, would effectively train children to respond aggressively to social situations. An alternative explanation would be that exposure to live aggression, especially family violence, is a much stronger force in the shaping of behavior.

Another issue in the literature is whether tendencies toward violent behavior have a genetic basis. Studies which compare identical twins reared apart have supported the notion that there is a genetic predisposition to a violence-prone personality (Eley et al 2003). On this view, some individuals are prone to interpret situations as threatening and are more likely to respond violently. The environment is the basis for some learned responses, but this only enhances or suppresses an innate disposition. Some investigators interested in media violence have used this theory to suggest that the correlation between playing violent video games and aggressive behavior is explained by a third underlying factor: the innate disposition. Video game violence (and other violent entertainment), these investigators have argued, has a negligible effect in the formation of an aggressive personality.

These different theories of aggression have been tested both inside and outside of the laboratory. In the lab, it is easy enough to expose subjects to violent or non-violent video games. The trick is to find a way of identifying aggression in an experimental setting. The investigator cannot simply instigate a fistfight, obviously, so some sort of proxy must be used. Some studies administer a questionnaire after gameplay, asking subjects to report their feelings or thoughts. Another sort of protocol seeks to identify aggressive thoughts by asking the subjects to complete open-ended stories. The stories describe a frustrating situation, such as being involved in an auto collision, and ask the subjects to list possible actions, feelings, or dialogue for the characters. Another test identifies aggressive action more directly. In this protocol subjects are told they are playing a computer game against an opponent. The winner of each trial gets to set the volume and duration of a noise blast heard by the loser. They are, in fact, playing only against a computer. Louder and longer blasts are taken as more aggressive.

In correlational studies, investigators use surveys to look for a relationship between playing violent video games and various forms of aggression. Again, while it is easy to understand how a questionnaire might ask about what video games a person has played, it is more difficult to see how aggression might be measured. Direct measures would look at actual events, such as arrest records. Aggression is a larger phenomenon than criminal activity, of course, so investigators must cast a wider net. Surveys of attitudes are a common way of indirectly measuring aggression. In contemporary survey methodology, questions are divided into groups which correlate highly with each other. The identification of such "factors" is an important (and challenging) part of developing a useful survey instrument. Each factor is supposed to explain or account for a significant portion of the variation in answers. The idea behind the construction of factors is that while a phenomenon like aggression is manifested in a variety of ways, these different manifestations arise from a smaller number of underlying properties. The factors should identify these deeper structures.

The Buss-Perry Aggression Questionnaire (Buss and Perry 1992) is a typical survey instrument. It has twenty-nine statements, and the subjects are asked to rate them on a scale of 1 (extremely uncharacteristic of me) to 7 (extremely characteristic of me). While the subject answers the questions in a randomized order, the investigators know that questions divide into groups corresponding to four factors: physical aggression, verbal aggression, anger, and hostility. For example, there are five questions that compose the verbal aggression factor (Buss and Perry 1992, 454):

- I tell my friends openly when I disagree with them.
- I often find myself disagreeing with people.
- When people annoy me, I may tell them what I think of them.
- I can't help getting into arguments when people disagree with me.
- My friends say that I'm somewhat argumentative.

A subject's answers on the scale of 1–7 are combined to create a single verbal aggression score for that person. A typical question of correlational research on video game violence, then, is whether subjects who report higher levels of exposure to violent video games have higher levels of physical aggression, verbal aggression, anger, and hostility as measured by factors of the questionnaire.

The study of video games and aggression raises a number of important philosophical questions, and we have already noted several of them. Is it really possible to measure things like aggression? The methodology of survey research presumes that indirect measures can capture the relevant patterns which will help us understand, explain, and predict aggressive behavior. Do these substitutes ("loud" blasts punishing a computer, answers to the Buss-Perry Aggression Questionnaire) really capture the concept of aggression? And what *is* the concept we are trying to capture, and how would we know that we have it right? Does it matter if the teen gamers think about aggression differently than the social scientists who study them?

We will discuss these questions in the next two sections. Others arise as well. The question with which we began is about causes: do violent video games cause aggressive behavior? How can a questionnaire be evidence for a causal association? And even if we could discover something like a causal law linking video games with aggression, could it really explain why Fred punched his little brother? The problem of whether human action can be explained causally will be discussed in Chapter 5, while the more general issues about the metaphysics and epistemology of causality will be discussed in Chapters 11 and 12.

3.2. Defining Theoretical Concepts

The Empiricist View of Concepts and Theory Structure

The body of empirical research briefly described in the previous section asks whether there is a causal relationship between playing violent video games and aggression. One of the philosophical questions that arises from this research is: what is "aggression" as defined by these studies, and how is it measured or empirically identified? The theories of aggression discussed earlier all postulate that aggression arises from an enduring feature of a person: an "aggressive personality." The difference between the social learning theories and the innate/genetic theories is primarily a difference about the causes of this kind of personality and the degree to which it is environmentally malleable. The aggressive personality is a *theoretical entity* or *posit*. It is not directly observable; it is something known only through knowledge of the theory. In this respect, theorists in this area are adhering to a philosophical picture of scientific theories and concepts that goes back at least to the scientific revolution. The empiricist view of theory was formulated in a strong and clear way by mid-20th-century philosophers of science, but the central ideas can be found in a broad range of philosophical and scientific writing. It has been commonly expressed by social scientists in their writing about theories and theory construction.

On the empiricist view of theory, a theory is a structure of general statements that explains some phenomena and permits predictions about them. These statements are often called "laws" or "nomological generalizations." Newton's mechanics were taken as an exemplar of a scientific theory. Given knowledge of some initial conditions (such as mass, force, position, or velocity), Newton's laws of motion explain current motions of an object and predict its future motions. The statements of the theory are deductively related and form a logically unified structure. The generalizations of a good scientific theory should be precise enough to permit the deduction of testable hypotheses. The theory can be epistemologically justified by comparing these consequences of the theory with observation.

The concepts of a theory are expressed by the substantive words that appear in the theory's general statements. In precisely quantified theories, the concepts are often associated with the variables of the laws. Newton's second law of motion is that $F=ma$. It relates force, mass, and acceleration, which are three of the central concepts of Newtonian mechanics. The concepts of a theory might be more or less directly observable or measurable. We learn in high school physics that *mass* and *weight* are different. Weight is what I feel when I pick up a barbell. Mass is a technical concept of Newton's theory. In the absence of gravity or acceleration, the barbell is weightless, yet it retains its mass. Weight is easily observable, but mass must be calculated, via the statements of the theory, from weight in a gravitational field or some other observables. What are often called "theoretical concepts" are those that are relatively remote from observation. On the empiricist view, the statements of the theory give content to (we might even say "define," but here we must be careful not to beg important questions) the theoretical concepts. Thus, in Newton's theory, the theoretical concept of mass is the quantity that is equal to force divided by acceleration (if $F=ma$, then $m=F/a$), the quantity that is equal to momentum divided by velocity (since $p=mv$, $m=p/v$), and so on.

Returning to the studies of aggression, "aggressive personality" is a theoretical concept. Having an aggressive personality is not directly observable in the way that playing a video game or punching someone in the nose is observable. That some people have an aggressive personality is a theoretical posit. The different theories of aggression agree that there is such a thing, that an aggressive personality causes aggressive behavior, and that aggressive behavior is relatively observable. They differ in their specific accounts of internal structure and etiology of "aggressive personality." These theoretical disagreements result in differences in what "aggressive personality" means in the different theories. For a social learning theory, an "aggressive personality" is a set of memories, behavioral scripts, and learned affective responses to the environment. These are created by the person's experiences, and they cause a person to perceive some actions as threatening and to react to those threats. Aggressive personality is an inner state. The central question of behavioral-genetic theory is the relative proportion of the contributions of genes and environment. Hence, for a behavioral-genetic theory of aggression, "aggressive personality" is a *phenotype* in the same sense as songs are part of the phenotype of a bird species. That is, it is a pattern of behavior created jointly by the individual's genes and the environment.

Research on the question of whether violent video games cause aggression, and the underlying research on aggression and personality, can be fit into the empiricist view of theory. Both social learning and behavioral-genetic theories are systems of generalizations about how aspects of personality are developed, maintained, and expressed. Through this system of law-like generalizations, they give content to concepts like "aggressive personality." To test the theory, the investigators derive hypotheses that satisfy two criteria: (1) the hypothesis should be logically entailed by the theory; and (2) it should include concepts that are amenable to direct or indirect observation. The logical relationship between hypothesis and theory makes the test possible. If observation shows that the hypothesis is false, then as a matter of logic alone, some proposition of the theory must be false. The second requirement means that the hypothesis can be observationally determined to be true or false. Here, however, there is a substantial challenge. "Aggressive personality" is not the sort of thing which can be directly observed. How can social scientists identify or develop reliable observation concepts?

Realism, Instrumentalism, and the Problem of Construct Validity

Survey responses seem to be a simple and clear species of observable behavior, and as a result, they are a common method of theory testing. The vagueness and ambiguity of everyday life is neatly carved into distinct components. Each question has an answer chosen from a discrete set of options. The uniformity of the answers permits direct comparison among responses of different subjects. Moreover, since the answers can be counted, investigators can calculate probability, correlation, risk, odds ratios, and a host of other relationships. Patterns of survey response among the participants are therefore a popular observational basis for testing hypotheses. However, it would be pointless to formulate hypotheses that directly described patterns of survey response. After all, we do not learn much from the observation that 43% of the respondents answered "yes" to question 7. The discussion of the Buss-Perry Aggression Questionnaire shows how these patterns are turned into concepts that are more closely related to the theories that social scientists want to test. The concepts are defined by responses to the questions and called "factors," "latent variables," or "constructs," and the hypotheses tested by a survey are expressed in terms of these constructs. These scientific practices raise several philosophical questions: why should we think that these patterns of survey response *represent* anything? Why should we think that a higher score on the physical aggression factor of the Buss-Perry Aggression Questionnaire means that the person is physically aggressive?

In the methodological literature, these philosophical questions are often called problems of "construct validity." There are two broad philosophical positions for us to evaluate. A *realist* position about construct validity holds that a valid construct is one that measures what it purports to measure. In other words, real features of the world correspond to theoretical concepts or constructs, and valid surveys (or other tests) can measure them. While this position may seem like common sense, it is not the most common philosophical view. The dominant tradition in methodology has been *anti-realist*. We will meet several varieties of anti-realism in this book. What they share is a suspicion about metaphysical claims in the sciences, and the idea that unseen entities correspond to our theories is suspiciously metaphysical. The variety of anti-realism relevant to the present discussion is *instrumentalism*. An instrumentalist view of construct validity holds that a valid construct is one that simplifies and systematizes our past observations and permits accurate predictions of the future. Commitment to the "reality" of theoretical constructs is simply unnecessary.

The canonical expression of construct validity is Cronbach and Meehl's essay "Construct Validity in Psychological Tests" (1955). They articulated a position on theoretical concepts in the social sciences that is consistent with the empiricist view of theory. Again, on this view, a concept has specific defining attributes because of its role in the theory. The question of construct validity, then, is to show that the specific attributes of the concept are found in the observational evidence. Consider the construct of "verbal aggression" in the Buss-Perry Aggression Questionnaire. Verbal aggression is treated as a theoretical posit, like "aggressive personality," but "verbal aggression" is closer to the surface of observable behavior. As a theoretical posit, verbal aggression is part of a network of concepts (including physical aggression, anger, and hostility) related by generalizations. Sometimes these are rough or pre-theoretical generalizations; sometimes they may be substantiated by earlier research. This is a theory (Cronbach and Meehl call it a "nomological network"), and it makes predictions about how the different factors should correlate. Roughly, if the factors do not correlate in the way that theory predicts, then the theory must be modified, which means that the content (definition) of the concepts is modified.

Cronbach and Meehl take an instrumentalist approach to construct validity. The goal is to find a theory that fits the observation, and the only real question is whether the data points correlate or cluster in ways that fit the concepts. The lure of instrumentalism lies in the way it resolves the epistemic predicament of the scientist. The predicament arises when the theory postulates the existence of something and we have no way of directly observing or measuring it. The only epistemological resources are more observations: more tests, more surveys, more experiments, and so on. The best we can do is to compare these observations with each other, using them to rule out theories that do not conform to the data. In the end, a good theory is one that accounts for all the observations. We can ask no more, yet a realist seems to want more. The realist wants to ask whether the theoretical constructs *really* correspond to the hidden properties or structures. The instrumentalist replies that since there is nothing but observations that could answer that question, the realist demand cannot be satisfied.

In response, realists have argued that there is something incoherent about the instrumentalist approach to concept validity. The idea of measurement requires two commitments, and instrumentalism violates both. First, measuring the properties of an entity requires commitment to its existence. For example, it is impossible to design an instrument that would detect the presence of Santa Claus in the chimney. The problem is not that we have no theory of Santa Claus (we do!), but that we think Santa Claus does not exist (sorry, kids). Therefore, it is incoherent to say, "This instrument measures aggression" and at the same time deny that aggression exists. Instrumentalism thus seems to be an inconsistent position. Second, any measurement instrument must be causally related to the things measured, such that changes in the object cause changes in this instrument. This is true of mechanical measuring devices, like thermometers, as well as all kinds of surveys and tests. Denying such a causal connection renders insignificant any claim that a difference in test score (etc.) means that there is some difference in the things measured, and it would make measurement irrelevant to both theory and practice. To adopt an instrumentalist attitude toward theoretical concepts, the realists argue, is to deny the very thing which makes measurement possible.

A practical consequence of this debate is that some social scientific research seems to be superficial precisely because the constructs are so thin and under-developed. Starting with a large enough pool of questions, it will always be possible to find correlations among them and to derive "factors" from those correlations. Of course, survey developers never start with random questions; they start with questions which they guess will capture the phenomena in which they are interested. But if these initial concepts are weakly developed, ambiguous, or vague, the surveys cannot yield significant results. The instrumentalist understands this line of criticism as showing that good research requires good theories. Without well-developed and carefully articulated theories to support the constructs, the surveys will be superficial. The realist will respond that the criticism goes deeper. Some social scientific research tries to measure entities which we have, as yet, no good reason to believe exist over and above patterns of correlated survey responses. The result is studies which are methodologically sound but theoretically vacuous.

The debate between realism and anti-realism is a conflict between two broad views about the project of science. A realist takes the goal of science to be the discovery of truths, including mechanisms and entities that are not directly observable. The anti-realist denies that the goal of science could be the discovery of truths or theory-independent facts. Anti-realism takes many forms, depending on the grounds for rejecting realism. Instrumentalism is a form of anti-realism which arises within an empiricist framework for theory construction. We have seen in this section how the difference between realism and instrumentalism has important consequences for the way social scientists understand their research.

3.3. Interpretivism

You may already have had the thought that the research on aggression does not capture the way the subjects think about, react to, or feel aggression. For example, context seems to matter. If I were to say, "That is an incoherent statement" to my daughter over breakfast, it would be taken as aggressive: it was unnecessarily harsh and argumentative. If I say the same thing later in the day to my colleague while talking philosophy, it may be understood as an unremarkable moment of intellectual give-and-take. Whether an act is aggressive depends on how the subjects understand "aggression," as well as their views about contextually appropriate behavior. The problem with instruments like the Buss-Perry Aggression Questionnaire, one might think, is that pre-selected survey items stand in for the subjects' points of view. Indeed, some have argued that the whole empiricist apparatus of law-like generalization and hypotheses testing is blind to the subjective character of social reality. Therefore, some have concluded, the social sciences need concepts and forms of theory that are different from those of the natural sciences.

Following common philosophical usage, this form of anti-naturalism will be called "interpretivism."

Ideal Types and Verstehen

Max Weber, the great social theorist of the late 19th and early 20th centuries, articulated an influential vision of social inquiry. Central to his methodological approach was the notion of an "ideal type" (Weber 1949 [1904], 85–110). Concepts of the social sciences, Weber argued, need to capture the meanings and motivations that are significant for the subjects. To do so, the social scientist should first describe the actions to be explained in terms of their typical motivations. The concept is then formed by abstracting characteristics of the action from a variety of observations. The unique character of social inquiry is that ideal types must include typical motivations, attitudes, and meanings. Ideal types therefore relate observable behaviors by identifying the motivations that stand behind them. The concept of "aggression," Weber would say, must be developed as an ideal-type concept. It is not sufficient to define it solely in terms of observable behavior, such as selecting the loudness of a sound blast. The concept needs to identify the typical feelings, beliefs, and social meanings that stand behind the behavior. In this respect, the definition of aggressive behavior in terms of the "intent to cause harm" (Anderson and Bushman 2002, 28) is on the right track because it picks out a typical motivation. However, since the common understanding of aggression also involves other feelings, motivations, and responses, Weber would say that the definition remains incomplete.

How would an investigator determine that their concepts are incomplete or otherwise inadequate? We have seen the empiricist answer: concepts get their meaning from their role in a theory, and a theory is a system of laws. The meaning of a concept develops as the theory is modified in response to testing. Weber could not accept this account because he rejected laws as a necessary basis for social scientific understanding. While the discovery of law-like generalizations might be important and useful in some contexts, he argued that the expression of laws in the social sciences already required well-developed ideal type concepts. Ideal types are thus independent of and prior to generalizations. Weber emphasized that ideal types were idealizations; they were tools for the identification of central aspects of a phenomenon (Weber 1949 [1904], 90). Yet, unlike the idealization of a "frictionless surface," ideal types are to be compared with the evidence and modified in its light. An ideal type predicts actions, historical changes, or social developments based on the particular motivations it identifies. If these actions do not arise in the expected context, there is reason to modify the ideal type.

The concern with which this section began was that a naturalistic perspective on the social sciences, particularly the empiricist view of theory and associated methods, failed to capture the subjective character of the social world. Weber's ideal types go some way toward addressing this concern, but one might argue that they do not go far enough. Ideal types treat the subjectivity of the agents as a construction of the social scientist. It is the social scientist, after all, who chooses to emphasize one aspect or another of the social environment. This replacement of the subject's view with the scientist's theory, some have felt, is precisely the problem with survey research and similar methods. Weber's idea might be pushed further by recognizing that the subjects have their own ideal types. That is, as participants in a social group, we have our own understanding of the possibilities for action. We know the expectations, regulations, roles, and institutions that make up our social reality. Alfred Schutz called this "common-sense thinking," and he argued that *verstehen* is "the particular experiential form in which common-sense thinking takes cognizance of the social cultural world" (Schutz 1954, 264). A full-blooded *verstehen* approach to the social sciences would thus capture the subjects' own understanding of their world.

Schutz suggested that the social sciences require two levels of ideal types. The first is the level of common-sense thinking, and it contains the "theories" used by a group of people to understand each other. The second is the social scientific models of motivations, feelings, and meanings. The social scientist's theory construction proceeds with the second-level ideal types. Since the aim of social science, on the *verstehen* view, is to understand the subjects' perspective, the second level must reflect the first level in some way. Articulating this relationship between first- and second-level idea types is a difficult philosophical problem. Schutz proposed that the second-level ideal types had to be "consistent" with the common-sense thinking. As he phrased this "postulate of adequacy" it required that:

> Each term in a scientific model of human action must be constructed in such a way that . . . the typical construct would be understandable for the actor himself as well as his fellow-men in terms of common-sense interpretation of everyday life.
>
> (Schutz 1953, 34)

While this arguably does more than Weber's ideal types to capture the subjective dimension of social concepts, it too has its challenges. The postulate of adequacy seems both too strong and too weak. It is too strong if it requires that *every* concept of a scientific theory be "understandable to the actor himself." Some concepts might require mathematical formalism or other technicalities not normally known by the subjects. Moreover, it seems to forbid social scientists from trying to discover something about our social lives that we do not already know. There is no room for deception (including self-deception), concealed deployment of power, structural inequalities, and so on. One might reply that Schutz only requires that the agents be able to understand the constructs, not that they agree with them or use them in their daily lives. On this reading, the requirement is too weak, because we lose any sense of how the second level ideal types correspond to the first level.

Hermeneutics and Meaning

What is the role of *language* in common-sense thinking about social reality? Another way of representing Schutz's problem is that there are two languages involved in the social sciences: the subject's own and the social scientist's. Even if the scientist comes from the same social milieu and speaks the same language as their subject, the social scientist is developing a technical terminology (ideal types) with which to describe and explain social events. What is the relationship between the subject's language and the specialized language of the scientist?

Empiricist approaches treat the problem of relating the scientist's technical language to the subject's language as the problem of relating theory to observation. We saw the outline of this view in Section 3.1. At the outset of social research, we do not know the subject's motivations, feelings, meanings, and so on. Inquiry, empiricists argue, must therefore begin with a neutral description of behaviors. From this perspective, one can see the attraction of survey and testing methods, since they need only a very thin description of the action, e.g., that the person selected "Very like me" in response to question 14.

Interpretivists have been very suspicious of the idea that such an impoverished observation language could possibly support interesting social scientific research. Language, many have pointed out, is deeply integrated into social life. Events of social life get their identity—even their very existence—because of the way in which language and action are mutually embedded. Charles Taylor's essay, "Interpretation and the Sciences of Man" (1971), uses this point about the relationship between language and action to argue against any naturalistic approach to the social sciences.

Taylor distinguishes "rule-governed" from "rule-constituted" activities. Consider two players at a game of chess. Suppose one player moves their knight two squares up and one over, and we want to explain why. A neutral observation language would let us describe the state of the board and the regularities of motion of the pieces. But simply saying that the horsey-shaped pieces generally move two up and one over will not suffice. While true, it misses the normative character of the move. Knights are not just pieces with a particular shape which happen to move in this way. The knight has a role which *requires* it to move in a particular way. We might try to capture this aspect of the game by adding that the players believe that the knight moves in an L-shaped path. Even so, this belief is unlike the belief that the fastest route from New York to Washington, DC, is via Highway 95. The game of chess, Taylor says, is a rule-constituted activity, not merely a rule-governed activity. In a rule-governed activity, the actions already have a particular character, and rules are brought to bear on this character. Laws govern behavior in this sense: it is because we already know what walking is that a rule can forbid walking on the grass. In rule-constituted activities, the actions get their identity from the rules. To be the move of a knight requires more than moving in an L-shaped path. What it is to be a knight and what it means for a knight to move are both defined by the rules of chess. (We will return to this idea and develop it further in Section 10.3.)

Taylor argues that a neutral language restricted to the motions of bodies, answers on a survey, or even descriptions of the beliefs and attitudes of the agents would be unable to capture rule-constituted activities. To express these, both the players and the social scientists must *interpret* the motions *as* conforming to the rules. Interpretations, Taylor contends, are never neutral. What is interpreted in one way can always be re-interpreted by arranging the meanings differently. Thus, if our two players stop interpreting each other as playing chess and begin to think of themselves as, say, making an aesthetically pleasing pattern, they will stop playing chess. And they might even continue to conform to the rules! To interpret behavior, Taylor concludes, requires taking a stand on what the action means.

While natural language is not constituted by strict rules in the way that chess and other games are, many have argued that language has a very strong normative character. Utterances may be grammatical or ungrammatical, meaningful or nonsensical, and appropriate or inappropriate in the context. Any identification of *the* use of a word or phrase presupposes a difference between correct and incorrect use. Taylor's argument identifies a problem with concept construction that is shared by the empiricists and Weber's ideal-types. Both think of the concepts of social science as part of a theoretical project. While Weber and Schutz highlighted differences between concepts of the natural and social sciences, the aim is still to find an adequate theoretical representation. Taylor's alternative suggestion is that we must think about social scientific concepts as more like *translations* of the subject's language than like representations of their beliefs.

Thick Description and Its Challenges

One of the clearest articulations of the idea that social scientific concepts are translations is found Clifford Geertz's essay "Thick Description: Toward an Interpretive Theory of Culture" (Geertz 1973b). Geertz is an anthropologist, and while his primary goal in this essay was to articulate a conception of culture and account for the epistemology of ethnography, his ideas have been adopted by social scientists in a variety of fields. The challenge of writing ethnography, it has often been remarked, is that it needs to render another way of life intelligible to the audience without losing its foreignness. Ethnographic description is thus akin to translating novels or poetry. Geertz's notion of "thick description" aims to meet this challenge.

The key idea, of course, is "thick description." The difference between "thick" and "thin" description is a matter of degree. A maximally thin description would be something like the behaviorist observation language criticized by Taylor. To describe a person as simply walking be a thin description. Thin descriptions have minimal relationships to other descriptions. That is, to say person is walking is to say almost nothing about the person's goals and motivations. A thicker description of the same event would be that the person is *walking to Bowden Hall*, or that she was *walking to class*. These are thick descriptions because they show how the action is related to other aspects of the person's life and social environment. *Hurrying to class* suggests a possible set of motives and specific relationships to prior and subsequent activities. It invokes the idea of getting to class on time, the possible alternative modes of transportation, and the reasons why a person would prefer walking to driving or taking the bus. Thick descriptions of actions, events, or even socially significant objects, have, in virtue of their meaning, specific relationships to other actions, events, objects, motivations, possibilities for response, outcomes, strategies, and so on.

The conceptual relationships expressed by thick description are already embedded in the language, symbolic system, and actions of the subjects. They thus correspond to Schutz's common-sense thinking. However, Geertz does not follow Schutz in regarding common-sense thinking as the subject's *theories* about their own society. Following Wittgenstein, Geertz treats the meaning of a word as its conditions for use in a community. This notion of meaning can be generalized to symbols of all kinds, and to the meaningfulness of actions as well (cf. Winch 1958). Because meaningfulness depends on patterns found across the whole community, thick description captures what the members of the community have in common— their culture. Culture is, in Geertz's phrase, an "acted document" (Geertz 1973b, 10). Schutz's common-sense thinking becomes nothing more or less than the totality of actions, utterances, and social events that make up the culture. The goal of interpretive social science is to thickly describe the culture, and thereby express in the interpreter's language the relationships that make the subjects' social world meaningful.

Interpretivism has several consequences that have troubled both philosophers and social scientists. Thick descriptions are generalizations about a group, and some have found generalizations about "the" culture problematic. There is a strong tendency in interpretive social science to understand the beliefs, values, meanings, symbols, norms, and actions of a group as a single coherent system. Against this, one might point out that social groups are typically riven by conflict and contradiction. Different people do not find the same meaning in a social event or symbol; they do not understand the demands of a rule or norm in the same way. Moreover, differences in interpretation can be closely tied to social relationships of power and domination. By presenting a single narrative of "the" culture, the interpretation not only misrepresents the social reality; it takes up a position within the power structures of the society. One group's common-sense is highlighted as the true account, while other, dissenting voices are eclipsed. Thick description, some conclude, is inevitably a political act. In the terms of Section 2.3, interpretations are not value-neutral. One criticism of earlier anthropologists has been that they were not sufficiently sensitive to the unintended political consequences of their work. As a result of these criticisms, contemporary interpreters are often concerned to represent conflict and difference of voice in the interpretive description of a group. It has also resulted in a demand for *reflexivity* on the part of the interpreter, a requirement that will be examined in Section 4.1.

The problem of generalization goes deeper still, insofar as it questions whether cultures have clear identities at all. Social groups not only dispute meanings, but they also borrow meanings and practices from each other. Any thick description depends on the interpreter's decisions about which meanings, values, symbols, and so on are typical of the culture. In an important sense, then, "the culture" is nothing more than the artificial creation of the anthropologist, or so it has been argued. This dispute raises some very difficult philosophical questions: are cultures bounded entities with typical features? And if cultures or social groups are always artificial, what consequences does this have for the social sciences?

Realism and Relativism About the Social World

The questions with which the last section ended raise the issues of realism and anti-realism again. When taking an interpretivist stance, it is natural to adopt what Martin Hammersley characterizes as "naïve realism." This is the doctrine that "there is a reality independent of the researcher whose nature can be known and that the aim of research is to produce accounts that correspond to that reality" (Hammersley 1992, 43). The ethnographer is concerned with a social world which in some way is the product of human activity. A naïve realism about the social world holds that there is a *social* reality independent of the researcher. The subjects have a culture composed of concepts, beliefs, values, and norms, and that culture exists independently of the researcher. Culture is out there, waiting to be discovered by the ethnographer.

Two points canvassed earlier seem to argue against naïve realism about the social world. First, the porous character of human interaction seems to show that there are no clear cultural boundaries. The appearance of these boundaries is a product of distinguishing "us" from "them," which is a political distinction, not one based in reality. Second, the elements that compose "the culture" seem to be determined by the ethnographer, not by any facts about culture. These reasons motivate many who adopt interpretivism to adopt an anti-realist, relativist stance. On this view, the aim of the social sciences is not to grasp an independent reality—even a social reality—but to inhabit different realities. Hammersley characterizes the position this way:

> In their work ethnographers create a social world (or worlds), rather than merely representing some independent reality (more or less accurately). And, it may be concluded, this world is no more nor less true than others; for instance, than the perceptions and interpretations of the people studied.
>
> (Hammersley 1992, 45)

Ethnography (and other "qualitative" methods we will explore in Chapter 4) are thus taken as not discovering a social world but creating it.

The ideas that motivate relativism are compelling, yet to many social scientists and philosophers, the conclusion is troubling. Taken literally, the proposed relativism effaces the difference between ethnography and fiction. Why spend all that time and effort to visit a place, when you can just sit in the armchair and make it up? The difference between ethnography and fiction, a realist will argue, turns on the idea of evidence. Ethnographers observe social events and spend a lot of time analyzing field notes. If it were really the case that each version of a social world was just as real as any other, then this effort seems pointless. The challenge for a realist is to explain how one interpretation can be better than another while acknowledging that cultural boundaries are fluid and that the ethnographer makes a significant contribution to the social reality they study.

In response to the relativist challenge, a realist might make two points. First, a realist might back off the strong claims about cultural boundaries that character-ized early anthropology. What are identified as "cultures" from the outside are better understood as overlapping and intersecting sets of practices. A practice is something like a habit; it is learned, reproduced, and sometimes reflected upon. The practices of a group of people need not be consistent or coherent, and individu-als may reject the practices of their community. While we the idea of a practice needs more elaboration (and we will do so in Section 9.3), the point here is that it does not presuppose the rigid boundaries commonly associated with the idea of culture. Second, the existence of practices does not depend on the ethnographer. The social world will indeed be different when the ethnographer engages their subjects, but the ethnographer is not creating the subjects' social world through their ethnography. Rather, according to the realist, the ethnographer is gathering evidence to support an interpretation of those practices in which the ethnographer was participating. The success of this realist response clearly turns on the way in which interpretations are based on evidence. This is the subject of the next chapter.

3.4. Wrap Up

Chapter Summary

This chapter has surveyed one of the fundamental debates about epistemological naturalism. Does human subjectivity require that the concepts and theories of the social sciences be different from the natural sciences? Or, as the naturalists claim, is there a single form of scientific knowledge? Many research programs within the social sciences emulate the natural sciences by adopting an empiricist conception of theories and concepts. The survey methodologies discussed in Section 3.2 are just one example of how the empiricist view of theory influences social scientific practice; we will discuss research on causes and correlations in Chapters 11 and 12. The strength of the empiricist view of theory is that concepts can be identified or measured and the theories can be tested.

Interpretivists criticize research based on an empiricist view of theory, arguing that it develops inadequate concepts. Social scientific concepts must encompass the ways in which the social world is meaningful to the agents. Interpretivists share several commitments. First, there is no neutral, uninterpreted, "brute data" which can form the basis of social scientific theorizing. Social phenomena are already interpreted by the subjects. Second, social worlds are partly constituted by norms, rules, and values. For interpretivism, then, the goal of social inquiry is to articulate these meanings and norms and to systematize them in a way that shows their inter-connectedness. This is the essence of Geertz's thick description.

A second question that has run through the chapter is whether we should take a realist stance toward the social sciences. A realist view of the social sciences would take its concepts to correspond to real social entities. Where the natural sciences discover natural kinds, the social sciences discover social kinds. We saw two forms of anti-realism in this chapter: instrumentalism and relativism. We will return to the issues raised here in Chapters 4 and 8.

This chapter is the opening salvo in a larger battle between naturalist and anti-naturalist views. The debate between interpretivism and the empiricist conception of theory will reappear in Chapter 5. Some of the most damaging critiques of the empiricist conception of theory come not from interpretivists but from naturalists who want to develop causal theories. Chapter 6 will look at modeling practice in the social sciences. The social sciences, many argue, are better understood as cre-ating models than as creating empiricist-style theories. In Chapters 11 and 12, we will discuss the critique of the empiricist conception of causality and law, and we will look at some recent alternatives. Interpretivism faces troubles of its own, and in Chapter 4 we will look at the epistemological and methodological issues which it raises. How can we come to *know* what the subjects believe or how they concep-tualize their activities? Interpretivism is not based on a neutral body of observa-tion. What, then, are the evidential constraints on interpretation? What makes one interpretation better than another? These are questions for the next chapter.

Discussion Questions

1. Compare instrumentalist and realist interpretations of the construct "aggres-sion." Which view seems the most plausible to you? Which view can help understand whether violent video games cause aggression?
2. Both the United States census (discussed in Section 2.1) and research on aggression require measurement. What are the differences between measuring "aggressive personality" and measuring the number of people in a country?
3. Schutz's postulate of adequacy holds that social scientific must be closely related to those used by the subjects. Can surveys be designed so that they satisfy Schutz's postulate of adequacy? Must they be so designed? Why?
4. To what extent can (or should) social science discover features of a society that are hidden from the members of that society? What would be an example of such hidden social structure? Would your example violate Schutz's postu-late of adequacy?
5. Does thick description require that the group under study be clearly delin-eated? Can it be applied in modern societies where group identity is fluid, and where people often inhabit multiple cultures, ethnicities, races, or genders?
6. It was argued in Sections 3.3 that interpretation cannot be value-neutral. Does this form of value-ladenness weaken the epistemic status of interpretations?

Further Reading

For a review of the literature and discussion research on aggression, see Anderson and Bushman (2002). Ferguson and Kilburn (2009) have a critical meta-analysis of this research, which is updated and analyzed in Bushman and Anderson (2015). Longino's *Studying Human Behavior* (2013) is a philosophically informed critique of the various fields that study aggression.

The classic statement of the empiricist view of theory in the philosophy of social science is in Book VI of Mill's *System of Logic* (1987 [1872]). While focused on the natural sciences, Hempel's little textbook *Philosophy of Natural Science* (1966) has clear and nuanced presentations of the standard view, and Nagel's monumental *Structure of Science* (1961) has an extensive discussion of the social sciences. Merton's *Social Theory and Social Structure* (1957) embeds these philosophical ideas into its methodological discussion. Hage's *Techniques and Problems of Theory Construction in Sociology* (1972) is a well-known text; Hage updates and reflects on this view in Hage (2007).

Measurement is a large topic in the methodology literature, and it involves substantial technical complexities. Cronbach and Meehl's seminal presentation is surprisingly accessible, and the philosophical ideas are close to the surface (Cronbach and Meehl 1955). Trout's *Measuring the Intentional World* (1998) relates the technicalities of measurement theory to the deeper philosophical questions, and Michell gives an overview of the issues (2007).

Martin's *Verstehen: The Uses of Understanding in Social Science* (2000) is an extensive overview and critique of different conceptions of *verstehen* in the social sciences. Weber presents his conceptions of *verstehen* and ideal types in several places. "Objectivity in Social Science and Social Policy" (Weber 1949 [1904]) is a readable presentation. Interpretation of Weber's ideal types can be found in Aronovitch (2011) or Ringer (1997). Classic arguments against the empiricist conception of theories and concepts is found in Schutz's "Concept and Theory Formation in the Social Sciences" (1954) and Taylor's "Interpretation and the Sciences of Man" (1971). For an historical overview and appraisal of these arguments, see Outhwaite's "Phenomenological and Hermeneutic Approaches" (2007). Naturalistic responses to this critique include Rudner's "On the Objectivity of the Social Sciences" (1966) and Føllesdal's "Hermeneutics and the Hypothetico-Deductive Method" (1973).

Geertz's essays "Thick Description: Towards an Interpretive Theory of Culture" and "Deep Play: Notes on the Balinese Cockfight" are important programmatic statements of contemporary interpretivism (both in Geertz 1973a), and Winch's *The Idea of a Social Science* (1958) was treated as a philosophical ally of the position. Critiques relevant to the topics of this chapter are Jarvie, "Understanding and Explanation in the Social Sciences" (in Jarvie 1972); Roth, "Pseudoproblems in Social Science: The Myth of Meaning Realism" (in Roth 1987); Kincaid, "A Science of Interpretation?" (in Kincaid 1996); Little, "Interpretation Theory" (in Little 1991); and Bohman, "Interpretation and Indeterminacy" (in Bohman 1991).

See also Feleppa, *Convention, Translation, and Understanding* (1988) and Ris-jord, *Woodcutters and Witchcraft* (2000). In anthropology, the interpretivist program came under severe criticism from the essays in Clifford and Marcus's *Writing Culture* (1986). See also Asad, *Anthropology and the Colonial Encounter* (1973) and Hammersley, *What's Wrong with Ethnography?* (1992). These anthropological disputes are put into historical and philosophical context in Risjord, "Models of Culture" (2012) and Palecek "The Evolution of 'Culture'" (2020).

Bevir and Blakely's *Interpretive Social Science* (2018) is a systematic defense of interpretivism that intersects with many of the themes of this book. It is noteworthy for its defense of the idea that interpretivism can absorb—carefully!—many of methods espoused by naturalists.

4   Interpretive Methodology

Interpretivists argued that the meaningful character of human life prevents the social sciences from adopting notions of theory structure, concept development, and objectivity from the natural sciences. In this chapter we turn away from concepts and theories to the evidence which supports them. After all, interpreters base their interpretations on fieldwork; they do not invent cultures from nothing. Those who maintain that interpretation is a distinctive form of inquiry need to articulate how interpreters acquire knowledge of others' experiences, meanings, and values. The interest and importance of these epistemological questions is not limited to those anti-naturalists who believe in the epistemic distinctiveness of interpretation. The reliability of a survey or an experiment depends on whether the subjects understand the questions and instructions. During survey development, social scientists standardly use interviews and focus groups to gauge the subjects' understanding of the survey. Independently of the issues debated in the last chapter, the epistemic soundness of social science depends on the soundness of the "qualitative" methods associated with interpretation. In this chapter we will address these epistemological questions: what is the evidence for an interpretation? What makes one interpretation better than another? What are the constraints on interpretation?

4.1. Evidence for Interpretation

At the end of the last chapter, we saw the realism issue arise for interpretivism. The issue may be posed as a dilemma. On the one hand, it seems that a community has a determinate set of experiences, values, attitudes, and beliefs that an interpretation aims to understand. As we saw, this sort of realism need not reify culture, but it does hold onto a notion of *authenticity*. Qualitative methods aim to understand the participants' own (authentic) experience, and the challenge is to remove the interpreter's biases and preconceived ideas. On the other hand, the interpreter contributes to the construction of the meanings they purport to uncover. If so, authenticity is unattainable since all interpretation will be co-created. A consequence of the co-creation of interpretation is that a different interpreter will produce a different interpretation and there will be no grounds on which to say that one is more accurate than the other. Does the rejection of authenticity require us to give up on a difference between good and bad qualitative research?

DOI: 10.4324/9781003207795-4

Qualitative Research Methods and Their Presuppositions

The research methods associated with interpretation are often called "qualitative" research, and thereby distinguished from "quantitative" social science. While commonly used in the methodological literature, the distinction between qualitative and quantitative research is quite problematic. It is difficult—perhaps impossible—to state the distinction clearly. More importantly, there are complex questions about how the social and natural scientific methods are related. Insisting on a dichotomy compresses these multi-faceted problems into a dogma. As used here, then, the phrase *qualitative methods* refers only to a loose collection of research techniques. Interviews, participant observation, and focus groups are paradigmatic examples, but qualitative methods also include life histories, production and analysis of video or audio recordings, discourse analysis of conversations, photography and the analysis of visual images, and so on. In recent decades, it has expanded to include analysis of social media and virtual communities. Before we can engage the epistemological issues that such methods raise, we need an understanding of what the methods are and what they presuppose about the subjects of study. While there are many methods, we will here introduce three iconic qualitative methods: interviews, focus groups, and participant observation.

Interviews are, perhaps, the most prevalent of the qualitative methods. The many textbooks on social scientific research methods note that interviews may be more or less structured. Structured interviews standardize each encounter by strictly following an ordered list of questions, while unstructured interviews begin with an open-ended question and let the conversation follow its own internal logic. Semi-structured interviews occupy the middle ground, following a set of questions but leaving the investigator latitude for follow-up questions.

The epistemic advantage of an interview is supposed to be that it provides:

> . . . access to the participants' understanding of the world and their experiences. Qualitative interviews give participants the opportunity to describe experiences in detail and to give their perspectives and interpretations of these experiences. The interviewer has the opportunity to discuss and explore with the participants and to probe more deeply into their accounts.
>
> (Taylor 2005, 40)

The methodological discussion of interviews typically focuses on ways in which a clumsy interview can keep the subject's "perspectives and interpretations" from emerging. Choices of clothing, interview location, ordering of questions, linguistic competence, and so on are typically cited as important determinants of the quality of the interview. Notice how such recommendations seem to presuppose authenticity: there is a determinate, if subjective, "understanding of the world and their experiences," and the object of the interview is to get a glimpse of this world.

Focus groups are familiar because of their role in developing advertisements or political campaigns. Originally developed as a way of assessing audience response to TV, movies, and consumer products, they have become an important scientific research tool. Unlike interviews, which are one-on-one conversations, focus groups encourage subjects to interact. Sophisticated users of the method look not only at the product of the group (e.g., the transcript of what was said), they also look at the process by which the group disputed, questioned, and (perhaps) reached consensus. Like interviews, focus groups may be structured by a specific protocol of questions. A focus group is often led by a professional moderator because a focus group requires careful management of the participants. If one or two people dominate the conversation with forceful opinions, or if some participants never become comfortable expressing their views in front of the others, the results may be one-sided, truncated, or biased. Some proponents of focus group methods argue that they can reach a deeper level of social reality because they are more dynamic and intensive than interviews or participant observation. Again, notice how realism has emerged into the characterization of the method.

Participant observation was articulated by Bronislaw Malinowski in the early 20th century as a way to "grasp the native's point of view, his relation to life, to realize *his* vision of *his* world" (Malinowski 1922, 19, emphasis in original). It was quickly adopted by sociologists in their studies of urban communities, and it is now used across the social sciences. In anthropology, ethnographers have typically followed Malinowski by taking up residence among the people whom they are studying. In other disciplines, the interaction might be more casual. In all cases, the investigator engages with the subjects across a broad range of everyday behavior. The investigator may take a role within the group, perhaps as an apprentice or volunteer in an organization. The investigator will, of course, be talking with the subjects, and some of these conversations may be indistinguishable from unstructured interviews. The participant observer places herself in a position to either witness or be part of the social processes she is studying. Participant observation, therefore, can rely on non-verbal behavior and natural interaction in a way that is inaccessible to either interview or focus group methods. Again, note the apparent presupposition: "his vision of his world" is as clear an expression of authenticity as one could want.

All three of these research methods take the interpretivist critique of naturalist social science seriously. Using these methods, social scientists learn the subject's interpretation of the events, practices, roles, and institutions that make up their social world. That is, they aim to uncover what Schutz called "common sense thinking" about the social world (*cf.* Section 3.3). The realism they presuppose is not the realism of a naturalist who is concerned with the causes or mechanisms of social process. Rather, it is a realism about meaning. Communities have their own distinctive experiences and social worlds. Discussion of the possible biases and mistakes of qualitative research in the methodological literature make it clear that the goal is to get an *authentic* presentation of these experiences and social worlds. They therefore presuppose that the subjects of a study have a clear view of their own experiences, motives, and perceptions.

Authority and Authenticity

The idea that qualitative methods can provide an authentic glimpse into a society or into a person's experience has its roots in our everyday experiences of communication. If I want to know what someone is thinking, I should ask them. Of course, people sometimes dissemble, especially to outsiders or those with whom they are unfamiliar. A good qualitative researcher establishes rapport. Rapport makes it more likely that the research participants will be honest, and it gives the researcher context to spot elisions or partial perspectives. The deep relationship between researcher and subjects is expressed in an interpretation through establishing interpretive *authority*. Like an eyewitness, he or she was present and part of the social milieu, talking with the subjects, perhaps living among them, and listening to their stories. Like a journalist, the interpreter can report "I was there." An interpreter's authority, then, seems to be one of their strongest epistemic credentials.

Several authors have argued that the common view of the interpreter's authority, expressed in the previous paragraph, is naïve. Establishing the interpreter's authority is fundamentally a rhetorical problem, and it is resolved through rhetorical devices. The literary device known as "realism"—the use of vivid, concrete detail—is a common tactic. Textbooks on qualitative research methods advise researchers to develop the details: "Sufficient description and direct quotations should be included to allow the reader to enter into the situation and thought of the people represented in the report" (Patton 2002, 503). Critics of authenticity argue that by rendering their experience in writing, the interpreter is constructing the very object which is to be interpreted. Moreover, the interpreter may create a sense of place by pulling together events and details that did not really co-exist. To protect the identity of informants, textual characters may be fictional, a mosaic created from aspects of many individuals. Particularly "informative" quotations are carefully selected from a longer text and presented to the reader. These are not sins against veracity in interpretation; they are necessary to its creation. But this means that the interpreter's authority is established by a sleight of hand. The interpreter creates the text to be interpreted and then disappears into the background, as if the text were a naturally occurring object to be observed.

The issues get more complicated when we think about the ways in which interviews, focus groups, and so on are special-purpose creations by the subjects as well. In their essay "Interview Society" (1997), Atkinson and Silverman point out that interviews are pervasive in the contemporary, global media culture. No sporting event is complete without interviews with the winners and losers; entertainment stars are interviewed about everything from their favorite cooking techniques to their political opinions. Subjects therefore come to an interview prepared to construct themselves through the conversation:

> The authenticity of a life is not to be understood simply in Romantic terms. There is no guarantee of biographical or narrative unity. The artifacts and memorabilia of a life—memories, documents, images—are themselves achievements. Life

narratives, whether they be retrospective or prospective accounts, are always pastiche, as it were. They are pieced together, always changeable and fallible, out of the stock of mementos. By examining how a biography is constructed, we move from the modernist theme of representation to the postmodern theme of strategies for the cultivation of the self.

(Atkinson and Silverman 1997, 319)

If we take this line of thought seriously, we lose touch with the idea of authenticity entirely. There is no authentic experience to be captured in the interview. The interview is nothing more than a moment in the changing, flowing narrative co-created by interviewer and subject.

One response to this critique of qualitative methods has been to embrace an anti-realist stance toward the social sciences. One might argue that the interpreter's construction of interpretations is a concern only if one were committed to the idea that the aim of interpretation is to represent an independent reality truly or falsely. Construction of a text which is then interpreted looks like a sleight of hand only if we are committed to a conception of objectivity which demands that the object of study be entirely independent of the inquiry. In other words, the response concludes, these epistemic worries arise only if one adopts a realistic stance toward the social sciences. However, even if we accept this response and admit that interpretations and their subject matters are textual through and through, the qualitative researcher owes us an account of why one interpretation is better than another. What *does* distinguish fieldwork from fiction?

A different response to the critique of authenticity looks more carefully at the notion of "experience" which is employed in most discussions of interpretive methodology (Sangren 1988). To think that "description and direct quotations" could somehow "allow the reader to enter into the situation and thought of the people" (Patton 2002, 503) is to reach for the unattainable. The mistake was to move from the (correct) thought that humans are self-interpreting animals who create meaningful social worlds, to the (mistaken) goal of representing *experience* in an interpretation. This mistake is doubled when experience is regarded as somehow uniform across the community, constituting the "thought of the people" or "the natives' point of view." Instead of thinking that qualitative methods provide a glimpse into experience, we should think of qualitative methods as producing evidence about how people interact with each other. The interview text, focus group process, or activities of participant observation are all forms of human interaction shaped by the social background of the specific participants. The goal of interpretation is to characterize those social relationships, and the interpreter's encounter is evidence for that characterization.

The second response to the problem of authenticity does not give up entirely on realism about the social. It agrees that we should not think of interviews, focus groups, and so on, as providing a particularly authentic presentation of "the native's point of view." Any meaning that comes out of qualitative methods is the co-creation of the researcher interacting with the subjects. Transcripts, field notes, and other forms of qualitative documentation are evidence of the interpreter-sub-ject interactions, not evidence of a hidden, subjective world. What the interpreter comes to understand, then, is independent of the interpreter's efforts to understand it, though not independent of their interactions with the subject. Just as you can come to realize that you misunderstood a social situation in which you participated (think of a dispute with your roommate), an interpreter can realize through examin-ing notes and transcripts that they misunderstood a social process. Understanding can be more or less accurate without presupposing a problematic notion of authen-ticity. Recognizing the interpreter's hand in the creation of the text to be interpreted leads us toward a more nuanced, but still realistic, view of qualitative methods.

Reflexivity

Some social scientists and philosophers have recommended that attention to "reflexivity" can compensate for the challenges articulated in the previous section. Sandra Harding once expressed this as the demand that "the researcher be placed in the same critical plane as the overt subject matter, thereby recovering for scrutiny in the results of research the entire research process" (Harding 1987a, 31). Reflex-ivity is a response to the recognition that, in the social sciences, the researchers are subject to the very same social forces they are studying. Interpreters come to the research project with background beliefs and values, as well as a social position. The interpreter's interaction with the subjects relies on specific forms of social engagement. The claim is that if the interpreter can somehow recognize and reflect on these background conditions of the research, the research will be more episte-mologically robust. Some have even claimed that it can achieve a distinctive kind of objectivity appropriate for interpretation, different from the objectivity of the natural sciences. The philosophical problem is to unpack "reflexivity." We need to understand what is being asked of the interpreter and why it is relevant to the epistemology of interpretation.

Bracketing is one form of reflexivity found in the qualitative research method-ological literature. Qualitative researchers are advised to identify their beliefs, val-ues, interests, feelings, and social roles relevant to the subject of study. Researchers are urged to reflect on the way that these might influence the data collection and analysis. The exercise is supposed to be the "means by which researchers endeavor not to allow their assumptions to shape the data collection process and the persis-tent effort not to impose their own understanding and constructions on the data" (Ahern 1999, 407). Thinking through one's presuppositions is, no doubt, a useful exercise for any researcher. And interpreters do want to avoid simply reading their preconceived ideas into the interpretation. However, the significance of bracketing to enhance validity or objectivity is dubious for several reasons.

First, there is no reason to suppose that interpreters are especially good at under-standing their own biases. Recall from Section 2.3, for example, the way that evaluative presuppositions are embedded in thick moral concepts. It is easy not to notice that a concept like aggression has a negative moral valence and to treat it as if it were a simple description of the facts. The most worrisome biases in research are transparent to those who hold them. Hence, if used as recommended, the exercise of bracketing is more likely to instill a false confidence than to uncover a problematic bias. More deeply, bracketing assumes that the interpreter's assumptions (etc.) are a veil that distorts a clear understanding of the subjects. Hence it presupposes the kind of authenticity criticized in the previous section. Qualitative methods produce evidence through an interaction of interpreter and subjects, and all the parties' backgrounds and perspectives contribute to the result. It is a mistake, then, to think that the interpreter's contributions can be filtered out, leaving only the pure substance of the social object.

A different kind of reflexivity has appeared in the way interpretive monographs are written. Traditional narratives in the interpretive social sciences tried to adopt the stance of a neutral, objective documentation of social reality. We saw the argument that such presentations create an illegitimate sense of authority by erasing the interpreter from the interpretation. The result of this critique has been a trend of self-conscious writing which puts the interpreter in the center of the narrative. Rather than describe the social group from the standpoint of a socially invisible and omniscient narrator, the narrative is written at least partly in the first-person. The interpreter's experiences, feelings, and mistakes are explicitly described and integrated into the analysis and description. Unlike the exercise of "bracketing," this kind of reflexivity takes seriously the role of interpreter in the creation of the phenomenon to be understood. It tries to make the production of the narrative self-conscious, thereby highlighting the way the "text" to be interpreted is the joint product of the interpreter and the subjects. Therefore, it is argued, reflexive interpretation establishes the epistemic credentials of the interpreter without fabricating an illusory authority.

In assessing this sort of reflexivity in writing, Paul Roth has argued that it does not live up to its epistemological aspirations (Roth 1989). The epistemological problem is whether the interpreter has both established a position in the society from which to report, and whether those reports are reliable. The interpreter may have established an epistemically responsible position even if the position is not articulated, and the articulation of position provides little additional epistemic confidence. Moreover, first-person disclosure by the interpreter is another way in which an author can construct a picture of themselves. Just as it is a mistake to think that the results of an interview can be an "authentic" presentation, there is little reason to think that an interpreter's construction of themselves in a monograph is authentic. It is not enough, then, to simply include the interpreter's social position, reactions, and feelings in the text.

The foregoing criticisms of reflexivity have not undermined the claim that the evidence for interpretation is jointly produced by the interpreter and subject. This point has clear epistemic significance and does not depend on dubious claims about authenticity or self-transparency. Another way to approach the issue of reflexivity, then, is to ask whether the interpreter was aware of the ways in which the qualitative methods produced their results, and whether these modes of production were included in the analysis. Charles Briggs argued that interviewers do not typically understand how the interview is a joint production, and this kind of failure of reflexivity has serious effects (Briggs 1986). Interview subjects apply culturally specific communicative norms to the interview, and these "metacommunicative" frameworks may be at odds with framework of the interview. A simple example is provided by Ingrid Monson's (1996) enthnomusicological study of New York jazz musicians. Her subjects were quite familiar with interviews, but they understood them within a journalistic framework. In their experience, interviews had been a couple of questions about their approach to the music, their motivations, and so on. Such interviews might be conducted by telephone or after a concert. They were quite surprised, then, when Monson wanted extended discussions, and when she asked them to comment on specific elements of recorded performances. The musicians came to the interview prepared for a very different kind of self-presentation than what Monson was asking for. Both interviewer and subject had to adjust their expectations and responses to make the interviews work. A reflexive interpreter, then, needs to both adjust such local norms of communication and to explicitly recognize their influence on the final product (the interview text) in the analysis.

These reflections on reflexivity challenge the common-sense idea that if we want to know what someone is thinking or feeling, one should simply ask. The debates over authenticity and reflexivity have shown, at least, that such a naïve realism is inadequate. At the same time, the flight to anti-realism seems unjustified. By being careful about how we think about "experience," and recognizing the researcher's role in creating meaning, we can preserve the idea that there are better and worse interpretations. A sophisticated realism about qualitative research requires a more nuanced understanding of the way in which qualitative evidence is produced. This puts a heavy burden on investigators to understand the subjects' point of view *on the research process*, not just on their social world.

4.2. Rationality, Explanation, and Interpretive Charity

The Problem of Apparent Irrationality

Understanding beliefs and practices that are profoundly different from one's own is one of the deepest challenges of the social sciences. One of the reasons for the popularity of works of anthropology and history is that they present forms of behavior that are at once utterly bizarre, yet comprehensible after the anthropologist or historian has explained them. But how is the transition possible? This is a somewhat different kind of epistemic question than those that concerned us in Section 4.1. The problem here concerns how interpretations should change. A form of behavior can seem "utterly bizarre" only because it has been interpreted in a particular way. If it later seems "comprehensible," it is because a better interpretation has been offered. What makes the latter *better*? In general, what makes one interpretation superior to another?

Consider, as an example, the puzzles about Azande witchcraft which we encountered briefly in Chapter 1. Unlike European witches, Azande witchcraft was not deliberate. It was the unintentional result of a person's malevolent feelings. When an unfortunate event occurred, such as a tree falling on a child or the unexpected death of a cow, the Azande explained it as due to witchcraft: a malevolent force left the witch's body and caused the harmful event. To be accused of witchcraft had social consequences because the affected persons could demand retribution from the witch. The Azande therefore used oracles and autopsy to determine whether witchcraft accusations were true. So far, the beliefs seem odd, perhaps, but not incomprehensible. Belief in witches is not much different from the belief that forces I do not understand cause my computer to freeze and crash. The deeper puzzle arises from (apparent) logical incoherencies in the Azande belief system. In Section 1.1, we discussed the apparent incoherence which arose out of the practice of consulting oracles. Evans-Pritchard found that Azande witchcraft was puzzling in other ways too.

The Azande believed that the capacity for witchcraft was heritable. A male witch's sons were all witches, as were a female witch's daughters. Evans-Pritchard noticed that, if there had been enough verified cases of witchcraft, then all Azande people would be implicated. Everyone should be a witch. When Evans-Pritchard inquired about this consequence, the Azande apparently agreed that there had been enough verified cases of witchcraft to implicate every family; yet they denied that all Azande are witches. The Azande thus apparently accepted an inconsistent triad of beliefs. What makes this case deeply puzzling is that, according to Evans-Pritchard, when he pointed out the inconsistency, the Azande were unmoved:

> Azande do not perceive the contradiction as we perceive it because they have no theoretical interest in the subject, and those situations in which they express their beliefs in witchcraft do not force the problem upon them.
>
> (Evans-Pritchard 1937, 25)

For Evans-Pritchard, this failure to think logically was an indication that Azande thought was taking a specific form. In some domains, such as gardening or house-building, their beliefs were empirically based common-sense. In the domain of witchcraft, Azande thought was "mystical," and mystical thought has "its own logic, its own rules of thought" (Evans-Pritchard 1937, 79). The failure to conform to empirical common sense was thus an indication that another sort of explanation was required.

Evans-Prichard's interpretive practice, therefore, treated true belief and logical inference differently than false belief and illogical inference. True beliefs, such as the belief that the crops need rain, require no special interpretation; logical inferences, such as the inference that the crops are not growing because there has been no rain, are understood at face value. False beliefs and illogical inferences require explanation in terms of mystical thinking, esoteric doctrine, the social function of the practice, or something similar. Evans-Pritchard was thus committed to what later came to be called the *asymmetry thesis*: the idea that false belief and illogical inference need explanation, while true and logical beliefs do not.

Relativism and Rationality

In "Understanding a Primitive Society," Peter Winch criticized Evans-Pritchard for his asymmetrical treatment of true and false belief (Winch 1964). Asymmetry, Winch contended, presupposes that truth and rationality are language- or culture-independent standards against which interpretation can be judged. Winch argued that this presupposition is mistaken. All languages make a distinction between what is real and unreal (or between rational and irrational), but the precise way in which these distinctions are drawn depends on the other practices available to support the distinction. For us, science is the primary example of reasoning from empirical evidence to unseen causes. To say that something is (or is not) real invokes criteria that are rooted in scientific practice. For a social group that does not use controlled experiment or statistical analysis, the distinction between what is real and what is unreal must be drawn on different grounds. As Evans-Pritchard himself notes, the Azande distinguish among events for which humans are responsible, natural accidents, and witchcraft. The interpretive problem is to understand the Azande criteria for identifying *real* witchcraft. Uncritical deployment of our distinction between "real" and "unreal" is bound to miss the point of the Azande distinction between real witches and those falsely accused.

For Winch, then, whether a belief is true or false, rational or irrational, by our lights is irrelevant to the interpretation. The interpreter needs to examine the subjects' practices of distinguishing reality from illusion, magical causation from natural causation, reasonable from unreasonable inferences, and so on. The interpreter thus needs to add local criteria of reality and rationality to the thick description. Doing so treats true and false belief, and rational and irrational inference, as *symmetrical* in the sense that all stand in equal need of interpretation. It is just as much of a challenge to explain why the Azande have true (according to us) beliefs about their gardens as to explain why they have false (according to us) beliefs about witches.

Winch's argument has been taken to support a form of cultural relativism about reality and rationality. There are many doctrines associated with relativism, but they have two commitments in common. First, any form of relativism must claim a dependence relation: X *is relative to* Y. Both the character of the dependence and of the things related (what X and Y might stand for) vary among forms of relativism. The conclusion of Winch's argument is that rationality and reality depend on culture. Others have argued that morality depends on culture, or they have suggested that rationality might be relative to historical period. Dependence alone, however, is not sufficient to constitute relativism. One might recognize cultural differences in what counts as real or rational yet still insist that some cultures are correct while others are mistaken. The second commitment of relativism, then, is *incommensurability*: there is no common standard or independent arbiter of what is real, rational, right, or whatever it is that is said to be relative. By contending that the criteria for what is real or rational are always embedded in a particular set of practices, Winch's argument denies that there are language- or culture-independent grounds to determine whether one culture is correct in its assessment of rationality or reality.

Winch's argument therefore establishes a form of relativism, and the argument for it flows from the interpretivist framework. The enterprise of thick description supposes that the meaning of words, actions, symbols, and so on is constituted by the practices of which they are part. This applies to the distinction between reality and illusion, or good and bad inference, as well as it applies to witches or rituals. An interpreter is thus bound to seek out and apply local criteria. Notice however, how Winch's account seems to presuppose that there is a well-defined group who "has" these criteria of reality and rationality. In both Sections 3.3 and 4.1, we saw reasons to be skeptical of this kind of reification of cultures or communities. While it does not directly undermine Winch's argument, it may begin to undermine the very problem of apparent irrationality. We will return to this concern at the beginning of Section 4.3.

The Principle of Charity

In response to the interpretivist position, several philosophers have argued that by denying the asymmetry thesis, Winch makes interpretation impossible. The interpretivist position puts no limit on the differences between any two languages; anything that is regarded as true according to one could be regarded by another as false. Against this, some have argued for the necessity of a *principle of charity*. A first pass at the principle of charity is: interpret so that your interlocutors have mostly true beliefs. One argument for the principle of charity begins from the idea that beliefs and sentences have content insofar as they are about something, and a belief can be about something only insofar as it is truly described. As Donald Davidson put the point:

> How clear are we that the ancients—some ancients—believed that the earth was flat? *This* earth? Well, this earth of ours is part of the solar system, a system partly identified by the fact that it is a gaggle of large, cool, solid bodies circling around a very large, hot star. If someone believes *none* of this about the earth, is it certain that it is the earth that he is thinking about?
>
> (Davidson 1984, 168)

If the attributed beliefs were entirely false, Davidson argues, the interpreter would have no grounds for saying that they were about one thing rather than another. To interpret at all, the interpreter must attribute some true beliefs. And because beliefs form a network, the whole set must be largely true. Attribution of false belief is, of course, possible, but the content of disagreement is sharpened by the background of agreement.

Not only must the interpreter and the subjects agree, at least in large part, they also must have very similar criteria of good reasoning (logic). Martin Hollis argued (1967) that if "mystical beliefs" are to be attributed to a culture, then those beliefs must be reasonable in the light of their other beliefs. But, he asks, whose criteria of "reasonable" are to be used? The criteria must be discovered, and at the outset of the inquiry, the only criteria available to the interpreter are their own. Once those criteria of rationality are applied, however, it is too late to "discover" a different form of reasoning. For interpretation to be possible at all, then, there must not only be broad agreement about the content of beliefs, but also about their reasonableness.

The principle of charity should not be understood as making disagreement impossible. People obviously do disagree about the truth and reasonableness of many things. The principle of charity makes the most sense when understood as constraining the early stages of the inquiry. An interpreter must assume that the people with whom he or she speaks are competent users of their own language. They will generally use words when it is appropriate. For declarative sentences in ordinary contexts, this means that the sentences are taken to be true. Interpretation therefore requires a *bridgehead*, as Hollis called it, of true and rational belief about simple, everyday matters. As Hollis punned: "If the natives made no statements about the cat on the mat and the cow in the corn which can be translated to yield truths, the anthropologist has no way into the maze" (Hollis 1967, 232).

Understanding disagreement, then, especially about deep matters, must come at a later stage of the inquiry when the interpreter has some confidence in the translations about ordinary matters. When it comes to interpreting areas of disagreement, the recommendation to attribute mostly true beliefs is not terribly helpful. Philosophers have therefore understood the principle of charity as requiring that the interpretation minimize *inexplicable* disagreement. It is no conflict with the principle of charity to say that the Azande believe in witches, which do not exist according to the interpreter, as long as the interpreter is able to explain why they have this belief. What other beliefs or social forces support the belief in the efficacy of witchcraft? Why *don't* they have a "theoretical interest" in the consistency of their beliefs about witchcraft?

The arguments for the principle of charity thus try to reestablish the asymmetry between true and false, rational and irrational, that Winch criticized in Evans-Pritchard's work. Notice how the principle of charity both puts limits on possible interpretations and provides criteria for evaluating them. We would expect the subjects of interpretation to have true and rational beliefs about the great mass of ordinary, everyday phenomena. These will be true and rational, and the principle of charity—according to earlier arguments—entails that there will be agreement between interpreter and subjects about what is taken as true and rational. The interpreter is not obligated to give any special explanation for why these beliefs are held. It is sufficient that they are true and rational. False or irrational belief, on the other hand, can be attributed to the subjects, but it must be accompanied by a special explanation. The relativism that follows from interpretivism is defeated by showing that an interpretation that portrayed a group as using radically different criteria of truth or rationality would never be the best interpretation.

Some have pointed out that once we start thinking of translations and belief attribution as explanatory, it leads to a breakdown of the asymmetry thesis which Hollis and other critics of Winch wanted to reinstate. That someone holds a true belief stands in just as much need of explanation as a false belief. The difference is that the explanations for true belief are often trivial: Jones believes that there is a rabbit in the garden because there *is* a rabbit in the garden, and she can see it. But true belief might be puzzling too. Suppose an untrained person correctly judges that another person has cancer. How did that happen? Was it a lucky guess, or something else? The demand to minimize inexplicably false belief becomes the demand to simply minimize inexplicability. The best interpretation, then, would be the best explanation. Mark Risjord goes on to argue that if interpreters can appeal to norms of rationality in their explanations of why the subjects make an inference or hold a belief, we have returned to something like Winch's original conclusion (Risjord 2000). The principle of charity, in this view, ceases to be a substantive constraint on translation. This sort of view faces challenges of its own, of course. "Explanation" needs to be understood so that meaning and value are the kinds of thing that can be explained. Also, this view relies heavily on explanations that appeal to social norms and rules. As we will see in Chapter 9, accounting for the normativity of the social world is a complicated issue.

4.3. Cognition, Evolution, and Interpretation

Philosophers and anthropologists are not alone in their interest in human reasoning. Experimental psychologists have produced a variety of results which are directly relevant to both social scientific and philosophical understanding of social phenomena. They challenge the presuppositions of the philosophical debates, and they suggest new strategies for understanding the social world. We will be considering these challenges and questions throughout the chapters which follow. In this section, we will begin with the way psychological experiments challenge the problem of apparent irrationality and the interpretivist project more generally.

Bounded and Unbounded Rationality: Consequences for Interpretivism

The problem of apparent irrationality arguably gets its purchase from a surprising difference between the way people do behave and the way they ought to behave. Both sides of the debate over rationality in interpretation presumed that humans ought to reason according to rules of logic; their difference concerned whether such rules could be discovered by, or had to be presupposed in, interpretation. But is the notion of rationality presupposed in this debate intelligible? Recent work in psychology sheds new light on the relationship between rationality and interpretation.

One interesting and much discussed result experiment from the study of reasoning is the Wason Selection Task. The standard setup goes like this. You are shown four cards arranged as in Figure 4.1. Each of these cards has a shape on one side and a solid color on the other. As you can see, two cards show their shape side and two show their color side. Which card or cards must you turn over to determine the truth of the proposition "If a card has a circle on one side, then it is black on the other side"? The answer is in the footnote to this sentence (no peeking!).[1]

Chances are, if you genuinely tried to answer the question before reading the footnote, you got it wrong. Most people do—as many as 90% get it wrong in some studies—yet the answer in the footnote clearly follows the rules of elementary logic. Subjects who get the answer wrong typically accept the explanation when it is given. That is, while they are apparently able to think through the logical problem, they make mistakes anyway. The result is surprisingly robust: even mathematicians and logic teachers get it wrong 50% of the time. The Wason Selection Task is just one of several results which seem to show that humans tend to systematically and reliably fail to conform to the simplest norms of deductive and inductive inference. Studies have shown that humans ignore sample size, forget base rates, imagine illusory correlations, and make a hash out of conditionals.

Now, the professor who is teaching your logic course will nod knowingly if you present them with this psychological data. They have seen students commit every fallacy in the book. Nonetheless, they will say, these results do not tell us much about logic. Logic is the study of how we *ought* to reason, not how we do, in fact, think. The rules of logical inference are normative in this sense. It is common to use the distinction between *bounded* from *unbounded* approaches to make sense of the relationship between logical rules and human inferences. Logic, probability theory, decision theory, and game theory abstract away from the messy particularities of human thought processes. They treat reason as an ideal system, and reasoners as if they were not subject to limitations of time, memory, or ability to calculate. Such approaches to reasoning and rationality are unbounded. A bounded approach,

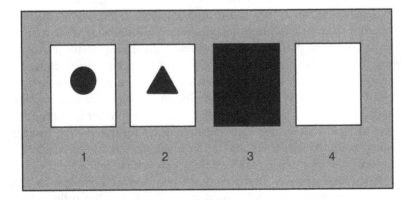

Figure 4.1 Wason Selection Task

by contrast, understands human reasoning as having limited resources and as being robustly prone to systematic mistakes. Models of bounded rationality aim to provide a realistic presentation of human reasoning or decision-making processes. The psychological results which show patterns of inference at odds with classical logic or decision theory are the data for such models, and a good model explains why we make good inferences under some conditions and bad ones under others (where "good" and "bad" are judged from the point of view of classical logic and decision theory).

Interpretative research has traditionally supposed that to understand a social group is (in part) to understand its norms, rules, and values. Cultural rules tell members of a culture how they ought to reason or act, and deviations from these norms are treated as mistakes. The relativist idea that what is "real" and "rational" might vary among cultures relies on the idea that cultural rules specify correct ways of reasoning. Interpretivism thus relies on an unbounded model of rationality. The philosophers and anthropologists who were concerned to make sense of "alternative ways of thinking" accepted this distinction between norms of reasoning and the descriptions of psychology. The problem of apparent irrationality arose against the background of the interpretivist project. As a result, it asked: do we need to postulate other norms, different forms of rationality, to make sense of people in other places and times?

Considered from the perspective of a bounded model of rationality, the problem of apparent irrationality disappears, or so Mark Risjord argues (2021). We remarked in Section 4.2 about the way in which both the relativists and the rationalists in the apparent irrationality debate assumed that cultures or communities are well-defined and bounded. Sections 3.3 and 4.1 gave us reasons to be suspicious about such a reification. In this section, we have seen that *nobody* always makes the inferences dictated by classical logic and probability theory. So, it is unsurprising to find pervasive deviations from these rules in other times and places. Evans-Pritchard should not have been so impressed by the Azande's lack of "theoretical interest" in the contradiction he pointed out to them. In this way, the Azande are no different from the subjects of Wason's experiments. There are two important conclusions to be drawn from this point. First, against the relativist side of the interpretivist project, a phenomenon like Azande witchcraft is not a sufficient reason to postulate that other social groups use norms of reasoning different from classical logic, and the notion of a "group" is not clear. There may reasons to recognize a variety of perspectives on reasoning, of course, such as the existence of an alternative tradition of logic such as we find in classical Buddhism. Second, against the rationalist side of the interpretivist project, the principle of charity cannot be used as an argument for interpreting humans as necessarily conforming to the norms of classical logic. A "bridgehead" of true and rational belief is a bridge too far. If these conclusions are correct, *both* sides of the debate over apparent irrationality are mistaken, and perhaps we should think that the problem was badly posed in the first place. But if that's not the right question, what is?

Cognitive Roots of Culture

One might argue that an interpretivist can accept the conclusions of the fore-going section. While the project needs to be modified to include a bounded perspective on reasoning, the fundamental notions of interpretivism remain untouched. We should still see humans as self-interpreting beings. Social phenomena are already meaningful and rule-constituted, and therefore thick description remains the goal of understanding human groups. Theorizing about human cognition, however, is not limited to the Wason Selection Task. A broad range of experimental results in cognitive psychology seem directly relevant to understanding human sociality, and they suggest explanations of many social phenomena. Do theories which invoke psychological underpinnings of culture supplant interpretivism?

Consider again the Wason Selection Task. It may have struck you that the low rate of success by subjects is a consequence of the way in which the problem is presented. Perhaps subjects can reason perfectly well, but they got confused by the presentation. To exclude this possibility, experimental psychologists present the task in a variety of ways and test whether the variations make a difference to the outcome. It turns out that *content* makes a difference. The previous example posed the problem in terms of shapes and colors. Suppose the problem was posed with Figure 4.2, and the subjects are now given this instruction:

> You are a bouncer in a bar, and you'll lose your job unless you enforce the fol-lowing law:
>
> "If a person is drinking beer, then he must be over 21 years old."
>
> The cards above have information about four people sitting at a table in your bar. Each card represents one person. One side of a card tells what a person is drinking, and the other side of the card tells the person's age.
>
> Indicate only those card(s) you definitely need to turn over to see if any of these people are breaking the law.
>
> (based on Cosmides 1989)

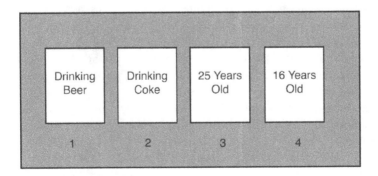

Figure 4.2 Social Selection Task

When the problem is presented in social terms, performance dramatically increases. In some experiments while less than 25% of subjects correctly choose both cards 1 and 4 when the problem is presented abstractly, 75% do so in the drinking-age problem (Cosmides 1989). Leda Cosmides and John Tooby concluded that human reasoning is domain-specific in the sense that we are hard-wired to quickly solve problems of a specific sort (Tooby and Cosmides 1992). We have evolved in a specific natural and social environment, and to survive we had to be able to reason about the problems this environment presented. Detecting cheaters is one such problem. Our capacity to reason about problems like the Wason Selection Task may be part of a cognitive process which is primarily designed to solve social problems like the detection of cheaters.

It is not news that the human mind might have specific mechanisms or capacities that make humans suitable for social life. Nineteenth-century social theorists postulated the "psychic unity of mankind," holding that the evolution from simple, "primitive" forms of culture to more complex civilizations was an evolution of the human mind. (This was the context of the question about "primitive mentality," which we saw in the discussions of Azande witchcraft in Sections 1.1 and 4.2.) While late 20th-century theorists share a commitment to evolution, they differ from 19th-century theorists in several ways. First, they take the psychological foundations of human sociality to be more-or-less fixed after the emergence of modern humans 200,000 years ago. Culture has changed since then, but the basic architecture of the mind is unchanged. Second, contemporary social science tries to link specific features of human psychology with particular social phenomena, thus explaining aspects of human society by reference to psychological mechanisms.

An interesting example of the recent work connecting cognition to culture is Scott Atran's *In Gods we Trust* (Atran 2002). Atran sets out to explain the universal human belief in the existence of supernatural agents. Ghosts and zombies, gods and demons, are found everywhere. Atran's explanation draws on several well-established features of human cognition. First, from infancy, humans distinguish between agents and non-agents in their environment. That is, we identify some events as arising from intentions or motives, and others to be the result of blind causes. This "agency-detection module" is sensitive and tends to over-identify agency. (In the language of Chapter 2, it produces false-positive results.) After all, it is better to hear the wind as the pad of a tiger than to think the pad of a tiger is just the wind. Atran argues that when the agency-detection module misidentifies an agent, the result is a representation violating innate expectations about object kinds. Trees are not supposed to speak, so when whispers are heard in the rustling of leaves, it is a striking event. Representations of agents with supernatural powers are thus naturally invented and re-invented by people. Some of these representations are communicated and remembered, and Atran draws on features of memory and communication to explain why some representations stick.

Interpretation and Cognitive Explanation

Work like Atran's sets up a conflict between psychological explanations of social phenomena and traditional social scientific interpretations. On an interpretivist view, gods and spirits need to be understood as part of a system of ideas. They get their meaning from religious discourse on one hand and ritual practice on the other. Whatever the virtues of a universal explanation like Atran's, it seems doomed to miss much of what makes humans unique. An interesting question of contemporary philosophy of social science, then, is to understand the relationship between cognitive explanations of social phenomena and their interpretation.

Anti-naturalist programs in the social sciences have held that studies of the social world should be methodologically and theoretically isolated from facts of human psychology and biology. An interpretation of, say, ritual practice neither requires nor benefits from theories of cognition. While these anti-naturalist views postulate a gap between interpreting culture and understanding psychology (or evolutionary biology), they must make some psychological assumptions about learning and socialization. Interpretivists take culture to be prior to individual psychology in two ways. First, cultures and social structures are temporally prior to any individual. The individual is socialized into the culture and adopts the local ways of living. Culture is thus prior to the individual in the second sense that the features of personality, belief, and ways of acting are derived from the culture (not *vice versa*). This priority of culture over the individual presupposes that culture is written onto individuals who are largely a blank slate. While there may be some innate learning propensities, such as the human's unique ability to learn language, these are content-neutral. They have little or no influence on the characteristics of a culture. Interpretivists conclude that there is no methodological or theoretical need to pay close attention to the details of human psychology, biology, or evolutionary history when trying to interpret social groups.

In "The Psychological Foundations of Culture" (1992), Tooby and Cosmides argue against the psychological presuppositions of interpretivism. Postulating content-rich psychological mechanisms has been a very successful explanatory strategy. The hypothesis that we have agent-detectors, capacities to detect cheaters, propensities to remember certain kinds of representations, and so on, is inconsistent with the assumption that our learning mechanisms are perfectly general. It also supports better explanations of the same phenomena, and it garners support for the social sciences from psychology and evolutionary biology. Interpretation must therefore be replaced with the alternative view that:

> The human psychological architecture contains many evolved mechanisms that are specialized for solving evolutionary long-enduring adaptive problems and that these mechanisms have content-specialized representational formats, procedures, cues, and so on. These richly content-sensitive evolved mechanisms tend to

impose certain types of content and conceptual organization on human mental life and, hence, strongly shape the nature of human social life and what is culturally transmitted across generations.

(Tooby and Cosmides 1992, 34)

Interpretivists and other anti-naturalists have some possible responses to this strong position. First, one might argue that even if we accept the value of using cognitive mechanisms to explain cultural phenomena, these hypotheses will still have to be tested by looking at the variety of the world's cultures. Understanding the content of the ideas will require interpretation, perhaps even thick description. Therefore, cognitive theorizing could not completely replace interpretation, on pain of having no methodology for discovering content at all. Moreover, Tooby and Cosmides's alternative seems to change the subject. Where interpretivists were interested in questions of difference— the nature and scope of human variation—the proponents of cognitive and evolutionary explanations are interested in human universals. It may be true that interpretivism has retained an out-of-date psychology of learning and socialization. It remains to be seen, one might argue, whether updating that psychology will completely undermine the methodology of interpretation or the specific interpretations based on it.

There is a middle ground between the interpretivist view that cognitive explanations can be ignored and Tooby and Cosmides's view that cognitive explanations supplant interpretation. One might hold that the social sciences need both interpretive and explanatory approaches. Tomas Lawson and Robert McCauley call such a position "interactionism," and they characterize it this way:

Explanation and interpretation are, then, different cognitive tasks. They supplement and support one another in the pursuit of knowledge. . . . Specifically, interpretations presuppose (and may reorganize) our systematic, empirical knowledge, whereas successful explanatory theories both winnow and increase it. Interpretations uncover unexpected connections in the knowledge we already possess; the success of new explanatory theories establishes new vistas.

(Lawson and McCauley 1990, 30)

Rather than replacing interpretation, the interactionist view recognizes that any attempt to explain social phenomena in psychological terms is going to require substantial interpretive results. We need some set of concepts with which to begin any inquiry. Interpretation is required for developing these in the context of the wide variety of human cultures. At the same time, interpretation alone does little to develop or refine social theories. On the interactionist view, the job of explanatory social science is to propose and test new theories, and to link together different lines of inquiry. In this section, we have seen the relevance and importance of cognitive explanations. We will encounter these again, along with other explanatory paradigms, in subsequent chapters. The ongoing challenge, for both philosophers and social scientists, is to blend interpretation and explanation in ways that are conceptually sound and empirically fertile.

The New Questions of Naturalism

In Chapter 3, the problem of naturalism was posed in terms of the conflict between interpretivism and an empiricist view of theory. Empiricism imported ideas about theory structure, concept development, and hypothesis testing from the natural sciences into the social domain. Interpretivism resisted this on the grounds that empiricist methods did not penetrate the meaning of actions and social events. To uncover intentions, values, norms, and meaning, different kinds of methods and theories were necessary. The debates over interpretive methodology we have surveyed in this chapter have led us to a new perspective on the question of naturalism. Research in social psychology, cognitive science, neuroscience, and animal ethology has begun to uncover the psychological and biological underpinnings of human sociality. This research does not rely on the sort of "brute data" of thin description criticized by the interpretivist. It challenges interpretivism by undermining its implicit psychological assumptions, thereby closing the gap between human psychology and social meanings. Cognitive theories also seem to show common patterns within and limits to the range of human beliefs and attitudes. One might argue that these universal patterns should limit the range of possible interpretations.

The rise of the cognitive sciences and their apparent relevance for questions about the social world brings out the question of naturalism in a new way. We can think of naturalism as raising several specific challenges for interpretivism. First, interpretivism needs to respond to Tooby and Cosmides's charge that it rests on a bad psychology. While it is true that many of the classical proponents of interpretivist views seemed to hold views like those criticized, the idea that the social world is meaningful does not entail any particular psychology. The challenge here is to figure out whether the results of recent work in the cognitive sciences can be made compatible with some version of interpretivism.

At the same time, interpretivists will not want to take the results of cognitive science at face value, nor should they. A second challenge, then, is to reach a critical understanding of exactly what the evidence is showing us. Experimental and other results need to be interpreted, and the interpretations rest on theoretical and philosophical commitments. To what extent and in what precise ways does current research undermine the presuppositions of interpretivism? One of the important issues in this area concerns the way in which social norms are understood, an issue we will discuss in Chapter 9.

A third challenge arises out of the suggestion that interpretive and explanatory approaches are complementary. How, exactly, is the interaction supposed to work? How should theories about cognitive processes inform research based on surveys, interviews, participant observation, and so on? In the methodology literature, the problem of bringing different approaches together in one study is sometimes called the problem of "triangulation." It seems likely that different methods will yield a wider range of data, and this would appear to be a good thing for social inquiry. But what happens when the different methods produce conflicting data? Do interpretive methods trump experimental methods? Do surveys trump interviews? It may be that these questions do not have perfectly general answers. They can be addressed only in the context of particular studies where we can use what we know about the people under study and the context of their action to get some purchase on the issue. If so, the sweeping battle between empiricism and interpretivism seems to disintegrate into small skirmishes and local truces.

4.4. Wrap Up

Chapter Summary

This chapter has been concerned with a set of broad questions about the epistemology of interpretation. Interpretation is associated with several distinctive "qualitative" methods of gathering and analyzing data. We have seen that demands for authenticity and reflexivity involve dubious assumptions about shared meaning and experience. Shorn of some of the more problematic commitments, interpretive methods are important, even indispensable, ways of gathering information about the social world. Section 4.2 explored the limits of interpretation. Is it possible to interpret others as having different conceptions of truth, reason, and moral rightness? Some interpretivists have argued for relativism, holding that what is true, rational, or moral depends on culture. In opposition to relativism, some have argued that there are limits to the ways in which humans should be interpreted. The principle of charity is one such limit, holding that people should be interpreted as holding mostly true and rational beliefs about a shared world. We will encounter these questions about rationality again in the next chapter when we turn to questions about intentional action.

In Section 4.3, we began a discussion of whether and how results from cognitive psychology are relevant to the methodology of interpretation. Interpretivism has tended to treat human reasoning as unbounded in the sense that it can be described by abstract rules. If reasoning is unbounded, interpreters need not attend to limitations of memory, processing capacity, and so on. A range of experimental studies have shown that humans do not reliably conform to the rules of logic. Bounded approaches to rationality try to model human reasoning more directly, reflecting our limitations. Some have argued that cognitive explanations (along with neurological and evolutionary explanations) should supplant traditional methods of interpretive analysis. We will encounter bounded rationality, cognitive, and evolutionary explanations in many places in the chapters which follow. These explanatory approaches have proven very important in the contemporary social sciences, and they raise new questions in a number of areas. Indeed, as we saw at the end of Section 4.3, they change the character of the debate over naturalism. As the social sciences begin to absorb both methods and theories from biology, psychology, and neuroscience, it becomes more difficult to postulate a bright line separating natural from social sciences. The new questions concern how we are to relate and integrate interpretive and explanatory approaches to the social sciences.

Discussion Questions

1. Can interpretations capture an "authentic" experience of the subjects? Why or why not? If not, then what is the point (if any) to using qualitative methods? If so, how? Does reflexivity help?
2. Are truth and reality culture-relative? Can one adopt an interpretivist position without being a relativist?
3. Think of some examples where the rationality of the subjects seems questionable. Use them to evaluate the relative merits of the "symmetry thesis" and the "asymmetry thesis" discussed in Section 4.2. Do false belief and illogical inference require a different kind of treatment than true belief and logical inference?
4. Does the problem of apparent irrationality arise only in the study of other cultures? Or does it arise for our neighbors (or roommates . . .) as well?
5. When trying to interpret apparently irrational behavior, can we distinguish between genuine differences in forms of rationality (or rules of logic) and merely pervasive mistakes or psychological biases? How?
6. Do the experimental results of the Wason Selection Task undermine Winch's approach to the problem of apparent irrationality? Do they undermine Evans-Prichard?

Further Reading

Anyone interested in the epistemology of interviews must read Briggs, *Learning How to Ask* (1986). Kratz's "In and Out of Focus" discusses the methodology of focus groups (2010). The classic justification for participant observation is in the first chapter of Malinowski's *Argonauts of the Western Pacific* (1922). For a philosophical critique of participant observation see Zahle, "Practical Knowledge and Participant Observation" (2012) and "Participation Observation and Objectivity in Anthropology" (2013).

The critique of authenticity and authority in qualitative research is clearly presented in Clifford's "On Ethnographic Authority" (1983). Clifford and Marcus's *Writing Culture* (1986) was a very important body of critical appraisal of ethnographic writing and methods.

Rosaldo's "Grief and a Headhunter's Rage" (1989) is a classic argument for the importance of reflexivity, and Tedlock's "From Participant Observation to the Observation of Participation" (1991) is a good discussion of the significance of reflexive writing in ethnography. For critique of reflexivity, see Roth, "Ethnography Without Tears" (1989); Salzman, "On Reflexivity" (2002); and Karp and Kendall, "Reflexivity in Fieldwork" (1982).

The debate over how to interpret apparent irrationality begins with Winch's work, both *Idea of a Social Science* (1958) and "Understanding a Primitive Society" (1964). Important contributions to the debate started by Winch are contained in Wilson's *Rationality* (1970). Davidson's essays "Belief and the Basis of Meaning" and "The Very Idea of a Conceptual Scheme" (both in Davidson 1984) changed the rationality debate in important ways. Hollis and Lukes's *Rationality and Relativism* (1982) collects a number of essays which take up the problem in ways inspired by Davidson's work. See also Root, "Davidson and Social Science" (1986); Henderson, "The Principle of Charity and the Problem of Irrationality" (1987); and Risjord, *Woodcutters and Witchcraft* (2000). Explorations of the consequences of bounded rationality are found in Polonioli's "Blame it on the Norm" (2014), Risjord's "Rationality and Interpretive Methodology," (2021), and Feleppa's "Rationality Assumptions and their Limits" (Forthcoming).

The epistemological questions about interpretation are deeply tied to issues in the philosophy of language, and they have implications for the issues discussed in Chapter 3 as well. Books which pursue these themes include Roth's *Meaning and Method in the Social Science* (1987), Henderson's *Interpretation and Explanation in the Social Sciences* (1993), and Risjord's *Woodcutters and Witchcraft* (2000).

Tooby and Cosmides's "The Psychological Foundations of Culture" (1992) is an extensive argument against interpretive social science. A somewhat different critique of interpretivism which also argues for the importance of psychological mechanisms is found in Sperber's *Explaining Culture* (1996). Lawson and McCauley argue for interactionism in the first chapter of *Rethinking Religion* (1990). Responses to these arguments can be found in Tanney (1998) and Risjord (2004). The idea that reasoning might be domain-specific has been developed by Gigerenzer into the idea of "fast and frugal" algorithms; see the first chapter of *Rationality for Mortals* (2008). For an overview of contemporary research, see Fessler and Machery, "Culture and Cognition" (2012). Mercier and Sperber's (2017) *The Enigma of Reason* has important—and as yet largely unexplored—consequences for the issues discussed in this chapter.

Note

1   The correct answer is cards 1 and 4. Here is the reasoning: the statement "If a card has a circle on one side, it is black on the other" is false only if there is a card which has a circle on one side and is *not* black on the other. In other words, only a card with a circle on the front and a white (non-black) back would be a counterexample to the proposed statement. There are two cards on the table which might be this counterexample: numbers 1 and 4. QED, as they say.

5   Action and Agency

The interpretations we have been discussing so far have focused on social or cultural phenomena. What about the interpretation of individual actions? The notions of agency and intentional action stand at the intersection of several important themes in the philosophy of social science. The idea that individual actions are the root of all social-level phenomena is the motivation for reductionist programs in the social sciences. Treating individual actions as fundamental to the social sciences also directly engages the questions of naturalism. Can intentional actions be explained in ways familiar to the natural sciences? For instance, can scientifically established laws explain the actions of an individual? Or again, are action explanations a species of causal explanation? If intentional actions fall within the domain of cause or law, then the case for epistemological naturalism is significantly bolstered. On the other hand, if action explanation is not causal, or makes no reference to general laws, then a crucial aspect of social scientific explanation would be shown to be *unlike* the natural sciences. The question of how intentional action is to be explained or understood is thus central to the philosophy of social science.

Our discussion in this chapter will fall largely within the theme of naturalism, leaving the questions of reductionism for subsequent chapters. We will begin in Section 5.1 by examining the question of whether the explanation of intentional action can be understood as analogous to explanations in the natural sciences. The idea of instrumental rationality will loom large in this discussion. Instrumental rationality is usually regarded as the primary form of understanding action: if an agent wants to achieve a goal, and believes that doing A is the best means of doing so, then an instrumentally rational agent will do A. Much economic theory has been developed from refining the idea of instrumental rationality. The tools of microeconomics, especially game theory, have become prevalent in the social sciences. Game theory considers the interactions of multiple agents, and it shows how stable patterns can emerge out of individually rational choices. Some have gone so far as to argue that game theory is foundational for the social sciences. We will outline the basic ideas of decision theory and game theory in Section 5.2. The concepts of decision theory and game theory will continue to appear in Chapters 6, 7, 9, and 10.

Agents are beings who act. Different ways of understanding intentional action, then, support different ways of thinking about who we are as agents. Because instrumental rationality is a pervasive framework for explanations of action, its

DOI: 10.4324/9781003207795-5

conception of agency is common in the social sciences. One might be concerned that this conception of agency is too narrow. Trying to get what one wants is only one color in the palette of human motivations. Is instrumental rationality adequate to accommodate the full range of human motivations and intentions? Recent work in cognitive psychology and experimental economics presents important challenges to the notion of instrumental rationality. Human beings are remarkably cooperative and strongly oriented toward others. Other humans have a special place in our mental representations of the world around us. What does this tell us about who we are as agents? How should it influence our conceptualization of action explanation? This chapter will begin, but not complete, our discussion of agency. The human cooperative orientation toward others manifests itself both in the presence of norms, rules, and laws in human society and in the capacity for joint action. These topics will be taken up in Chapters 7, 9, and 10.

5.1. Explaining Action

Admiral Tryon and Instrumental Rationality

Historical narratives often provide explanations of individual action. To be sure, contemporary historians are skeptical of explanations which make large-scale events depend on the decisions of a "great man." Nonetheless, understanding the motivations of historical figures is often an important aspect of understanding the events of which they were part. It is hard to understand the American Civil Rights Movement, for example, without understanding why Rosa Parks refused to give up her seat on the bus. Understanding intentions is even more important where the actions were a failure. Just what were Lord Raglan's intentions when he ordered the ill-fated charge of the light brigade? The sinking of the HMS *Victoria* in 1893 is a less well-known, but more puzzling, historical example of military failure (Hough 1959). Vice-Admiral George Tryon, commander of the British Mediterranean fleet, ordered two iron-clad battleships equipped with rams to turn toward each other. They collided, sinking the *Victoria*. What was he thinking?

Britain was at peace in 1893, but because of the strategic importance the Mediterranean Sea, it kept a large force of its best ships there. On the day of the tragedy, the 11 ships of the fleet were steaming toward Tripoli, where they would anchor for the night. As they approached the coast, Tryon told the captain of his flagship (the flag-captain) and his staff-commander "I shall form the fleet into columns of two divisions, six cables apart, and reverse the course by turning inwards" (Hough 1959, 66). (A "cable" is a nautical unit of measure, roughly equal to 600 feet or 180 meters.) This meant that the lead ships of each column would turn toward one another. The other ships in each column would follow the lead ship in a half-circle, and the fleet would have reversed its course. Tryon's officers knew that the combined turning radius of two the battleships was eight cables. Hence, if the lead ships turned toward each other, they would collide. They asked for clarification, and Tryon insisted that the divisions should maintain a separation of six cables.

Admiral Tryon was a notoriously demanding commander who often presented his subordinates with difficult problems to solve on their own. His flag-captain and staff-commander did not ask for clarification a second time.

Orders were transmitted between the ships by flag signals. The fleet divided into two divisions, the HMS *Victoria* leading one column and the HMS *Camperdown* leading the other. Two and a half miles from shore, Admiral Tryon ordered the signals for the reversing maneuver hoisted. They read: "Second Division alter course in succession 16 points to starboard, preserving order of the fleet" and "First Division alter course in succession 16 points to port, preserving order of the fleet" (Hough 1959, 70). To preserve the order of the fleet meant that since the Second Division was the port (left) side column at the beginning of the maneuver, it would also be on the port side at the end.

On the *Camperdown*'s bridge, Rear-Admiral Markham saw the potential danger and waited for further instructions. After Admiral Tryon signaled "What are you waiting for?" the ships turned inwards, toward each other. On the *Victoria*, Admiral Tryon was looking astern, watching the rest of his fleet. He initially ignored his flag-captain's requests to change course, and by the time he turned around to see the danger, it was too late. The *Camperdown* rammed the *Victoria* amidships. The other ships quickly began to lower rescue boats, but Tryon signaled "Anull sending boats." The *Victoria* rolled and sank with shocking speed. Over 300 sailors drowned, including Admiral Tryon. His last words were, "It was all my fault" (Hough 1959, 134).

What was Admiral Tryon trying to do? One hypothesis is that he simply took leave of his senses. As one of his contemporaries put it: "Everyone who knew and esteemed the late Sir George Tryon must feel that, though bodily he was present on the afternoon of June 22 last, the guiding brain which made him so dear to us was absent" (Hough 1959, i). This interpretation reads Admiral Tryon's behavior as not fully intentional. Explaining Admiral Tryon's behavior as the result of drunkenness or fever-induced delirium does not provide *reasons* for Admiral Tryon's actions. One might suppose that any hypothesis giving reasons for Admiral Tryon's actions must make him *instrumentally rational*. To be instrumentally rational is to have some kind of goal or desired outcome, and then to do the action or sequence of actions which is the best way under the circumstances to achieve that goal. In the different explanations of what Admiral Tryon intended, it is generally agreed that his goal was to reverse the direction of the fleet by 180°. The more difficult interpretive question is what he took to be the best means of doing so.

The flag-captain of the *Victoria* understood Admiral Tryon as intending that the two columns should each make a U-turn, ending up side by side and traveling in the opposite direction (Figure 5.1a). This interprets Admiral Tryon as having made two mistakes. First, the two divisions were sailing too close to each other. If the ships were to turn in upon each other as in Figure 5.1a, they would need to begin at least eight cables apart. Second, the order of the fleet would not be preserved. Note the small mark indicating the port (left) side of the lead ships in Figure 5.1a. The division which begins the maneuver on the port side ends it on the starboard side. Hence, if Admiral Tryon intended a maneuver like Figure 5.1a, his flag signals were mistaken.

a.

b.

c.

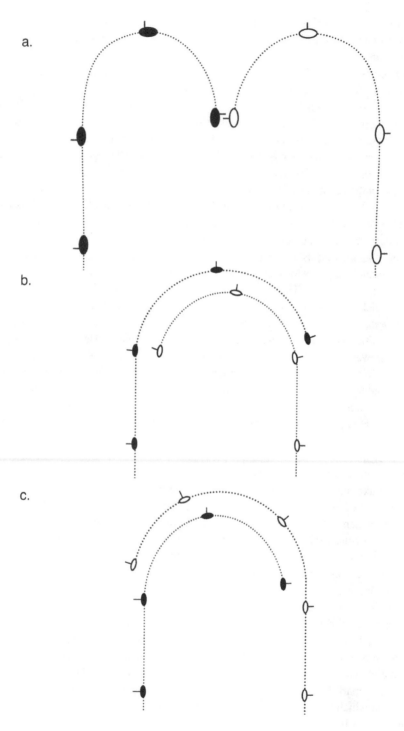

Figure 5.1 Sinking of the HMS *Camperdown*

Rear-Admiral Markham understood Admiral Tryon as intending to bring the *Victoria* and the first division in a slightly wider circle than the *Camperdown* and the second division (Figure 5.1b). Markham was cognizant of a "rule of the road" which said that he should not pass on the portside. He therefore kept turning as tightly to starboard as he could. The divisions would then file past each other, ending up six cables apart and preserving "the order of the fleet." The advantage of this explanation over the first is that it does not interpret Admiral Tryon as making mistakes. On the other hand, the problem with this explanation is that Admiral Tryon did not order the *Victoria* to pass outside of the *Camperdown*. Rather, it too continued to turn as tightly as it could. A third explanation is that the captains of both the *Camperdown* and the *Victoria* misunderstood Admiral Tryon. Historian Richard Hough provides some evidence that Admiral Tryon believed that the *Camperdown* would pass outside of the *Victoria*. This best explains why both the *Camperdown* and the *Victoria* kept turning as tightly as possible: each thought the other would pass outside.

Hough closes his history of this naval tragedy with the remark:

> No one will ever know for sure what Tryon's intentions were when he gave the order which resulted in the sinking of the *Victoria*. Individual theories can start and end with the possible interpretations of those five words he spoke on the chart house, . . . "It was all my fault," he said. Did Sir George Tryon mean, "It was all my fault. I have made an appalling miscalculation and this is the result"? Or did he mean, "Markham is a greater fool than I had imagined him to be. But now that my ship is to sink and many of my men are to die, I shall die with them and it is better that I should take the blame"? Or is the true interpretation something between these two extremes?
>
> (Hough 1959, 168)

These questions arise because the action was a failure. Were it a success, we would not wonder what Admiral Tryon was *trying* to do. And as long as we assume that he was trying to do something, one might argue, we will be fitting the possibilities into the schema of instrumental rationality.

One might conclude that the presumption of instrumental rationality makes an explanation of intentional action deeply different from an explanation of events involving non-agents. If we ask why the *Victoria* filled with water and sank, we do not need to ask about the goals or beliefs of the ship. In this sense, the HMS *Victoria* was not "trying" to do anything. If we ask why Admiral Tryon gave the order to turn inward, we must ask about his goals and beliefs. One might argue that Admiral Tryon's actions are explained *causally* only if we say something like "His brain left him." This dispenses with the assumption of instrumental rationality, but in so doing it also dispenses with the assumption that his actions were intentional.

As a first pass at the idea of an action explanation, then, we might say that the explanation of an intentional action presents the agent's reasons, and these reasons make the action instrumentally rational. Intentional action explanations are not causal because a causal explanation does not assume that its subject is instrumentally rational. This line of thought has clear implications for both the naturalism and reductionism debates. With respect to naturalism, the concern with agents and actions means that the social sciences require a different form of explanation than the natural sciences. With respect to reductionism, the concern with intentional action means that there is something special about the level of agency. Reduction to the causal realm of cognitive psychology or to biology will change the subject. And explanations which explain social-level phenomena without any reference to agents or intentional actions will be leaving out something important.

The Function of General Laws in History

Any attempt to contrast the forms of explanation in the natural sciences with the social sciences requires some conception of "explanation." What is an explanation in the natural sciences? One very common answer is that an explanation shows how an event to be explained satisfies a law or regularity. Explaining why the *Victoria* sank depends crucially on Archimedes's law of buoyancy. An ironclad ship like the *Victoria* floats because it is hollow. The weight of the water displaced is greater than the weight of the ship. When the water was allowed to spread throughout the ship, it reduced the amount of water displaced, and the *Victoria* was no longer buoyant. Notice how this explanation fits with the empiricist conception of theory which we discussed in Section 3.2. A scientific theory is a set of laws on this view. General laws, like Archimedes's law of buoyancy, entail more specific regularities, such as why solid iron sinks while iron ships float. Individual events are explained by showing how they fit into a lawful pattern or regularity. The standard empiricist analysis of causality is Hume's, and Hume held that one event caused another when there was a regular association between them. To show how an event is related to its antecedents in a lawful way is therefore to causally explain it. (We will discuss Hume's analysis of causality in Section 9.3.) On this view, then, scientific explanation is both law-governed and causal.

In the middle of the 20th century, when empiricist views of theory were common, Carl Hempel refined this picture of explanation (Hempel 1942). According to Hempel, a scientific explanation must have three features. First, it must provide a law or set of laws which express a general relation between an antecedent or initial condition and the event to be explained. Appealing to a law makes the explanation "nomological." Second, it must describe the initial conditions. Finally, it must show how the law and the initial conditions logically entail the event to be explained (hence, the explanation is "deductive"). Note that logical entailment includes mathematical calculation, so when we plug values into Archimedes's law and calculate how much water intake is required to sink a battleship, it is a deduction in the sense Hempel intended.

Scientific laws express generalizations by relating properties or types of events. In its modern form, Archimedes's law relates density of the fluid, volume of displaced fluid, and weight of the object. Any deductive-nomological explanation will therefore explain a specific event by showing how it exemplifies particular properties. Any event or object has innumerable properties. This means that any event can be explained in many ways. In the case of the *Victoria*, the ship also capsized. To explain why, we need laws relating the ship's center of gravity to its center of buoyancy, as well as initial conditions about how the water flowed through the compartments, changing the center of gravity. Since any event can be explained in many ways, Hempel drew the conclusion that an explanation never explains the entirely of an individual event. Rather, it explains only the particular properties of the event described by the law.

Hempel argued that if we adopt the deductive-nomological analysis of scientific explanation, there is no difference between the explanation of intentional actions and the explanation of other kinds of events. The last section argued that intentional actions are instrumentally rational. To explain an action is to show how it fits with the agent's goals and beliefs about the situation. This means that we can fit it into the following pattern:

1.   If a person S wants to achieve goal G and believes that doing action A is the best way to achieve G, then S will do A.
2. S wants to achieve G.

   Therefore, S does A.

Hempel argued that the principle of instrumental rationality expressed in (1) is nothing more than a well-confirmed, empirical law of human behavior. Since (2) is an initial condition, and since together (1) and (2) entail the description of the event to be explained, intentional action explanations fit the deductive-nomological pattern of explanation. The difference between explaining why Admiral Tryon ordered the battleships to turn toward each other and explaining why the *Victoria* sank is only a difference in the laws to which we appeal. To explain Admiral Tryon's actions, we use the principle of instrumental rationality. To explain why the *Victoria* sank, we appeal to Archimedes's principle of buoyancy. The difference in laws is just what we would expect to differentiate scientific disciplines. Contrary to the conclusions of the previous section, human actions are just as susceptible to causal explanation as non-human events.

The conclusion that intentional actions are explicable in lawful, causal terms also contradicts the conclusions of interpretivism, which we discussed in Section 3.3. The interpretivists hold that that the meaningful character of the social world frustrates any attempt to apply the sort of theory found in the natural sciences. Hempel's application of the deductive-nomological explanatory form to intentional actions shows that a social scientist can bring at least some aspects of meaning and value into scientific explanation. The explanation refers to precisely those aspects of an action which make it meaningful: the agent's goals, values, and beliefs. Epistemologically, it may take qualitative methods to come to know *what* an agent wants and believes. But once we know the content, the explanation proceeds along causal lines. Contrary to the interpretivist view, a naturalist might

conclude, theories in the natural and social sciences have the same logical structure. Both postulate laws and causes, and both explain by fitting individual events
into general patterns.

Reasons and Causes

Many philosophers and social scientists have felt that there is something troubling
about the assimilation of reasons for action to causes and laws. The creativity and
unpredictability of human action, one might argue, means that there could be no
laws of the social sciences. We will consider the more general arguments against
laws in Section 9.2. For now, notice that Hempel's argument depends on treating
instrumental rationality as a law. Of all the candidates for laws of human action,
instrumental rationality is surely the most plausible. Nonetheless, one might still
think that there is something wrong with treating the principle of instrumental
rationality as just another law of nature.

One might begin by meditating on the differences between *reasons* and *causes*.
There are two differences between reasons and causes which suggest that it is
a mistake to treat the principle of instrumental rationality as a causal law. First,
because it invokes rationality, the principle of instrumental rationality is normative. It says what an agent ought to do, not what he or she will do. For example,
suppose you want to get an A in your philosophy class, and you know that the best
way to do so is to study tonight for the exam. It might be irrational to go out with
your friends anyway, but sometimes we act irrationally. Rules can be broken; laws
cannot. Therefore, one might conclude, the principle of instrumental rationality is
a norm or rule for rational action, not a law.

The second difference between reasons and causes harkens back to the arguments of Chapter 3. There we encountered the argument that social scientific
knowledge is like a translation. The most important premise in that argument was
that there are two sets of concepts in the social sciences, whereas in the natural
sciences there is only one. In the social sciences, the subjects of our inquiry have
their own language, and they have ways of thinking and talking about their actions.
These first-level concepts include the subjects' reasons for action, and the second-
level, social scientific concepts refer to them. Causal laws need make no reference
to meaning or motive.

Peter Winch used these two differences between reasons and causes to argue that
human action cannot be explained by laws (Winch 1958, 66–94). Indeed, treating
the principle of instrumental rationality as if it were a causal law is to misunder-
stand the very idea of a reason for action. The principle of instrumental rationality
is normative; to say that something is a reason is to say that that it makes appropriate or justifies the action. The criteria for what is appropriate or inappropriate, Winch argued, are found in the community of which the agent is a part. The
possible motives for Admiral Tryon's actions are the sort of reasons which 19th-
century naval officers and sailors would have regarded as reasonable. There is
thus a normative relationship between reason and action, and that normativity is

embedded in the subjects' activity and language. Treating the relationship between actions, beliefs, and goals as a general law effaces the normative relationship in terms of which the agents understand their actions. It treats a rule as if it were a mere regularity. What is rightly expressed in first-level normative concepts (the agent's reasons) is improperly expressed by second-level causal concepts alone (social scientific theories). Winch and others concluded based on these considerations that the explanation of intentional action cannot be assimilated to causal explanation in the way that the Hempel suggested.

In his essay "Actions, Reasons, and Causes" (1963), Donald Davidson presented an important response to Winch's argument that reasons could not be causes. Davidson pointed out that while there may be many reasons that would justify an agent's action, only one of these will be *the* reason why he or she acted. Admiral Tryon may have been testing his subordinates' capacity for problem solving, the sailors' ability to handle their ships, the strength of the sea currents near Tripoli, the maneuverability of his battleships, and so on. Any and all of these might have been features that counted in favor of the action and would have been regarded as reasonable by his comrades. Nonetheless, Davidson argued, only one of these was *the* reason which moved him. Davidson calls this the "primary reason" for the action. Fitting an agent's action into a pattern of actions which are treated as appropriate by one's community does not, therefore, explain it because the context does not identify the primary reason. The primary reason is the belief and attitude which actually moved the agent to action. "Moved" is a causal notion, and any alternate expression we chose would also suggest a causal relationship between primary reason and action. Without some kind causal relationship between belief, goal, and action, then there is nothing to make the primary reason *primary*. This means that the primary reason for an action is its cause. To explain an action, therefore, we need to find the reason which was also the cause. Contrary to the interpretivist position, no amount of thick description will show why an agent acted in a particular way.

Davidson thus disagrees with both Hempel and Winch. Against Winch, he holds that action explanations must be causal. The primary reason is the cause of the action. At the same time, Davidson agrees that action explanations show what the agent took to be desirable or appropriate about the action. Because he agrees with Winch on this point, Davidson disagrees with Hempel about the status of the principle of instrumental rationality. The principle does not describe a regular association between motives and actions. Actions are not explained by fitting them into a regular pattern of belief-attitude-action associations any more than they are explained by thick description. Davidson holds that the principle of instrumental rationality expresses what it would be rational for the agent to do, given their beliefs and attitudes. As we have already noted, norms can be violated while laws cannot. Agents may fail to do the instrumentally rational thing, and they may fail to act for reasons recognized as appropriate in their communities. This means that there can be no deduction of the sort Hempel envisioned. It is entirely possible for S to want G, believe that A is the best way to achieve A, and yet fail to do A.

Therefore, while primary reasons are causes, action explanation does not follow the deductive-nomological pattern of explanation.

One might feel that Davison's position is inconsistent. On the one hand, reasons are causes; on the other hand, reasons do not fit into causal laws. Contrary to first appearances, these two points are consistent. Davidson points out that not every causal relationship is captured by strict laws of the sort found in the natural sciences. To use Davidson's example, hurricanes *cause* disaster. But we don't expect there to be a natural law associating hurricanes with disasters. The laws relate properties of a different sort: wind velocity, sheer strength, and so on. The work of destruction is done by the myriad particular interactions, each of which can be explained with strict laws at the mechanical level. Hurricanes and disasters can take many forms, and we cannot identify hurricanes or disasters with any determinate set of lower-level events. So, while hurricanes cause disasters, there are no laws relating the two. Similarly, while reasons are causes, there are no laws at the higher (rational) level of description. The laws will presumably be expressed in neuro-physiological terms.

Davidson's work on action theory thus represented a new position in the debate over naturalism in the social sciences. Because explanations of intentional action describe the events in terms of reasons and rationality, and because they do not appeal to laws, action explanations are different from natural scientific explanations. Rationality of thought and action thus make social scientific theorizing take on a different form than the natural sciences. While the position is anti-naturalistic (in the epistemological sense of "naturalism"), human action is not outside of the causal realm. Davidson holds that humans are a part of the natural world and that the causal powers we have are discoverable by the natural sciences. The position is thus naturalistic in the metaphysical sense of "naturalism." Davidson's position is also anti-reductionistic. While the causal laws exist at a lower level of description, the principle of instrumental rationality cannot be reduced to these causal laws. Davidson's position is thus a sophisticated form of naturalistic anti-reductionism.

Re-Enactment: Verstehen Revisited

In the debate over reasons and causes, the different parties agree that the principle of instrumental rationality should be part of the theory of human behavior. The dispute is about the form of the theory and about the relationship between theories which rationalize action and theories which explain non-human events. There is a longstanding tradition in the philosophy of social science which stands in opposition to all parties of this debate. It rejects the idea that the understanding of human action is theoretical in either the empiricist's sense of theory as a set of laws or the interpretivist's sense of theory as thick description. In somewhat different ways, R. G. Collingwood and Wilhelm Dilthey argued that theoretical descriptions of behavior ignore the inner, subjective character of the action. In Section 3.3 we encountered the idea of *verstehen*: that social scientific understanding must capture the meaning the events have for the subjects. The idea of *verstehen* also appears in Dilthey's and Collingwood's writing, though they use it in somewhat different ways than Weber and Schutz. Dilthey and Collingwood argued that theoretical descriptions treat the thought objectively, from the outside. To properly understand an agent's reasons in their capacity to move the agent to action, the action needs to be understood subjectively, from the inside.

The metaphor of *inside* and *outside* (not to mention the slippery word *subjective*) can be made more precise (following Stueber 2002, 30ff). Grammatically, the principle of instrumental rationality is a sentence in the third person. It says what an agent should do, given their goals and beliefs. There is something special about the first-person pronoun in thinking about action. I can recognize that a combination of beliefs and attitudes would be a reason for action, but unless I also understand that they are *my* beliefs and attitudes, I have no reason to act. Suppose I know, for example, that if Risjord wants a cup of coffee and believes that the pot is fresh, then Risjord will get a cup of coffee from the pot. And suppose I also know that Risjord wants a cup of coffee. This fulfills the first two premises of Hempel's explanatory form, but this knowledge has no motivational force at all unless I also realize that *I am Risjord. I* want the cup of coffee, etc. This means that Hempel's form of explanation could not express a motivation or reason for action because the explanation is entirely in the third person. (Notice that the same argument works against Winch's and Davidson's views too.)

If the foregoing argument is correct, then no kind of contextualization of an action description will capture the motivation for action. Neither laws, thick descriptions, nor primary reasons will show why the reasons motivated the action. The motives must be understood in a first-person sort of way. Collingwood concluded that the subjectivity of thoughts entailed that a historian must "re-enact" the thoughts of historical figures:

> Suppose, for example, [the historian] is reading the Theodosian Code, and has before him a certain edict of the emperor. Merely reading the words and being able to translate them does not amount to knowing their historical significance. In order to do that he must envisage the situation with which the emperor was trying to deal, and he must envisage it as that emperor envisaged it. Then he must see for himself, just as if the emperor's situation were his own, how such a situation might be dealt with; he must see the possible alternatives, and the reasons for choosing one rather than another; and thus he must go through the process which the emperor went through in deciding on this particular course. Thus he is re-enacting in his own mind the experience of the emperor; and only in so far as he does this has he any historical knowledge, as distinct from a merely philological knowledge of the meaning of the edict.
>
> (Collingwood 1946, 283)

In Collingwood's re-enactment there is an ineliminable use of the historian's own ability to act for a reason. The historian must imagine the situation facing an agent, including the environment, the costs, and benefits of different courses of action, the reactions of others, and so on. Then the historian thinks the problem through for him- or herself.

Collingwood's notion of re-enactment (and to a lesser extent, Dilthey's version of *verstehen*) has undergone a recent revival in the light of new psychological and philosophical theories. Developmental psychologists have documented changes in children's ability to understand the psychological states of those around them. By three years of age, most children understand that others have desires and that these desires differ from their own. But three-year-olds do not seem to understand that others have different beliefs. This part of their "theory of mind" normally emerges during the fourth year. The psychological question is: how are we to understand the cognitive capacity of humans to represent the mental states of others? There are, broadly speaking, two camps. The "theory-theory" holds that children learn about mental states in the same way as they learn about any other part of the world. Children observe the events around them and inductively arrive at generalizations. The generalization that individuals act because of their beliefs and attitudes is thus on a par with the idea that kittens like milk and birds fly. The alternative "simulation theory" is like Collingwood's re-enactment. On this view, my capacity to represent my own reasons for action and my capacity to represent other's reasons are two uses of the same psychological mechanism. To understand you, I take an as-if stance to your situation. I imagine that I have the same goals and the same beliefs about the environment. I then process these beliefs and attitudes as reasons for action, but I do so in an off-line or pretend sort of way. My ability to reason about what to do in the light of my own beliefs and attitudes thus produces conclusions about what I would do in that situation. I thereby understand why you acted as you did.

The dispute in cognitive psychology between the theory-theory and simulation theories of "mind reading" (as it is called) parallels the dispute between theoretical explanations of action and *verstehen*. Some of the virtues which attend the simulation theory are also virtues for re-enactment. One challenge for the theory-theory is that humans can understand motives and attitudes where there is no known theory. Humor, for example, is notoriously hard to theorize about. What makes something funny? Yet, even without a theory, we can quickly decide whether a joke will be funny to others. Moreover, we can tell whether a joke will be funny to others even if those others have a different sense of humor. Simulation theory explains how we can do this: I put myself in the other's position, perhaps with their sensitivities and background, and then see whether I think the joke is funny. Similar points can be made about our capacity to predict the emotions of others and to anticipate what another person would do in a novel situation. In all these cases we can formulate no theory, yet we are able to understand. Therefore, the simulation theorists conclude, simulation theory is superior to theory-theory. Analogously, re-enactment is superior to theoretical explanations of action.

One challenge for a re-enactment view of social scientific understanding is that it needs to find an appropriate role for evidence, historical or otherwise. It is obviously not sufficient for me to simply sit at my desk and imagine what Admiral

Tryon was thinking. Historical imagination must be informed by historical evidence. In Admiral Tryon's case, we have already seen the large number of historical specifics necessary to understand his action: hierarchies among officers and sailors, flag signal systems, the physics of ironclad steamships, rules of the road, and so on. Unless the historian knows these things (and more), it will be impossible to imagine Admiral Tryon's situation. The historian knows a lot about the time and place, and this knowledge must be empirically supported in the same way as any theory or interpretation. One might challenge the re-enactment view, then, by arguing that re-enactment is not sufficient for historical (and other social scientific) understanding. At the very least, re-enactment must be supplemented by social scientific theories or thick description.

In response, most proponents of simulation or re-enactment agree that theorizing of the ordinary sort is also necessary for social scientific understanding. The quotation from Collingwood suggests that historical reconstruction begins where the texts leave off. While this response is plausible, it shrinks the role of simulation. The earlier argument contended that simulation is necessary for understanding an individual's motivations. If this is the only role for simulation, then re-enactment or simulation plays little or no role where our inquiries do not involve the actions of specific individuals. Many social scientific projects are not concerned with individuals. The limited role for reenactment therefore weakens the simulation theorists' argument against naturalism.

5.2. The Games People Play

The principle of instrumental rationality is at the center of one of the most powerful explanatory paradigms in the social sciences. Rational choice theory (RCT) has its roots in economics and the formal theories of decisions, games, and social choices. It is not concerned with uncovering the best interpretation of an individual's actions, like Admiral Tryon's. Rather, it uses instrumental rationality to explain recurring patterns of interaction. By treating individuals as rational actors who seek to maximize their expected utility, rational choice theory explains social phenomena as the (often unintended) outcome individual choices. Rational choice theory thus links intentional action explanations to social explanation.

It is important to bear in mind that rational choice theory is not a single, complete theory. It is a body of definitions and constructs that are useful for *modeling* a variety of social phenomena. There are two goals of this section. First, it will introduce some of the main concepts of rational choice theorizing. It aims to help you understand some key ideas used in the literature and get the flavor of game-theoretic modeling. With these concepts in hand, we will be better equipped to understand a wide range of philosophical arguments concerning normativity, collective intentionality, and causal modeling. If you have studied microeconomics, this will be familiar territory. Second, it will provide some insight into the workings of an important theoretical framework in contemporary social science. Economics was the first discipline to use and develop the theoretical tools of rational choice theory.

It was quickly adopted by political scientists and is now used by a range of social sciences. Since rational choice theory enshrines the principle of instrumental rationality, the philosophical issues to which the RCT framework gives rise are directly relevant to the way we understand agency and intentional action.

Rationality and Utility

In the discussion so far, the principle of instrumental rationality has been left as an informal bit of common-sense: if a person has goal G and believes that doing A is the best means to achieve G, then the person will do A. This formulation is problematic in at least two ways. First, it ignores the fact that people have many goals, and they are sometimes inconsistent. When he was exercising the fleet, for example, Admiral Tryon may have also had the goal of taking a nap or retiring back to England. We all have multiple desires, values, likes, and aversions. As ordinarily understood, some attitudes are stronger than others. Love is a stronger motivation than affection, duty stronger than inclination. We would expect an instrumentally rational agent to be acting for the sake of their most important goal. This means that to refine the principle of instrumental rationality, we will have to tackle the difficult problem of ranking subjective feelings. Second, there is the phrase "best means." Here again there is a problem of ranking. Different means to a particular goal may be more or less likely to succeed. Presumably, probability of success and failure is partly what makes one factor the "best." And there may be other considerations which make one course of action better than another, even if we hold the goal fixed.

The problem of ranking goals and means is made more difficult by the fact that they interact. An observer can only note what the agent does. There is no way to observe what the agent was intending. Assuming that the agent is instrumentally rational, there are different possible combinations of goals and beliefs that would have rationalized any given action. Admiral Tryon could have had the goal of steering the *Victoria* to the outside of the *Camperdown* and believed that his orders would bring it about. Or he could have been trying to steer the *Victoria* inside of the *Camperdown* and believed that is orders would bring *that* about. Moreover, the strength of different desires interacts with the probability of success. One might reasonably prefer a sure path to a less desirable goal to a risky path to a more valuable one.

Economists of the early 20th century cut through these complexities with a very simple idea. It is common sense that if Fred's motive to eat salad is stronger than his desire for chocolate cake, then one would expect him to choose the salad when standing in the cafeteria line. At the moment of actual choice, the possible goals and beliefs collapse into a preference. Fred prefers salad to cake. A preference must involve two objects or courses of action: one prefers x to y. The simple idea is to identify the preference for x over y with the choice of x rather than y. We can ignore, for the present purposes, whether Fred relishes the taste of salad or eats it out of a sense of duty. In either case, he must prefer salad to cake because he chose the salad, not the cake. Now, it is easy to imagine that Fred has such preferences among each pair of choices available in the cafeteria. A rational agent, on this conception, doesn't just have a "goal *G*." He or she has an ordered set of preferences among all available options. By adding some assumptions, economists can use the concept of revealed preferences to define *utility functions*.

One of the simplest utility functions is an ordinal utility function. It ranks a set of possible objects of choice from highest to lowest. Imagine Fred standing in the cafeteria, and the choices are chocolate cake, chicken and rice, mystery meat in general utility brown sauce, and salad. This is his set of alternatives. We can turn Fred's preferences into a utility function by making two main assumptions. First, we assume that his preferences are *complete*. That is, for every pair of alternatives in the set, he either prefers one to the other or he is indifferent between them. Moreover, his preferences must be *transitive*: if he prefers *x* to *y* and *y* to *z*, then he must prefer *x* to *z*. With these assumptions, we can order the preferences in the set from his least preferred items to the most preferred. An ordinal utility function represents the ordering by assigning an ordinal number to each item of the set of alternatives. Fred's utility function might be as represented in Figure 5.2. Notice that the salad and the mystery meat are both assigned the value "1." This means that Fred is indifferent between them, preferring either one to the chocolate cake and the chicken stew to everything else. Also notice that, since the scale is ordinal, it provides no information about the magnitude of his likes and dislikes. For all we know, Fred just craves chicken and rice and would eat at the salad bar only if he were starving. Or perhaps he hates them all but hates chicken least of the bunch. The ordinal utility function only tells us how preferences—understood as one item preferred to another "all things considered"—are rank ordered.

The first refinement of the intuitive principle of instrumental rationality, then, is to replace the idea that rational agents pursue "a goal." A rational agent is one who acts act to maximize their utility, where "utility" is defined by an ordinal utility function. Of course, the notion of ordinal utilities is a dramatic over-simplification. It matters, one might think, whether Fred is a fool for chicken and rice, while

Fred's Utility Function

Alternative Set	Ordinal Utility
Chicken and rice	2
Salad bar	1
Mystery meat	1
Chocolate cake	0

Figure 5.2 Fred's Utility Function

hating chocolate. It is possible to create more sophisticated models of utility functions, as we will see momentarily, and these permit more sophisticated models of behavior. Nonetheless, even this very simple picture of preference is quite powerful. Our discussion of game theory, which follows, will be entirely conducted in terms of ordinal utility.

The simple model of utility as ordered preferences illustrates two important points about the economist's treatment of instrumental rationality as the maximization of utility. First, notice that in the example about food preferences, money was not a factor. Therefore, maximization of utility is not the same thing as maximization of profits. Though, obviously, levels of profit can be items in a preference set. Really, anything can be an item in a preference set—affection of friends, bottle caps, feelings of satisfaction from having done a good turn, the health of your parents—and this is the second point. While preferences are always the preferences of a particular agent, they do not need to be self-regarding. They are *my* preferences, but they do not have to be *about me*. It is therefore incorrect to regard the utility-maximization conception of rationality as selfish. It is entirely possible that to have an altruistic preference set that ranks gains for others (monetary, emotional, or what have you) higher than any gain for oneself.

Where the first refinement of the principle of instrumental rationality concerned the goal of the action, the second concerns the agent's beliefs. We often do not know whether what we want will be attainable. Life's choices are not like items in a cafeteria, there for the taking. Rather, we must consider the chance that our choice will not materialize. To explain why an agent took a particular course of action, then, we need to know something about how the agent evaluated the chances of success. As noted earlier, one of the difficulties here is that the assessment of risk and the evaluation of the benefit determine the action together. How can we tease apart the agent's utilities and beliefs about the probability of success? The trick is to think of the agent as making choices among *prospects* of satisfaction, or *lotteries*.

Suppose that Fred's food preferences are as represented in Figure 5.2. Now we look for gambles among which he is indifferent. For example, perhaps we offer Fred a choice between the certainty of getting a salad and a gamble where he gets chicken with probability p and nothing with probability $(p - 1)$. Then we adjust p until Fred doesn't care; he is indifferent between the sure thing and the gamble. Using this information, it is possible to construct a cardinal utility function, one which shows how much Fred prefers chicken to salad. It is also possible to deduce Fred's beliefs about the probabilities of different outcomes. If you have had courses in economics, you have probably worked through the construction of an *expected utility function*. Since our discussion will not depend on them, the details of the construction are beyond our scope. The crucial upshot is this: the construction of an expected utility function lets us treat an instrumentally rational agent as one who maximizes their expected utility.

Games and Strategies

So far, our examples have considered agents making choices among objects or lotteries. When the probability of success depends on what other agents will do, the situation becomes very different. Consider the following example.

In the winter of 1943, the battle for New Guinea had reached a critical point. The Japanese forces needed troop reinforcements from their base on nearby New Britain Island. General Imamura was charged with responsibility for the convoy. He had two routes to choose from. The northern route would take him across the Bismarck Sea, where the weather reports predicted storms and low visibility. The southern route across the Solomon Sea was predicted to be clear. Each route would take three days. General Imamura's primary concern was to protect his convoy from attacks by the American air force. The weather in the Bismarck Sea might delay their observation and thus reduce the number of days the convoy was exposed to bombing. The rational choice seems to be to go north. But General Imamura knew his opponent, General Kenney, could follow the same line of reasoning to predict that convoy would go north. General Kenney would therefore send all his forces to intercept the convoy in the Bismarck Sea. Would it be better, then, to go south? Or would Kenney follow the same logic and anticipate such a move?

The problem faced by Generals Imamura and Kenney (who were real generals in this situation, by the way) is the kind of problem modeled by game theory. Game theory is the formal treatment of rational agents who can maximize their utility only by anticipating and responding to the actions of other rational agents. If General Imamura's decision depends only on the relative value of a speedy crossing and the probability of bad weather slowing down his convoy, the situation can be modeled by looking at the expected utility of the different options. But General Imamura is facing a rational agent. General Imamura thus needs to respond to the various possible actions, that is, the *strategies*, of his opponent to find his own best strategy.

Game theorists model such situations by specifying the *players*, their possible *actions*, the *payoffs*, and the *information* available to them. The first three elements are represented in the standard matrix presentation of a game in Figure 5.3. Strictly speaking, no narrative is required, but adding one will help make sense of what is going on. Imagine that this is a TV game show where the two contestants, Smith and Jones, are in competition. In this game, they have each been given a pair of

The Simple Card Game

		Jones	
		Red	Black
Smith	Blue	$200, $0	$300, $200
	Green	$100, $100	$0, $300

Figure 5.3 The Simple Card Game

cards. Jones's cards are red and black, while Smith's are blue and green. They sit at a table facing each other, and they are to simultaneously play one of their cards face up. The pairs of dollar amounts represent what the players will receive if each were to play the appropriate card. Smith's payoff is first, then Jones'. So, the pair of numbers in the upper left payoff cell says that if Smith plays blue while Jones plays red, Smith receives $200 while Jones receives nothing.

Putting the game into this *matrix form* helps us think through the strategies from each player's point of view. From Smith's perspective, suppose Jones plays red. Then blue would be the better play because Smith would get $200 if he played blue, while he would get only $100 if he played green. If Jones played black, then blue is the better play for Smith again; he would get $300 if he played blue and nothing for green. From Smith's perspective, then, the best strategy is to play blue. It is a better play, no matter what Jones does. In this situation, where the player has a strategy that brings him higher utility than any other strategy, no matter how the other agents act, the player is said to have a *dominant strategy*. Now let's look at it from Jones's point of view. She too has a dominant strategy. If she plays black, she is better off, no matter what Smith does.

Equilibria

In the simple card game, the strategies form an *equilibrium*. An equilibrium is a set of strategies composed of the best strategy for each player. In the simple card game of Figure 5.3, the set would be {Blue, Black}. Since all the strategies in the set are dominant strategies, the equilibrium is called a *dominance equilibrium*. As we will soon see, not all games have a dominance equilibrium, and not all equilibria are unique, so the simple card game should not be regarded as a typical game. Perhaps the most well-known game with a unique dominance equilibrium is the Prisoner's Dilemma, represented in Figure 5.4. Imagine, the standard story goes, that Smith and Jones have been picked up by the police and accused of a crime. If both keep silent, there is still sufficient evidence to convict both on a lesser charge. The payoff in the upper left cell shows that if they cooperate and keep silent together, they would each get one year in prison. If one confesses while the other keeps quiet, the confessor gets to go free (zero years) while the silent partner gets 10 years. If both confess, both get five years. The dominance equilibrium is {Confess, Confess}.

The Prisoner's Dilemma

Jones

		Keep Silent	Confess
	Keep Silent	1 year, 1 year	10 years, 0 years
Smith			
	Confess	0 years, 10 years	5 years, 5 years

Figure 5.4 The Prisoner's Dilemma

Many people find the prisoner's dilemma troubling because the equilibrium is not efficient. The best payoff for the pair is one year of jail time; but instrumental rationality seems to demand that they both choose to confess and get more jail time. As you think about this, there are a couple of points to bear in mind. First, notice that it does not matter how many years of jail are threatened if the order of the player's preferences stay the same. In other words, we need only an ordinal utility function for the prisoner's dilemma. The same structure is represented in Figure 5.5 using the numbers 0, 1, 2, and 3. Only order of preference is represented, and 0 is the lowest utility. We do not care whether they are preferences about years in jail, amounts of money, or lunches. Changing the action set to "Cooperate" and "Defect" illustrates why the prisoner's dilemma has been so fascinating to philosophers and social scientists. It models cases where there are benefits to cooperation, but since each party has a motivation to be a "free rider," rationality seems to demand non-cooperation.

A common response to the prisoner's dilemma is to object that it portrays humans as paranoid and selfish. One might suppose that Smith and Jones care about one another. It would pain Smith greatly to defect alone and please him to know that both he and Jones got minimal jail time. Describing the player's motivations in this way suggests that the model is inaccurate because years in jail are not the only relevant payoff. However, this objection has little traction because only the order of the payoffs matters. If the payoffs are sufficiently altered to change the order of the preferences, then the strategic situation is no longer a prisoner's dilemma. The objection amounts to nothing more than telling a different story about a different situation. We can add care and feelings of commitment to the model, but if the order of the payoffs remains the same, the dominant strategy for both will still be to defect (perhaps with a wistful tear in the eye).

The narrative that goes along with the prisoner's dilemma often adds that the prisoners cannot talk to one another. It turns out that this is irrelevant. This game supposes that the players have *symmetric information* in the sense that both know the payoff schedule and possible strategies available to each. Since each prisoner knows that it would be irrational for the other to cooperate, each knows it would be irrational to keep any promises to cooperate. The apparent irrationality of promising in this situation highlights an important feature of game theory as we have developed it so far. We have presupposed that there are no binding agreements in the rules of the game. If any agreements arise, they do so because it is in the

Prisoner's Dilemma (Matrix Form)

		Jones	
		Cooperate	Defect
Smith	Cooperate	2, 2	0, 3
	Defect	3, 0	1, 1

Figure 5.5 The Prisoner's Dilemma (Matrix Form)

interest of each party to adhere; the agreements must be self-reinforcing. The kind of game theory we are surveying here is often called *non-cooperative*, and one of the interesting questions is whether and how group-level phenomena can arise out of the minimal assumption of instrumental rationality alone. *Cooperative* game theory assumes the existence of binding agreements, but it is beyond the scope of this brief survey.

So far, we have supposed that the players choose simultaneously. Would it matter if their actions were sequential? If Smith chose to cooperate, and Jones knew that she had already done so, then would that change the outcome? To model a game with sequential moves, we need to use an *extensive form* representation, as in Figure 5.6. In a game tree, each node (the circles in Figure 5.6) is a choice. The first move of the game is the top node. Here we represent Smith as choosing to cooperate or defect first. The two nodes at the next level represent the two possible situations in which Jones may find himself. At the left node, Smith has cooperated, and Jones must choose whether to cooperate or defect. On the right branch, Smith has defected, and Jones again must choose. The payoffs are at the bottom, again using the convention of putting Smith's payoff before Jones's and using ordinal payoffs like the last example. This representation makes it clear that even if Smith moves first and Jones knows what Smith has chosen, the strategy to defect dominates. Smith, being rational and knowing the payoffs, will know this and reason that Jones must defect. Smith's best strategy, then, is to defect. Even if the game is sequential, the strategy set {Defect, Defect} remains a dominant strategy equilibrium for the prisoner's dilemma. Note that this is not a general feature of game theoretic models. Often, changing the sequence of moves or changing the information available to the players will change the equilibria.

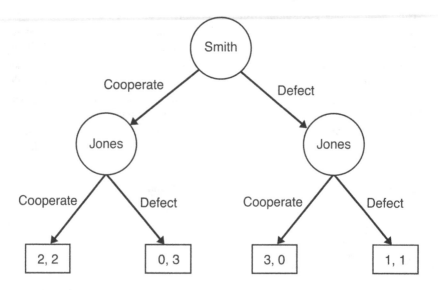

Figure 5.6 The Prisoner's Dilemma (Extensive Form)

Nash Equilibria and the Battle of the Bismarck Sea

With tools we have developed so far, let us return to 1943 and the war in the Pacific. The Generals Imamura and Kenney do not have information about each other's moves, so we can treat them as moving simultaneously. A matrix (Figure 5.7) can represent their strategic situation (Haywood 1954, 370). Recall that the northern route was obscured by clouds, making Kenney's reconnaissance more difficult. If both convoy and reconnaissance go north, the clouds make it likely that the convoy would not be discovered until the second day of the three-day journey, leaving only two days of bombing. Similarly, if reconnaissance goes north while the convoy goes south, the convoy would not be discovered until the second day. If the convoy went north and the reconnaissance went south, the convoy might escape with only one day of attack. If both went south, immediate discovery would make three days of bombing likely.

The payoffs are interesting in this case because a day of bombing is a benefit to Kenney and a loss to Imamura. Their utility functions are inverses; every good for Kenney is a bad for Imamura. This makes the situation a *zero-sum game*. While we could represent this with a pair of pay offs with numbers (e.g., +2,−2 for the upper left cell), this presentation is equivalent and more intuitive. What is the best strategy for each player? Let's begin with General Kenney. Unlike the two examples we have seen so far, General Kenney does not have a dominant strategy. If he sends the reconnaissance north, he is guaranteed two days of bombing. But whether two days of bombing is his best outcome depends on what General Imamura does. From General Imamura's perspective, he is indifferent among the payoffs in the top row; if General Kenney goes north, it doesn't matter what Imamura does. The payoffs in the bottom row are different, and General Imamura has a clear preference for one day of bombing. So General Imamura does have a best strategy. Sending the convoy north is at least as good as going south if General Kenney goes north, and better if Kenney goes south. This is General Imamura's best strategy, but notice that it is not a dominant strategy because the payoffs are not *always* better than an alternative. Such a case, as when General Imamura's strategy of going north is

Battle of the Bismarck Sea

		General Imamura	
		Send convoy north	Send convoy south
	Send reconnaissance north	2 days of bombing	2 days of bombing
General Kenney	Send reconnaissance south	1 day of bombing	3 days of bombing

Figure 5.7 Battle of the Bismarck Sea

sometimes better (when Kenney goes south) and never worse (when Kenney goes north) than the alternatives, is often called a *weak dominant strategy*.

Since neither player has a strongly dominant strategy (General Kenney does not even have a weak dominant strategy), there is no dominance equilibrium for the game. Recall, however, that an equilibrium was defined as the "best strategy" for all players, given the strategies available to the other players. The best strategy for a player need not be dominant. A broader conception of equilibrium is the *Nash equilibrium*, which captures a wide variety of strategic interactions. In a Nash equilibrium, no player can do better by unilaterally changing strategies. We thus ask of each set of strategies whether one of the players could do better if he or she changed, while holding the other players' strategies fixed. If no player can do better, then the set of strategies is a Nash equilibrium.

In the case of Generals Kenney and Imamura, there are four strategy sets:

1.   {Kenney goes north, Imamura goes north}
2.   {Kenney goes north, Imamura goes south}
3.   {Kenney goes south, Imamura goes north}
4.   {Kenney goes south, Imamura goes south}

Let's think our way through them. For strategy (1), if Kenney switched his strategy to south, and Imamura stayed with north, Kenney would be clearly worse off, since he would trade two days of bombing for one. On the other hand, if Imamura switched his strategy to south while Kenney stuck with north, he would gain nothing; there are two days of bombing either way. Neither player gains from a unilateral change in strategy, and therefore set (1) is a Nash equilibrium. In fact, it is the only Nash equilibrium in this game. In a case like (2), Kenney would do better by going south. Hence (2) is not a Nash equilibrium. Similarly, for (3) and (4), in each case, one of the players could do better by unilaterally switching. While it may seem a bit strange, the best strategy for both players, given the strategies of the others, is for them both to send their forces along the northerly route. As it happened, both generals took the rational choice. The American bombers intercepted General Imamura's convoy on the north side of New Britain on March 2, 1943, and the Battle of the Bismarck Sea was a decisive victory for the allied forces.

Multiple Equilibria and Coordination Problems

Every dominance equilibrium is also a Nash equilibrium, since in a dominance equilibrium (even a weak one), no player would be better off with another strategy. But not all Nash equilibria are dominance equilibria, as the Battle of the Bismarck Sea shows. More importantly, many Nash equilibria are not unique. For example, we will run into the "Ultimatum Game" several times throughout these chapters. The two players are to divide a good, say, a pile of 100 one-dollar bills. Player 1 decides how to divide the pile and offers that division to Player 2. She can split the pile 50–50, keep them all for herself and offer nothing, keep 99 for herself and offer 1, and so on. Player 2 can only choose to accept or reject the offer. If the offer is accepted, the payoffs are awarded according to the offered split. If Player 2 rejects the offer, then both players get nothing. There are as many possible splits as there are items in the pile (plus one: 0-all), and there are as many strategies for each player as there are splits. For Player 1, each strategy will have the form: offer n to Player 2. Player 2's strategies will take the form: accept an offer of n or greater, reject otherwise. Every strategy set with the form {offer n, accept n or more and reject otherwise} will be a Nash equilibrium. If we fix Player 2's strategy, then Player 1 would be worse off by offering $n-1$ (because she gets less) and by offering $n+1$ (because it results in a zero payoff). Given that Player 1 will offer n, Player 2 will be worse off by accepting at level $n-1$ or at $n+1$ for the same reasons. There are as many Nash equilibria as there are dollars in the pile.

Now, you might think that there is an obvious best choice for Player 1: one-for-you-and-the-rest-for-me. Player 2 would be irrational to accept nothing rather than something. So, this equilibrium seems like the obvious solution. This illustrates one important kind of response by game theorists to multiple equilibria: modify the "solution concept" or the definition of "best response" so that there is only one equilibrium left. In this case, the suggested solution can be formally developed as a "subgame perfect Nash equilibrium" (which we will not further describe here). We have only seen some of the many ways in which game theorists have tried to solve strategic interactions, and it shows something important about game theory. Game theory does not provide an algorithm or set of axioms for rationally resolving all games. Indeed, for every proposed solution concept, there are examples for which the definition is counterintuitive. This unreduced variety in of definitions of a crucial concept shows that game theory is less of a "theory" than it is a related collection of very powerful analytical tools.

Coordination games are an interesting class of games that have multiple equilibria. In these strategic interactions, players have a preference to coordinate, but different coordinations will suit them. Consider, for example, the problem faced by the captains of the *Victoria* and the *Camperdown* as they turned on a collision course. As illustrated in Figures 5.1b and 5.1c, there were two possible ways for the ships to pass each other while preserving the order of the fleet. If the *Camperdown* had passed outside of the *Victoria*, all would have been well. As it was, both ships tried to go on this inside part of the arc, and they collided.

Inside/Outside

HMS *Victoria*

		Inside	Outside
HMS	Inside	0, 0	1, 1
Camperdown	Outside	1, 1	0, 0

Figure 5.8 Inside/Outside

As Figure 5.8 illustrates, there are two equilibria. In the case of the sinking of the *Victoria*, Admiral Tryon's orders required the two ships to move simultaneously. When the moves are simultaneous, there is no rational way to achieve coordination. Choosing sequentially resolves the dilemma, since the rational choice for the second player will be to follow the first. Even so, it is impossible for an outsider to predict which equilibrium will result, since the first player is indifferent among the choices.

A somewhat more interesting game with multiple equilibria is the Stag Hunt (Figure 5.9). In this game, the players can cooperate for a high payoff or work separately for lower payoffs. The 18th-century philosopher Jean-Jacques Rousseau discussed problems of this type. In Rousseau's narrative, the hunters can either cooperate to kill a stag or hunt independently for rabbits. Two hunters are required to kill the stag. So, if one hunts stag while the other hunts rabbits, only the rabbit hunter succeeds. There are two Nash equilibria. One might think that, unlike the Inside/Outside game (Figure 5.8), this one has an obvious solution. Each hunter's highest utility is served by hunting stag. However, Jones might worry, "I know that the best option for Smith is to hunt stag, but what if Smith makes a mistake and chooses to hunt rabbits? Since I'd be left with nothing in that case, it is better to pick the sure thing and hunt rabbits." If Smith reasons the same way, the two would fall into the {Rabbit, Rabbit} equilibrium. This is known as the "trembling hand" problem. Even if the other players are fully rational and informed, they are not infallible. I can't be guaranteed that the other players won't make a mistake, and I should act accordingly.

One of the interesting questions about cooperative games is whether they can be solved within the game theory's framework of assumptions or whether they require appeal to external factors. Those who pursue the first option develop more sophisticated solution concepts than Nash equilibria, and some games can be solved this way. An appeal to externals, on the other hand, would look to psychological, historical, or cultural factors that lead agents to settle on one equilibrium rather than another. (We will discuss this idea further in Chapter 7.) Finally, we should note that all the games we have presented in this section have been treated as one-shot games among strangers. Does it matter whether the players have a prior history together? Does it matter if they will be in the same situation in the future? The study of repeated games has been very important, and we will discuss it in Section 6.4.

Stag Hunt

		Jones	
		Stag	Rabbit
Smith	Stag	2, 2	0, 1
	Rabbit	1, 0	1, 1

Figure 5.9 Stag Hunt

5.3. Agency

The Psychological Plausibility of Rational Choice Theory

It has probably already struck you that rational choice theory makes some rather implausible assumptions about human beings. Normal people don't calculate expected utilities. When deciding which movie to see with your date, you don't work out an optimal strategy with a complicated game-theoretical argument. A more profound concern is that rational choice theory puts all goals, values, and desires onto a single scale. I have a duty to my family, and I like coffee. But it is absurd to think that if you offered me a really, *really* good cup of coffee, I'd give away my family for it. The two simply aren't commensurable, or so one might argue. This casual observation is apparently supported by research in the growing field of behavioral economics. In Section 4.3, we encountered Herbert Simon's notion of bounded rationality. In the laboratory, subjects who play games like the prisoner's dilemma do not behave as game theory predicts. This kind of evidence is taken to show that humans do not, in general, act to maximize their expected utilities. The psychological costs of gathering the relevant information, evaluating, and arranging a consistent set of preferences are too high, and they may be out of reach for brains like ours. For reasons like these, some philosophers and social scientists have argued that rational choice theory is psychologically implausible and concluded that it is of little use in social scientific explanation.

Rational choice theorists recognize that decision theory or game theory do not do justice to the richness of human motivations. There are two quick responses to complaints about psychological implausibility. First, defenders will argue that decision theory and game theory are not meant to be complete theories of human behavior. All scientific theories highlight some aspects of the phenomenon to be explained and ignore others. When an explanation in physics ignores friction or heat loss, we do not reject physics. We simply note the limitations of the model. Similarly, rational choice theory should not be rejected just because it simplifies the picture of human motivation. The second response is that RCT explains *typical* human behavior, not the actual behavior of a specific individual. The limitations on human reasoning seen both in the lab and in ordinary life are like other kinds of individual variation. As we aggregate individuals, the errors cancel each other out. Of course, in some cases the psychological biases or informational constraints are strong enough to make the aggregate perform sub-optimally or irrationally. Nonetheless, the success of RCT in a wide variety of contexts shows that psychological deviations from the ideal of instrumental rationality can often be treated as mere noise.

Rejecting rational choice theory because it does not entirely match our experience does not cut very deeply into the theory. The critique can be deepened if we turn our attention to the underlying conception of agency. As we have seen, rational choice theory treats agents as beings who maximize their expected utility. This is a formalization and refinement of the notion of instrumental rationality, which is a framework for informal explanations of action. Is there reason to think that the underlying conception of agency is flawed? If the flaws are deep enough, we might conclude that theories which take instrumental rationality to be the core of agency are fundamental misrepresentations. Because agency is such a central concept, any revision will have far-reaching consequences. We will continue to pursue the issues of agency in Chapters 7 and 8, where the question of who we are intersects with issues of normativity and joint action.

Rational Fools?

Both informal and rational choice explanations of action represent motives as a combination of belief and a desire, value, or goal. Actions are thus always means to achieve something, and agents are those beings who act for the sake of their ends. There is a sense in which this conception of agency is fundamentally egoistic. Of course, rational choice theory does not constrain what agents may take to be valuable. I may value the welfare of my children and therefore choose to protect them over protecting myself. From the standpoint of utility maximization, such action is perfectly intelligible. My own pain is simply lower on my utility scale than the pain of my children. There is a sense in which this choice is altruistic: I act for the benefit of others at cost to myself. But notice that the costs *to me* are outweighed by the benefits *to me*. All the utilities are mine. Just as I like coffee more than tea, I dislike my children's pain more than I dislike my own. I prevent pain to my children because that outcome is high on *my* utility scale, not because pain is low on *theirs*. In this sense of "egoistic," utility maximization and its informal cousin, the principle of instrumental rationality, give rise to an egoistic conception of agency.

The egoistic conception of agency emerges from standard rational choice theory because all values are put on a single scale and indexed to an individual. No distinction is made between taste, preference, duty, or compulsion. Amartya Sen argued that conceptualizing motivation in terms of utility maximization conflates two different kinds of reason for action. He distinguished "sympathy" from "commitment."

> The contrast between sympathy and commitment may be illustrated with the story of two boys who find two apples, one large, one small. Boy *A* tells boy *B*, "You choose." *B* immediately picks the larger apple. *A* is upset and permits himself the remark that this was grossly unfair. "Why?" asks *B*. "Which one would *you* have chosen, if you were to choose rather than me?" "The smaller one, of course," *A* replies. *B* is now triumphant: "Then what are you complaining about? That's the one you've got!" *B* certainly wins this round of the argument, but in fact *A* would have lost nothing from *B*'s choice had his own hypothetical choice of the smaller apple been based on sympathy as opposed to commitment. *A*'s anger indicates that this was probably not the case.
>
> (Sen 1977, 328)

In this story, *B* understands all motivations in terms of "sympathy." Each individual has particular desires and acts to obtain those desires. As a result, *B* interprets *A* as desiring the smaller apple. It is the preference revealed by the hypothetical choice which *B* presents to *A*: which one would *you* choose? Since *A* would have chosen the smaller, *A* should have no complaint. And yet *A* does have a complaint. The issue, he might say, is not the size of the apple. It is about how we treat other people. There is something about human relationships which is being missed if all choices are treated as maximizing one's personal utility. As Sen remarks, "The *purely* economic man is indeed close to being a social moron" (Sen 1977, 336).

Choices based on commitment, according to Sen, may run contrary to self-interest. In these cases, the subject will choose "an act that he believes will yield a lower level of personal welfare to him than an alternative that is also available to him" (Sen 1977, 327). This means that given a utility scale where x is ranked more highly than y, acting from commitment will result in choosing y. My choice to tell the truth because duty demands it, even though the truth is embarrassing and will cost me my job, would be a presumptive example. While Sen's notion of commitment seems to capture an aspect of our motivation, rational choice theorists have a ready response to his argument. In cases like these, the agent appears to be choosing the outcome with lower utility only because we have misunderstood the agent's utilities. In Sen's story, the payoff is not just the apples. Boy *A* also gets satisfaction from offering *B* the larger apple when he has an opportunity to take it for himself. The payoff is thus the small apple plus the smug satisfaction of the altruist, and this is higher than the value of the large apple alone. Boy *B* is apparently not moved by such feelings, and he therefore values the large apple more highly. What Sen distinguishes as two kinds of motivation, the rational choice theorist might conclude, is nothing more than different objects taken as valuable. If doing my duty is ranked highly enough, then I will do so even if it costs me my job.

Game Theory in the Laboratory

Sen's suggestion that rational choice theory misrepresents the character of agency has gained force in recent years from the experimental research. Lab subjects have played all manner of choice and bargaining games. These experiments have seemed to show that human subjects routinely and dramatically deviate from the predictions of rational choice models. For example, consider a sequential prisoner's dilemma game. In this set-up, the payoffs are arranged as a standard prisoner's dilemma (Figure 5.5). The first player chooses to cooperate or defect. The second player then chooses with full knowledge of the first player's choice. In one experiment (Clark and Sefton 2001), the first-movers chose to cooperate more than 50% of the time. In response to an opening move of cooperation, second-movers chose to cooperate more than 30% of the time. The subjects seem to have some propensity to forego the payoffs in favor of cooperating and reciprocating cooperation.

These experiments have not been interpreted as refuting game theory for reasons exactly like those given in the response to Sen. The fact that some subjects do not choose the "defect" strategy shows that their utilities are not limited to the monetary payoffs offered by the experimenter. Perhaps their utility functions include the value of kindness, fairness, or reciprocity. When we change the utility functions of the subjects in the experiment, the payoffs change. And when the payoffs change, the game changes. This means that the subjects were behaving exactly as game theory predicts. They were just playing a different game than the experimenters thought they were playing.

The possibility of refining utility functions raises a question about the empirical testability of rational choice theory. There is no theoretical restriction on the preferences of an agent. This means that whatever an agent does must therefore have had the highest utility at the time. Some have tried to argue that this makes rational choice theory empirically empty. No test is possible because every result can be accommodated by adjusting the utilities attributed to the agents. We give the subjects of our experiment a game to play, then adjust our estimation of their utilities to match whatever they do, thus determining what game we gave them in the first place. This circle can be broken by separating the measurement of what agents want from the predictions of game theory. We need a way to determine the agent's preferences independent of the strategic game. If we knew the preferences, we could use those as the game payoffs. We would thereby hold the preferences fixed while we test game theory's predictions.

Francesco Guala has argued that the standard way of identifying preferences in rational choice theory does not permit refinements which would accommodate the kind of reciprocity seen in experimental economics (Guala 2006). Guala discusses a series of experiments conducted by Gary Charness and Matthew Rabin (2002). In these experiments, subjects played versions of the dictator and ultimatum games. In their version of the dictator game, one player (Player 2 in Figure 5.10) has a choice between two allocations of money. Player 1 must simply accept what Player

Allocation Game 1

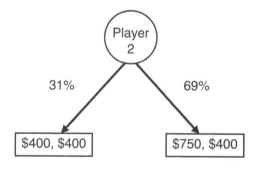

Figure 5.10 Allocation Game 1

2 dictates. The first choice gives Player 1 $400 and Player 2 $400; the second choice gives Player 1 $750 and Player 2 $400. The percentages in Figure 5.10 show what proportion of the subjects made each choice (Charness and Rabin 2002, 829; cf. Guala 2006, 259). This very simple game is a direct application of the standard definition of preferences. We are determining which of the two outcomes Player 2 prefers by looking at Player 2's choices. Monetary benefits to Player 2 are the same, so any difference should reflect extra-monetary utilities. And it turns out that a substantial number of the subjects seem to place some value on benefitting Player 1.

In Allocation Game 1 (Figure 5.10), the pool which Player 2 will divide is given to Player 2 by the experimenter. It is manna from heaven to be divided in one of two pre-determined ways. In a variation of the game (Figure 5.11), Player 2 is given the same choice, but the choice takes place at a later stage of play. Player 2's choice is determined by Player 1, and Player 2 knows Player 1's decision. In Allocation Game 2, which is a version of the ultimatum game, Player 1 has the choice of either taking $750 and leaving Player 2 with nothing or letting Player 2 make an allocation. Notice that the pattern of choice by subjects in the Player 2 position changes dramatically. Almost all prefer to reward Player 1 for giving them some

Allocation Game 2

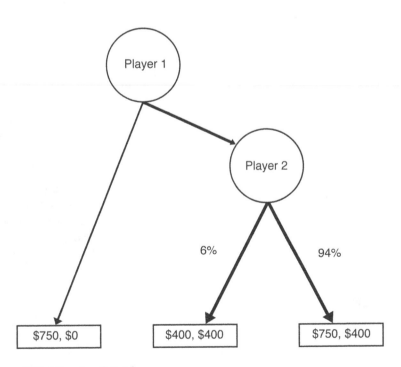

Figure 5.11 Allocation Game 2

benefit. Charness and Rabin account for these results by creating a sophisticated formula describing how subjects' utilities change. Guala points out that in their theory, the subject's utility function must include consideration of choices that the other player could have made: Player 1 *could* have allocated Player 2 nothing at all. This means that giving people simple choices among possible goods, as is done in the standard definition of preferences and utility functions, is inadequate. The value depends on what game is being played. In other words, agents care about how the choices came about. This means that it will be impossible to define a utility function that will determine an agent's values across all social contexts.

Guala's argument supports Sen's view that rational choice theory inappropriately treats agents as egoistic. Not all motives can be understood simply as a stronger preference for one outcome over another. What matters is not just the size of the apple, but the process of interaction by which the result came about. This means that it is not enough to treat agents as utility-maximizers. To understand action, we need a more complicated picture of motivation. Guala is careful to point out that the argument is not a blanket condemnation of game theory. With respect to particular situations, game theory may show something important about how agents interact. The conclusion is that the limitations of the theory prevent us from treating it as a fully general theory of action.

Realism, Instrumentalism, and Structural Modeling

Defenders of classical decision theory and game theory have made several moves in response to the argument that RCT is psychologically unrealistic. Historically, some economists have argued for a thoroughgoing instrumentalism of the sort we discussed in Section 3.2. On this view, RCT should not be construed as referring to real psychological states. Preferences, beliefs, utility functions, and the like are merely constructs of a theory which help us make accurate predictions. We saw earlier that instrumentalism is problematic for several reasons. In this context, one of the largest concerns is the way that instrumentalism segregates different sciences. For an instrumentalist, micro-economic theory is one sort of prediction instrument and cognitive psychology is another. There is no need for their constructs of micro-economics, political science, and sociology to be linked or even consistent. This flies in the face of much scientific practice and undermines some of the most powerful reasons for taking rational choice theory seriously. Mediated by game theory, social scientists have discovered important relationships between micro-economics, cognitive psychology, and evolutionary biology. Rational choice theory is important precisely because it can travel among different fields and link them together. Such cross-fertilization is difficult to understand on an instrumentalist construal of science.

Short of a retreat to instrumentalism, RCT can be defended from charges of psychological unreality by re-thinking the relationship between its claims and the facts of individual psychology. Despite its common name—rational choice *theory*—most social scientific research in this tradition consists of building models.

Rational choice theory explains large-scale social phenomena by showing how agents typically respond to the features of their environment. The model postulates idealized agents who are responding to specific costs and benefits. A kind of social event is then explained by showing how it arises as the result of the rational choices and strategic interactions of these ideal agents and the idealized resources available to them. The model is "structural" in this sense. Since the model does not describe the motivations of actual agents, the question of its psychological plausibility is moot. A further advantage of treating RCT as a structural theory is that it can take a larger variety of objects as "rational agents." In the discussion of revolutions (Section 7.1), we will see theorists who want to treat trade unions and churches as the agents of rational choice theory. In economics, it is common to treat firms and families as agents. Treating rational choice theory as a structural theory thus distances rational choice explanations from the explanation of (individual) intentional action.

While treating rational choice theory as structural goes some way toward defusing Guala's and Sen's critique, structural theories cannot be cut off from empirical testing. If we are concerned only with the predictions of the model, and not at all with the mechanisms it postulates, we fall back again into instrumentalism. If we are not to be instrumentalists, we must evaluate whether the mechanisms postulated by the model are realistic. It is at this point that Guala's and Sen's concerns become vivid again. As Lehtinen and Kuorikoski have argued (2007), much depends on the details of the model. When rational choice models are used structurally, we need to pay careful attention to the aspects of the agent's decision-making that are being ignored. If there is reason to believe that the social phenomenon being modeled depends on some feature which has been left out of the model, then the model's explanations are inadequate. This means that the epistemology of rational choice modeling will need support from social scientific research which lies outside of the model. Cognitive psychology, ecology, history, social theory, and even philosophy may be necessary to support rational choice modeling.

Like a map, we do not expect a model to be accurate in every respect. Models must abstract or idealize some of the features of the system being modeled. But how can we learn from models if they are so unrealistic? We will explore this question in the next chapter.

5.4. Wrap Up

Chapter Summary

Instrumental rationality plays a prominent role in our common sense thinking about intentional action. We understand the actions of others by looking for their goals and their beliefs about the environment. Rational choice theory formalizes the intuitive idea of instrumental rationality into the more precise conception of expected utility maximization. The philosophical debates in this chapter have questioned the character of the principle of instrumental rationality, its psychological plausibility, and its function in action explanation. The debate between Hempel, Winch, and Davidson surveyed in Section 5.1 concerned the character of the principle of instrumental rationality. Is the relationship between beliefs, goals, and actions a causal, law-like relation, or is it normative? Can reasons be causes? When the principle of instrumental rationality is formalized in rational choice theory, the problem of psychological plausibility comes to the fore. While this problem has been recognized since the inception of rational choice theory, it has received new impetus from research in behavioral economics. In the laboratory, people tend to be much more cooperative than game theory predicts. This raises important epistemological questions about how rational choice theory could be empirically tested, and more generally, how any model which contains abstractions and idealizations can be tested. It also puts the spotlight on human cooperation. Clearly, cooperation is fundamental to human society. Game theoretical equilibria are one way to understand cooperation, but the problems of multiple equilibria, trembling hands, and so on point toward important difficulties. Moreover, part of the psychological implausibility has to do with game theory's failure to predict human cooperative tendencies. How should the experimental evidence about cooperation bear on social scientific theories?

In this chapter we have seen two challenges which strike to the heart of the picture of agency implicit in instrumental rationality. Collingwood's challenge was that action explanation must capture the first-person character of belief and attitudes if it is to portray motives as motivational. The challenge is epistemic. Our understanding of agents must include their subjectivity, and it requires a kind of simulation or re-enactment. Agents thus cannot be represented in the same way we represent other objects. Sen's critique was more metaphysical. He pointed out that decisions are less self-regarding than can be accommodated within either rational choice theory or standard intentional action explanations. Agency must be represented in richer terms. These questions about agency will return in Chapter 9 when we consider how to understand the normativity of the social world and in Chapter 10 when we look at actions that only can be done in groups, such as winning a football match.

Discussion Questions

1. Apply Hempel's deductive-nomological form of intentional action explanation to Admiral Tryon's actions. Is anything left out? Does this form of action supplant a broader interpretivist approach?
2. Apply Hempel's deductive-nomological form of intentional action explanation to studies of aggression. Suppose that there are strong correlations between playing violent video games and aggressive behavior. What does this explain? Would it explain why Jimmy punched Tommy in the nose?
3. Contrast Davidson's position with Hempel's and Winch's views. How do they agree, and on what points do they disagree? Who has the most convincing view of action explanation?

4. In Section 5.1, humor was used as an example of something that is easy for a simulation theory to explain but difficult to theorize about. Is it true that we have no theory of humor? On a simulation theory, how could we come to understand the humor of people very different from ourselves?
5. Do the forms of the strategic interaction discussed in Section 5.2 apply to other any real-world social situations? When you confront problems of these forms, how do you solve them? What does that tell you about the use of game theory to represent and analyze these strategic interactions?
6. Sen distinguished between choices based on sympathy and choices based on commitment. Find some examples of each. Can they be adequately explained by standard rational choice theory? If not, then what is the "commitment" found in your examples? What is the conception of agency which stands behind your examples?

Further Reading

The story of Admiral Tryon and the sinking of HMS *Victoria* is told in *Admirals in Collision* (Hough 1959). In "Imperfect Rationality," (1970) Watkins uses Admiral Tryon to discuss a number of the issues about rationality and action explanation which are the subject of this chapter.

Hempel's "The Function of General Laws in History" (1942) is an important starting point for late-20th-century debate over the character of social scientific explanation. Dray famously responded to Hempel in his *Laws and Explanation in History* (1957). Hempel and Dray continued the debate (Dray 1963 and Hempel 1963). The argument that reasons cannot be causes is found in Chapter 3 of Winch's *Idea of a Social Science* (1958). Anscombe's *Intention* is a must-read for anyone interested in action explanation (1963). Davidson's "Actions, Reasons, and Causes" is reprinted in his *Essays on Action and Events* (1980) along with further relevant essays. Important contributions to the continuing debate over reasons and causes include Goldman's *A Theory of Human Action* (1970), Von Wright's *Explanation and Understanding* (1971), and Bratman's collected essays (Bratman 1987 and Stueber 2013). Gallagher's *Action and Interaction* (2020) is perhaps one of the most important recent works on this topic.

The notion of re-enactment has its source in Collingwood's and Dilthey's work. For discussions of their work with reference to the consequences for the philosophy of social science, see Dray, *History as Re-Enactment* (1995); Stueber, "The Psychological Basis of Historical Explanation: Reenactment, Simulation, and the Fusion of Horizons" (2002); and Makkreel, *Dilthey: Philosopher of the Human Studies* (1975). The contemporary reappraisal of these arguments in terms of simulation theory is explored in Goldman's "Interpretation Psychologized" (1989); Kögler and Stueber's (eds.) *Empathy and Agency: The Problem of Understanding in the Human Sciences* (2000); and Stueber's *Rediscovering Empathy* (2006). Khalifa's "Is Verstehen Scientific Understanding?" (2019) is a provocative challenge to the verhstehen approach.

The presentation of game theory in this chapter generally follows Rasmusen, *Games and Information: An Introduction to Game Theory* (2007). Bonano's entry on "Game Theory" (Jarvie and Zamora-Bonilla 2011) goes beyond the discussion in this chapter by introducing the representation of differential information among the players. Ross's entry on game theory in *The Stanford Encyclopedia of Philosophy* is a superb introduction to the philosophical significance of game theory (2011). For more on the philosophical presuppositions and consequences of these constructions, see Reiss *Philosophy of Economics: A Contemporary Introduction* (2013b).

Gintis, *The Bounds of Reason: Game Theory and the Unification of the Behavioral Sciences* (2009) and Coleman, *Foundations of Social Theory* (1990) provide programmatic orientations toward rational choice theory for the social sciences. For general discussions of rational choice theory in the social sciences and its challenges, see Pizzorno (2007) and Paternotte (2011). Hechter and Kanazawa's "Sociological Rational Choice Theory" (1997) provides a critical overview of rational choice theory in sociology. In political science, debate about rational choice theory can be found in Green and Shapiro's *Pathologies of Rational Choice Theory* (1995); see Cox (1999) for a reply. Philosophical critiques of the use of rational choice theory in the social sciences include Sen, "Rational Fools" (1977); Sanchez-Cuenca, "A Preference for Selfish Preferences" (2008); Kuorikoski and Lehtinen, "Economics Imperialism and Solution Concepts in Political Science" (2009); Lehtinen and Kuorikoski, "Unrealistic Assumptions in Rational Choice Theory" (2007). Satz and Ferejohn defend rational choice theory against some of these charges in "Rational Choice and Social Theory" (1994); see also Little, *Microfoundations, Method, and Causation* (1998).

Tversky and Kahneman's research documented important ways in which humans deviate from the expectations of instrumental rationality as well as other forms of logical reasoning. "Judgment Under Uncertainty: Heuristics and Biases" (1974) is the seminal study. Gigerenzer (1991) suggested alternative explanations for Tversky and Kahneman's results and presented his own program (2008). Kahneman won the Nobel Prize for his work, and his Nobel lecture, "Maps of Bounded Rationality" is a good introduction to his work (Kahneman 2002). The field of behavioral economics has taken off in recent decades. Camerer's *Behavioral Game Theory: Experiments in Strategic Interaction* provides an excellent overview of experimental results (2003). Henrich et al (2005) test the predictions of game theory cross-culturally. Explorations of the philosophical significance of behavioral economics include Woodward's "Experimental Investigations of Social Preferences" (2009), Guala's "Has Game Theory Been Refuted?" (2006), and Heidl's *Philosophical Problems of Behavioural Economics* (2016).

6   Modeling and Explaining

While it seems counterintuitive, science often proceeds by *ignoring* known causes. For example, every massive object in the solar system gravitationally attracts every other. But by considering only the pair-wise attraction between each planet and the sun, Newton successfully explained the orbits of the planets. In the last chapter, we saw some attempts to explain human behavior by treating agents as simple utility maximizers. Humans are obviously much more complex, but analogous to Newton's simplifications, proponents of game theoretic and other sorts of modeling would argue that by isolating just a few of the factors that determine our behavior, we can get a deeper understanding. Models always either ignore known factors (abstraction), or they treat them as having values or features that they do not (idealization), and often they do both. Models thus misrepresent. But if they misrepresent, how can they be used to understand and explain? This is the central puzzle of modeling. And since so much social scientific inquiry today is concerned with model building, the puzzle strikes to the heart of the social sciences.

The analogy between models and maps sharpens the puzzles presented by modeling. Like models, maps both abstract and idealize. The map on your GPS navigation app represents streets and highways, and perhaps it also depicts railways, rivers, and lakes. However, it does not represent the hills and valleys; it abstracts away from these features. While to abstract is to ignore something, to idealize is to distort. Map scale distorts distance in a systematic way. On pain of absurdity (which authors like Jorge Luis Borges and Lewis Carroll have playfully explored), a map must not be the same size as the territory it represents. The scale shrinks the map proportionately. If the scale of the map is 1cm=10km, and two points are a centimeter apart on the map, then they lie 10 kilometers apart in the countryside. And notice that not everything on the map will be to scale, so some idealizations distort to the point of complete misrepresentation. For example, a road is typically about 7 meters wide. So, if the lines representing roads were drawn to the 1cm=10km scale, they would have to be .0007 centimeters wide, which is smaller than a human hair! So, the lines representing roads do not represent their width. Thus, even very simple maps systematically misrepresent their territories, and they must do so if they are to be useful at all. Nonetheless, we use them with confidence. Can we say the same thing about social scientific models?

DOI: 10.4324/9781003207795-6

A large part of our confidence in the use of maps derives from our understanding of the idealizations and abstractions involved in their construction. When one knows how to read a highway map, one knows that one can infer the distance between two cities, but not the width of the roads or the steepness of the hills. This puts a sharper point on our question about social scientific models. What analogous constraints apply to social scientific models? How do we know when inferences from a model are reliable? The example of the Newtonian model of the solar system suggests that perhaps a well-confirmed theory needs to generate the model, and the theory tells us what inferences are reliable. Alternatively, perhaps we need to attend carefully to the purposes of the model or to the relationships between the model and system represented. After presenting an example of social scientific modeling in some detail (Section 6.1), Section 6.2 will explore these questions.

While the analogy between maps and models might make social scientific models seem more familiar, it does not touch the fundamental question about models. Models provide explanations of social scientific phenomena. Maps represent a territory, but they do not explain. Explanation is a relationship: the lightning explains the forest fire. But if there was no lightning, then the fire is not explained by lightning. Because models idealize, some of what they say about their target systems will be false (recall the thickness of the lines representing roads). But if what the model says is false, and falsehoods cannot explain, then models cannot explain. Such a result is paradoxical: the value of models seems to be that they explain, but their dependence on idealization means that they cannot. We will discuss this paradox of explanation in Section 6.3.

6.1. Modeling Segregation

Segregation Studies in the US

The end of slavery in the US presented the enormous challenge of integrating an enslaved population into the society of the slaveholders. In some southern states, Black residents significantly outnumbered White. The White response, especially in the south, was to create a system of laws and often violent practices that enforced a separation of Blacks from White society and that limited access to education, employment, and political participation. In the latter part of the 19th century, Black Americans began to move to northern cities, both for the higher wages and to escape the oppressive "Jim Crow" laws, violent repression, and White supremacy of the southern states. Between the end of the First World War and 1970, more than 6 million Black Americans migrated north. While the northern industrial cities offered opportunities, the new immigrants faced substantial racial discrimination in housing and employment as well as poor police protection. While some prospered, many Black communities were plagued by unemployment, crime, and poverty. Moreover, the quick rise in the Black population led to tensions with Whites that frequently broke into open violence. The Tulsa Massacre of 1921—one of dozens of such examples—killed 300, injured 800, and burned down 35 city blocks of a prosperous Black neighborhood. The questions of how to prevent such violence and how to ameliorate the problems of poverty, crime, undereducation, and unemployment were consuming political problems of the 20th century, and we feel the reverberations today.

Some of the earliest empirical work in American sociology focused on describing the condition of urban Black residents and explaining why they faced the problems they did. W. E. B. Du Bois's *The Philadelphia Negro* (Du Bois 1996 [1899]) was one of the first studies to use methods clearly recognizable to contemporary sociologists: extensive interviews, surveys, residence mapping, and descriptive statistics. He identified segregation as fundamental to the problems faced by that community:

> In Philadelphia, as elsewhere in the United States, the existence of certain particular social problems affecting the Negro people are plainly manifest. Here is a large group of people—perhaps forty-five thousand, a city within a city—who do not form an integral part of the larger social group. This itself is not altogether unusual; there are other unassimilated groups: Jews, Italians, even Americans; and yet in the case of the Negroes the segregation is more conspicuous, more patent to the eye, and so intertwined with a long historic evolution, with peculiarly pressing social problems of poverty, ignorance, crime and labor, that the Negro problem far surpasses in scientific interest and social gravity most of the other race or class questions.
>
> (Du Bois 1996 [1899], 5)

For Du Bois and the sociologists who followed him, the pressing question was to explain why segregation persisted. They were concerned with this question for two reasons. On the surface, as the quotation from Du Bois indicates, the social problems of crime and poverty, undereducation and unemployment, needed solutions, and segregation seemed to be a causal factor. Indeed, for much of the 20th century, most sociologists would follow Du Bois in supposing that "racial segregation in residential areas provides the basic structure for other forms of institutional segregation" (Johnson 1943, 8). More deeply, these sociologists were engaged in the larger debate over whether race was biological (a question we will discuss further in Chapter 8) and thus whether the differences between Black and White educational and socio-economic achievement could be attributed to racial differences. The sociologists sought to explain the problems by appeal to the environment, not heredity. Hence, by identifying the social causes of segregation, they could identify the social forces that kept Black communities impoverished and undereducated.

By the 1970s, several detailed studies of residential segregation had been completed, often comparing different cities and regions in the US. Three possible explanatory factors for the persistent segregation by race emerged from this research. First, racial prejudice, animosity, and discrimination figured prominently. Both officially sanctioned and informal racial discrimination were common in America, and their effects were quite obvious. Both institutionalized discrimination, such as racial zoning laws, and informal discrimination in banking and real estate narrowed the options for Black residences. However, in American cities, like cities around the world, neighborhoods were segregated by economic status (or class) and occupation. Immigrants to and within the US—of all backgrounds—first occupied neighborhoods where rents were low and unskilled jobs were available. As they moved north, Black Americans also followed this pattern. Economic segregation was thus a second possible explanatory factor. Discrimination potentially played an indirect role in this second factor too, of course, since discrimination in education and employment opportunity would keep Black residents in less-prestigious jobs with lower wages. Finally, many sociologists included individual choice as an explanatory factor. Immigrant groups often found comfort in living near those who shared familiar language and customs. For Black Americans, where interactions with the White majority could be dangerous, a Black neighborhood also provided security. By the 1960s, then, the main questions in the study of residential segregation were to understand how these three factors interacted to explain the persistent segregation of Black neighborhoods in American cities.

Schelling's Checkerboard Model of Segregation

Thomas Schelling came to the questions of residential segregation with an economist's sensibilities, and he had two fundamental ideas. First, he noted that there were "many macrophenomena, like [economic] depression and inflation, that do not reflect any universal desire for lower incomes or higher prices" (Schelling 1969, 488). Economic models aggregate preferences, and they show how a macrophenomenon, whether desirable or undesirable, can arise from everyone pursuing their best interest. Second, he noticed certain logical, or better, topological, constraints on spatial arrangements. Suppose we are arranging black and white counters on a grid. Each counter is surrounded by eight others, as is the counter marked "A" in Figure 6.1. If we want each counter surrounded by an equal number of black and white counters, the total neighborhood of all *nine* squares will be either majority black or majority white. And if there is more of one color than another, then an even distribution is obviously impossible: some "neighborhoods" will necessarily be dominated by the majority.

Schelling's model combines these two insights in a clever way. The model is composed of a grid of squares on which are distributed two kinds of agents. Several squares are left unoccupied so that movement into unoccupied squares is possible. Figure 6.2 illustrates such an arrangement with randomly distributed black and white circles (agents) on a 6x6 grid. To eliminate problems about the edges, we treat the grid as continuous: the left and right sides connect (as if the grid were rolled into a tube), as do the top and bottom (forming a doughnut-shaped surface). Each agent has a neighborhood and a preference for their neighbors, and we can vary these parameters, setting the size of the neighborhood and the preference for living among other agents who are the same or different. To illustrate, let us set the neighborhood of an agent to be the eight adjacent squares, as in Figure 6.1. Agents prefer a percentage of black or white neighbors. If a given agent is in a

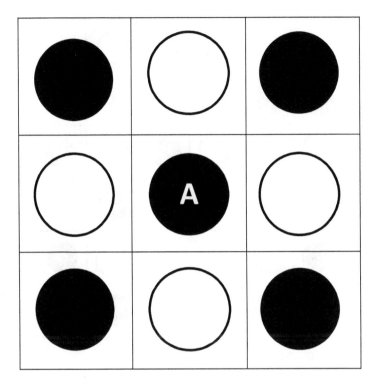

Figure 6.1 A Schelling Neighborhood

neighborhood that is at or above this "tolerance level," then that agent is "satisfied." When a neighborhood of an agent is below the tolerance level, they are "unsatisfied." Let us begin with a tolerance for 50% neighbors of the same color. The agent marked "A" in Figure 6.2 is thus satisfied, since they have three black and two white neighbors (remember, the board wraps around top to bottom). Agent B, however, is unsatisfied with their three black and one white neighbors.

Schelling's model lets us look at how different patterns of residence can evolve based on the tolerance threshold and neighborhood size of the agents. To do so, we let unsatisfied agents move to the nearest open space that satisfies them. For agent B, this would be the space marked "C," where they have three black and two white neighbors and thereby meet their 50% threshold. The mechanism of Schelling's model is to go through the entire grid, one agent at a time and give each a chance to move. If the agent is unsatisfied, they move to the nearest open space where they are satisfied. Obviously, each move affects both the neighborhood that the agent left and the neighborhood into which they move. When agent B moves to space C, agent A is now in a neighborhood with three black and only one white neighbor. We continue letting agents move with further rounds and look at the resulting patterns. After one round of movement (starting in the upper left corner and working to the right and down), the pattern of Figure 6.3 results.

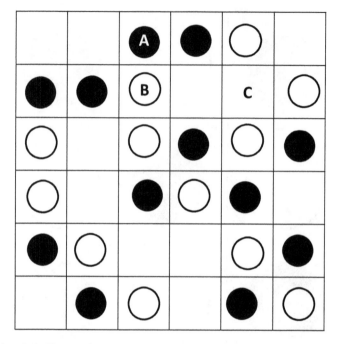

Figure 6.2 A Schelling Model Initial Arrangement

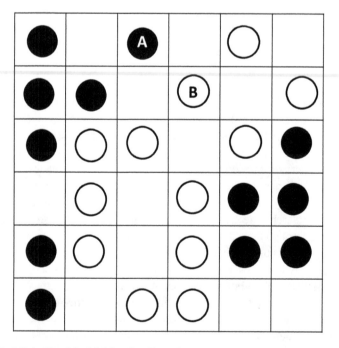

Figure 6.3 A Schelling Model After One Round

The result is quite striking, even after just one round of movement. If you remember that the left and right sides of the grid are continuous, then the agents have already moved into two clearly defined groups. But not all agents are satisfied yet. Figure 6.4 shows the result of one further round. The earlier pattern has consolidated. Moreover, all the agents are satisfied. The model has thus reached an *equilibrium*, where each agent's preference is satisfied. Notice that the agents ended up rather strongly segregated. Only 3 of the 36 are in 50–50 neighborhoods; all the rest are in majority white or majority black neighborhoods. Yet no agent preferred to live in a neighborhood with a majority.

What happens when we manipulate the parameters? Suppose we start with the same initial random arrangement of Figure 6.2 but change the tolerance. Suppose the agents are happy being in a minority, but they don't want the minority to be too small. Let them be happy with three similar neighbors out of the eight (a tolerance of 37.5%) but move if they find themselves in a neighborhood where they are in a smaller minority. After two rounds, equilibrium is reached again, and a very similar pattern emerges, as we see in Figure 6.5. This result is rather surprising: segregation is an equilibrium even when all agents are satisfied being in the minority.

Schelling's model shows that the interacting preferences of agents and the topology of their movement put constraints on the overall patterns that can emerge.

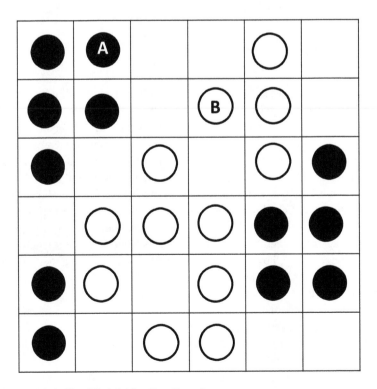

Figure 6.4 A Schelling Model After Two Rounds

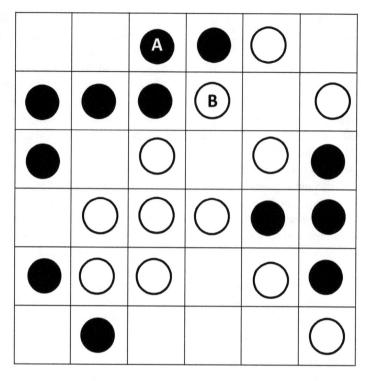

Figure 6.5 Equilibrium of Tolerant Neighbors

Even when no agents prefer segregated neighborhoods, segregation emerges anyway. We could have varied a different parameter, such as the proportion of agents of each type, the proportion of blank spaces, or the size of the neighborhood, but the result is surprisingly robust. Over many of these variations, segregation is an equilibrium. But not always: if the tolerance is set below about 30% (depending on the other variables), the agents may not settle into an equilibrium. And if the neighborhood is quite large compared to the size of the grid, some of the equilibria are quite integrated. Schelling extended the basic ideas of the checkerboard model to look at what happens under two further conditions. In this model, there are equal numbers of agents of each kind and all the agents have the same tolerance. If one kind is in the minority, however, it is impossible for all the neighborhoods to be integrated proportionally. There will have to be some all-majority neighborhoods. What happens if the minority agents have one tolerance (say, a 50% tolerance), but the majority has another (say, a 30% tolerance)? In most of these cases, but not all, segregation is again an equilibrium.

Schelling's checkerboard model is highly abstracted and idealized. It ignores many factors that we have good reason to believe influence patterns of residence. There are no natural boundaries to neighborhoods, like railroad tracks or rivers. There are no centers of employment, like factories or central business zones. There are no costs associated with moving, no run-down houses, no tiny neighborhoods. The agents, their preferences, and their environments are highly idealized. The model makes no distinction between a White preference for a majority White neighborhood because of racist attitudes and non-racist preference for similarity, nor between a Black preference for a 50–50 neighborhood because it reduced the risk of White violence and a Black preference for integration. The model idealizes away from such variation and treats all motivation as simply a tolerance level. The model is thus extremely unrealistic. Proponents of such modeling, of course, will regard the abstractions and idealizations as a strength. Just as experiments shield the phenomenon in question from all possible causes but one, so that the contribution of that one cause can be identified, a model lets us see how just one factor can influence an outcome. The question for critics and proponents alike is: what does such an artificial set-up tell us about the real world?

Critiques, Tests, and Extensions of Shelling's Model

Schelling's model was not immediately noticed by social scientists. In the 1980s and 90s, however, the questions surrounding residential segregation changed somewhat. Legislation and court rulings during the 1950s and 60s made explicit discrimination in housing, education, and employment illegal. Proponents of such legislation anticipated that, as legally sanctioned discrimination was eliminated, Black Americans would integrate. Their expanded educational and occupational opportunities would give them greater income, and without barriers on their choice of residence, Black Americans would purchase or rent in the higher-income neighborhoods previously dominated by Whites. However, this did not happen. In the 1970s and 80s, segregation by race persisted. While Black Americans joined the middle classes in greater numbers and moved to more desirable housing, those neighborhoods remained strongly segregated.

Against this background, several social scientists looked to Schelling's model for an explanation. A study of Black and White attitudes toward neighborhood integration in Detroit revealed that for 62% of the Black respondents a 50–50 mixed neighborhood was their first choice, and for a further 20%, it was their second choice (Farley et al 1978, 328). Among White respondents, 20% said they would be uncomfortable if there were *one* Black family in a neighborhood of 15 houses, and 72% said they would be uncomfortable if the neighborhood were 50–50 (Farley et al 1978, 333). Given such attitudes, the Schelling model predicts that neighborhoods would be segregated. In a review of the available evidence, William Clark argued that of the four possible explanatory factors for residential segregation, "economic status (affordability), social preferences, urban structure, and discrimination" (Clark 1986, 95), economic status and social preferences, acting in concert, were by far the most important. Urban structure, by which he meant things like the distance between one's place of residence and place of employment, was less important. As for discrimination, he concluded: "Assertions that discrimination is a major factor causing the segregation of housing patterns in metropolitan areas must be treated as unproven until further research is conducted" (Clark 1986, 122).

Other social scientists took issue with these explanations. In a response to Clark, George Galster argued that the Schelling model abstracted away from crucial explanatory factors:

> It assumes: (1) housing prices in the neighborhood remain constant for all racial compositions; (2) whites in the neighborhood will always move out when the percentage of minorities which they can tolerate is exceeded (i.e., they are always able to find another dwelling/neighborhood which is both superior and affordable); (3) all in-movers are minorities, all out-movers are white; (4) the distribution of preferences of whites originally in the neighborhood is identical to those of whites in the larger community.
>
> (Galster 1988, 100)

These other factors can override any preferences for neighborhoods with a particular racial composition. If segregation persists, he argues, it is because discrimination is playing an important role. In *American Apartheid* (1993), Douglas Massey and Nancy Denton argued that a discriminatory mechanism was necessary to explain residential segregation. While they accepted that the Schelling model captures an important dynamic, Whites can flee a neighborhood where Blacks have entered only if there are other majority White neighborhoods to go to. And these neighborhoods will exist only if Blacks are unlikely to enter certain neighborhoods. "Some method must exist, therefore, to limit black entry to a few neighborhoods and to preserve racial homogeneity in the rest" (Massey and Denton 1993, 97).

Criticisms like Galster's and Massy and Denton's contend that specific abstractions and idealizations in the Schelling model keep it from explaining the real-world phenomenon of segregation. By ignoring the way prices are set (Galster) or by idealizing movement in and out of neighborhoods (Massey and Denton), the model ignores factors related to active discrimination against Black residents. By the 1990s, then, the social scientific debate over segregation came to focus on the relative importance of discrimination over economic status and preference as causes. An obvious response to criticisms by proponents of Schelling's model is to add other possible explanatory factors to the model. A more complex model will let us examine the interaction among the possible causes and determine their relative importance, the conditions under which they are determinative, and so on.

Schelling's model was simple enough to explore with coins and a checkerboard. To consider all the variables mentioned, substantial computer power is required to implement the dynamics of the model. The tradition that emerged out of Schelling's work is called "agent-based modeling." Schelling's agents were very simple. They decided whether to move based on their tolerance threshold and information about the racial composition of the neighborhood. More complicated agents would have to seek more than one kind of information about the environment and weigh multiple criteria to determine an outcome. In agent-based modeling, then, agents make decisions based on sophisticated algorithms. This permits the modeler to control more variables and experiment with their interaction.

Responding to those contending that racial preferences required mechanisms of discrimination to produce neighborhood segregation, Mark Fossett developed an agent-based model (Fossett 2006). Where Schelling's model defined the neighborhood as the squares around a given agent, realistic neighborhoods are geographic areas, not just the houses around an individual. Fossett captures this by dividing the overall grid into smaller neighborhoods that contain 49 families each. The overall landscape of his model had 112 neighborhoods and 5,488 housing units (Fossett 2006, 232). Each housing unit varied in quality, and higher quality residences were located toward the edge (the suburbs) with lower quality units closer to the center. Schelling's agents had only one property (color), which created two kinds: black and white. By contrast, Fossett's model gives agents both ethnicity (Black, White, and Hispanic) and a socioeconomic status. Socioeconomic status means that some agents of each ethnicity can afford high quality housing while others cannot. The proportion of the three ethnicities were 60% White, 20% Black, and 20% Hispanic. In each cycle of the model, then, agents could decide whether to move their residence based on three factors: preferences for housing quality (limited by affordability), preferences for neighborhood status, and preferences for neighborhood ethnic composition (Fossett 2006, 332). The cycles themselves were slightly different from Schelling too. Where all of Schelling's agents considered moving every cycle, 25% of Fossett's agents were randomly selected to look for a residence that better satisfied their preferences. And rather than looking for equilibria, Fossett's model ran for 30 cycles, and the resulting patterns were inspected and measured. While Fossett's model abstracts and idealizes in significant ways, it is clearly much more realistic than Schelling's.

Fossett's model allowed him to "turn on" and "turn off" factors influencing the agents' decisions to move. This meant that he could compare the relative contributions of the agents' three preferences. As we saw earlier, some suggested that the ethnic segregation we observe is the result of individuals seeking the best residences in high-status neighborhoods. If income and status are not distributed equally among ethnic groups, then ethnic segregation will result. Fossett's model permitted him to test this hypothesis. In his simulation, an unequal distribution of socioeconomic status (with Whites at the higher levels) did not produce strong levels of segregation, suggesting that the hypothesized mechanism for segregation is inadequate. High levels of segregation did not appear until agents used ethnic preferences in their decision making. Fossett concludes that "the results show that ethnic preferences clearly have the theoretical capability, at least under the conditions specified in these simulation experiments, of produce [sic] substantial levels of ethnic segregation in the absence of housing discrimination" (Fossett 2006, 250).

Defenders of discrimination-based explanations of segregation were not entirely convinced. John Goering (2006) pointed out that Fossett's model city had no history. Hence, it abstracted away from the history of bias, discrimination, and interracial or inter-ethnic violence that characterize real American cities. As a result, the agents' preferences are artificially insulated from discrimination. Fossett, he argues, "has simulated a sociologically misleading world of options" (Goering 2006, 309). Hence, the model fails to be a genuine test of whether such purified, non-discriminatory ethnic preferences would be effective in a world with discrimination. Moreover, the model does not include any discriminatory causal factors, such as steering by real estate agents, discriminatory lending practices, and so on. Hence, it is unable to determine the relative importance of discrimination and preference in the real world. And since Fossett agrees that there are multiple factors in play in the real world, including discrimination, the model does not let us infer that preferences for ethnic similarity are a significant causal factor in real-world segregation.

The Schelling model and the controversies around it highlight the philosophical issues that arise from modeling in the social sciences. While the model can be made more realistic by adding possible explanatory factors, all models idealize and abstract. These idealizations and abstractions enable the model to show us *something* about the processes that lead to or maintain residential segregation, but what? In virtue of what do social scientific models produce knowledge of social systems? In virtue of what do they explain?

6.2. Learning From Models

Models and Theories

One way to understand the scientific utility of models is to look at their paradigmatic use in the natural sciences, specifically in mechanics. In this domain, models appear to stand between the theory and the phenomenon to be explained. The puzzle about how we can learn from models would thus be resolved by looking at how the model is supported by a well-established theory, on the one hand, and by its application to observed events on the other.

Consider, for example, an apparently simple question about billiard balls. As any billiards player knows, when the cue ball hits another ball—let's say that it is the 8-ball—the latter may move at an angle to the cue ball's trajectory and with a different velocity. Players can control the direction and velocity of the 8-ball with the cue ball. Since it is a simple mechanical system, Newton's three laws of motion explain this pattern, but they are extremely general. How would the law that force equals mass times acceleration, or that objects in motion tend to remain in motion, tell us anything about the trajectory of the 8-ball? To apply the laws, we build a model. A model in this sense is a specification of objects and relationships that satisfy the laws of motion. To apply to the billiard ball system, that model would need two elements (balls A and B in Figure 6.6) and an angle of collision (Θ in Figure 6.6). In addition, we ascribe properties to the balls that accord with Newton's laws: each ball has a mass, and a velocity and direction of travel before and after the collision. In Figure 6.6, the velocity and direction of travel are represented by the vectors V_{1A} (ball A before the collision), V_{2A} and V_{2B} (balls A and B after the

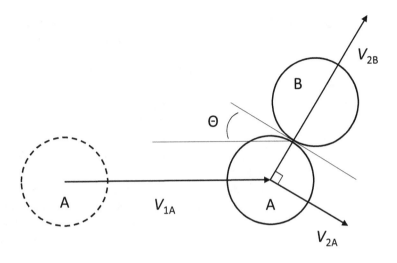

Figure 6.6 Model of a Billiard Ball Collision

collision). Newton's laws, along with some geometry, entail that $V_{1A}^2 = V_{2A}^2 + V_{2B}^2$ when the masses are equal and the collision is perfectly elastic. Using this model, we can explain why, after the collision, the balls move as they do.

Like the Schelling model, the Newtonian model of the billiard balls abstracts and idealizes. In a real billiard ball collision, the balls would be rotating, and there would be energy lost in the collision. Their masses would not be exactly equal, and they would not be perfectly spherical. All such details *could* be added to the model, but the model idealizes them. It sets the values of variables for rotation and friction to zero and stipulates that the balls are spherical and their masses are equal. The model ignores (abstracts away from) other possible forces that might act on the balls, such as your friend bumping into the table just as you make the shot. Despite these misrepresentations, the model seems to provide a deep understanding of the patterns of motion.

There are plausibly two sources of understanding for our billiard ball example: it is built from an extremely general and well-confirmed theory, and it could be "de-idealized." The model was constructed by deducing the consequences of Newton's laws, given the stipulation that two billiard balls collide. We stipulate further that the masses are equal and that the collision is elastic. Newton's theory of motion, of course, is an extremely well-supported theory. The capacity of the model to explain the motion of real billiard balls seems to consist in the fact that the model is a direct consequence of the theory. The model does nothing more than apply the theory to a specific situation. Generalizing from this case, one might argue that we learn from models because models let us link existing theoretical knowledge to a specific case. Of course, calculations were facilitated by the model's idealizations. By treating the masses as exactly equal, they dropped out of the conservation of momentum formula, leaving only the velocity-direction vectors. Similarly, by setting the energy lost to the collision equal to zero, a further variable falls out of the equations. These values, of course, *could* have been included. The model could have been "de-idealized" by supplying the variables and equations that take them into account. When the difference between the idealized model and the de-idealized model is small, we can safely ignore these idealizations. Where they are large, we can say that the idealized model has provided a partial or all-things-being-equal explanation. It seems that we can learn from models because they are derived from well-confirmed theories and can be de-idealized.

Unfortunately, the foregoing picture of modeling does not fit social scientific practice. De-idealization does not seem necessary for models to be instructive. To be sure, one can see Fossett as de-idealizing aspects of Shelling's model. He makes the neighborhoods more static, the housing units qualitatively different, and so on. However, it is not the case that *all* the idealizations could be removed without destroying the capacity of the model to provide understanding. In many theoretical models, the central construction is an idealization, and without the idealization, the model does not explain. In the Shelling case, the decision procedure of the agents is such a construct. If we made this realistic and included all of the factors that agents really use to make decisions about whether to move, then the role of preferences for similar neighbors would become completely invisible. The idealization of the agents is crucial to the capacity of the model to show us something about the possible role of preferences, so it cannot be de-idealized. Hence, while de-idealization may provide some confidence about a model in some cases, it cannot be the main reason why scientific models are instructive.

More fundamentally, neither Schelling's nor Fossett's models were derived from a theory. Schelling's model seems to draw on no empirically established generalizations. He simply stipulated that the agents had a tolerance threshold and a neighborhood. Fossett expands the information available to the agents and gives them a more complicated algorithm for deciding whether (and where) to move, but again, these did not follow from any established theory. In general, models in both the social and natural sciences are constructed from a variety of materials, including generalizations of theories from different domains, known patterns, existing data, suggestive metaphors, and the working of mechanical objects (Morgan and Morrison 1999). The social sciences simply do not have an analogue of Newton's mechanics. Yet, they have an active and robust practice of modeling, especially in economics, political science, and sociology. *Prima facie*, these models provide a rich understanding of social phenomena. So, the capacity of models to generate knowledge cannot be attributed to the power of a larger theory.

Notice that this insight—that the social sciences generate informative models in the absence of theory—speaks directly to the larger question of the role of theory in the social sciences. In Section 3.2 we encountered the empiricist view of theories, and in the mid-20th century, many philosophers supposed that generating general theories was the primary mark of scientific knowledge. The fact that the social sciences (not to mention natural sciences like biology) proceed by developing and testing models in the absence of overarching theories casts doubt on that conception of science. Looking at social scientific practice, a very different picture emerges: research programs produce a plurality of models, each of which seems to pick out important aspects of social phenomena. Returning to the analogy between maps and models discussed earlier, we would not expect there to be a master, universal map that depicted every aspect of a territory. Rather, there are many kinds of maps satisfying many kinds of purposes. Perhaps the social sciences—and the sciences more generally—are better understood as an overlapping and only partially related library of maps, rather than a single theory that explains everything.

Models, Simulation, and Thought Experiments

If models are not just ways of applying existing theory to examples, then what are they? Another way to understand models is by analogy with experiments. Uskali Mäki (2005) and Mary Morgan (2005) have explored the relationship in some detail, noting several points to the analogy. First, both models and experiments create a situation that is a *representative* of some real-world phenomenon. Representatives are stand-ins that function in the place of something (or someone) else. In both theoretical models and experiments, we learn about a real-world phenomenon (the "target system") by manipulating the experimental apparatus or the parameters of the model. The phenomenon is presumably too messy and complicated to work with directly, or perhaps the intervention would be unethical. The capacity of a model or experiment to be a representative also requires that it *represent* the target system. Mäki suggests that "models represent by resembling those real systems in certain respects and to certain degrees" (Mäki 2005, 304). The question of *which* respects and degrees, Mäki proposes, is answered by looking at the function of the model in a scientific context. Models do not represent on their own; they represent a target system because scientists use them to do so for specific purposes.

A second point of analogy between models and experiments is that both isolate the system from external influences. In an experiment, we want to be sure that the experimental and the control conditions are identical except for the experimental intervention. This typically means that the experimental apparatus must be shielded, the participants randomized into control and experimental groups, the experimenters blinded to outcomes, and so on. Analogously, the abstractions and idealizations of a theoretical model impose constraints. In Schelling's model, he isolates his agents from any preferences except the tolerance threshold by making it the only factor in the decision to move. The model is insulated against environmental factors too, since the checkerboard has none of the features of a real city that influence residence patterns, such as business districts and housing costs. In both models and experiments, the point of the isolation is to identify the effects of a very small number of potential causes, operating independently of the complex web of causes and conditions found in the real world.

Finally, both models and experiments are manipulated to study the different possible outcomes. Such manipulation is important when establishing causal relations. An experiment is convincing when it shows that in the absence of any other factors, the dependent variable changes when the independent variable changes. (We will further explore the idea of causality and how causal models are tested in Chapters 11 and 12.) Similarly, Schelling's model lets the theorist manipulate the strength of the tolerance threshold. Doing so shows that, under a wide range of preferences, segregated patterns of residence emerge.

Given these points of analogy, one might argue that we learn from models for the very same reason that we learn from experiments. The primary difference is that experiments are done with real people or things, while models are constructed in the mind of the theorist. Models are literally thought experiments. When we want to understand a social phenomenon, we imagine (or write down in prose or mathematical formulae) a small number of potential causal factors. We assume that other possible factors do not exist (abstraction), or we shape them so that their influence is neutralized or controlled (idealization). Doing so isolates the potential causes, and using rules or mathematical formulae that govern the interaction of the causes we calculate how changing the potential causes changes the effects.

While she endorses the analogy between models and experiments, Morgan (2005) points out some disanalogies. These potentially temper the conclusion that we learn from the two in the same way. A model like Schelling's is entirely artificial; it is a *simulation* of a real-world process, not an instance of the process itself. Experiments, on the other hand, exhibit the actual causes, albeit in an artificially isolated context. When two real people play a prisoner's dilemma game in a laboratory, they are using their actual understanding of the rules of the game and the payoffs to make choices. The experimenters will have isolated them from any factors relevant to their decision except the payoffs, e.g., by physically separating them so they cannot make eye contact or being sure that they have no shared history. Even so, their choices are brought about by real human decision-making processes, whatever those are. In a game theoretic model, by contrast, no real choices are made; the "decisions" of the "agents" are driven only by the rules. While experiments *replicate* the phenomenon in a controlled and isolated environment, models *simulate* the phenomenon.

The fact that models simulate while experiments replicate has two consequences. First, models are subject to a kind of complete, deterministic control in the way that experiments are not. The mathematical formulae or rules that make up the model typically fix the possible outcomes. The result of manipulating the values of the variables, like the value of Schelling's tolerance threshold, might be surprising, but only in the sense that we had not seen this consequence of the model assumptions in advance. In experiments, on the other hand, the results might not only be surprising, but they can be confounding (Morgan 2005, 321). That is, they might show us new phenomenon, unrelated to the original target of our inquiry, and they may even be at odds with the way we have previously understood that phenomenon. For example, a game theoretic model of the prisoner's dilemma shows that there is a dominant strategy. However, experimentation showed that humans do not always play the dominant strategy, even when they fully understand the game and its payoffs. The experiments thus brought to light a new phenomenon that could not have been predicted by the experimental set up. The upshot of this argument is that while we learn from both experiments and models, we do so in somewhat different ways.

The second consequence of the difference between model simulation and experimental replication is that models must *represent* their target systems in a different way than experiments do. We learn from experiments because the same causes identified in the controlled and isolated context of the experiment also exist in the wild, uncontrolled world. The experiment represents the larger phenomenon because it is an instance of it. For models, there is no such identity. It seems that we can draw inferences about a model's target system only if it represents the system in the way that a linguistic description or picture represents its object. This means that much depends on the rather vexed concept of "representation." Mäki suggests that we understand representation in terms of resemblance, where resemblances depend on the function of the model and the purposes of the modelers. Resemblances are not fixed or given. Indeed, whether a model represents a given system is often at stake in scientific disputes. In Section 6.1 we saw some of the disputes that arose over the application of Schelling's model to residential segregation. Clark used Schelling's model to explain patterns of residential segregation. On Mäki's view, then, Clark took the model to resemble real cities insofar as preferences were a cause of segregation, while the history of discrimination was not. Galster's rejection of Clarke's explanation denied that the model resembled real cities in these respects.

A potential problem with Mäki's account of resemblance is that it seems to reduce the dispute about representation to a dispute about individual preferences for resemblance. In this case, the two disputants have the same purposes (to understand the causes of segregation) and appear to take the model as functioning in the same way (as identifying a cause of segregation). So, what, one might wonder, is the basis of the dispute? If purposes become too idiosyncratic, then whether Schelling's model represents anything seems to become a matter of personal choice or taste. To make the representation relation more objective, further specification is needed. While there is much more to be said on this topic, we must leave the matter here.

A further issue with treating models as experiments returns us to the way models idealize. According to Mäki, the function of idealization and abstraction is to isolate only a few possible explanatory factors, analogous to the way that experiments isolate just one cause. As we noted earlier, an experiment presupposes that the isolated cause also exists in the real world. The isolation merely cuts out the noise so that the cause can be studied. By contrast, models sometimes *create* the purported explanatory factor through idealization. In Schelling's model, the potential explanatory factors are the tolerance threshold along with a rule that one must move to the nearest open space if the threshold is exceeded. These are themselves idealizations—distortions of real-world phenomena. The idealization does not just shield the purported cause; it *is* the purported cause. This means that there is a much larger gap between the model and the real world than there is between an experiment and the real world.

Models, Fables, and Conceptual Exploration

Many philosophers and social scientists have been struck by the way that models like Schelling's are distanced from any empirical evidence. While the model might be applied, as we saw Clark do in Section 6.1, the model itself is apparently not being tested by such applications. We noticed that, in models like Schelling's, the central potential cause—the tolerance threshold—is itself an idealization and does not directly correspond to any real causes. Models are thus unlike maps. A representation like a map might abstract and idealize, and thus falsify aspects of its depiction. But there remains a core representative content in virtue of which map is accurate or inaccurate. Unlike a map, some have suggested, a highly idealized model like Schelling's has no such core representative content. Some have concluded that models are not representations at all. Theoretical economist Ariel Rubenstein put the idea this way:

> As economic theorists, we organize our thoughts using what we call models. The word "model" sounds more scientific than "fable" or "fairy tale" although I do not see much difference between them. The author of a fable draws a parallel to a situation in real life. He has some moral he wishes to impart to the reader. The fable is an imaginary situation that is somewhere between fantasy and reality. . . . In this unencumbered state, we can clearly discern what cannot always be seen in the real world. On our return to reality, we are in possession of some sound advice or a relevant argument that can be used in the real world.
>
> (Rubinstein 2006, 881)

While drawing an analogy between a scientific model and a fable may seem to trivialize the research, Rubinstein is suggesting that if we take it seriously, it shows the value of modeling. Perhaps models are useful *because* theorists are not constrained by the need to accurately represent social phenomena. Without being pejorative, let us call this perspective on modeling "fabulist:" theorists are makers of fables.

Before considering the fabulist perspective in more detail, we should note at the outset that its proponents are not proposing that *no* social scientific models represent their targets and are independent of empirical evidence. Many models make extensive use of empirical data to determine their content and structure. Indeed, Fawcett's modification of Schelling's model began to move in this direction by making many of the parameters more realistic. Other models begin with a data set and look for the mathematical expressions that best fit them (as in statistical data modeling). So, to take the fabulist perspective on modeling is to acknowledge from the outset that there are multiple kinds of models with a variety of purposes. The question before us is how to understand the highly idealized "theoretical models" we find in game theory, decision theory, and macro-economics.

The question, then, is to understand the value of theoretical modeling if the goal is not to represent a social system. While he never called models fables, Daniel Hausman proposed that in theoretical economic modeling, "one is saying *nothing* about the world" (Hausman 1992, 80 emphasis in original). Instead, Hausman suggested that we should think of models as developing concepts or definitions:

> One might take the claims . . . that agents' preferences are complete, continuous, and transitive and that agents choose the option they most prefer, as providing a model of rationality. In so doing, one is just defining rationality.
>
> (Hausman 1992, 77)

A concept or predicate like ". . . is rational" does not describe anything; it is neither true nor false. So, in providing a definition of economic rationality the theorist has not yet said that any economic behavior is or is not rational. Theorists explore models to understand their definitions. By creating a model of, say, a market, the theorist can deduce consequences of the assumptions that created the model. Understanding these consequences lets theorists see how the fundamental concepts of economics are related. And on occasion, finding inconsistencies or troubling consequences can lead theorists to alter their initial concepts.

Anyone who denies that models represent social systems needs to provide an account of how models can be useful in understanding social systems anyway. On Hausman's account, the concepts developed in models are applied by using the same concepts in theory. In Section 5.2, we modeled the strategic situation of Generals Imamura and Kenney in World War II. The "theory" is the statement that this strategic situation *is* a zero-sum game with a weakly dominant strategy. In making this theoretical statement, we applied the concepts of instrumental rationality, payoff, and weakly dominant strategy to a particular historical event, treating the event as an instance of those concepts. While the game theoretic model itself is not testable, since it is a definition, the theory that the definition applies to this historical event is testable. In this case, the theory correctly predicts both generals' actions.

Returning to the Schelling model, Hausman's perspective would treat it as working out the concepts of preference and residential segregation. Given a particular set of definitions (neighborhood, tolerance threshold, movement rules), we can see what consequences follow. On Hausman's reading, Schelling has said nothing about residential segregation in the US with his model. In reply, Robert Sugden (2000b) argued that it would be "disingenuous" to read Schelling in this way. According to Sugden, Schelling is not merely offering up a logically consistent set of concepts nor simply showing what consequences follow from some assumptions. He is offering a potential explanation of residential segregation. Sugden's point is even more clear when we look at Fossett's development of the Schelling model. Fossett uses his model to test different explanations of residential segregation. Arguably, Hausman's perspective does not account for all highly theoretical modeling work in the social sciences.

A defender of Hausman's perspective, however, has at least two reasonable responses to Sugden's objections. First, as Hausman points out, modeling and theorizing are not strictly separated activities, and most theorists do both. We can understand both Schelling and Fossett as both making models, which spell out some conceptual relationships, and postulating the *theoretical hypothesis* that residents of American cities have tolerance thresholds (etc.) in the sense defined by their models. Second, both Schelling and Fossett might be understood as testing *conceptual* hypotheses. Schelling shows that it is possible for the preference to not be in the minority, which can bring about segregation by itself. This is important insofar as people previously thought that some other mechanism, such as discrimination, was required. Understood this way, Schelling's contribution is entirely conceptual: something we thought logically impossible is shown to be possible. Fossett too can be understood as evaluating different conceptual possibilities.

6.3. The Explanation Paradox

Models always abstract and idealize, and often the potential explanatory factors they describe are themselves products of dramatic idealization. Nonetheless, many social scientists take models to be explanatory. Julian Reiss (2012a) pointed out a tension between the idealized character of models and their explanatory power. We noticed earlier that explanation is a relation, and if the explanation is to be successful, the explanatory factor exists and is truly described. Again, lightning can't explain the forest fire if there was no lighting. If a model is explanatory of some event or phenomenon, then the model must truly describe the causes (or reasons, cf. Section 5.1). For example, to say that Schelling's model explains segregation is to say that the model describes a cause (a tolerance threshold) and that this cause explains the pattern of residential segregation. But we have also seen how the Schelling model idealizes human decision making, collapsing a complex cognitive process into a tolerance threshold. Because human decision making is not just a preference threshold (or even just a utility function), the model misrepresents decision making. In this sense, one might say that Schelling's model is *false*, and in this same sense, all models are false (because all models idealize). Reiss argues that this is not just a tension between idealization and explanation; it is an out-and-out paradox. The following three sentences are *each* true, but they cannot *all* be true (Reiss 2012a, 49):

1. All models are false.
2. Models are explanatory.
3. Only true accounts can explain.

This paradox strikes to the heart of modeling in the social sciences. It is hard to give up the third statement. It is also difficult to see how models could fail to idealize. But this means that models could not explain, which seems to be the point of building models in the first place.

There are two ways to escape a paradox. One might deny the truth of one of the claims, or one might show that when the claims are properly understood, they do not conflict. In this section, then, we will consider each of the three branches of the explanation paradox to see whether any offers a way out.

Are All Models False?

A first response to this question is that "All models are false" is misleading. While there is no doubt that models misrepresent in various ways, they correctly represent in others. Recall our earlier discussion of maps. On a standard highway map, the *width* of a line representing a road is not to scale, but the length of the line is. So, assuming the map is accurate, the map gives us a true description of the distance between New York and Philadelphia but a false description of the width of US Highway 95. Models are similarly true in some respects and false in others. When a model is used to explain, we obviously must rely on the model elements that correctly describe the social system.

In response, Reiss (2013a) argues that there are two disanalogies between models and maps. First, models do not "decompose" in the way that maps do. Maps can be neatly decomposed into the parts that are to scale and the parts that are not. Similarly, experiments can be decomposed into the cause we are manipulating and the various ways we have isolated that cause from outside influence. As we saw earlier, the idealization of models seems to be different from the isolation of causes. On a map, the line representing the road has a length, and a simple transformation relates the length of the line to the length of the road. In an experiment, the same cause exists in the experiment and in the wild. In a theoretical model, by contrast, the purported cause is *itself* the product of idealization, and no simple transformation will map it onto part of a real social system. There is no such thing as a "tolerance threshold" in human cognition.

Second, unlike maps and experiments, the consequences of a theoretical model depend on *all* the assumptions and idealizations that create the model in the first place. An experiment is designed to show a relationship between cause and effect when all other interfering factors have been excluded. A theoretical model is a logical or mathematical construction. The assumptions that "isolate" the factor of interest are necessary for deducing the consequences. Thus, the relationship between the tolerance threshold and the segregated patterns in the Schelling model does not just depend on the tolerance threshold; it depends on all the idealizing assumptions. So again, the true and false aspects of a theoretical model cannot be neatly separated.

In response, one might argue that not all models are as highly idealized as Schelling's. Fossett's model already makes the decision-making more realistic. In a further move toward realism, Babak Ardestani and colleagues have created a model of residential segregation that takes even more possible factors into account (Ardestani et al 2018). Their goal was to model segregation in Auckland, New Zealand. Rather than a checkerboard, they used Auckland's own neighborhoods and territorial authorities as the map within which agents would move. And the information for agents' decisions was based on measured vacancy rates in the different neighborhoods among other more realistic factors. While the model still idealizes in substantial ways, it is much easier to identify those places where the model is inaccurate and those places where it is accurate.

One might agree that in a very empirical model like Ardestani's, it is possible to identify ways in which the model is accurate, and hence yields explanation. But Reiss points out that this leaves the paradox in place for highly theoretical models like Schelling's. And Schelling's model is not an outlier; *many* models in economics are highly idealized mathematical constructs. These models are not as easily de-idealized as Schelling's. So, we still need to understand whether and how highly theoretical models can be explanatory.

Are Models Explanatory?

In response to this branch of the paradox, one might say that "models explain" is not literally true. It is a figure of speech that simplifies what is in fact a more complicated process. Those who propose this idea begin by noting that models must be applied to social systems before any explanations are forthcoming. To apply the model, we need to make an inference from what the model says to a description of the social system. In Section 6.2 we saw this idea recur in different ways, depending on the perspective being offered. On Hausman's perspective, where models were only conceptual explorations, a theoretical hypothesis was necessary to connect the model to the social system. Mäki, on the other hand, held that models resembled social systems. Exactly *how* the model resembled a given social system, that is in which respects it resembled the system and which respects it did not, was an empirical question to be worked out by the scientists. In both Hausman's and Mäki's perspectives, then, an inference is made from the model to a statement about a social system. This statement about the social system is the basis for the explanation, not the model itself.

On this view, then, "Schelling's model explains segregation" is short for a longer inferential process. First, calculations are made with the model and a result is calculated, e.g., preference thresholds above 30% by a majority group result in segregated equilibria. Then, we make an inference from this model result to a statement about a particular city, e.g., "In Detroit the White preferences for segregation are above 30%, and this causes the residential segregation in Detroit." This statement, of course would have to be tested. If there were evidence for the hypothesis (something that we saw Clark and Galster debating in Section 6.2), then the preferences would explain segregation, not Schelling's model *per se*.

In response to an escape route like this, Reiss notes that while models sometimes serve as the basis for empirical hypotheses, this is less obviously true for the highly idealized models. Schelling's model might be misleading in this respect. It is already set up in terms of psychologically plausible "preferences" and socially plausible "neighborhoods," which make the inference rather obvious. When the models get more abstract, as they do in economics especially, they have fewer direct connections to real social systems. The basis for the inference becomes quite slim. Why apply the model in one way rather than another? Models this abstract become little more than heuristics that inspire empirical hypotheses. But if the models are no more than inspiration, then it is hard to see why economists put so much effort into building them. Why not just study the economic systems themselves? We did not need Schelling's model to suggest the hypothesis that preferences might cause segregation. As we saw in Section 6.1, that hypothesis was among the explanatory factors considered by sociologists before Schelling even came on the scene.

The burden on someone who wants to escape the explanation paradox by this route is to explain how the inferred hypotheses are related to the models. The connection between the results of calculating with the model and the empirical hypothesis must be more robust than mere inspiration. But what justifies such inferences? And why is the model necessary at all? Ultimately, Reiss challenges this response to explain why models have epistemic value to the social sciences.

Do Only True Accounts Explain?

While it seems obvious that an explanation must cite a cause or reason that actually occurred, if the explanation is to be successful, notice that this focuses our attention on one kind of explanation. We can explain by describing a cause or reason for action, but there are other sorts of explanation as well. Till Grüne-Yanoff (2013) has suggested that by demonstrating a possible cause of segregation, Schelling's model explains how segregation could possibly come about. It thus provides a "how-possibly" explanation, rather than a "how-actually" explanation. When we explain how an event actually came about, we must assume that the cause existed and that it was sufficient (in the context) to bring about the event. While we can't explain a forest fire by appeal to lighting if there was no lightning, the *possibility* of lighting explains how the forest fire *could* have come about. A how-possibly explanation is particularly important in a scientific context where the possibility is not recognized. Grüne-Yanoff argues that, before Schelling

> it was widely believed that racist preferences were a necessary cause of segregation. Schelling's model shows that segregation patterns might be produced by another cause, which is an actual property of agents in many real-world populations. . . . The model result thus justified changing one's confidence in hypotheses about racist preference being a necessary cause of segregation.
>
> (Grüne-Yanoff 2013, 856)

On Grüne-Yanoff's view, then, models do more than provide conceptual understanding. We learn about real social systems from them.

Grüne-Yanoff's account of models as providing how-possibly explanations has been criticized on two points, both developed by Roberto Fumagalli (2016, 444–445). First, it is not really the case that social scientists who studied residential segregation thought that racism was necessary to explain the racial segregation found in American cities. Indeed, they recognized that many groups exhibited a preference to live in communities where they were not the minority. So, exhibiting the possibility alone was not what made the Schelling model relevant to understand residential segregation. Second, learning from a how-possibly explanation requires substantial additional information. As Grüne-Yanoff says, one of the reasons that Schelling's model was compelling is that we believe that people often prefer not to be in the minority in social situations. This, of course, is not part of Schelling's model; it is background knowledge. So, the possibility is compelling in the actual world not just because of the conceptual possibility, but because we have evidence that it is a *real* possibility.

While Grüne-Yanoff may have overstated the state of the science when Schelling introduced his model, a defender of how-possibly explanation can accept Fumagalli's points. The fabulist perspective treats modeling as part of a broader scientific inquiry. A highly idealized theoretical model has significance only when we can use it along with our current knowledge of the social system. Schelling's checkerboard model was important, one might argue, precisely because preferences were already recognized as a possible explanatory factor. However, they were generally treated as a minor factor, and Schelling's model showed that they could possibly be determinative. After Schelling's model, the character of the debate changed, and the question became whether preferences and economic status were more important factors than the history of racist discrimination.

Even if we accept that how-possibly explanations are useful in the social sciences, and that they escape the explanation paradox, there is a sense in which this escape route just sidesteps the main question. Social scientists treat models as providing actual causal explanations, not just how-possibly explanations. While Schelling does show a possible way in which segregation could come about, the debate in sociology after Schelling was about the actual causes of segregation. For this debate, the explanation paradox remains in place. The defender of a how-possibly explanation has to hold either (1) that all model-based explanations are how-possibly explanations, in which case the debate over Schelling's model was confused, or (2) that there are some how-actually explanations based on models, in which case the paradox remains unresolved.

Instrumentalism: Living With the Paradox

Reiss concludes that none of the possible escape routes will be successful. The paradox is genuine. If we can't escape, then we need to learn to live with the paradox. Reiss points out that the paradox arises from treating models as realistic. The proponents of the various escape routes treat models as analogous to maps of real places, like a map of Stockholm. But perhaps we should treat models as maps of imaginary places, like a map of Middle Earth. The paradox of explanation shows, Reiss suggests, that we should be *instrumentalists* about models, at least highly theoretical ones. We encountered instrumentalism in Sections 3.2 and 5.3. As you might recall, instrumentalists deny that scientific theories (concepts, or models) really represent what they seem to represent. A model seems to represent a hidden mechanism. The instrumentalist denies this. Models (and similar scientific constructs) are better understood as tools. While our models invoke exotic constructs, these do not correspond to anything real. Their object is only to help us systematize, unify, and predict observable phenomena. We care about systemizations and predictions of observable phenomena for practical reasons: we want to predict economic downturns, for example, or find ways to mitigate the effects of residential segregation. To use a model to explain a phenomenon, on this view, is to show that it contributes to the kinds of predictions and interventions we want (Reiss 2013a, 290). The mistake—which is illuminated by the explanation paradox—is to think that the mechanisms in the model somehow correspond to real mechanisms.

Of course, and Reiss himself admits, the explanation paradox has its clearest application to highly idealized, theoretical models. Many models in the social sciences are much more empirical, and in these cases, it is not so difficult to distinguish between the parts of the model that are accurate and those that are not, or to specify what inferences about real social systems are justified by a model. The required instrumentalism, then, may take one of two forms. A modest, or localized, instrumentalist would take the instrumental stance only toward highly idealized theoretical models and be realistic about more empirical models. This kind of instrumentalist would need to account for the difference between theoretical and empirical models. What is the difference that justifies an instrumentalist stance toward one and an empirical stance toward the other? While this is certainly feasible, if there is not a clear, bright line here, then the difference just seems to collapse into the escape routes that Reiss has rejected. That is, it becomes a matter of saying, for any model, how to identify its accurate aspects or how to justify inferences about the social system. The other option is to be more globally instrumentalist, about economics in general or about science in general. In this case, we can only say that more argument is needed (and Reiss begins to provide those arguments in 2012b). The explanation paradox might be beginning, but the instrumentalist case needs to be made for empirical models, as well as other kinds of scientific constructions.

6.4. Wrap Up

Chapter Summary

Modeling is a common social scientific practice, and the central question of this chapter is: how can we learn from models? We have seen that answers to this question depend on three others. What are models, and how are they related to theories? What is the relationship between the model and the social system it models? And how can models provide explanation?

With respect to the question of what models are, we have seen three answers. First, models might be thought of as closely related to theories. Models apply theories to observable phenomena, supply specific parameters, and work out the details of the theory in a specific case. On this view, theories remain the primary product of scientific inquiry, and models are a useful adjunct. While this view has a long tradition, it fails to account for many modeling activities. Schelling's model did not draw on any established theory; it was *autonomous* in this sense. The possibility of autonomous models calls into question the priority of theory. Since the social sciences lack general and broadly applicable theories, the autonomy of modeling is welcome. It shows that perhaps the social sciences do not need the "grand theories" for which they strove in the past.

The autonomy of models from theory makes the questions of how we learn from models and whether they are explanatory even more pressing. In Section 6.2, we saw two ways of conceptualizing models, and each has consequences for how we learn from models. The first relied on an analogy between models and experiments. In both cases, a potential causal factor is isolated. Where experiments physically isolate the causal factor, models do so by idealizing and abstracting. On this view, we learn from models by manipulating the causal factor and deducing various possible consequences. We then infer that in real social systems, the causal factor behaves is a similar way. The parallel is illuminating, but it must be squared with some of the relevant disanalogies. A central problem (which returns in Section 6.3) is that models frequently idealize the causal factor itself. Indeed, in highly idealized models like Schelling's, the potential cause (the tolerance threshold) is a construct of the model. For the analogy between experiments and models to work, the model needs to represent the social system, which means that an account of representation is required.

The second way to conceptualize models does not treat them as representing social systems. Rather, the point of modeling is to explore conceptual consequences and relationships. The conditions of the model are entirely artificial, but they are designed to let us calculate or deduce the consequences of particular conceptual configurations. On this view, Schelling's model is simply a device for understanding the relationship between preferences for similar neighbors and residence patterns. We learn from models by connecting them to theories. Theories describe social systems, and by working out conceptual relationships, we can formulate better hypotheses to test. One of the main problems with this sort of view is that it does not account for the broad range of social scientific practice wherein models seem to be used to explain rather directly.

In Section 6.3 we confronted the paradox of explanation: models are too idealized to be true; and if they are not true, then they cannot explain—yet they are used to explain social phenomena. In the section, we considered the consequences of denying (or modifying) each of the three branches of this paradox. One of the upshots of that discussion was that theoretical, highly idealized models are more easily trapped by the paradox than empirical models that draw extensively on data. This gives us reason to distinguish theoretical from empirical models. And when we look back at the discussion of Section 6.2, we might draw the conclusion that the different conceptions of what models are is also made clear by this distinction. One might treat theoretical models as "fables" that let us explore concepts, while empirical models are more like experiments. Of course, making such a distinction demands that the difference between empirical and theoretical models must be made clear. The challenge of understanding models—whether there is one kind or many—remains an important area of inquiry for the philosophy of social science.

Discussion Questions

1. Consider the prisoner's dilemma as a model. How should we understand what this model tells us about human behavior, especially in light of the evidence from behavioral economics showing that many research subjects choose to cooperate? What do we learn from this model?
2. Consider the prisoner's dilemma as a model again. Can this model be used to *explain* any aspect of human behavior? How do such explanations escape the paradox of explanation?
3. We noted in this chapter that Schelling's model might be a special case, and other models cannot be so easily de-idealized. Find some examples of highly theoretical models in a discipline with which you are familiar (economics and political science have many). How are these models similar or different from Schelling's model? Are they easier to apply, or harder? Do any escape the explanation paradox?
4. The analogy between maps and models is often invoked. How are they related? Are all maps a kind of model? Or are there important disanalogies between maps and models?
5. Several companies have developed software for agent-based modeling. They provide demonstrations on their websites for free. Search "agent based models" and look for some of these simulations. Are they reductionist? What are the elements of the mechanisms? Is what they leave out important?
6. This chapter repeatedly touched on a possible difference between theoretical models and empirical models, but it never gave definitions or explained the difference. The author, apparently, was too lazy to figure it out. Help him by finding criteria that differentiate theoretical and empirical models.

Further Reading

The philosophical literature on modeling is enormous, and a variety of issues criss-cross the literature. The entrée provided here is designed for students of the social sciences, and so it foregrounds works that highlight social scientific modeling. Most of this literature concerns models in economics or political science because those disciplines have long-standing practices of theoretical modeling. The following works are selected to help the reader begin from the narrow set of issues discussed in this chapter and use that as a springboard to broader concerns about modeling in science.

Beginning with general treatments of modeling, Morgan and Morrison's *Models as Mediators* (1999) is a classic collection of essays exploring a variety of themes about how models are related to theory and how we can learn from them. Morgan's *The World in the Model* (2012) provides historical perspectives and philosophical insight into the ways modeling has become central to economics. Clark and Primo's *A Model Discipline* (2012) argues for a model-based approach to political science. Collections of essays about the methodological and conceptual issues involved in analytical sociology are Demeulenaere (2011) and Hedstrom and Swedberg (1998). Hedström's *Dissecting the Social* (2005) is a systematic argument for model-based social science.

Mäki is a prominent proponent the representational view of models. Of his many essays, "MISSing the world" (2009) stands out because it contains a succinct characterization of his position and relates it to other prominent approaches. Sugden's "Credible Worlds" (2000a) agrees with Mäki that we can draw conclusions from models, but it does not treat them as representations. Alexandrova's "Making Models Count" (2008) is an original and distinct take on how models apply to real-world systems. Veit (2019) defends the idea that inference from models requires pluralism. The question of how models can represent real-world systems has been the subject of an extensive literature and long debate. Frigg and Nguyen's *Modeling Nature* (2020) provides a systematic and critical overview.

Among those who follow a line like Hausman's and deny that models represent real-world social systems, Johnson (2021) applies the view to political science. Grüne-Yanoff has developed the notion of how-possibly explanations and replies to Fumagalli's (2016) objections in Grüne-Yanoff and Verreault-Julien (2021).

The paradox of explanation was discussed in a special issue of the *Journal of Economic Methodology* Volume 20 Issue 3 (2013) with essays by Alexandrova, Grüne-Yanoff, Rol, Sugden, Hausman, and Mäki. Reiss replies in (2013a).

7 Reductionism

Structures, Agents, and Evolution

The social sciences seem to investigate two kinds of objects. On the one hand there are individual persons with their beliefs, values, emotional responses, choices, and actions. On the other, there are fire departments, university administrations, churches, laws, customs, and cultures. One might wonder, since churches and cultures are composed of people, are there really two kinds or levels of phenomena here? Can the social level be *reduced* to the individual level? Or is something lost when we treat a church as nothing more than the set of its members? These questions were posed by the earliest social scientists and the philosophers who reflected on their work, and reductionism remains one of the central philosophical issues in social inquiry.

The question of whether the social level reduces to the individual level spans a variety of theories and methodological strategies in the social sciences. Indeed, most of the remaining chapters of this book will relate to the problem of reductionism in one way or another. Rational choice theorizing has provided, at least since Adam Smith's *Wealth of Nations* (Smith 1937 [1776]), a model for reductionist programs in the social sciences. RCT appears to explain social phenomena such as markets, institutional structures, or social norms as the outcome of many individual decisions. We will begin in Section 7.1 with a social scientific research program which relies on the resources of RCT modeling. While rational choice theory is not the only motivation for reductionism, it highlights the main arguments for and against reduction, which we will survey in Sections 7.2 and 7.3.

Evolutionary explanations of social phenomena are another motivation for reductionism. Evolution has a checkered history in the social sciences. In the last several decades, however, some robust research programs have explained the emergence of cooperation, social norms, and institutions in evolutionary terms. These programs are philosophically interesting in their own right, and Section 7.4 will ask whether the use of models from evolutionary biology provides convincing arguments for reductionism.

7.1. Explaining Revolutions

When people struggle under oppressive regimes, why don't they just revolt against the unjust officials or dictator? Sometimes, of course, they do, as witnessed by the French and Russian Revolutions as well as the host of independence struggles

DOI: 10.4324/9781003207795-7

against colonial powers. Sometimes they don't, and that is just as interesting. Oppressive regimes often manage to keep people under their control despite the most appalling conditions. The question of how a community can move from a state of widespread discontent to active rebellion has been fascinating for political scientists, historians, anthropologists, and sociologists.

In his study of the French Revolution, Alexis de Tocqueville proposed a rather simple and striking theory (Tocqueville 1955 [1856]). One might expect that revolutions occur when people become impoverished and desperate. De Tocqueville found that, surprisingly, the French Revolution occurred after a period of unprecedented prosperity. De Tocqueville suggested that during a period of rising prosperity, expectations rise. If the economy takes a downturn, there will be a gap between what people expect and what they have. When this gap gets sufficiently large, people will revolt against their government. As articulated by James Davies, the theory says that:

> Revolutions are most likely to occur when a prolonged period of objective economic and social development is followed by a short period of sharp reversal. The all-important effect on the minds of people in a particular society is to produce, during the former period, and expectation of continued ability to satisfy needs—which continue to rise—and during the latter, a mental state of anxiety and frustration when manifest reality breaks away from anticipated reality. The actual state of socio-economic development is less significant than the expectation that past progress, now blocked, can and must continue in the future. . . . Political stability and instability are ultimately dependent of a state of mind, a mood, in a society.
>
> (Davies 1962, 6)

The shape of the curve representing rising prosperity followed by a sharp decline led theorists to call this the "J-curve" theory of revolutions.

In Davies's presentation, psychological characterizations play a crucial role: anxiety, frustration, expectation, and mood. As Davies uses these terms, they do not seem to characterize individual attitudes. Rather, the terms are used as if the society as a whole was anxious or frustrated. This sort of language often motivates arguments for reductionism. What could it mean for a society to have a mood? A charitable interpretation of Davies would be to take "mood" and "expectation" to be the average of individual expectations. This would reduce the talk of social-level needs, expectations, and states of mind to the individual-level. Reduced in this way, it is possible to see revolutions as the unintended consequence of many individual actions. Each individual acts based on their personal motivations, and as a result, the whole society changes.

Considered from the perspective of rational choice, revolutions and social movements are quite puzzling. Why should an individual join the rebellion? Revolution is a risky venture, and participation has costs. Joining the revolution risks one's own safety, as well as the safety of family and friends. Should the revolution succeed, the new government will (presumably) improve the lives for all citizens. This means that each citizen will benefit from the revolution whether or not he or she participated in bringing it about. The fruits of the revolution are a *non-exclusive good*. It is something that all enjoy whether or not they contributed to its creation. As a result, each person gets a higher net utility from sitting idly than from joining the barricades because they can reap the benefits without paying the costs. This is known as the problem of "free riders," and it plagues any attempt at collective action. Using game theory, the situation can be modeled as a prisoner's dilemma (Figure 5.5). The equilibrium which results from free-riding is sub-optimal: everyone "defects," and no one joins the revolution. If a revolution is understood as the individually rational actions of many people, it is hard to see how revolutions could ever happen.

Whether the choice to join the revolution is best represented as a prisoner's dilemma depends on the players' preferences. If the change in the payoffs is so great that the order of the preferred outcome changes, the game changes. For example, suppose that we change the narrative of the prisoner's dilemma to include a strong bond between the prisoners. Their solidarity is such that despite the risks of a longer prison term, they would rather go to prison together than to be free alone. This raises the utility of the cooperation strategy for each party. It therefore changes the prisoner's dilemma situation into the assurance game represented in Figure 7.1. (Again, the utilities are ordinal and "3" is the highest.) In the prisoner's dilemma we noticed that communication did not matter; because the strategy to defect dominated, neither prisoner could trust the other's promises. The assurance game is a coordination problem with two Nash equilibria. Each player prefers to use the same strategy as the other, and the problem is to settle on the right choice. Since the payoffs of mutual cooperation are superior to mutual defection, an agreement to cooperate becomes self-reinforcing. Promises are not needed.

Applied to the problem of revolutions, the foregoing line of thought suggests that strong norms of solidarity, such as bonds of ethnicity or feelings of nationalism might explain how some revolutions overcome the free rider problem. Discontent is turned into action when our solidarity leads us to value joint action, and we see that acting together against the regime is the bigger pay off. When we look at actual historical revolutions and rebellions, however, this theoretical solution faces some challenges. It works best where the rebellion is small, like a ship mutiny.

Assurance Game

| | | Player 2 | |
		Cooperate	Defect
Player 1	Cooperate	3, 3	0, 1
	Defect	1, 0	2, 2

Figure 7.1 Assurance Game

Face-to-face interaction can reinforce the norms of solidarity, spread information about cooperation, and keep everyone on task. When the revolution is larger, however, a new kind of defection arises. Why, a potential revolutionary might ask, should I choose to value nationalism, when so many others are already risking their lives for the Fatherland? The individual is asking whether to cooperate with or defect from *the norms of solidarity*. This new game looks like a prisoner's dilemma all over again, and the problem of free riders threatens to scuttle the possibility of revolutionary action.

An interesting solution to the problem of defection from the norms of solidarity was proposed by Jack Goldstone (1994). He suggested adding a middle level of aggregation between individuals and the larger revolution. We have been posing the problem as to why an individual should join something big, like the Russian Revolution. Goldstone noted that individuals do not normally make this choice. Rather, they are already members of some group which has an interest in promoting (or preventing) the goals of the revolution:

> [I]nvestigations of crowd actions in the revolutions of 19th century Europe show that those who manned the barricades were not random assortments of individuals, but groups of individuals recruited and organized along neighborhood lines. . . . The same appears to be true of workers and peasants in the Russian revolution, where local communities provided the framework for organizing and taking revolutionary action.
>
> (Goldstone 1994, 141)

Goldstone applies the rational choice framework at two levels. Individuals make choices to join groups, and groups make choices whether to join the revolution. Groups like churches, trade unions, and neighborhoods are sources of solidarity for the individuals. The problem of whether to join a group can be represented as an assurance game. Group membership is thus individually rational and self-reinforcing. Groups are also treated as rational choosers. A group such as a church will decide whether to engage in revolutionary action if the probability of success is high and the action furthers its goals. Moreover, groups that can mobilize many people make substantial contributions to the success of a revolution. A relatively small number of groups who engage in revolutionary protests are thus very likely to succeed in achieving their individual goals. The problem of individual free riders is solved at the level of the group, and the revolution is explained by the actions of these groups.

The theoretical developments we have been discussing are no more than a glimpse of a large and complex literature on revolutions and social movements. These examples illustrate how rational choice modeling figures in the understanding of large-scale social phenomena. Revolutions, one might argue, are ultimately nothing but the outcome of many individually rational choices. In this way, the RCT model of revolutionary action appears to reduce a social-level event to individual actions.

7.2. Social Theory and Social Ontology

The Individualism-Holism Debate

The debate over reductionism may be framed as a dispute between two camps. Those who propose that the social level reduces to the level of agents are often called "individualists." Their opponents, who resist such reduction, are often called "holists." A classic statement of individualism is found in John Stuart Mill's 1872 *System of Logic*:

> The laws of the phenomena of society are, and can be, nothing but the laws of the actions and passions of human beings united together in the social state. Men, however, in a state of society, are still men; their actions and passions are obedient to the laws of individual human nature. Men are not, when brought together, converted into another kind of substance, with different properties; as hydrogen and oxygen are different from water, or as hydrogen, oxygen, carbon, and azote, are different from nerves, muscles, and tendons. Human beings in society have no properties but those which are derived from, and may be resolved into, the laws of the nature of individual man.
>
> (Mill 1987 [1872], 65)

In *The Rules of the Sociological Method*, Emile Durkheim responded to Mill's position and argued for holism. He contended that it is

> in the nature of society itself that we must seek the explanation of social life. We can conceive that, since it transcends infinitely the individual both in time and space, it is capable of imposing upon him the ways of acting and thinking that it has consecrated by its authority. This pressure, which is the distinctive sign of social facts, is that which all exert upon each individual.
>
> (Durkheim 1938 [1895], 128)

Mill is denying that the social world is a kind of thing over and above the individual human beings who make it up. There are no social properties that are not already properties of individual humans. Durkheim, on the other hand, is saying that a social science needs to postulate the existence of "social facts," which go beyond (or "transcend") the properties of any collection of individual humans.

The careful reader will have noticed that these two authors are basing their claims on rather different assumptions. Mill is making an ontological claim about the composition of social entities. Social phenomena are entirely composed of humans and their actions. No new properties emerge from the interaction of agents. Ontologically, social entities or properties reduce to individual entities or properties. Mill is also making a claim about the relationship of laws of the social world to laws of psychology. A proper science, in Mill's view, should be able to derive specific or local laws from more fundamental laws. This would mean that, in principle, we could make predictions about social-level events based on knowledge of the psychology of the individuals involved. Durkheim, by contrast, is making a point about explanation. To explain social phenomena—including the actions of individuals within a social setting—we need to invoke social facts.

Within the quotations from Mill and Durkheim, then, we can discern three different points of contrast between an individualist and a holist position:

> **Theoretical**: individualists hold that the theories of the social sciences can be derived from theories of psychology, while holists hold that social scientific theories are logically independent of lower-level theories.
>
> **Ontological**: individualists hold that only human agents and their properties exist, while holists hold that social entities and properties also exist.
>
> **Explanatory**: individualists hold that explanations in the social sciences must refer to individual actions, while holists also accept social-level explanations.

The difference is presented here in overly dramatic terms. As you will see when we dig into the arguments, much effort has been put into refining these positions and determining exactly what the commitments of individualism and holism should be. For example, is the property of being married a property of an individual agent, or is it a social property which needs individualistic analysis? Is individualistic reduction a long-range goal to be pursued by the social sciences, or is it a criterion for rejecting some current theories as unscientific? You will also see that authors link the positions together in different ways. Mill, for example, accepted a view of explanation very much like the deductive-nomological view we discussed in Section 5.1. His acceptance of theoretical reductionism thus entails explanatory reductionism, and Mill ends up being an individualist on all three points. We will also see some sophisticated positions that affirm holism in some areas but individualism in others.

Definition and Theoretical Reduction

When presenting the problem of reductionism, it is natural to distinguish between higher-level (social) theories and lower-level (psychological) ones. A good point of entry into the discussion, then, is theoretical reductionism. How do social-level theories relate to psychological-level theories? In the discussion of theories of revolution (Section 6.1), we noticed that one presentation of the J-curve theory seemed to invoke expectations and moods at the social level. It is a bit odd to say that there are expectations and moods of a nation which are not the expectations and moods of any person. Nonetheless, the theory needs something at the social level to do this work. After all, a change in Robespierre's expectations alone did not cause the French Revolution. Something happened to the French citizens, and as a result the revolution occurred. As suggested in Section 6.1, a good solution is to *define* the expectations of the nation in terms of the expectations of the citizens. This solution gives us a picture of reductionism: each term of social-level theory would be defined in terms of individual-level theory. "Expectation" in social-level theory might be an average of individual expectations, for example.

Mill demanded that social-level theory be derived from individual-level theory. A deduction of this sort would require social-level terms to be defined by individual-level terms. (In the literature, these definitions are sometimes called "bridge laws.") Of course, full reduction of social theory to individual theory would succeed only if all the social terms can be defined by individual terms. We have seen how "expectation" might be defined. What about "revolution"? This is more troublesome for two reasons: the problem of the remainder and the problem of multiple realizability. Both problems have been taken as important arguments against individualism (and in favor of holism).

The problem of the remainder was clearly stated in Maurice Mandelbaum's classic essay "Societal Facts" (1955). In Goldstone's explanation, for example, the revolution is the product of middle-level actors: trade unions, churches, and the like. If this theory is to be reduced to an individual-level theory, then terms like *trade union* and *church* will have to be defined in individual terms. The problem is that these groups do not decompose directly into individuals. If trade unions and churches are to make decisions as Goldstone's theory requires, they must have an internal structure. Union leaders have the authority to speak for the group and call a strike, for example. Defining *trade union* therefore requires use of terms for roles like *shop steward*. Additionally, there will be decision-making processes within the group, and these are likely to be defined by norms or rules. This means that we will need to define further social-level predicates such as *voting* and *union rules*. Each new attempt at a definition adds a new social-level term which must be defined. Mandelbaum concluded that any definition of a social-level terms by individual-level terms will leave some social remainder. The goal of deriving social theories from individual theories is therefore impossible.

Multiple realizability is the fact that many social-level terms apply to an open-ended variety of individual arrangements. For example, a revolution can be constituted by many different arrangements of individual actions: the Russian Revolution involved one set of individuals with their various interests and situations, while the French Revolution involved another. Revolutions, churches, labor unions, ethnic groups, and so on are all *types* of human action which can be exemplified by many possible *token* aggregates of actions and attitudes. Most terms that appear within social scientific theory are multiply realizable in just this way. Multiple realizability blocks theoretical reduction because there is no determinate set of individual-level aggregates which will serve as the definition. Suppose one tried to list all the possible ways of organizing individuals into a church. The definition would be then a list of all these alternatives (*A* or *B* or *C* or . . .). The problem is that there is no way of knowing how to continue the series. What if someone organizes a church in a way we hadn't foreseen? Does it fail to be a church? Or must we change our definition with every new example? None of these options seem satisfactory, and holists conclude that individualistic reduction of theory is impossible.

Both the remainder argument and the multiple realizability argument depend on a distinction between social-level and individual-level terms. What sorts of terms are supposed to count as individual? In other words, since priests are individual people, why isn't "being a priest" something which can appear in an individualist theory? Julie Zahle has contended that arguments like the two discussed here unfairly narrow the range of individual descriptions (Zahle 2003). It would be impossible to explain individual action without relational terms like *mother of* or *lives in the same household as*. An individualist must be able to describe individuals in terms of their relationships to each other. Social-role terms are relational and ought to be part of the individualist's descriptive repertoire as well.

As Zahle recognizes, the remainder argument is the reason social role terms like *priest* or *shop steward* are usually denied the individualist. Being a priest is not an individualistic property because being a priest depends on the existence of the church. Why, Zahle asks, is this a problem for the individualist? The holist and individualist can agree that *priest* cannot be defined in terms of the actions, beliefs, or attitudes of the individual who is a priest. It must be defined by the actions, beliefs, and attitudes of the parishioners as well. The definition will also depend on the church hierarchy. So, the individualist is taking on a definitional burden. To define a priest in individualistic terms will require reference to the beliefs and attitudes of many individuals, some of whom may be long dead (think of St. Paul's role in establishing the Catholic Church). The remainder argument correctly points out that defining one social-level term will require defining some others. However, Mandelbaum's argument does not *guarantee* that there will always be a remainder. Perhaps clever definitions can be found.

Zahle's argument highlights the importance of articulating the descriptive resources of the lower-level theory. Notice that this will differ among social scientific theories. Rational choice theory is one of the main contenders for an individual-level theory to which social-level theories can be reduced. Rational choice theory is quite austere in its commitments. Game theory, for instance, appeals only to the player's utility functions, beliefs, game payoffs, and the game rules. Social roles like shop steward have no place in this theory except as part of the description of a person's beliefs or utilities. A reductionist who relies on classical rational choice theory, then, is taking on a rather large definitional burden. A reductionist who treats rational choice as a structural theory has somewhat different commitments. Zahle argues that, in the end, whether a social-level theory can be successfully reduced to an individual-level theory is an empirical problem to be decided on a case-by-case basis.

Supervenience

Does failure of theoretical reduction entail ontological holism? One might think so. If the theories are irreducibly different, one might conclude, they must be about different things. Hence, each theory has its own ontology. While it is tempting, this quick argument from different definitions to different ontologies is not sound.

It assumes that every different noun refers to a different object. On the contrary, we often have different ways of describing a single thing. The possibility of multiple descriptions appeared in Davidson's argument that descriptions in terms of reasons do not reduce to descriptions of neurological processes (Section 5.1). On his view, reasons and causes are two ways of characterizing one thing. Similarly, one might accept the multiple realizability argument and still contend that each revolution, church, or trade union is made up of a particular constellation of agents and actions. The decision of a trade union to join a general strike and the beliefs, attitudes, and actions of the union members are therefore just two descriptions of one event. Multiple realizability is thus consistent with a commitment to ontological reduction.

In response, the holist might argue that the multiple realizability of social-level predicates points to a special relationship between social and psychological properties. It is different from other cases of multiple descriptions. For example, describing a ball as round, describing it as moving at 50 mph, and describing it as just having been kicked by Pelé are three ways of describing the same thing. These descriptions are independent: something can be round without being kicked by Pelé, and Pelé probably kicked a few things besides footballs. By contrast, when we describe an event as a revolution and we describe the individuals as taking up arms and heading for the hills, etc., there is a dependency relation between them. Without some set of individual actions, the revolution could not exist. This dependency of revolutions on actions, of course, is precisely what ruling elites count on when trying to stop a revolution. They kill, arrest, or placate the individuals to get them to stop their revolutionary activities. If individuals stop staging protests, etc., then the revolution will end.

The dependency of higher-level properties on lower-level properties has been called "supervenience" in the philosophical literature on reductionism. Roughly, properties of type A supervene on properties of type B if and only if any change in A properties or any difference between A properties requires a change or difference in B properties. A revolution can begin or end only through changes in the way the participants are acting. Or again, a trade union is different from a church only insofar as there is some difference between the beliefs, attitudes, and actions of union members and those of church members. Notice that supervenience has been described in terms of *properties*, not words or concepts. Supervenience is an ontological relationship of dependence between properties. A single object (or aggregate of objects) can have many different properties. According to proponents of supervenience, a single object can have properties at different levels, and where some properties supervene on others, the higher-level properties of the object depend on its lower-level properties.

For example, cuckoo clocks keep time, run fast or slow, and mark the hours with a distinctive sound. The clocks' gears do not keep time, run fast or slow, or say "cuckoo" on the hour. These are properties of the whole clock. Yet, we do not think that there are two *objects* on the wall, the set of gears (etc.) and the clock; the clock *is* the set of gears (etc.). There is a single object which manifests different properties. The clock-level properties depend on the mechanism-level properties. Note that the property of "chiming 12:00" is multiply realizable (think of electronic clocks) and therefore not definable in terms of the motions of gears. The multiple realizability of clock-level properties means that these properties must be distinct from the mechanism-level properties.

Analogously, the actions of a crowd of people manifest many properties. Some of these are individual-level properties which would be describable in terms of the agents' beliefs, attitudes, and actions. No individual is staging a revolution, but the individuals in the crowd may also have a social property, e.g., convening a general strike. The combination of supervenience and multiple realizability permits a sophisticated holist position which admits that there are no social *objects* but insists that there are non-reducible social *properties*. Keith Sawyer has called this view "non-reductive individualism" (Sawyer 2002). The position is individualist in the sense that it contends that social-level entities do not exist. It is non-reductive in the sense that it holds that social-level properties do not reduce to individual-level properties and that social theories cannot be derived from psychological properties.

Methodological Localism

Non-reductive individualism, like other forms of ontological holism, permits social scientists to make causal generalizations at the social level. This raises the question of how higher- and lower-level properties could be causally related. For example, on the J-curve theory, revolutions occur when there is a gap between expectations and levels of prosperity. One empirical study of the J-curve theory used gross national product (GNP) to measure the change in economic prosperity prior to revolutions. With some caveats, it found that historical revolutions were preceded by a rise and abrupt fall in GNP (Tanter and Midlarsky 1967). Given non-reductive individualism, *GNP* and *revolution* are social-level properties which are ontologically distinct from individual-level properties. Revolutions supervene on the actions of individuals. This means that, somehow, the change in GNP must cause individuals to act in revolutionary ways. Non-reductive individualism is thus arguably committed to so-called downward causation: changes in social-level properties cause changes in individual behavior.

Downward causation has struck many philosophers as a bit strange. How can a fact about the whole country—a change in GNP—cause *me* to go out and join a street protest? Suppose Fred knows nothing about economics and has never heard of "GNP." In that case, a change in GNP won't figure as a reason for him. The causation must somehow work without Fred's awareness. It's downright spooky. It seems more plausible to say that Fred can't afford the payments on his car anymore, and this is his motivation to join the protest. What causes *Fred* to take to the streets is the gap between *his* expectations and economic situation, and the same is true of each of his fellow revolutionaries. So, all the causation happens at the individual level. If this argument is correct, supervenient properties like GNP and revolutions do not pick out causally effective properties. And if they are causally impotent, the individualist concludes, it is meaningless to say that they "exist."

One way to respond to the problem of downward causation is to provide an account of how social-level properties could cause changes in individuals. There is a hint of an answer in the quotation from Durkheim which opened this section. Durkheim mentions a "pressure" exerted by social facts on individuals. Chances are, you feel guilty after driving through a stop sign on a deserted street late at night. Durkheim would say that you are experiencing the effect of a social fact (the law) on you. This is not particularly mysterious. You have noticed many patterns of behavior around you. For instance, you have noticed that police officers often patrol the streets after dark. You have experienced their rebuke before and don't want to be stopped again. When you learned to drive, you learned about the traffic laws. And because you had a good upbringing, you learned to feel guilty when breaking the law. Your ordinary capacities for perception, memory, and learning give you information about social properties. Daniel Little has developed this idea into a position he calls "methodological localism:"

> There is no action at a distance in social life; instead, individuals have the values that they have, the styles of reasoning, the funds of factual and causal beliefs, etc., as a result of the structured experiences of development they have undergone as children and adults. On this perspective, large social facts and structures do indeed exist; but their causal properties are entirely defined by the current states of psychology, norm, and action of the individuals who currently exist.
>
> (Little 2007, 347)

For a methodological localist, social properties form both the framework for individual decisions and the character of the agents. Individuals learn to perceive the social properties of their environment, including norms, social roles, institutions, and so on. They respond to these features of their environment, and through their action, new social properties emerge.

Little's methodological localism denies that there are causal relationships between social-level properties. All the causes occur at the individual level, and this ontological view has important consequences for explanation in the sciences. Two features of Little's view are worth highlighting before we move to a discussion of explanatory reduction. First, Little's view focuses attention on the important "structure and agency" problem in the social sciences. Social structures shape agents by informing their beliefs, values, and perceptions. They also constitute the environment for action—the institutions, roles, rules, and regularities to which agents must respond. At the same time, all social properties supervene on action. This means that the very same social properties which shape agents and action are themselves shaped by individual action. Structures and agents create each other, so to speak, and an important project for social scientists is to determine in particular, local contexts how this interaction works. Second, Little's view suggests that mechanistic explanation is particularly important for the social science, and it is to questions of explanation that we now turn.

7.3. Agents and Social Explanations

Methodological Individualism

Students of the social sciences are likely to come across questions about reductionism under the heading of "methodological individualism." Roughly, it is the claim that social phenomena should be explained as the outcome of individual choices and actions. The earliest use of the phrase was in the work of Sir Karl Popper and Friedrich Hayek, who wrote on this topic in the mid-20th century. Their positions in the philosophy of the social sciences were partly influenced by political concerns. Many 19th- and early 20th-century social theorists held that there were laws of social development which worked independently of individual actors. Holistic explanations sometimes justified restricting the scope of individual freedom in the name of group goods. In a time when communism and fascism seemed aligned against democracy, one can understand why Popper and Hayek would worry about the political implications of the social sciences. Their arguments for methodological individualism were thus part of a larger critique of political systems which privileged the community over the individual.

Popper and Hayek recognized that explanations suggest how to control the phenomenon explained. We seek explanations of crime and poverty, for example, because we want to prevent them; we seek explanations of peace and prosperity because we want to promote them. Social-level explanations suggest social-level interventions. Explanations in terms of the agent's choices suggest interventions that change individual incentives. If the J-curve theory of revolutions, for example, is accepted, then the natural way to prevent political upheaval is to keep citizens satisfied. According to Goldstone's theory, by contrast, a politician who wants to prevent revolutions should work with churches and trade unions (etc.) to be sure that their goals are being met. However, it would be a dramatic oversimplification to align holistic and individualistic explanations with the political left and right respectively. It would also be a mistake to think that the arguments for methodological individualism are primarily political.

To help sort out the political and epistemological issues, consider the so-called broken windows theory. Its main idea can be succinctly stated: "Failing to address disorderly conditions in certain areas has been hypothesized to spark a wave of serious crime within those needy neighborhoods or communities" (Gau and Pratt 2010, 758). The theory postulates that orderliness in a community communicates a message of control. Tidy streets and well-behaved citizens show that social norms are being upheld in the community. This message deters disorderly behavior and thereby reinforces the norms. Figure 7.2 shows how one commentator diagrams the theory (Harcourt 1998, 308). Notice that the causal relationships are all macro- or social-level properties.

Now, consider how you might use this theory if you were a police chief or mayor. You might spend resources cleaning up litter and fixing windows, but these measures will be ineffective unless people also stop tossing litter and breaking

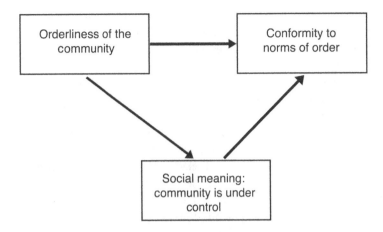

Figure 7.2 Broken Windows Theory

windows. To change orderliness of the community, you need to change behavior. This point is one of the primary premises in an argument for methodological individualism: only *agents* have causal powers. Broken windows don't steal purses. Any causal relationship that might exist between crime and orderliness is produced through individual actions. It will not suffice, therefore, to explain changes in the crime rate by appeal to rates of broken windows. The explanation must show how changes in individual belief, attitude, and action brought about the larger-scale changes. This argument for methodological individualism is relatively independent of political value and motivation. Indeed, it is interesting to note that the political criticism of the broken windows theory attacked *both* the social-level and the individual-level explanations.

Jon Elster characterized methodological individualism in these terms:

> In principle, explanations in the social sciences should refer only to individuals and their actions. In practice, social scientists often refer to supraindividual entities such as families, firms, or nations, either as a *harmless shorthand* or as a *second-best approach* forced upon them by lack of data or of fine-grained theories.
> (Elster 2007, 13)

Elster is proposing a strong criterion for social scientific explanation. Since there are many different proposals for "methodological individualism," it is handy to have a name for this one. We will call positions like the one Elster suggests "strong methodological individualism" and define it this way:

Strong methodological individualism: finished or rock-bottom explanations in the social sciences must always refer only to individuals, their actions, and properties.

In the broken windows theory, there is a mix of harmless shorthand and second-best description. "Orderliness" may be construed as a compact way of describing a range of petty crimes and minor social issues. This is the sort of thing that Elster might call harmless shorthand. "Social meaning" and "norms" are more complicated. Exactly what are the processes by which individuals recognize disruptions of order, and how do these change their attitudes? How do social norms influence behavior? We do not have detailed theories about these processes. Understanding normativity from either a social scientific or philosophical perspective is particularly difficult (and we will devote Chapter 7 to the problem). In these cases, the explanation needs to appeal to social-level terms. But since the causal relationship is carried by agency, we must treat these social-level terms as placeholders for individualistic analyses. We have not finished the job—reaching "rock-bottom" explanations—until we can explain the broken windows correlation in terms of individual action and motivation.

All forms of methodological individualism stand opposed to holism. Since we are concerned here with explanation, the opponent of methodological individualism is:

> **Explanatory holism:** explanations in the social sciences need make no reference to individuals; they may appeal only to social-level entities or properties.

An explanatory holist would allow orderliness or social norms to explain low crime rates. Drawing on the argument for multiple realization, discussed in Section 6.2, the explanatory holist can argue that strong methodological individualism demands the impossible. The argument begins by granting the individualists' assertion that the causal powers of social-level entities are carried by the agents, just as the causal power of a clock to chime "cuckoo" is carried by its particular mechanism. A social-level predicate like "orderliness" will be instantiated in each neighborhood by a different set of activities. In one neighborhood public drunkenness may be the problem; in another it might be dog owners who don't clean up after their dogs. Some neighborhoods may have explicitly codified rules or laws; others may rely on informal norms. Multiple realizability means that each individual-level explanation would have to be different. Abiding by the strong individualist requirements on explanation would therefore lose the generality of the original broken windows theory. The explanatory holist has a response to the earlier argument for methodological individualism. Individualists contend that interventions must target individuals, since only they have causal powers. The explanatory holist can reply that without the generalizing power of terms like *orderliness*, we would not know which set of individual actions to intervene upon. Therefore, our capacity to implement social policy depends on a holistic approach.

Microfoundations and Moderate Explanatory Individualism

Both the strong individualist and the explanatory holist have important points on their side. The multiple realizability of social-level terms seems to block the usefulness, or perhaps even the possibility, of explanations that refer only to individuals. At the same time, it seems right to agree with Little that there is "no action at a distance" in the social world. Causal relationships among social-level phenomena are mediated by individual actions. These two insights can be brought together. In *Foundations of Social Theory*, the sociologist James Coleman expressed a compromise view:

> No assumption is made that the explanation of systematic behavior consists of nothing more than the individual actions and orientations, taken in aggregate. The interaction among individuals is seen to result in emergent phenomena at the system level, that is, phenomena that were neither intended nor predicted by the individuals. Furthermore, there is no implication that for a given purpose an explanation must be taken all the way to the individual level to be satisfactory. . . . This criterion will ordinarily require an explanation that goes below the level of the system as a whole, but not necessarily one grounded in individual actions and orientations.
>
> (Coleman 1990, 5)

This clearly stands opposed to explanatory holism, since holism would say that reference to individuals is not necessary at all. And it makes weaker demands than strong explanatory individualism. A full explanation requires some reference to these processes, but the failure to explain away supra-individual phenomena does not always invalidate social scientific explanation. Following Harold Kincaid (1986, 493), we may define the middle position as follows:

Moderate methodological individualism: explanations in the social sciences must make some reference to individuals.

To see what this might mean, consider again Goldstone's explanation of revolutions. As you'll recall, his explanation invoked rational choice theory at two levels. Individual agents chose to join local organizations, such as schools, churches, and trade unions. Once individuals are part of these institutions, the norms, rules, and social sanctions of those organizations set payoffs which made it rational for the individuals to continue to participate and to not defect. The institutions then chose to participate or not participate in revolutionary activities, depending on the risks and benefits for the group. This sort of use of rational choice theory does not refer to the psychological states of the actors. Rather, it characterizes the payoffs for typical individuals and institutions. Goldstone's explanation is an example of a structural use of rational choice theory. The typical situations of actors and groups are not just "harmless shorthand," nor are they adopted because he lacks the data to fill in the detail. Goldstone needs middle-level agents because appealing to individual rational choices alone leads to the problem of free riders. Goldstone's explanation thus seems to be a case where a social scientific explanation refers to institutions without being either shorthand or a second-best explanation. At the same time, agent choices and actions are shouldering most of the explanatory load.

One program for implementing a moderate form of methodological individualism is what Daniel Little calls the "microfoundations" program (Little 1998,
2007). It follows the idea, expressed in the quote from Coleman, that an explanation should go "below the level of the system as a whole." A good explanation
exposes the mechanism which stands behind a larger phenomenon. This sort of
mechanistic explanatory structure is often presented in a diagram like Figure 7.3.
"Macro 1" is the description of the environment which the agent apprehends. In
the broken windows theory, for example, this will be patterns in the environment:
whether there is litter or broken windows, how other agents generally respond
to such misdemeanors, etc. Agents recognize this situation, and they form intentions based on their past experiences and knowledge (Micro 1). These intentions
result in actions (Micro 2). The aggregate of the individual actions is the rate of
crime later (Macro 2). Microfoundational research often draws on the resources
of rational choice theory to explain the transition between micro-level states, but
it is not limited to those austere resources. Micro-explanations may draw on theories of emotion or communication to explain how individuals interact. Again, the
microfoundational program typically treats rational choice theory as structural, and
therefore it sees no need to replace descriptions of typical situations and responses
with actual (or psychologically realistic) perceptions and choices.

Notice that Goldstone's explanation implements the schema of Figure 7.3 twice.
First, it treats trade unions and other institutions as crucial decision-makers in the
revolution. Then it looks at how individuals bind themselves together into institutions like trade unions in the first place. Little argues that this is exactly what we
should expect from mechanistic explanations in the social sciences. The simple
distinction between "the social level" and "the individual level" was questioned
in Section 7.2. The Russian Revolution involved social entities, institutions, and
agents at a variety of scales. Some of these nest in the way that Goldstone's explanation portrays; others may be related in more complicated ways. Little draws a
further conclusion from the multiple realizability of macro-level properties and
events (Little 2009). An institution like a church or trade union may require different micro-level explanations at different places and times. A trade union might

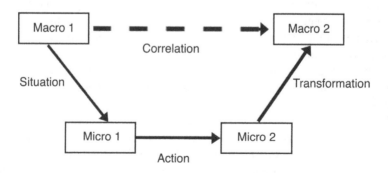

Figure 7.3 Microfoundations

have slightly different institutional norms in different cities, perhaps, and these could affect the costs and benefits of membership. The microfoundations program thus emphasizes the heterogeneous character of the social world and of the explanations needed to account for it.

Agency and Mechanistic Explanation

In the discussion of the microfoundations program, we invoked the idea of mechanism and mechanistic explanation. While it grew in prominence during the last decade or two of the 20th century, mechanistic explanation in the social sciences is not entirely new. Microeconomic modeling is a longstanding research program, and rational choice theory has supported mechanistic explanations in political science. The changes have been more striking in sociology and anthropology. The program of "analytic sociology" has tried to turn sociologists' attention away from correlational research and toward models which explain the internal dynamics of social phenomena (like the models of segregation in Section 6.1). In anthropology, cognitive psychology has provided new resources for understanding both human evolution and contemporary cultural phenomena (we saw examples in Section 4.3 and will see more in Section 7.4).

For physical objects, we have a relatively clear conception of what a "mechanism" amounts to. If I take the back off an old cuckoo clock, I can see the mechanism. It is the "entities and activities organized such that they are productive of regular changes from start or set-up to finish" (Machamer et al 2000, 3). When the clock strikes the hour, the internal mechanism of cogs and wheels make the cuckoo pop out. We can extend our artifactual image of mechanism into the natural world, understanding, say, the replication of DNA as *unzipping* the double helix molecule into two strands, each of which then serves as a *template* for a new molecule. When we turn to social phenomena, it is not so obvious how to extend the metaphor. What in social life is analogous to the cogs and wheels of the cuckoo clock? Must the mechanisms behind social phenomena involve choices, beliefs, utilities, and other personal-level properties? Or should they be sub-personal cognitive processes? And what about norms, rules, or social roles; can they be the elements of social mechanisms? Finding the right level for mechanistic explanations has obvious implications for our understanding of reductionism and more broadly for the metaphysics of the social world. Some of these issues will occupy us in Chapters 9 and 10. Here we will focus on one prominent contender for the rock-bottom of micro-level explanations: individual agency.

Many social scientists and philosophers have held that in the social world only agents have causal powers. This premise is shared by both strong and moderate individualists. There are two objections to treating agency as a privileged level of social scientific analysis. First, there may be some kinds of action which cannot be understood as products of individual intentions. An individual cannot dance a waltz, win the World Cup, land on the moon, or invade Poland. These actions require groups to act in concert, and arguably, the intention to, say, win the World

Cup is not an individual intention. It is something that *we* intend as a team, not something that *I* intend as an individual. We will discuss this interesting dimension of social ontology in Chapter 10. For now, suffice it to say that if the explanation of joint action requires joint or collective intentions, then the basic elements of mechanistic explanation should include social groups as units of analysis.

The second objection is somewhat more profound since it threatens to dissolve the very conception of an agent. We have seen several explanations and theoretical programs in the social sciences which open the black box of agency. In Section 4.3 we discussed the use of cognitive mechanisms to understand cultural phenomena, such as Atran's explanation of why belief in supernatural beings is so widespread and Tooby and Cosmides's account of the Wason card task. Social scientists like these have challenged our ordinary conceptualization of belief, desire, reasoning, and intentionality. They propose a variety of mechanisms to explain both individual action and social events in terms of *sub-personal* cognitive processes. With these explanations in the background, one might argue that agents themselves are the products of underlying causal mechanisms. They get their powers of thought and action from more fundamental processes. This means that we must look to the cognitive sciences for our micro-level processes. The result of this argument is a somewhat unsettling picture: mechanistic explanation in the social science should directly link social macro-phenomena with sub-personal micro-phenomena. The realm of agency, along with the folk-psychological language of belief, desire, and intention is bypassed entirely. What were three levels—the social, personal, and sub-personal—become two, the social and the sub-personal.

This objection forces the proponent of the agency argument to defend the leading premise of the argument: only agents have causal powers. Why should we think that there is something theoretically privileged about agents? In the philosophy of social science, this premise is often taken for granted. As discussed earlier, part of the original motivation for methodological individualism was political. From a political perspective, individuals are the seat of rights and responsibilities and thereby have a special status. But even if individual liberty is a fundamental political good, it does not follow that social scientific models must be restricted to personal-level variables. Alternatively, the proponent of mechanistic explanation might look to the interpretivist for help. If we bypass the level of agency by modeling social phenomena with sub-personal processes alone, we seem to eliminate any role for cultural meaning, value, and intentionality in the social sciences. Such an alliance between mechanistic explanation and thick description is certainly possible. In Section 4.3 we discussed Lawson and McCauley's "interactionism" as a philosophical way of bringing together interpretive and explanatory programs. This would allow us to embrace the sub-personal level and integrate mechanistic explanations across the spectrum of sub-personal, personal, and social level properties. This last gambit, it should be recognized, has the effect of giving up on a special status for agency. No longer can one say that only agents have causal powers. Either causal powers are found across the spectrum, or we must hold that all causal powers reside at even lower levels of organization. We will pursue this issue further in Chapter 11.

7.4. Evolutionary Explanations

So far, our discussion of reductionism has focused on the relationship between the social sciences and psychology. What about biology? Humans are biological creatures, so one might expect that biological modes of explanation would apply to humans in the same way that they apply to other creatures. The distinctive mode of biological explanation, of course, is evolution. The social sciences have had a long and complicated relationship with evolutionary explanation. Nineteenth-century social science was strongly evolutionary. The central questions were about how societies developed from one form to another. For several reasons, evolutionary explanations fell from favor early in the 20th century, replaced by synchronic studies of different cultures and social structures. During the same period, evolutionary explanation underwent a revolution in which genetics became part of the evolutionary toolkit. Today, evolutionary explanations are not limited to studies of human prehistory; they are found in a wide range of social scientific inquiries.

A number of philosophers and social scientists have argued that explanation in terms of natural selection unifies biology and the social sciences in a deep way. Alexander Rosenberg presented a powerful form of the reductionist argument from natural selection in his provocative essay "Lessons from Biology for Philosophy of the Human Sciences" (Rosenberg 2005). Both social and biological properties, Rosenberg points out, are functional. To describe something functionally is to characterize it in terms of its purpose. To say that a part of an organism is its ear, for example, is to say that the organ is for hearing. What it is supposed to do—its purpose—is to provide auditory information. Similarly, social roles (police officer, teacher) and institutions (bank, church) are functional characterizations. They describe the social entity in terms of what it is supposed to do. Natural selection, Rosenberg argued, is the "only game in town" for explaining functional types. It is only through natural selection that we can explain why something with a particular function arises, persists, and has its distinctive characteristics. Therefore, explanations in both biology and the social sciences must be based on natural selection.

Rosenberg contends that the resulting unification of the social and biological sciences is a form of reductionism:

> Reductionism does not mean that the explanatory regularities of social science (i.e., the principles of natural selection) be derivable from those of physical science. That is perhaps a project for biologists or philosophers of biology. Nor does reductionism here mean genetic reductionism. No one, least of all biologists, supposes that they provide the underlying mechanisms for human affairs or the evidence that can choose between narratives about them will always be genetic. Reductionism here is a thesis about how to test the links between the particular initial conditions social science sites to explain and its *explanantia*. Reductionism

requires us to seek mechanisms, not necessarily genetic mechanisms. For each of the real patterns—transitory or persistent—uncovered in the human sciences, there must be a set of underlying mechanisms put in place by natural selection.

(Rosenberg 2005, 19)

Rosenberg's reductionism is analogous to the microfoundations program discussed in the previous section. Both assume an ontological stance of non-reductive materialism. Every macro-level type is instantiated in a micro-level token. And the macro- and micro-levels are relative in the sense that what is a micro-level mechanism in one explanation is a macro-level phenomenon to be explained in another. Both also see an explanatory unity across levels. For the microfoundations program, explanations appeal to the rational choices of typical decision-makers. For Rosenberg, the explanatory unity comes from natural selection. It not only unifies explanations of the social and individual levels, but it also encompasses psychology and biology as well.

Rosenberg's argument raises several issues which we will pursue in this section. First, what is the character of explanation by natural selection? Rosenberg claims in the earlier quotation that natural selection does not require a genetic basis for behavior. In other words, social scientific explanations can rely on natural selection as a mechanism without assuming that each behavior or social form is correlated with a gene. Contemporary philosophers and social scientists largely agree on this point, but it is surprising, and we will want to look at it closely. Second, functions and their explanations have been a longstanding issue in the philosophy of the social sciences. Why is natural selection the only game in town for understanding function? And finally, what would the social sciences look like if they were treated as biological in this way?

Functions in Evolutionary Perspective

To say that something has a function or is a functional kind is to describe the entity in terms of what it is supposed to do. The purpose explains both the entity's presence in a system and its characteristics. For example, Chicago has a police force to keep civil order. The institution of a police department exists because it has this effect on the community. And it has certain features because of those effects, e.g., police officers conduct regular patrols and investigate crimes *so as* to keep civil order. Notice that what a function is supposed to do and what it does in fact do may diverge. The function of a police department is to keep order, even if it is so corrupt that it fails to do so. (Compare: the function of your ears is to hear, even if you cannot do so now.) Some early social scientists (such as Durkheim, Kroeber, and Radcliffe-Brown) were sufficiently impressed with the importance of functional explanation that they thought of societies as analogous to organisms. Like organisms, the parts of a society work together to preserve the whole. Social scientists who accepted this analogy were strongly anti-reductionist.

A curious feature of functions is that the existence or characteristics of an entity are explained in terms of its *effects* rather than its *causes*. Many have thought that this made functions both metaphysically and epistemologically distinct from ordinary causes. Aristotle distinguished functions as a separate sort of causality, calling them "final causes" or *telos* (whence *teleology*) as distinct from the "efficient causes" described by natural laws. The prevalence of functions in the social world has therefore been taken as a reason for thinking that the social sciences must be distinct from the natural sciences. If functions are metaphysically distinct from ordinary, efficient causes, and if they cannot be reduced to efficient causes, then the social sciences do not reduce to psychology, biology, or any other natural science.

Because of their causal peculiarities, functional explanations have struck many philosophers and social scientists as problematic. There are three common objections to functional explanation. First, since the social entity must exist in order to have any effects, functional explanations appear to require a mysterious backward causality; the effects somehow bring the cause into existence. Second, functions are just too easy to find. An institution or social practice will have many, many effects. For instance, the Chicago police department annoys motorists who want to speed. Presumably, this is not its function. Why, then, is the function of the police department to restore order rather than to annoy motorists? These first two problems might be countered by thinking of social functions as products of evolution over time. Some of the effects of a trait cause the organism to be more fit in its environment and so to pass its traits on to the next generation. We will explore this idea presently, but it seems to raise a third problem for functional explanation. Societies are disanalogous to organisms in at least two crucial ways. There are no genes for a society. This means that there is nothing to carry information from one generation to the next. Moreover, societies are not bounded in space and time in the way organisms are. There is nothing analogous to a "generation" in a society. When does a society "die"? As we saw in Section 3.3, social scientists do not like to think of cultures as having neat boundaries. Cultures are fluid and permeable, and therefore we cannot identify earlier and later generations.

Two conceptual developments have helped defenders of functionalism answer these challenges. First, some philosophers have tried to define functions so that they fit within the nexus of efficient causality. Second, the character of evolutionary explanations has been explored, clarifying the role of genes and populations in the explanation of functions. Let us consider functions first. Harold Kincaid has proposed that functional explanations satisfy three criteria (1996, 111). The function of a part or property A is to B when:

1. A causes B.
2. A persists because it causes B.
3. A is causally prior to B.

To see how this works, consider the example used earlier: the function of a police department is to maintain civil order. Since police departments cause civil order, they satisfy the first condition. Second, the police department persists because it preserves civil order. If for some reason police departments stopped doing so, it is very likely that municipalities would stop funding them. The third condition guarantees that there is no backward causation involved. Peace may reign in a community, but that situation does not cause a police department to come into existence.

The distinctive feature of functional analysis is captured by Kincaid's second condition. In a causal chain like the one in Figure 7.4, the second condition is satisfied. *A* continues to exist because it keeps causing *B*, which in turn brings about *A* again later. Note that the third condition of Kincaid's analysis is consistent with the causal chain of Figure 7.4. In that case, *B* causes *A*, but the chain is initiated by *A*, not *B*. Recall that something can have a functional explanation yet not be currently capable of exercising its typical effects. The police department is for maintaining order, even if it is in disarray. But if it is in disarray, how can it bring about order? To see how Kincaid's definition can accommodate this phenomenon, we need to remember the type/token distinction which figured earlier in this chapter. To explain non-functional police departments in functional terms is to explain them as *types*. This particular police department (token) cannot maintain order, but considered as a social kind (type), maintaining order is why police departments persist in communities. Recognizing that functional explanations deploy types, it becomes clear that Kincaid's condition (2) demands a causal history involving social types. Police departments in the past have maintained order, and they exist today because they did so in the past. There is, then, a natural relationship between functional explanations and evolutionary explanations.

Darwin's theory of evolution involves three key ideas: (1) variation in a population, (2) transmission of traits from one generation to the next, and (3) natural selection. The first point is fundamental, and it was not appreciated before Darwin. Traits can be selected for only if there is variation in the population. For a trait to evolve, therefore, members of a single species must be different from each other. Suppose we want to give an evolutionary explanation of why dogs' ears are sensitive to a particular range of frequencies. If so, there must have been variation in ancestral populations of dogs. Imagine, for instance, that some of the dogs could not hear sounds above 35 kHz, while others could. Selection is simply a difference in survival among the variants. If, for whatever reason, dogs which could hear above 35 kHz were more likely to survive and reproduce, the frequency of the distribution in the population will change over time. Dogs' hearing abilities will have evolved. Notice two important points about this evolutionary explanation (what is usually called "selectionist explanation"). First, selection works like a filter to change the distribution of a trait in a population over time. Anything that causes

Figure 7.4 Evolutionary Functions

differential reproduction will serve the purpose. Since humans selectively breed animals, the explanation for why Dachshunds have short legs involves human choice as the selective filter. While we distinguish selective breeding as "artificial" (as opposed to "natural") selection, the explanatory form is the same. Second, there must be some causal relationship between successive generations which transmits the trait. In biological evolution, genes play this role. Nothing in the selection-ist form of explanation, however, demands genetics. In the next section, we will explore the question of whether evolutionary explanations of cultural phenomena require something analogous to genes as the mechanism of transmission.

Selectionist explanations thus provide the kind of causal history which func-tional explanations require. When we provide a selectionist explanation of some property, A, we will need to pick out those effects, B, which caused the differential survival of earlier As. Clearly, all three of Kincaid's criteria will be satisfied: A will cause B, A will persist because of B, and A will be causally prior to B. A successful selectionist explanation, then, will provide the material for a functional explana-tion. And we will be able to explain a property functionally even if it now does not produce the relevant effects. My deaf old hound dog's ears are for detecting the 40 Hz to 60 kHz range because ears in ancestral populations had this effect.

The deep relationship between evolution and function provides resources for a defender of functional explanation to reply to the three objections mentioned ear-lier. Responding to the first two objections is relatively straightforward. First, on a contemporary analysis like Kincaid's, functions are a particular arrangement of ordinary, efficient causes. They are not an additional mysterious kind of causality. Second, Kincaid's analysis can distinguish the functions of a trait from its irrel-evant effects. The function of a hound dog's floppy ears is precisely those effects which caused differential survival among ancestral populations. Any other effects of floppy ears are irrelevant to the functional explanation. There are, of course, substantial empirical challenges to finding out exactly what these effects were in real cases. That is a different problem, and we will return to this issue later. The third objection concerned the legitimacy of the analogy between biological evolu-tion and social evolution. To get a grip on it, we need to look more closely at some of the ways that selectionist explanations have been used in contemporary social science.

Selectionist Explanations of Cooperation and the Evolution of Norms

Cooperation is a fundamental feature of human social life. Human beings are unique among animals for the depth and pervasiveness of their cooperative ten-dencies. From an evolutionary perspective, cooperation is difficult to achieve. The prisoner's dilemma (Figure 5.5) illustrates the problem. While cooperation is more efficient, the dominant strategy is to defect. And as we discussed in Section 6.1, where cooperation produces a non-exclusive good, free riders get the benefits without paying any costs. Still, the laboratory confirms common sense: humans have strong propensities to forego the benefits of defection and cooperate. Norms presumably play an important role in explaining human cooperation. But how did early hominids overcome the problem of free riding and institute stable systems of norms, institutions, and practices? These questions about cooperation are at the center of a lively research program.

In our earlier discussion of game theory (Section 5.2), we noted that the games under discussion were one-shot games. The players are strangers and will not meet again. Real life is different. Where a strategic interaction has the structure of a prisoner's dilemma, we are often interacting with people with whom we have a history and who we will meet again. What happens to strategies when prisoner's dilemma games are repeated among members of a population? When players repeat games, then, they can use knowledge of how the opponent played in previous games to determine what to do in the next game. Unlike classical game theory, there is no single strategy which is always best for the iterated prisoner's dilemma. The strategy of always cooperating is strongly dominated in classical game theory, but it will pay off in an environment where others are also cooperative. But if the environment contains some who always defect, defection may be a better policy.

In an early study of iterated prisoner's dilemmas, Robert Axelrod created a tournament for strategies (Axelrod 1984). He asked theorists to submit their strategies, and then he let these strategies play against each other. He created a computer model where simulated individuals were randomly paired to play an iterated prisoner's dilemma. A strategy's representation in the next generation depended on how well it scored in the previous rounds of games. Strategies that scored better were thus more likely to be reproduced in the next generation. One strategy which did very well under these conditions is "Tit for Tat." This strategy begins by cooperating and then imitates the other player's move on every other iteration. Of course, whether the proportion of Tit for Tat players grows depends on the characteristics of the environment. A strategy of Always Defect will do slightly better than Tit for Tat (since it reaps the advantage of defecting on the first round). But when Always Defect meets another defector, both do worse than when a pair of Tit for Tat individuals meet. Provided that there are not too many Always Defect players in the population, Tit for Tat will drive out Always Defect.

Evolutionary game theory studies populations of strategies which reproduce according to the payoffs they gain from playing strategic games against each other. Axelrod's tournaments for the prisoner's dilemma show how evolutionary game theory is importantly different from classical game theory. First, players need not be rational agents. The theorist does not need to postulate that the individuals are maximizing their utilities, have beliefs, or make decisions. The individuals simply adopt one strategy or another. Notice also that *strategies* survive into the next generation. One can, therefore, think of evolutionary game theory as modeling humans who try out different strategies over the course of their lives, keeping those which work and discarding others. So interpreted, the population is not a group of organisms but the number of people at a given time who are using the strategy. Second, when a game with a Nash equilibrium is modeled in evolutionary game theory, it is possible for the population to end up playing a strategy that would be dominated in classical game theory. A modification of the Nash equilibrium concept which is sometimes used in evolutionary game theory is the "evolutionarily stable strategy." A strategy is evolutionarily stable if it is difficult for it to be replaced by a small invasion of a different strategy.

Evolutionary game theory shows that under some conditions, cooperation between pairs of individuals can become evolutionarily stable. Tit for Tat works against alternative strategies because it "punishes" defection by defecting in return and "rewards" cooperation by continued cooperation. Many cooperative problems, however, involve more than two people. These too can have the structure of a prisoner's dilemma. We saw this sort of problem in the discussion of revolutions (Section 7.1). If all cooperate in the revolution, all are better off; if everyone defects, the unpleasant status quo remains. Mixes of cooperation and defection either result in a failed revolution (with the revolutionaries punished for their trouble) or free riders. Common sense dictates punishing defectors. But punishment is not normally free. Punishers may face retaliation or simply lose an opportunity to do something else. This results in a new strategic game with the form of a prisoner's dilemma again: cooperate with the punishment regime and everyone is better off, or free ride and let other punishers bear the cost. It is hard to see how systems of norms and social institutions could ever evolve.

One clue to unraveling this puzzle is found in the transmission of strategies from generation to generation. In the models we have discussed so far, a strategy is copied if it is relatively more successful than its competitors. This is called "payoff-based transmission." Consider a game where defectors can be punished at some cost to the punisher. Free riders who cooperate but do not punish defection will have higher payoffs than cooperators who punish. If payoff-based transmission is the only selection mechanism, then the non-punishing strategy will dominate. But humans do not imitate only successful individuals; we also have strong conformist tendencies. In conformist transmission, the most common strategies in a population are copied. These two mechanisms of transmission for strategies—imitation and conformism—push in opposite directions. Conformist transmission is conservative, tending to hold onto strategies which are relatively less successful. Joseph Henrich and Robert Boyd created a model where selection was determined both by imitation of successful strategies and by conformism (Henrich and Boyd 2001). It turns out that very small preferences for conformity make costly punishment of defectors an evolutionarily stable strategy. Hence, with the right mechanisms of transmission for strategies, cooperation can become evolutionarily stable.

Models like Henrich and Boyd's show that selection processes operating on strategies can create groups of individuals who cooperate and punish defectors. But what are they cooperating *about*? Human cooperation often involves activities that benefit the group, such as collective hunting or child-rearing. As has already been remarked, however, the equilibria possible in evolutionary game theory need not have the highest payoffs. As Robert Boyd and Peter Richerson put the point:

If everybody agrees that individuals must do X, and punish those who do not do X, then X will be evolutionarily stable as long as the costs of being punished exceed the costs of doing *X*. It is irrelevant whether *X* benefits the group or is socially destructive. It will pay to do *X*.

(Boyd and Richerson 2009, 3283)

So, why do beneficial norms and practices evolve? Notice that, without this piece of the puzzle, we will not have successfully articulated a selectionist account of the function of social practices. So far, the cooperation has no social function. The suggestion championed by Boyd, Richerson, and Henrich is that once different groups stabilize their norms and practices, selection among groups drives out less-beneficial practices. In other words, there must be cultural evolution as well as genetic evolution.

As articulated by Richerson and Boyd, among other theorists, the co-evolution of genes and culture explains why functional norms, practices, and institutions arise. The higher primates are very clever animals, as are some non-primate families, such as corvids and dolphins. The capacity for social learning distinguished early hominids. We learn by imitating both common behaviors and successful behaviors. These learning capacities permitted early hominids to adapt to the rapidly changing environment of the Pleistocene. Rather than solve a problem from scratch, early hominids could imitate successful solutions which were already present in their group. And, as we have seen, these forms of imitation are enough to stabilize norms and practices in a group. This makes cultural evolution possible. Human groups compete for scarce resources, and the groups may have had different solutions to the same problems of finding food, mates, shelter, and so on. Selection acts on the norms and practices which have been stabilized. In a given environment (which is both natural and social), some cultural variants are more likely to be transmitted than others. This permits us to say that a particular cultural variant has been selected because it is beneficial in a particular environment. We have arrived at a selectionist account of social functions.

On a co-evolutionary theory, both genes and culture evolve. This should not be understood as saying that fully modern humans evolved and then culture took over. Rather, early manifestations of culture—in the form of socially learned ways of solving problems—constituted a new environment for early humans. Where non-conformity began to be punished, it became another force of selection. Richerson and Boyd thus propose feedback between the evolution of culture and the evolution of pro-social attitudes and social cognition. As human groups which were more cooperative succeeded against groups which were less cooperative, psychological capacities and dispositions for cooperation became fitness-enhancing traits of individual humans. This raises the interesting question of what these cooperation-supporting capacities and dispositions might be. In Section 10.2, we will return to this topic when we discuss Michael Tomasello's comparative research on human infants and chimpanzees.

Consequences of Selectionism for the Social Sciences

The co-evolutionary story of Richerson and Boyd is not the only selectionist account of social function available today, but it nicely illustrates several of the common features of contemporary evolutionary thinking in the social sciences. To begin our philosophical assessment, let us return to an objection against evolutionary and functionalist explanation in the social sciences which was left hanging: that they depend on an illegitimate analogy between organisms and societies. There are two important disanalogies. First, that evolution requires analogs of a gene, and these are not present in societies, and second that societies are not bounded in time and space the way organisms are.

With respect to the first disanalogy, notice that in evolutionary game theory, strategies are transmitted, not genes. In Boyd and Richerson's theory of cultural evolution, the activities which have the payoffs are imitated and transmitted. Dan Sperber has argued forcefully that these evolutionary units do not need to behave like genes (Sperber 1996). Indeed, replication is the exception when it comes to cultural features like rules for behavior, beliefs, recipes, or practices. What exists in a population is a variety of similar variants on an idea, not the very same idea. For example, when an apprentice learns to process acorns into flour, the teacher and student may have different mental representations of how the process is "supposed to be done." And their activities may differ in many details. As long as the variants have the same sort of payoffs, the variation does not matter to the selection process. If any of the variants in my social group is substantially better than the process I have been using, I may adopt their practice too, adding my own idiosyncrasies along the way. Contemporary proponents of selectionist explanations thus do not seek social analogues of genes. Practices, norms, beliefs, and other cultural features must be similar, but they do not need to exhibit the sort of deeper identity found in genetics.

The second disanalogy between organisms and societies is that biological organisms have clear spatial boundaries (phenotypes) and temporal limits. Organisms are born from specific parents, they live to reproduce (or not), and they die. These features are crucial to evolutionary explanation in biology. Selection acts on phenotypes through the lack of reproductive success among maladapted creatures. Cultures do not have clear spatial boundaries, and the complete extinction of a culture is a relatively rare event. In responding to this objection, it is important again to point out that strategies, ideas, and behaviors are being selected, not whole cultures. Individuals may learn and simultaneously use many variants of an idea. It is entirely possible for individuals to deploy different values, ideas, or practices in different situations. (Again, there is no insistence that humans be instrumentally rational or logically consistent.) Indeed, Boyd and Richerson argue that the permeability of group boundaries through migration and assimilation have been important forces in spreading group-beneficial practices (Boyd and Richerson 2009). Contemporary accounts of social evolution thus do not seem bound to a view of cultures as organismic.

The disanalogies between societies and organisms illustrate one of the ways in which selectionist explanation may be said to be reductionist. Functions have been thought to involve metaphysical features which put them outside of the ordinary causal realm. Evolutionary accounts permit us to fit functions into systems of ordinary causes. While every functional type is multiply realizable in a variety of social, psychological, or physiological tokens, there is nothing more to social function than is provided by groups of individuals. Ontological holists may remain suspicious of this reduction. One of the sources of dissatisfaction concerns the treatment of normativity within evolutionary accounts. Functions say what a practice or institution ought to do, and evolutionary accounts turn this "ought" into an historical "is." In the next chapter, we will explore the questions about how norms, rules, and values are related to descriptions of social practice.

Evolutionary explanations in the social sciences are also reductionist in an epistemic sense. Richerson and Boyd make the bold claim that "nothing about culture makes sense except in the light of evolution" (Richerson and Boyd 2005, 237). Like Rosenberg, Richerson and Boyd are claiming that selectionist explanations unify the social sciences in the same way they unify biology. An evolutionary framework put the different projects of the social sciences into a single system. This point is well illustrated by Rosenberg's surprising argument that a thoroughgoing evolutionary approach is consistent with interpretivism. Interpretive methods will remain our best way to discover the patterns of beliefs, rules, practices, and institutional arrangements. And something like thick description will be necessary to articulate the patterns. What changes is how we understand what interpretive explanations are doing. In an evolutionary framework, patterns of culture are strategies which solve design problems. The cultural forms were selected in an evolutionary process. To understand why, we need to know what sort of advantages they provided over alternatives in the environment. Interpretation thus fits within a larger explanatory enterprise.

7.5. Wrap Up

Chapter Summary

This chapter has been concerned with the core arguments about reductionism in the social sciences. To sort them out, we distinguished between theoretical, ontological, and explanatory issues. Section 7.2 focused on the theoretical and ontological questions. As these arguments have developed over the last several decades, the concepts of multiple realizability and supervenience have taken on a crucial role. Multiple realizability blocks a simple definition of social-level theoretical terms by individual-level terms. As a result, it is unlikely that Mill's vision of a deductive relationship among theories can be realized. Indeed, this is another reason why the empiricist view of theory has lost its popularity among philosophers. This failure has turned attention to the ontological question of whether social entities or properties *exist* over and above individual people and their properties.

Contemporary debates about the ontological questions of reductionism focus on the notion of supervenience. Supervenience is a dependence relationship: there is no change at the social level without a change at the individual level. Anti-reductionists contend that this is a real difference and that social properties are distinct from individual properties. However, since this is claim about *properties*, not *entities*, it makes a non-reductive individualist position possible. Non-reductive individualism holds that there are no social objects, only individual agents. So, fire departments do not exist, only firefighters. At the same time, the property of being a fire department is not a property any individual can have (except, I suppose, in a *very* small town). The individualist challenge to the non-reductive individualist is: how can such supervenient properties be causally effective? Little's methodological localism solves the problem by keeping all the causal relationships at the individual level.

Reductionism about explanation is a prominent part of the methodological individualism debate in the social sciences. This debate is about whether social scientific explanations must *always*, *sometimes*, or *need never* mention individual agents, their properties, and their actions. Recent decades have seen a movement toward mechanistic explanations in the social sciences, explaining social phenomena in terms of how individuals respond to their social environments. The explanatory focus is thus on the relationship between the macro- and micro-levels. One commitment of moderate explanatory individualism, however, is that the level of agency is privileged. At the end of Section 7.3 we saw some arguments for further reducing agency to the sub-personal level of cognitive psychology or neuroscience. It ended with the rather unsettling suggestion that agents are nothing more than an interface between social-level properties and sub-personal level processes.

In the final section of this chapter, we turned to evolutionary explanations in the social science. Social explanations have often appealed to the function of an institution, norm, or practice. The most widely accepted gambit for understanding functions and functional explanations deploys a causal-historical account of function. Something has a function because it has a particular evolutionary history. Looking at the details of how selectionist explanations are used to explain the evolution of human cooperation, we saw that these explanations were reductionist in the sense that they appealed only to the interactions of individuals. Yet, they also invoked strategies, which are not the property of any individual. One of the important philosophical debates in this area remains whether there needs to be some*thing* passed among individuals to explain cultural evolution. If so, then an anti-reductionist element lurks at the heart of evolutionary explanations.

This chapter will not exhaust our discussion of reductionism. It will recur throughout the remaining chapters. The next two chapters consider issues that constitute challenges for a reductionist program. The apparent irreducibility of "ought" to "is" means that social norms, rules, customs, and other forms of normativity will be a particularly difficult challenge for any reductionist program. Normativity will be the topic of Chapter 9. Actions that a single person cannot intend to do, such as playing football, also constitute an apparent counterexample to reductionist claims. Chapter 10 will examine whether phenomena of collective action require a different sort of analysis than individual action.

The search for causes and causal explanations is another aspect of social science that bears on the question of reductionism. Proponents of "analytical sociology" and similar programs have argued that to understand social phenomena, we must be able to explain *how* they work, and this requires exhibiting the mechanisms. Causal explanations provide another *prima facie* case for reductionism. On the other hand, one might argue that some causal relationships operate at the social level. Moreover, mechanisms might be explanatory only if we presuppose a fixed environment or context, and in the social sciences the environment will be other social-level phenomena. Chapters 11 and 12 will explore these aspects of the reductionism question.

Discussion Questions

1. A revolutionary and a government official will both be interested in the question of why revolutions begin. Does reductionism matter to a policy maker who wants to intervene in social systems? What is the relationship (if any) between the political stance of the investigator and their position on reductionism?
2. Consider Goldstone's rational-choice explanation of revolutions. Does this example support an individualist perspective on reductionism? What are the definitional, semantic, or explanatory challenges to an individualistic reduction of revolutions? Can they be met within the confines of a rational-choice approach?
3. The broken windows theory uses social-level predicates in its explanations. Using this example or another with which you are familiar, address the following questions. Do the social-level predicates depend on individual action? How? Does the microfoundations account do an adequate job of analyzing the relationship between the individual and social levels in this case? Or is there something more to "downward causation"?
4. Recall Atran's explanation of the widespread belief in supernatural agents, discussed in Section 4.3. This appears to be an explanation of a social-level phenomenon in terms of sub-personal level mechanisms. Could all social scientific explanations bypass talk of beliefs, attitudes, goals, and values, relating cognitive mechanisms directly to social mechanisms? What sort of phenomena resist such reduction?
5. What are some examples of social function? Think of cases where we might say that a society has an institution, rule, social norm, or practice *in order to* bring about some benefit to the society. Do these satisfy Kincaid's three criteria? What sort of history would they need?
6. In the first part of Section 6.4, three objections were levied against the idea that social phenomena could be explained functionally. What were these three objections? Do selectionist explanations of function resolve these objections?

Further Reading

Nineteenth- and early 20th-century arguments for individualistic reductionism are found in Book VI of Mill's *A System of Logic* (1987 [1872]) and Popper's *Poverty of Historicism* (1957). Watkins's "Ideal Types and Historical Explanation" (1953) and Jarvie's *Concepts and Society* (1972) develop these ideas. Durkheim's *Rules of the Sociological Method* (1938 [1895]) is a classic presentation of holism, and Mandelbaum's "Societal Facts" (1955) develops the argument in response to Popper and Watkins. Lukes's "Methodological Individualism Reconsidered" (Lukes 1968) is a balanced treatment of the issue as it stood in the 1950s and 60s. Good overviews of the problem of reductionism are found in Zahle (2007) and Bouvier (2011).

Kincaid's arguments in "Reduction, Explanation, and Individualism" (1986) and Chapter 5 of *Philosophical Foundations of the Social Sciences* (1996) remain important critiques of individualism. The problem of the remainder is pursued further in Zahle, "The Individualism-Holism Debate on Intertheoretic Reduction and the Argument from Multiple Realization" (2003), and Epstein, "When Local Models Fail" (2008). Zahle and Kincaid reconsider the contemporary arguments for indivudalism in "Why be a methodological individualist?" (2019). Zahle and Collin's *Rethinking the Individualism-Holism Debate* (2014) has a number of excellent essays. Supervenience arguments for ontological anti-reductionism are found in Pettit, "Defining and Defending Social Holism" (1998); Sawyer, "Nonreductive Individualism: Part I—Supervenience and Wild Disjunction" (2002); and Epstein, "Ontological Individualism Reconsidered" (2009). Greve (2010) and Van Bouwel (2004) reply to these arguments. Elder-Vass appeals to a critical realist version of emergence to relate structures to agents in *The Causal Power of Social Structures* (2010). In *The Ant Trap* (2015), Epstein connects the questions of individualism to contemporary metaphysical concerns of social ontology.

Trying to move beyond the debate, List and Spiekermann (2013) argue for the consistency of both approaches, while Kincaid (2015) argues that the remaining issues in the individualism-holism debate are empirical, not conceptual, in his "Open Empirical and Methodological Issues in the Individualism-Holism Debate" (2015).

The microfoundations approach is articulated in Little's *Varieties of Social Explanation* (1991), as well as his more recent thinking about localism and microfoundations (Little 2009 and Little 2007). Elster has a sophisticated treatment of mechanistic explanation in *Explaining Social Behavior* (2007).

Analytical sociology is a field which is leading the way in micro-level explanations of social phenomena; see Hedström's *Dissecting the Social* (2005) for a systematic discussion. There are excellent essays collected in Hedström and Swedberg's (eds.) *Social Mechanisms* (1998) and Demeulenaere's (ed.) *Analytic Sociology and Social Mechanisms* (2011). The idea that only agents have causal powers is defended in Bhaskar (2008 [1975]) and Hedstrom (2005), and criticized in Sperber (2011). Marchionni and Ylikoski critique individualist arguments based on agent-based simulation (2013).

Kincaid's "Functional Explanation and Evolutionary Social Science" is a comprehensive and detailed discussion of the topic (2007), and his chapter on functionalism (Kincaid 1996) remains an authoritative treatment of the topic; see also Pettit's "Functional Explanation and Virtual Selection" (1996).

Axelrod's *The Evolution of Cooperation* (1984) and *The Complexity of Cooperation* (1997) are important works in evolutionary game theory. Skyrms's "Game Theory, Rationality, and Evolution of the Social Contract" (2000) includes a useful comparison of evolutionary and rational-choice game theory. Alexander and Skyrms's "Bargaining with Neighbors: Is Justice Contagious?" (1999) is a provocative application. Richerson and Boyd's *Not By Genes Alone* (2005) gives a general presentation of their gene-culture coevolutionary theory; see also their "Culture and the Evolution of Human Cooperation" (Boyd and Richerson 2009).

Several philosophers and social scientists have argued that explanation in terms of natural selection unifies biology and the social sciences in a deep way. See Zamora-Bonilla, "Why the Social Sciences are Natural, and Why They Can't" (2012); Rosenberg, "Lessons from Biology for Philosophy of the Human Sciences" (2005); and Ross, "Naturalism: The Place of Society in Nature" (2011).

8   Race and Other Social Constructions

The concept of "race" has a perplexing status in the social sciences. In the 19th century, it was a substantial part of anthropology's subject matter. Races were conceptualized as biological sub-species of *homo sapiens*, and race was used to explain a wide range of human variation. As both anthropology and evolutionary biology developed in the 20th century, however, it became clear that races in this sense did not exist. Human variation in language, religion, technology, social institutions, and so on were explained in social or historical terms, and the concept of culture emerged as a crucial part of these explanations. Human bodily variation came to be explained in genetic terms, and genetic variation correlates very weakly with the traditional concept of "race." And yet, while social scientists will affirm that there are no races, race continues to be a common independent variable in social scientific explanations. In the last chapter, we were wondering whether higher-level entities of the social sciences (e.g., institutions) might be reduced to lower-level entities and properties (e.g., agents and their actions). The ontological reductionist will say that only the lower-level entities exist. Race turns this picture upside down: at the lower, biological level races do not exist, yet we deploy the concept of race at the social level. Can race have explanatory power in the social sciences? Or is it a holdover from 19th-century social science that should be eliminated?

A common response to the puzzle about race is to say that race is "socially constructed." Race is nothing but a product of the way we talk and treat each other. The language of social construction has a range of meanings, and in Sections 8.2 and 8.3, we will try to sort out some of the possible commitments. Some talk of social construction has a debunking character. As we will see in Section 8.2, to say that something is a social construction is to deny that it is natural or inevitable. One might argue that since the concept of race is inextricably bound up with racism, the social construction of race tells us that we should eliminate the notion entirely from the social sciences. On the other hand, one might also argue, the fact that race has a history and is the product of social practices does not mean it is unreal. Many things that are socially constructed have demonstrable effects on our lives. College tuition is the product of the ways we talk and treat each other, but it would be fantasy to pretend that it does not exist. Some social constructionists, then, take a more realistic attitude, treating race as analogous to other social entities that are the product of human practices. Race then figures in social scientific explanations

DOI: 10.4324/9781003207795-8

in the same way that institutions and social roles do. Section 8.3 will explore this response to the puzzle about race in the social sciences.

8.1. Race in the Social Sciences: A Brief History

Science, Race, and Slavery in the 19th Century

The contemporary concept of "race" is heir to 18th- and 19th-century thinking about race, which had both scientific and political dimensions. From the 16th century forward, European economic and political power spread across the globe. Advances in transportation and other technologies enabled people to travel farther and faster than they ever had before. This led to global trade and a surge of colonial empire-building by the European powers. In the Americas, colonialism included slavery, primarily of Africans brought to North and South America. Such practices were justified by the alleged superiority of the European "civilization," a superiority which was supposed to include not only their technology but their religion, language, political institutions, and bodily form. A hierarchical understanding of human difference was thus central to colonialism and slavery.

But how should human difference be explained and understood? In the mid-18th century, Linnaeus attempted to create a taxonomy of all living things, and we still deploy his division of life forms into families, genera, species, and so on. Linnaeus divided the species *homo sapiens* into four sub-species, or races. They were distinguished by geographic and somatic features. Linnaeus's races were identified by their continent of origin: "Americanus," "Europaeus," "Asiaticus," and "Afer" (Linne 1964 [1758]). However, noting differences in bodily form alone did not explain the range of human variation, and accounting for the difference among human groups became an important anthropological problem in the 19th century. To the European scientists of this era, the differences among humans apparently clustered in a coherent way. Skin color and other aspects of bodily form seemed to vary with differences in language, technological development, social organization, and cultural forms. Race was postulated to be a kind of essence, that is, an underlying property of humans that explained the observed differences. In the 19th century, race was taken to be a powerful explanatory posit.

The theoretical project of 19th-century anthropology sought to explain difference not only by positing underlying properties but by putting these properties into a historical and developmental sequence. This anthropological theorizing was "evolutionary" in the sense that humans were supposed to have developed from more primitive forms to more advanced ones. Unlike contemporary evolutionary thinking, the framework was teleological and evaluative: later developments (the Europeans) were "higher civilizations," while earlier forms (the lower races) were "primitive" or "savage" or simply lower forms of civilization. The idea of race that emerged in the 19th century, then, was the idea of a hidden set of properties— a racial essence—that both explained human difference and put humans into a moral/political hierarchy.

The Demise of Racial Essentialism

While racial theorizing dominated 19th-century thinking about humans, some anthropologists opposed and criticized it. Franz Boas was one of the first to make empirical arguments against the way in which race had been conceptualized, and by the early 20th century, his arguments were widely accepted. The coherence of racial classification was the main target of Boas's critique. Identifying a taxonomic level in biology, such as a sub-species, requires "concordant" traits. This means that variation in one of the traits reflects variation in the others. For example, a bowl of fruit, say, apples, oranges, plums, and grapes, would divide naturally into sub-groups because their color, surface texture, seed size, and so on are concordant traits. Separating the fruits by color yields the same sub-groups as partitioning by surface texture or seed texture. Boas showed that bodily form, language, and culture are not concordant. People with different body types may speak the same language (all kinds of people are native English speakers); persons with the same bodily form may speak unrelated languages (Czech and Hungarian are from different language families). Similarly, culture and language vary independently (Boas 1911). Boas concluded that the three criteria (language, culture, and bodily form) together could not provide a consistent racial classification. This conclusion reduced the power of the concept of race to explain cultural differences and differences in technological achievement observed in the 19th century.

As already noted, the 19th-century concept of race included the idea of "higher" and "lower" races. Race was thus an example of what Section 2.3 called a "thick" evaluative concept. The concept of race was partly descriptive and partly evaluative. The descriptive component was the property of having racial essence, and the different phenotypic traits, etc. that the essence was supposed to cause. The evaluative component put these differences on a moral scale. To the Europeans, it was obvious that "civilization" was better than "savagery," and as we have already seen, this moral difference was part of the justification for colonialism and slavery. Boas stood against this moral evaluation. He thought that the idea of higher and lower races distorted the discipline of anthropology by inviting speculative histories of humankind. Boas's critique nicely illustrates one of the ways in which scientific research can dislodge problematic moral or political ideas. Boas found the notion of higher races odious, but he did not launch a moral polemic. Rather, he critiqued the descriptive side of the concept. Because of his efforts, and those of other early 20th-century anthropologists, culture replaced race as the explanation of human difference. And the notion of "a culture" carried with it a different moral perspective. Cultures did not fit into a moral hierarchy, and each needed to be understood and evaluated in its own terms.

Early 20th-century research in physical anthropology continued to undermine the viability of racial theorizing. Boas compared the children of immigrants to the United States to their parents, measuring the physiological features used to classify race, such as head size and stature. These changed within one generation, and Boas concluded that many of the observed physical differences among human groups depended on diet or other environmental factors, rather than an underlying racial essence. He also found that variation within racial groups on such measures was greater than the variation between them. Boas's conclusions were further supported by the new science of genetics. By 1936, Julian Huxley and A. C. Haddon were arguing that because of the continual contact and interbreeding among humans, there was too much genetic overlap for *homo sapiens* to have sub-species or races. While bodily forms like hair texture and skin color did have a genetic basis, their distribution did not correspond to racial categories. Appeal to genes did not substantiate the idea of racial essences. Haddon and Huxley concluded: "These considerations rob the terms race or sub-species, as applied to existing human groups, of any significance" (Huxley and Haddon 1936, 219).

While geneticists have continued to confirm Haddon and Huxley's earlier conclusion, the concept of race did not lose its significance in the 20th century. It continues to appear in social scientific (and medical) generalizations. This situation raises several fascinating philosophical questions. In what sense is "race" a social construction? Can a social construction ground robust causal generalizations? If so, how?

8.2. Reductionism and the Social Construction of Race

Claims that this or that sort of thing are "socially constructed" proliferated in the last decades of the 20th century and have become commonplace. Often, such claims are presented with a skeptical attitude, suggesting that because something is socially constructed, it cannot be real; such would be the force of saying that electrons or chemical elements are social constructs. On the other hand, some social constructions are undoubtedly real. The United States Constitution is a social construction in the sense that was created by historically contingent human decisions, practices, and ideas, but it seems no less real for all of that. Claims about social construction, then, are ambiguous in several dimensions, and in this section and the next we will try to sort out the various things that might be claimed when something is said to be socially constructed.

Social Construction of What?

In the 19th and early 20th centuries, race appeared to be a natural kind of thing, something inevitably found as we examine our environment, like water or tigers. While languages might differ, we would expect all languages to have a way of describing water (perhaps a single word) and distinguishing it from other things. Similarly, someone committed to the 19th-century concept of race would expect racial differences to be noticed by anyone who traveled far enough away from home. The history sketched earlier is already a bit unsettling to the idea that race is something natural. Race was not simply discovered; it emerged from a particular set of moral and political attitudes, as well as the economics of empire and exploitation. Knowing this, race does not seem so natural after all.

In *The Social Construction of What?* (1999), Ian Hacking argues that the primary purpose of making claims about social construction is to challenge the naturalness or inevitability of something. Hacking argues that a social constructionist about *X* holds that:

(1) *X* need not have existed, or need not be at all as it is. *X*, or *X* as it is at present, is not determined by the nature of things; it is not inevitable.

(Hacking 1999, 6)

When we come to understand how race emerged from a particular social milieu, it becomes quite plausible that race is not inevitable. And when we see that the idea of race no longer has explanatory power in human biology, it becomes obvious that race is not in the nature of things. Hence, social constructionism about race is a natural and plausible response to the history of race in the 19th and 20th centuries.

The claim that human races are a social construction contains an important ambiguity: is the *idea* of race said to be social constructed, or is it *race itself*, that is, the property of being Black or White socially constructed? Social construction claims thus have meaning in two dimensions: the construction of ideas and the construction of things. As Hacking points out, the claim that *X* need not have existed makes sense against a background where such a claim is surprising. Looking for the surprise factor can thus help us figure out which dimension of social construction is being emphasized. Saying that an idea is socially constructed can be quite surprising where the idea seems natural, inevitable, or determined by the facts of nature. This was the case for the idea of race in the 19th century. For a different example, consider the economic concept of "the market." It may seem like a natural concept, forced upon us by the nature of things. Every economy has a market, one might think, so we simply notice this and name it. To say that the concept of "the market" is a social construction that arose through a particular historical development in contingent social circumstances, then, is a startling claim. It suggests that an economic phenomenon could be conceptualized very differently, which would no doubt have consequences for both the discipline of economics and for our practical activity. On the other hand, since markets are obviously created by human actions in particular social circumstances, it is less startling to say that markets themselves—the things to which the word *market* refers—are social constructions.

By contrast, where the thing itself seems to be a natural fact about the world, it is surprising to find that it might be the contingent product of human practices and decisions. Gender has seemed to many to be a natural fact about humans. It is quite obvious that the *ideas* or conceptualizations of men and women vary across cultures and through history. So, the notion that our current ways of thinking about women and men in the early 21st century have a contingent history is unsurprising. It seems obvious that we could have conceptualized women and men differently, and we can change the way we think. On the other hand, to say that gender itself is a contingent product of social practices is more interesting. This means that what I am now is the contingent product of social forces, and that is an uncanny thought. The interesting claim about the social construction of gender, then, is that genders themselves are social products, not just that the ideas (concepts, beliefs, etc.) have changed or are changeable.

When a social constructionist claims that a kind of thing, not just the idea, is constructed, they owe us an account of how such a construction would work. How did decisions, attitudes, and practices bring about or constitute X in a given time and place? Such social constructionist claims are most easily supported where X is a feature of humans or human societies. Labeling is one of the simpler possible mechanisms: we create differences among people when we label them in one way or another. The label or idea of X has a history, and it gets a particular content from the social environment in which it was created. Then, labeling or describing people as X divides people into the Xs and the non-Xs. A "kind of person" is created in that time and place in the sense that the labeling has social consequences. Being X has certain privileges or subjects one to certain deprivations. Notice how, on this sort of view, Hacking's two dimensions of social construction come together. Both the idea and the kind of person are created at the same time. In the case of race, the idea emerged in the context of colonial empires and slavery, along with the scientific attempts to explain human variation. The idea of race is thus socially constructed. The 19th-century idea of race sorted humans based on bodily type and held that some races were inferior to others. On this labeling account, once race labels gained currency, races themselves came into existence.

A labeling account of the social construction of a social category is an instance of metaphysical reductionism in the social sciences. The higher-level concept of "being X" is reduced to a (lower-level) practice of labeling people as X and treating them differently on that basis. The example of race brings a new dimension to our discussion of reductionism in Chapter 7. In 19th-century science, to be a particular race was understood as a matter of having a racial essence. The concept of race thus was thought to correspond or refer to something. Subsequent scientific investigation showed that there was no such thing as a racial essence, hence the 19th-century concept of race referred to nothing. The labeling account explains the phenomena previously associated with race. Notice how reductionism in this case was motivated by scientific developments. The idea that having a race is nothing more than the practices of racial labeling gains significant support from the social and biological sciences, but for this reason it also raises new philosophical questions. Sometimes, when scientific developments show that nothing corresponds to a scientific concept, the idea is eliminated from scientific theorizing. Concepts like "the æther" or "phlogiston" no longer appear in explanations of light or heat. Should the concept of race be eliminated in this way? Alternatively, in some cases it might make better sense to say that the higher-level concept is "nothing but" the lower-level activities and to maintain the higher-level concept for descriptive and explanatory purposes. In Chapter 7, we looked at the suggestion that revolutionary action might be reduced to the strategic choices of individuals. In this case, social scientists continue to deploy the concept of a revolutionary action, but they understand it as a set of individual actions. Should race be understood in this way—that is, as a concept that remains useful for the social sciences, even though it does nothing more than capture a pattern of underlying labeling practices?

Elmininativism About Race

Hacking points out that social constructionists often go beyond contention (1) and argue for one or both of the following:

(2) *X* is quite bad as it is.
(3) We would be much better off if *X* were done away with, or at least radically transformed.

(Hacking 1999, 6)

Work in this vein often has a debunking or unmasking quality. For example, "hysteria" was a common medical diagnosis for women in the 18th and 19th centuries. Foucault and others have argued that this diagnostic label drew on and reinforced the conceptions of a woman's place in society and of what a virtuous, temperate, upper-class woman should be like. Such conceptions were part and parcel of a system wherein men maintained power over "the weaker sex." The Foucaultian argument is not merely that the idea of hysteria was socially constructed; hysteria itself was constructed. The scientific history of hysteria is analogous to the scientific history of race. Like race, the diagnostic category of hysteria was rejected as psychology and psychiatry developed. Psychiatrists are no longer committed to the existence of hysteria, and the labeling account of the social construction of hysteria explains why there seemed to be such a phenomenon.

When a reductionist attitude is combined with Hacking's points (2) and (3), it results in *eliminativism*. The label "hysteria" was part of a system of oppression that pathologized behavior falling outside of 19th-century gender norms. Since it does not refer to anything, both science and morality dictate that the use of the label should be discontinued. Insofar as there were forms of suffering captured by the diagnosis of "hysteria," these need to be identified with more accurate, less politically problematic, terms. Such would be an eliminativist response to the social construction of "hysteria." One is an eliminativist with respect to *X* when one holds that the objects *X* purports to describe do not exist, that we should stop using the term *X* and, if possible, replace it with terms that successfully refer.

In *The Philosophy of Science and Race*, Naomi Zack makes the following argument for eliminativism about race:

If educated people believe that scientists believe that something, in this case biological race, exists, and scientists do not believe that the thing exists, then there is a problem for educated belief. The problem can be solved in three ways: (1) Reject the findings of physical science in general; (2) reject the findings of physical science in this particular case; (3) remove biological race from secular ontology. The first option is not feasible. The second option requires making a special case for biological race, which cannot be done without begging the question of whether race has a biological foundation. The case for the non-existence of race is straightforward and consistent with (accepted) scientific cases for the nonexistence of many other things. The best option is the third: remove biological race from secular ontology.

(Zack 2002, 6–7)

Such a view proposes that any explanatory value that is attributed to race will be better captured by other variables, such as socio-economic, educational, or occupational status. Discovering such variables will take time, in just the way that it took decades for the medical concept of hysteria to disappear from the diagnostic vocabulary. In this respect, eliminativism is less a position about our current attitude toward the concept of race than it is a recommendation for, and prediction of, the course of future science.

One concern about eliminativism is political: if we were to transform the social sciences and eliminate the concept of race, we would be unable to describe, diagnose, and intervene on the varieties of racial oppression. Even if all the explanatory power of "race" is captured by either attitudes (like racism) or underlying variables (like socioeconomic status), to ask questions about the pressing social problems of our day requires us to use the vocabulary of race. For example, without it we could not form generalizations about the way in which segregation by race causes educational or occupational inequalities. The eliminativist can respond to this question by noting that it assumes that race *must* be used to describe the social problems we face. If these are really the result of other social processes, then they should be described in non-racial terms.

One might also argue that the language of race needs to remain in the social sciences as a characterization of what people believe and the way in which they categorize each other. As long as people believe that races are different and should be treated differently, the social scientist will need a concept of race. In response to this criticism, one might point out that Zack's argument concludes that race should be removed from "secular ontology." An eliminativist might strive to do so and recognize that until society changes, a science of society will need to appeal to racial labels used by that society and to its beliefs. After all, an eliminativist can agree that to understand human behavior, we must understand the way people think and speak about themselves. Notice how this makes the concept of "race" something like the concept of a "malevolent spirit." Such things "exist" only in the sense that people believe them to exist. The eliminativist about race can thus recognize that insofar as the people we are studying categorize each other with racial terms, social scientists will need to use the concept of race.

8.3. Is Race Real? From Social Construction to Social Kinds

Zack's argument for eliminativism concerns the "biological concept of race," which treats race as an essential property of each sub-species of *homo sapiens*. Most biologists and social scientists would agree that *this* is a concept that the sciences can dispense with. But as we noticed earlier, there is more than one possible response to the determination that a scientific concept fails to refer. Eliminativism is one response: we drop the word from our vocabulary and no longer use it to describe phenomena or theorize about them. A second alternative is to treat the concept as a useful way of capturing complex, lower-level patterns. This might be called the *nominalist* strategy: nothing corresponds to the higher-level concept, and its explanatory or descriptive value is exhausted by lower-level causes and effects. A third possible option is *realist*. This view would agree that the earlier scientific concept fails to refer but holds that the failure is conceptual in the sense that the earlier concept was inadequate. Once we have a new understanding of the concept in question, we see that it does refer to something. This section will explore the nominalist and realist responses to the puzzle of race in the social sciences.

Racial Nominalism

One way to argue for racial nominalism is to invoke a distinction between *natural* and *nominal* kinds. In a nutshell, the argument points out that the failure of the 19th-century conception of race shows that race is not a natural kind. And if it is not a natural kind, then the people who are called "Black" or "White" share no property. They are grouped together only based on human interests, that is, they are merely a nominal kind. And as a nominal kind, all the explanatory or causal force of the higher-level category, such as being Black, is found at the lower level, e.g., socioeconomic status, practices of discrimination, etc. Race does not exist, but using the concept of race in the social sciences helps identify problems to be investigated and explanatory factors. To unpack this argument, we must begin with the notions of a natural and nominal kind.

Natural kinds are enduring features of the world, like water, silicon, or tigers. They figure in causal generalizations and support a variety of inferences. If something is a tiger (*Panthera tigris*), we can infer that it is likely to have stripes and a long tail, to bear live young, and to eat meat. The kind "tiger" supports these generalizations because tigers have several properties that reliably occur together. Their co-occurrence is the result of underlying mechanisms, not only genetic, but epigenetic and environment-dependent processes of development. These mechanisms are "homeostatic" in the sense that the mechanisms ensure that the properties continue to cluster together over time and across individuals. That is, because of the mechanisms of evolution, genetic inheritance, and ontogenetic development, the properties of one tiger (e.g., having stripes) will be shared by all or most others. When a property cluster is supported by homeostatic mechanisms, it enters powerful causal generalizations and supports inductive inferences. Discovering natural kinds, then, is an important goal of the natural sciences.

Nominal kinds, on the other hand, are categories created by humans because we find it useful or convenient. In an obvious sense, all nominal kinds are socially constructed. The categories "object on my desk" or "plant commonly found on college campuses" would be examples of nominal kinds. Like natural kinds, they are labels that group objects together and distinguish them from others. Unlike natural kinds, nominal kinds do not figure in causal generalizations or support strong inferences. Thus, knowing that X is an object on my desk provides very little basis for causal generalizations. We don't know whether it is flammable, edible, or soluble. There are, of course, some inferences we could make: it is very likely that X weighs less than 10,000 kg and is cooler than 2,000 °C. Insofar as it does support generalizations or inferences, it is entirely because of human interests and practices. It is very likely that X is not extremely hot because humans tend not to keep extremely hot objects on hand. Nominal kinds are thus excellent candidates for metaphysical reduction in the manner of Section 7.2. Any causal powers attributed to the nominal kind are attributable entirely to the individuals grouped together.

We can now see the full force of the argument for a nominalist account of race. Nineteenth-century anthropology regarded race as a natural kind. When it was shown that racial traits were not concordant, and that there was no genetic mechanism that supported racial differences, this conception failed. The 19th-century conception of race is not a natural kind because there are no homeostatic mechanisms that maintain property clusters analogous to species or sub-species. The explanation for the persistence of the concept of "race" is that it is a social practice of labeling, and thereby distinguishing, people. But this is exactly what it means to be a nominal kind. Racial nominalism is thus a form of metaphysical reductionism. The term *race* does not refer to anything over and above the people categorized as being in the race. They are related only by the social practice of labeling, not through any inherent similarity or underlying essence.

One might wonder why nominalism does not collapse back into eliminativism. After all, both agree that "race" does not refer a kind of person, and the nominalist will agree that the concept of race and the related practices of white supremacy, slavery, exploitation, etc. are profoundly problematic. However, the eliminativist wants to treat "race" in the way that an anthropologist treats "malevolent spirt;" only the beliefs have explanatory power, not the sprits or races themselves. The nominalist, on the other hand, takes the social construction of race a bit more seriously. "Race" is not simply a concept that figures in the beliefs and language of a group of people. Distinguishing people by racial labels is a form of activity, and these activities have consequences over and above the beliefs of a group. For a nominalist, then, race—not just beliefs about race—can figure in the explanation of social phenomena. The explanatory power does not come from the existence of a natural kind, of course, but from the social practices associated with racial labeling.

So far, we have been relying on a rather simple account of how race is socially constructed. As a result, its explanatory power is quite limited. The story so far has turned on the idea of labeling: racial labels divide people, and these divisions have social consequences. Thus, for instance, if a social scientist finds that educational attainment correlates with race, this will have to be understood as saying that educational attainment correlates with racial labels. Now, if we are thinking of the effects of race in terms of discrimination, this replacement of "race" with "racial label" might make sense. Being labeled as "Black" in America (and other places) usually comes along with discriminatory treatment, so the explanatory force of identifying someone as "Black" is carried by the discrimination. This sort of approach is sometimes summed up in the slogan: there is no race, only racism.

It is not always noticed that the shift from "race" to "racial label" carries with it some deep methodological consequences. If we are to correlate race with something else, such as educational attainment, race must be measured. But measuring race is a very messy business. In the 19th and early 20th centuries, the US census required the *census taker* to identify an individual's race. The individual had no say in the matter. Today, the US census asks individuals to self-identify their race. Many people today regard the earlier practice as rather shocking. Race is at least partly an identity, and most of us are uncomfortable with the idea that someone else should impose an identity on us. But if measuring race is a matter of measuring the label put on someone, then it is the label by the census taker, not the individual, that should matter.

The idea that race is an identity points to another explanatory limitation of the simple labeling view of the social construction of race. That one is Black, White, Asian, or Hispanic provides a way of thinking about oneself. It can provide a scope of possible actions or be the recognition of a limited possibility for action. This way of thinking about oneself may exist because the ideas were introduced as labels, but they become more. As an identity, race can figure in explanations of action, and not just as a label imposed by others. Louis Armstrong, one might argue, recorded the song "(What Did I Do to Be So) Black and Blue" because he was Black and thereby wanted to call attention to the horrors of slavery for his ancestors and the current plight of his fellow Black Americans. Such an explanation invokes race as an identity and goes well beyond any labeling practices.

Finally, there are many ways in which we label and categorize each other, and not all of these have the kinds of effects that race seems to have. To explain these special effects of racial labeling, one needs to add more elements to the explanation: discriminatory practices that result from the labeling, institutional structures that maintain the labels, forms of practice that make such labels resilient to change, norms of differential treatment, and so on. The labels are part of a larger social structure that generates the specific effects of being one race or another.

A sophisticated nominalist can recognize these points and develop a more nuanced conception of how race is socially constructed. Kwame Anthony Appiah has suggested that race should be treated as an identity. Social identities have the following characteristics:

> There will be criteria of ascription for the term '*X*'; some people will identify as *X*s; some people will treat others as *X*s; and there will be norms of identification.
>
> (Appiah 2006, 368)

Appiah's account of the social construction of race clearly picks up the points made earlier about the way that race can figure in identity. It also stresses norms, and Appiah recognizes that some of these are norms concerning how members of a race ought to behave, while others concern how members ought to be treated. While nominalist, this conception of race seems to give it substantial explanatory power, both of individual action and social patterns. But because the view is reductionist, all the explanatory power of appeal to "race" will be carried by the underlying facts that individuals identify as a member of a race, receive differential treatment, and so on.

Since a sophisticated nominalism about race seems to provide the social sciences with explanatory and descriptive resources over and above mere beliefs about race, it is arguably distinct from eliminativism. But the opposite problem now looms: race starts to look less like a mere nominal kind and more like a cluster of properties with a homeostatic mechanism for maintenance. To be sure, the mechanisms are *social* mechanisms, not natural mechanisms. So, the sophisticated nominalist account does not make race into a natural kind. But one might argue that it is more than a nominal kind. One might call it a *social kind:* a cluster of properties that reliably occur together, where their co-occurrence is created and maintained by underlying *social* mechanisms. If it figures in causal generalizations and inferences because of this cluster of properties, then a reductionist attitude seems less plausible. The alternative would be to take an anti-reductionist stance and regard race as a real, albeit social, kind with causal powers over and above the underlying social practices.

Social Kinds and Realism About Race

When we come to questions of existence and reality, we sail onto the high seas of metaphysics. Fortunately, we can narrow the horizon by continuing to think in terms of metaphysical reductions, as we did in Section 7.2. When a metaphysical reductionist says that some property or object, X, does not exist, they are saying that any causal or explanatory power we attribute to X is really the causal or explanatory power of the things of which X is composed. The anti-reductionist (or holist) denies that all the causal or explanatory power of X is exhausted by its components. One of the main pivots of the argument between the reductionist and the anti-reductionist, then, is whether the property in question, be it race or revolution, has causal or explanatory force over and above the individuals who adopt the racial identity or participate in revolutionary activities.

Natural kinds are clear examples of entities where the kind has causal powers that are not just the causal powers of the components. Water is a natural kind, and its capacity to take both a liquid form and solid, crystalline forms are some of its more important properties. Water, of course, is made from hydrogen and oxygen. The explanation of, say, the crystal structure of water, will depend on the properties of hydrogen and oxygen, and neither of these elements alone creates the same kind of crystals. Ice crystals depend on the properties of the whole molecules of H_2O.

Notice how the relationship between water and its component elements is analogous to the "non-reductive individualism" discussed in Section 7.2. Non-reductive individualists hold that higher-level social entities (such as a revolution) do not reduce to their component parts (the actions of individuals). But, contrary to an ontological holist like Durkheim, they also hold that there is no additional social thing over and above the component parts. Similarly, a natural kind like water is nothing but hydrogen and oxygen. But when the elements combine in the right way, they become a homeostatic cluster of properties that have causal powers distinct from the elements alone. This is grounds for being a realist about water.

At the end of the last section, we noticed that to capture the phenomena associated with race, a sophisticated nominalist about race needed to invoke several social processes beyond mere labeling. The realist argues that when this story is fully spelled out, we will have identified social mechanisms that function to maintain the racial categories. Analogous to realism about the natural kind "water," the realist about race holds that the property of being a particular race has causal and explanatory power over and above the component people or social practices. And like the non-reductive individualist, the realist about race is not arguing for a biological conception of race, nor any other essentialist conception. There is nothing to being a race over and above the actions, practices, and norms that constitute such a social kind.

The realist position thus depends on two closely related claims. First, the social practices (etc.) that ground the social kind "race" are sufficiently robust to be analogous to the homeostatic mechanisms that ground natural kinds like "tiger" or "water." Second, the cluster of properties that constitute having a race (in a given time and place) support robust causal generalizations and explanations. We will consider these in turn.

Appiah's conceptualization of race as an identity characterizes it in terms of several dimensions of social practice. Realists like Michael Root (2000), Ron Sundstrom (2002a), and Ron Mallon (2016) have taken these to be potential mechanisms for the creation and maintenance of races. Sundstrom expresses these potential mechanisms as three "forces:"

> What unify human kinds are three social forces. These forces are: the force from above, the act of classification or labeling by some authority; the force from below, the intentional acting under the label by the so labeled; and the lateral forces, the normative standards that become attached to the label and are applied to those within and without the label.
>
> (Sundstrom 2002a, 95)

The first, labeling, has already figured prominently in our discussion. The realists emphasize that not just any act of labeling will serve to entrench a social identity (or more broadly, social status or social role) so that it becomes a social kind. The labels that distinguish social kinds cannot be idiosyncratic, so Mallon argues that the label must be common knowledge. For a label to be common knowledge, there must be some social processes by which it is regularly and widely communicated. In the case of race, 19th-century anthropology arguably played a crucial role in promulgating the idea of race and the justification of racial hierarchies. The labeling practices were also encoded in the laws and institutional policies of the time. These social mechanisms of communication, law, and policy serve to stabilize and maintain the use of racial categories.

Sundstrom's "force from below" highlights the way in which a social identity provides resources for self-understanding and motivation (a point also elaborated by Appiah). Ian Hacking has called this "the looping effect" (1995) and argued that it explains an important range of human behavior. Consider the social status or identity of being a college student. In a particular social context, describing oneself in this way has several consequences, that is, it has a social meaning. In the (temporally and spatially) local social environment where I grew up, being a college student involved living away from home, enrolling (typically full-time) in a college, and working in a temporary job during the summer. It also meant very casual dress and certain styles of socializing. Thinking of myself as a college student provided a framework of expectations for how I should spend my time. Later, when I began to think of myself as a teacher, the possibilities for action changed. Accepting a social identity thus changes behavior, and this explains how and why behavior changes as labels become available and widely known. And, of course, not all such identities are fully voluntary. During the Jim Crow era of US history, or South Africa under apartheid, being labeled as "Black" entailed a wide variety of expectations. On pain of various punishments and sanctions, those labeled "Black" had frameworks of expected actions, even if they were actively working to change what it meant to be Black in those times and places.

Sundstrom characterizes lateral forces in terms of norms. This encompasses informal expectations about how one ought to behave, institutional polices or rules, as well as laws. (In Chapter 9 we will explore norms and their role in the social sciences.) In the case of the identity of being a student, the lateral forces were primarily informal: I should go to class, I should talk philosophy in the pub. By contrast, being Black in the early 20th-century US was circumscribed by a wide range of formal laws of segregation, institutional rules and policies, as well as informal norms and expectations. These provide both rewards and sanctions for the behavior conforming to the social identity, and thereby reinforce and circumscribe the identity.

Mallon (2016) emphasizes the way in which these social mechanisms can work together and reinforce each other to make the social identity resistant to change. The laws constituting the "Jim Crow" system of racial segregation in the US relied on the idea of race propounded by 19th-century scientists. Many were passed as public health measures, based on (now debunked) scientific ideas about the propensity of Blacks to carry disease. The social processes that made it possible for racial labels to be widely circulated and accepted with a specific descriptive content (the force from above) thus also worked to support the lateral forces of segregationist laws and policies. These in turn influenced the social meaning of

"Black" at this time in US history (and it differed in different parts of the US). Hence, understanding oneself as "Black" (the force from below) came to influence the possible actions one might undertake in ways that were directly related to the lateral forces. Mallon suggests that these social mechanisms reinforce each other to the point that, were one lost, the others would compensate, and the social kind would remain.

The realist, then, concludes that social mechanisms or forces *can* create the context in which a social identity, status, or role becomes a social kind, analogous to a natural kind. Note that the realist does not make the blanket pronouncement that race is real. Race is a social identity, and in some times and places, the social mechanisms are such as to raise it to the level of a social kind. But not all social identities are supported by sufficiently robust mechanisms to constitute social kinds. For example, the identities of being a "jazz musician" or "*Dungeons and Dragons enthusiast*" provide very thin resources for thinking about oneself, are only weakly supported by social expectations, and are not subject to institutional rules or laws (at least in my community, now—things could change). Realists about race would argue that the social context of race—particularly being Black and White, but perhaps some others as well—in the US is very different, and as a result, race is real in the US now, and has been at least since the early 19th century.

What is at stake between realists and nominalists about race is whether race should figure in causal generalizations and whether it supports inductive inference. Recall that this was the central difference between natural and nominal kinds. Social kinds, we have seen the realist argue, have a structure like natural kinds: a body of social, not natural, mechanisms work to distinguish one group of people from another within a community. Once distinguished, being a member of this kind has consequences. It will be possible to generalize about the effects of being Black in the US, e.g., that having the social status of being Black in the US results in lower occupational status than being White. Realists about race are thus committed to the further claim that having a race supports robust causal generalizations and explanations. The nominalist doubts this further claim. As a reductionist, the nominalist about race holds that any explanatory power attributed to race is really working at the lower level: individual acts of discrimination, particular enforcement of the laws, socioeconomic status, and so on.

Realists and nominalists about race (in the US) agree that there is a large body of research establishing correlations between being labeled as "Black" and a host of disadvantageous social outcomes, including income, wealth, education, health, environmental risk, and incarceration. Their dispute concerns whether these outcomes are caused by race (considered as a real social kind) or whether they are best explained by several underlying factors. Paul Holland (2008), for example, argues that race itself is not a causal variable. Rather, when racial variables emerge as correlated with different social outcomes, the racial variables are capturing different experiences of people categorized in different ways, that is, they capture the effects of racial discrimination. Thus, while it may seem from such research that there is a correlation between race and social outcomes, other factors are causative.

Responding to Holland's nominalist interpretation, Kincaid (2018) argues that it is the result of adopting impoverished methods. It may be true that treating race as a variable in a multiple regression analysis will capture only current racism. But discriminatory treatment in the past has produced current differences in the other variables of the analysis. For example, in the 19th century, the United States government passed several "Homestead Acts" that gave free land to citizens. Blacks were initially not eligible, and later discrimination prevented their applications even when such applications were legal. As a result of this and other sorts of historical discrimination in land acquisition, there is now a significant difference in land ownership between Blacks and Whites. Land ownership is an important source of wealth. So, in a regression analysis, wealth may appear as a much more influential variable. But the difference in race has already been incorporated into the measure of wealth. The model is too simple to capture the effects of race. Kincaid argues that more sophisticated causal models, specifically those that capture the historical influence of discrimination, do show that race has a strong effect on social outcomes.

In reply to realist arguments like Kincaid's, Kareem Khalifa and Richard Lauer (2021) have argued that the empirical success of appeal to race as a real social kind is not so clearly assured. The realist, they argue, is not just committed to the explanatory success of race as a variable. The realist holds that race is real partly because it is constructed in a particular way. The construction described earlier appealed to what Sundstrom called "forces" and proposed that, acting on individuals, they constituted the social kind "race" in the way that the natural kind "tiger" is constituted by evolutionary and genetic mechanisms acting on specific organisms. Khalifa and Lauer point out that there have been no social scientific studies showing that the effects of race arise from the combination of mechanisms proposed to constitute the social kind. By contrast, with natural kinds, numerous studies connect the constituents (e.g., the tiger's genes) with macro-level outcomes. So, the realist is not entitled to conclude—as Kincaid does—that contemporary social science supports racial realism.

Both Kincaid's own conclusion that better models are needed to properly show the causal consequences of race (conceived realistically), and Khalifa and Lauer's argument, point to the conclusion that the crucial studies simply have not yet been done to support the racial realist's second commitment. The realist's commitment thus seems to be a kind of promissory note that the social sciences need to redeem. Doing so will depend on social scientists working through the differences between racial nominalism and racial realism and designing studies that will refine their conceptualizations of race.

Social Construction and the Reflexive Character of the Social Sciences

Nominalists and realists about social constructions agree that there is a dynamic relationship between behavior and the labels for social identities and social roles. This dynamic relationship has an interesting consequence for the character of the social sciences. As the social sciences find ways of describing their subjects, the subjects, in turn, adopt the descriptions as a basis for understanding themselves. As they do so, their behavior changes, and this further alters the basis of the social scientific description. In an important sense, then, the phenomena of the social sciences are always just out of reach.

The self-conscious adoption of (or resistance to) social scientific descriptions by the subjects of the social sciences differentiates the social from the natural sciences. The point is not simply that observation requires interaction with what is observed and thereby alters it; this is true in the natural sciences as well. The looping effect is a result of the self-interpreting capacity of human subjects. The social sciences must contend with the fact that their subjects may be aware of the theories used to explain their behavior. Any kind of social description can potentially be folded back into social reality. The social sciences do not merely alter their objects of study, they contribute to their creation. This reflexive character of social science has been used to argue that the social sciences are different from the natural sciences in other ways. Taylor (1973 [1967]) argued that prediction is a hopeless goal for the social sciences, and Giddens (1984) argued that there are no laws in the social sciences.

There is a further consequence of the reflexive character of social inquiry that brings us back to the discussion of the value-laden character of the social sciences. In Section 2.3, we encountered the argument that interpretation is political insofar as it takes a stand on the meaning of social events, and such meanings may reinforce or undermine existing power structures. The earlier arguments for the looping effect push this point further. As Anthony Giddens concluded:

> Every generalization or form of study that is concerned with an existing society constitutes a potential intervention within that society: and this leads through to the tasks and aims of sociology as critical theory.
>
> (Giddens 1979, 245)

Every generalization of the social sciences is a potential intervention in the sense that the descriptions can be adopted by the subjects. To study a society is, potentially, to change it through augmenting the subjects' resources for understanding their experiences and accounting for their actions. Giddens's sense of "critical theory" is thus somewhat broader than that discussed in Section 2.3. Social scientists are agents for social change whether they want to be or not. Yet, while social scientists ought to aim at beneficial outcomes for their subjects, looping effects are not easily predictable or controllable. And if they cannot be predicted, then it is hard to hold social scientists responsible for them.

Perhaps the moral is more practical: social scientists need to be aware of the effects that their activities of data gathering, analysis, and theorizing (or interpretation) can and do have on the society under investigation. Even if looping effects cannot be precisely predicted, they can be observed and to some extent anticipated. Whatever we ultimately make of the idea of objectivity, social scientific objectivity should not involve the pretense that social scientific practices are invisible. For better or worse, the social sciences are part of the process of social change.

8.4. Wrap Up

Chapter Summary

This chapter has focused on the social construction of race, particularly being Black in the US, but the issue is general, applying to all social identities and statuses. Being a teacher, a nurse, or a member of parliament are all social constructs. While eliminativism might not be tempting about a social role like being a teacher, it makes a difference both scientifically and philosophically whether one is a realist or a nominalist about it. The social status of having a race in the US is particularly interesting because of its origin in 19th-century social sciences and the economic and political context of slavery and colonialism. But many societies have had hierarchical social categories, such as caste or class, and these are often thought to be natural facts about humans. The arguments in this chapter thus have broad applicability.

This chapter has looked at social constructions through the lens of metaphysical reduction. It is uncontroversial that social identities and statuses are the products of the way we think about, talk about, and treat each other. They are thus social constructions in an unsurprising sense. The issue for the philosophy of social science is whether social identities and statuses have an explanatory role. We have surveyed three responses to this question. Eliminativism and nominalism are both reductionist about social identities and statuses, while realism is anti-reductionist.

Eliminativism is attractive when the social identity or status in question is, like race, both widely taken to be a natural kind and when the deployment of the identity has politically or morally troubling consequences. Showing that race is a social construction reduced the purported natural kind of race to an underlying body of social activities. The eliminativist takes such a reduction to show that the concept of race is empty. Addressing the morally problematic ways in which race has figured in society is a matter of political struggle. Eliminativists argue that getting rid of the idea of race entirely, at least in the sciences if not in the popular vocabulary, contributes to the moral and political goal of rectifying racial discrimination and oppression. Nominalists and realists agree with the eliminativist and recognize the moral and political trouble with racial (and other social) hierarchies. But they disagree with the eliminativist by holding that in order to identify and ameliorate the social problems caused by racism, social scientists must use the concept of race.

Nominalists, like the eliminativists, take a reductionist stance toward race. They treat it as a nominal kind: a term that collects a group of people, not because they have something in common, but because we have an interest in grouping them. Any explanatory power that race might have in the social sciences lies in the underlying real properties, not in race itself. The realist disagrees with the nominalist (and the eliminativist) by denying the metaphysical reduction they propose. To do so, the realist relies on two claims. First, the realist must show that race is a social kind. This means that the social mechanisms that underpin the social identity or status of race (at a particular time and place) are sufficiently robust to be analogous to the homeostatic mechanisms that unify natural kinds. Second, the realist must show that, as constructed, using race in social scientific inquiry provides explanations that go beyond those that only use underlying social practices and properties, such as socio-economic status or discrimination.

The debate over the reality of race thus has important consequences for both social scientific practice and for our political goals of addressing social injustices. Whether race can be reduced to other facets of society influences the kind of explanation offered in the social sciences. And different explanations lead to different ways of intervening on the social problems we seek to rectify. Since both the social problems and the social sciences are complex, we can expect the reality of race to continue to be subject to a lively debate.

Discussion Questions

1. What is the difference between race and ethnicity? Is there a difference? How would nominalists and realists respond to these questions?

2. What are some other examples of social roles besides race that fit Sundstrom's three forces? How are they similar to or different from race?

3. This chapter has focused on being Black in the US. Do other similar identities and statuses in the US, like being Asian or Hispanic, fit the realist or nominalist analysis? What about racial or ethnic identifications in other countries— are they similar or different? How should we think about "mixed race" as an identity?

4. Sophisticated social constructivists, like Appiah or Sundstrom, emphasize the way that labels for social identities are taken up and influence the behavior of those labeled. But labels for social identities and statuses are often imposed on people against their will, and they are actively resisted. What does this mean for the social construction of these identities? What does it mean for the account of social construction presented in Section 8.3?

5. Find a social scientific study where race is used in its generalizations or explanations, such as studies of segregation, educational attainment, or occupational opportunities as determined by race. What does "race" mean for these social scientists? Can their explanations be interpreted in nominalist terms, or does the appeal to race have explanatory power of its own?

6. Find several studies where race is used in its generalizations or explanations, as in question #5, but look at how they measure or identify race. You will quickly find that the number of races and the way they are named or clustered differs among different studies. What consequences does this have for the dispute between the nominalists and the realists?

Further Reading

Hannaford's *Race: The History of an Idea in the West* (1996) provides a comprehensive and fascinating account of race and racism in Europe. Zack's *Philosophy of Science and Race* (2002) also provides a historical perspective which emphasizes the role of the social sciences in creating the biological conception of race. Risjord (2007) is a detailed case study of Boas's deconstruction of the concept of race with an eye toward the philosophical issues.

Appiah's racial nominalism is articulated in his "How to Decide If Races Exist" (2006), and Sundstrom replies in "'Racial' Nominalism" (2002b). The discussion of realism in this chapter generally follows Mallon's lead in *Constructing Human Kinds* (2016). The chapter did not touch on the cognitive mechanisms that Mallon emphasizes, which are succinctly presented in Mallon and Kelly (2012). Other realist arguments are found in Root, "How We Divide the World" (2000); Sundstrom, "Race as a Human Kind" (2002a); Dupré, "Human Kinds and Biological Kinds" (2004); and Kincaid "Debating the Reality of Race, Caste, and Ethnicity" (2018). Hacking's "The Looping Effects of Human Kinds" (1995) is a succinct presentation of this fertile concept. Tsou (2020) critiques Mallon's arguments for social kinds.

Zuberi and Bonilla-Silva's *White Logic, White Methods* (2008) has an extended discussion of race in sociology and its methodological implications. The philosophical debate about whether realism is supported by contemporary social science is discussed in Sundstrom (2003), Kincaid (2018), Mallon (2018), and Khalifa and Lauer (2021). In a series of important essays, Spencer (2012, 2014, 2019) has drawn on contemporary biology to unpack, challenge, and ultimately defend conceptions of biological racial realism. While his view has evolved toward "radical pluralism" (2019), the earlier argument (2014) that the US government's racial categories correspond to biologically identifiable difference is particularly important for the social scientific questions about how race is to be measured.

9　Social Norms

Norms pervade the social world. States have laws, universities have regulations, and clubs have rules. Some codes of conduct are informal; as Captain Barbossa said, they're more what you'd call "guidelines" than actual rules. Others are so implicit that it takes violations to expose them: try keeping your eyes closed during a conversation. Social scientists routinely appeal to norms in their accounts. In the examples of social scientific research we have discussed already, norms have often played a role in the explanation. Goldstein invoked norms to explain why people follow their church leaders and join a boycott. The captain of HMS *Camperdown* would not turn in a wider circle because it violated a "rule of the road." Invoking norms in social explanation raises interesting questions. Why do people follow norms? Is it rational self-interest, habit, or something else? And what are "norms"? Do they exist over and above individual action, or are they somehow the product of belief, attitude, or action?

In philosophy, questions about the character and roots of normativity have traditionally been the domain of ethics. In the social sciences, the questions concern social norms, which are *prima facie* different. "Don't kill" (a moral norm) and "Place the fork on the left side of the plate" (a social norm) are both norms in the sense that they are prescriptive. They say what *ought* to be done. Yet there are many differences between moral norms and social norms. If you've had a class in ethics, you probably studied utilitarianism and deontology. These are two prominent views about the justification of moral norms. "Shake hands with your right hand" seems an unlikely candidate for justification by the greatest good (utilitarianism) or demands of rationality (deontology). Moral norms thus seem to have a deeper, perhaps more universal, justification. Social norms are also more variable. In some places people queue for the bus, while in others it is a mad scramble; some eat with forks, others with chopsticks. In the philosophy of social science, the paradigmatic examples of norms are the local rules of particular groups. While examples of moral norms are not the focus of the philosophy of social science, the distinctions among kinds of norms are an important topic.

The appeal to norms in social scientific theories raises issues of reductionism and naturalism. Norms are a kind of social phenomenon which seems particularly resistant to individualistic reduction. Norms of all sorts make demands on individual action. They sometimes require us to act against our self-interest.

DOI: 10.4324/9781003207795-9

For both explanatory and ontological individualists, then, accounting for the character of norms and their relationship to individual action is a crucial problem. With respect to naturalism, we have already seen how appeals to rules and rationality were used to draw a line between the social and natural sciences. Whether norms can figure in theories and explanations that are like those of the natural sciences depends in part on how normativity is understood. And if normativity cannot be fit into a fully causal picture of the world, metaphysical naturalism would fail.

9.1. Disenchanting the Social World

"Sociology begins by disenchanting the world," wrote Alvin Gouldner, "and it proceeds by disenchanting itself" (1968, 103). Here, "disenchantment" means demystifying appeals to norms and values by setting them in an explanatory theoretical framework. The image Gouldner is contemplating, then, is a value-free science of a value-free world. As we have already noted, social scientific research often appeals to values, norms, or rules in its explanations. If the social sciences are to "disenchant the world," they will need some sort of reduction or naturalization of values. One of the fundamental questions of this chapter, then, is whether social norms can be reduced or naturalized.

Is and Ought

Philosophers have often argued that the reduction of norms or values to facts is logically impossible. The formulation of the argument is often attributed to Hume in the *Treatise of Human Nature* (1978 [1740], 469). Descriptions, Hume argues, tell us something about what *is*. There is a significant difference in meaning between a statement of what *is* and a statement of what *ought to be*. A description can be true while the corresponding normative statement is not accurate. At a particular school, perhaps many students cheat. And yet there is no norm "we ought to cheat" at the school; indeed, their norm is quite the opposite. Therefore, in an argument about what ought to be, there can be no deduction from descriptive premises to a normative conclusion. If reduction is understood as a deduction of one theory from another, then no theory which included ought-statements could be reduced to a purely descriptive theory.

G. E. Moore provided another argument against any reductive naturalization of value (Moore 1993 [1903]). Moore was criticizing philosophical views which attempted to define values by features of the natural world. For example, some utilitarians identify right actions with those that produce the greatest net pleasure. Whether someone feels pleasure is a psychological or biological fact. Moore's challenge to this proposed definition of moral value is to ask, "Is pleasure *good*?" If this question makes sense, then the purported definition has not captured its target value. Something must have been left out. Moore argued that the question "Is *X* good?" always makes sense whenever a naturalistic description (*X*) is proposed.

Therefore, Moore concluded, values must be non-natural in the sense of not being part of the material and causal world.

To see how these philosophical arguments are relevant to the questions about normativity in the social sciences, let us consider two examples of norms in the social scientific theory. First, consider the Theory of Planned Behavior, a social-psychological theory which is widely used in the behavioral sciences. This theory is similar to the accounts of intentional action discussed in Chapter 5, where an intention is understood as the combination of beliefs and attitudes. Interestingly, the analysis of intention also includes a "subjective norm," which is "the perceived social pressure to perform or not to perform the behavior" (Ajzen 1991, 188). The Theory of Planned Behavior thus tries to include sensitivity to social norms as part of the cause of action. As a second example, consider the following proposal for a definition of social norms: "Social norms are shared ways of thinking, feeling, desiring, deciding, and acting which are observable in regularly repeated behaviors" (Critto 1999, 1). These theories answer two of the primary social scientific questions about norms. The Theory of Planned Behavior addresses the question "What is the relationship between norms and action?" It answers this question by treating norms as something represented in each individual's mind. Critto's definition, on the other hand provides a conceptualization of what norms are. It defines norms in terms of regularities. The definitions are both naturalistic and reductionist.

With the arguments of Hume and Moore in the background, one might contend that neither Azjen nor Critto succeed in naturalizing or reducing norms. In the Theory of Planned Behavior, the "norm" is nothing more than a perception of social pressure. It is a belief about what others expect. As such, it can say nothing about what the agent *ought* to do. When a person acts, according to the theory, beliefs about others' expectations are among their reasons. But the person is not thereby acting because they *ought* to do so; the person is not following a rule. Critto's definition of social norms suffers from a similar problem. It directly identifies what the agents *ought* to do with their actual patterns of behavior. The whole point of a norm is that actions or beliefs can be mistaken. An anti-reductionist will conclude that insofar as social scientific theories give us only descriptions of the agent's cognitive states or patterns of action, they will fail to capture normativity.

Normativism

The *normativist* believes that an adequate account of the social world must include norms. Normativists conclude from arguments like Hume's and Moore's that the social sciences should not be purely descriptive. The social sciences must not just describe patterns of belief or behavior; they must include genuine normativity in their theories. We have already encountered many normativist views in this book. In general, normativists hold that the social sciences should not be value-neutral, in the sense discussed in Section 2.3. Rather, social science requires substantial commitment to values, norms, and rules. These might figure in interpretations of communities where the interpreter's thick descriptions refer to conventions and social norms. Or the norms might be deeper and more universal, such as moral norms or norms of rationality. We encountered this deeper sort of commitment in Section 5.1, where Winch and Davidson argued that beliefs and attitudes explain action because they make it instrumentally rational. The social scientist explains action by showing what the agent *ought* to do in light of their beliefs and goals. We saw a similar commitment to norms of inferential rationality in Section 4.2, where Hollis argued that interpretation required a bridgehead of true and rational belief. All these views hold that, in some way, social science requires appeal to what subjects *ought* to do.

Normativism entails that the social sciences are deeply different from the natural sciences, and in this epistemological sense, normativism is anti-naturalistic. The point of the arguments about the role of rationality in the social sciences was to distinguish social understanding from natural scientific explanation. Insofar as the natural sciences study mere objects, not subjects who can feel the force of a rule, the natural sciences are descriptive. If no description can capture a norm, the normativist must conclude that the social sciences have different forms of theorizing (e.g., interpretation) based on different forms of evidence (e.g., qualitative methods). Normativists also tend to be anti-naturalistic in the metaphysical sense. One conclusion to draw from arguments like Hume's and Moore's is that values, norms, rules, and so on are ontologically different from any natural fact. Norms are not part of the natural realm, and the force of a rule is not the force of a cause. Insofar as the social world must include norms, some normativists conclude, the social world is distinct from the natural world.

Good Bad Theories

Normativists contend that many social phenomena are impossible to describe without normative language. Consider, for example, gift exchange. Since Marcel Mauss's seminal work (Mauss 2000 [1925]), gift exchange has been conceptualized in terms of mutual obligations. Gifts have consequences. In many times and places, to receive a gift is to incur obligations to reciprocate. A normativist will point out that the very idea of a gift is thus a thick normative concept. Any attempt to describe gift-giving without mentioning the network of obligations will seriously distort the phenomenon.

In *Explaining the Normative* (2010), Stephen Turner confronts the normativist claim that appeal to norms is indispensible in the social sciences. Turner agrees that Mauss's description invokes normative language, but asks: is this description the only one possible? Turner points out that Mauss himself describes the phenomenon in two ways. Mauss discusses the Maori concept of *hau*, in terms of which the Maori conceptualize gifts. In one characterization, Mauss writes in the voice of an imaginary Maori:

> Suppose you have some particular object, *taonga*, and you give it to me. . . . Now, I give this thing to a third person who after a time decides to give me something in

repayment for it (*utu*), and he makes me a present of something (*taonga*). Now this *taonga* I received from him is the spirit (*hau*) of the *taonga* I received from you and passed on to him. The *taonga* which I receive on account of the *taonga* that came from you, I must return to you. It would not be right on my part to keep these *taonga* whether they were desirable or not. I must give them to you since they are the *hau* of the *taonga* which you gave me. If I were to keep this second *taonga* for myself I might become ill or even die.

(Mauss 2000 [1925], 8–9)

In his second description, Mauss goes on to say that the Maori *believe* that gifts are animated by the spiritual power of *hau*. After all, Mauss does not believe that *hau* exists. He must therefore redescribe the phenomenon in terms that do not commit him to the existence of spiritual powers within gifts, so he invokes beliefs about *hau* to explain the behavior, not real spiritual powers. By transforming the normative characterization of gift-giving into a description of beliefs, Mauss can explain it.

The social sciences, on Turner's view, appeal to beliefs and other representations of normativity, but they are not committed to the existence of real norms or obligations. Having such beliefs helps humans coordinate their behavior. Indeed, it is likely that beliefs about rules, conventions, and moral obligations are necessary for human societies. In this sense, normativity is ineliminable from the social sciences. But the social sciences need not be committed to the truth of normative beliefs or other representations. The beliefs coordinate behavior whether or not they are true. Representations of normativity, whether those of the subjects (concepts like *hau*) or by the social scientist (concepts like *rule*), are what Turner calls "Good Bad Theories." They are bad theories in the sense that they are false, but good theories in the sense that believing them facilitates social interaction.

On Turner's naturalization of social norms, it is perfectly legitimate to treat norms after the fashion of the Theory of Planned Behavior. Norms are treated as representations and thereby rendered explanatory. As Turner sets up the problem, it is a matter of comparing normative explanations with naturalized explanations. Resolving the dispute between normativism and naturalism, then, turns on which sort of explanation is more successful. If the best social scientific re-descriptions and explanations fail to be adequate, and if normativist accounts explain better, then we would have to decide in favor of normativism. On the other hand, naturalism wins if its reconceptualization of norms and accompanying explanations are superior. This means that to adjudicate the issue of naturalism and normativity, we need to look more closely at how conventions and social norms have been analyzed, and at the sort of explanations they support.

Two broad traditions of social scientific explanation have been of special interest to philosophers interested in normativity. One tries to use the resources of game theory and decision theory to show how norms arise out of individual action. They generally treat norms as equilibria of strategic games. These will be the subject of Section 9.2. An alternative, to be explored in Section 9.3, is to analyze norms in terms of "practices." Practice theory looks back to Wittgenstein's reflections on rule-following in the *Philosophical Investigations* (1953) and was developed in anthropology by Pierre Bourdieu and in sociology by Anthony Giddens. As we will see, naturalist and reductionist programs face interesting challenges when they encounter normativity.

9.2. Norms and Rational Choices

Rational choice theory provides a powerful set of tools for explaining how stable patterns of social interaction arise out of individually rational choices. From this perspective, it is tempting to adopt individualism and treat all patterns of social interaction as the product of individual choices. Stable patterns of behavior emerge either as aggregate individual rational choices or as equilibria in strategic interactions. The challenge for this austere view is that some phenomena are not obviously just game-theoretic equilibria. There are two kinds of situation which seem to call for norms *in addition to* individually rational choice.

First, strategic interactions with multiple equilibria are apparently resolved with norms. The Inside/Outside game (Figure 5.8) has two equilibria, and players are indifferent between them. As long one ship circles to the inside while the other circles to the outside, all is well. Nothing in the strategic situation, however, determines which of the two equilibria the players will settle upon, and nothing guarantees that they will continue in the same way next time. Coordination problems like these are naturally solved by *conventions*. Many patterns of social interaction can be explained as conventions in this sense—rules of the road, shaking hands, appropriate dress, technological standards, even signaling conventions.

The second sort of situation involves mixed-motive games like the prisoner's dilemma (Figure 5.5). In these interactions, defecting has the highest expected payoff. *Social norms* can solve this problem, as we saw in the discussion of Goldstone's explanation of revolutions (Section 6.1) and Richerson and Boyd's account of the evolution of cooperation (Section 6.4). Social norms require sacrifice in the sense that an individual does not get the highest available payoff, and in this way, they are different from conventions. Notice that both social norms and conventions appear to be imposed from the outside of the game. Does this mean that rational choice theory cannot account for norms? Or can we use the resources of rational choice theory to explain how conventions and social norms emerge and why people choose to follow them? We will first consider whether conventions can be understood in game-theoretic terms and then turn to social norms.

Conventions

Conventions seem to have a couple of distinctive features. First, conventions are arbitrary. The British Navy had a convention that ships always pass on the port side, but it could just as well be the other way around. Conventions are also patterns or regularities. If ships pass each other sometimes on the port side and sometimes on the starboard side, then they have no convention. Finally, while conventions might be verbally articulated and explicitly adopted, they need not be. Conventions emerge in groups that are too large or anonymous to facilitate direct communication. Or perhaps communication is impossible: when our telephone conversation is cut off, we can't both call at the same time and we can't communicate. In situations like these, conventions seem to play an important role.

From the perspective of game theory, conventions can be modeled as game with two or more Nash equilibria. We have seen two such games already, Inside/Outside (Figure 5.8) and Stag Hunt (Figure 5.9). In these situations, our choices need to be coordinated, but payoffs of the game will not do the job alone. As a first pass at characterizing a convention, then, we might suppose that a convention is a common habit. It is a pattern of behavior whereby most people choose the same Nash equilibrium of a coordination problem.

While it is attractively simple, it won't do to treat conventions as aggregated habits. For example, in classrooms where there are no assigned seats, students often choose the same desk for every class. Finding a seat in a classroom is a coordination problem that is solved more-or-less by chance on the first day. After that, everyone might simply have the habit of sitting in the same place. While this would satisfy our initial characterization of a convention, it is a rather anemic convention. It is unlike more robust examples of conventions, such as shaking hands with the right hand or placing the fork to the left of the plate. In the classroom, each student sits in a certain seat because of an individual habit. I shake hands with my right hand because it is a convention, not just because I am in the habit of doing so. Full-blooded conventions should establish something like rules, and individuals should be acting *because* of the convention.

In an early and important application of game theory to the philosophical questions of social ontology, David Lewis strengthened the simple conception of a convention as a pattern of behavior. He suggested that regularities of behavior become conventions when there is a system of mutual expectations in place. He defined a convention as:

> A regularity R in the behavior of members of a population P when they are agents in a recurrent situation S is a *convention* if and only if, in any instance of S among members of P,

(1) everyone conforms to R;
(2) everyone expects everyone else to conform to R;
(3) everyone prefers to conform to R on the condition that the others do, since S is a coordination problem and uniformity to R is a coordination equilibrium in S.

(Lewis 1969, 42)

Conditions (2) and (3) make it instrumentally rational to follow the regularity once it is established. Each person wants to conform if the others do. And if the convention is in place, then each person also believes that the others will conform. So, each person is acting for a reason, and that reason includes recognition of the convention. Using this definition, we can distinguish between classrooms where everyone sits in the same place out of habit and those where there is a convention to sit in the same place. In the former, each person may satisfy only (1) and (2), and then choose an empty seat. The members of the class recognize the pattern in this case, but it is not their reason for acting. When the members of the class also have the preference to conform to the regularity on the condition that the others do too (3), a convention is in place. Notice also that once a convention exists, it is more stable than a mere aggregation of choices. Everyone in the group conditionally prefers to follow the convention. So if the regularity is not disrupted, members of the group will continue to conform.

Lewis's definition requires that a regularity is already in place. How could conventions get started? We might begin by a verbal agreement, but as we have already noticed, conventions can also get started in the absence of communication. Thomas Schelling suggested that *salience* can be the source of convention (Schelling 1960). Salience is sometimes a matter of perceptual bias or vividness. For example, many college campuses have a statue or large clock which serves as a conventional meeting place. Because they are eye-catching and memorable, these landmarks are salient coordination equilibria. Past practice is another way to make a coordination equilibrium salient. If we found each other by the clock tower last time we met, we have a reason to do so again next time. A random or accidental event that puts the parties into a Nash equilibrium can make a strategy salient.

Lewis's account explains how salience can be the seed of a rational response to coordination problems and, hence, how conventions can arise through the exercise of rationality. If we are separated on campus and we need to reunite, each of us will have to anticipate the other's reasoning. I know that you want to meet me, so I will go where you expect me to be. But the situation is symmetrical: you know that I want to meet you, so you will go where I expect you to be. We need a way into our circle of interlocking expectations, and the salience of something like the clock tower gives us a place to start. If I expect you to notice the clock tower, and I expect you to notice that *I noticed it too*, then I have a reason to go there. Existing regularities are also excellent sources of salience. The mere fact that others often meet at the clock tower can be a starting point for our reasoning too. Lewis's account thus shows how we can use the resources of rational choice theory to explain the origin and persistence of conventions. Conventions, of course, are not fully rational— salience is a non-rational push needed to get the convention started. Nonetheless, Lewis's work shows how social phenomena can arise through rational choices.

Conventionality and Normativity

Lewis's account of convention reduces conventions to regularities, and the reduction is both ontological and explanatory. A convention, for Lewis, is nothing but a regularity of behavior brought about by the right sort of mutual expectations and common knowledge. Any explanatory force that a custom might have is carried entirely by intentions of the individuals. When people conventionally queue for the bus, it is because everyone has the beliefs and expectations described in Lewis's definition. Conventions are a species of norm, so has Lewis succeeded in reducing "ought" to "is"? No, not at all: Lewis's account of convention depends on the instrumental rationality of the individual agents. Insofar as there is normativity to a convention, one ought to conform because it is the rational thing to do. Lewis's account is therefore reductive in the sense that it explains a social phenomenon (convention) entirely in individualistic terms (beliefs and preferences). It is not fully naturalistic, however, because it does not show how the normativity of rational action can be assimilated into a causal picture of the world. It simply reduces one sort of norm (the convention) to another (instrumental rationality).

Even if Lewis's account is normative, some have argued that it does not fully capture the normativity of convention. Conventions, like other sorts of norm, provide a ground for assessing the correctness of behavior. Table manners are an interesting sort of convention. In some communities, one is criticized for belching after a meal; in other places it expresses pleasure and satisfaction. As children are constantly made aware, people are criticized for bad manners. And manners are bad when they do not conform to the local conventions. Because Lewis's conventions are regularities, it is not clear how they make some actions correct and others mistaken. One ought to follow a convention, on Lewis's account, because it is individually rational to do so. If a person fails to follow a Lewis convention, then, he or she is not to be criticized for failing to conform to the regularity. The person has merely failed to act in their own interest. As Margret Gilbert put the point, Lewis's account does not capture the "ought" that is appropriate to convention, as opposed to the "ought" of self-interest or practical rationality (Gilbert 2008).

Another reason why Lewis's analysis does not seem to capture the normativity of convention is that he ties conventions to coordination problems. With apologies to both my mother and my children, I want to ask: is it *really* necessary that I eat my mashed potatoes with a fork rather than with my fingers? Why should I coordinate with my neighbor about table manners? Table manners do not solve any coordination problem. One might think that table manners play a role in establishing social identities. Andrei Marmor has argued that rules of etiquette or fashion are deeply different from conventions that resolve coordination problems. These conventions *constitute* the practices of which they are part. They are like the rules of games in the way that they create the very activities they regulate. The payoffs are thus internal to the convention: "purpose, point, or value is basically set by the conventions constituting the practice, and it is impossible to specify them independently and antecedently of the conventions themselves" (Marmor 1996, 366). Lewis's conventions, by contrast, only arise because the payoffs are arranged in a particular way, and the payoffs are external to the convention. If this line of argument is correct, then Lewis's conventions capture only a small part of the larger phenomenon of conventional rules or norms.

Lewis's reliance on regularities of behavior gives rise to another argument against his analysis of convention. One of the reasons why reducing an "ought" to an "is" seems impossible is that an obligation may persist even if it is rarely acknowledged. As your mother taught you, something might be *wrong* even if all your friends are doing it. Gilbert argues that it is easy to imagine examples of conventions that do not correspond to regularities of behavior (Gilbert 2008, 8). Suppose the philosophy club adopts a dress code for its formal dinner. Once the philosophy club has voted, the convention is in place. We need not wait and see whether the members conform. Suppose further that after adopting a dress code, they fail to follow it. (Philosophers are not known for their conformist behavior, after all!) One might argue that the convention was in place, but it was not being followed. Conventions, Gilbert concludes, do not need the sort of regularities that Lewis postulates.

The debate over whether conventions require repetition or regularity has been recently enlivened by empirical evidence. Francesco Guala and Luigi Mittone have devised an experimental protocol which seems to show that repeated interaction gives rise to "intrinsic normativity" (Guala and Mittone 2010; Guala 2013). In their experiment, subjects interact with each other only through a computer. Three players simultaneously choose one of two colored buttons (red or blue). They get the payoff only if all three players choose the same color. From the perspective of each player, the strategic situation can be represented this way as the Red/Blue game of Figure 9.1. (Note that because of the symmetry of the game, each of the three players can take the perspective of "self" in Figure 9.1.) The players are told that they will play the game together exactly ten times. They are also told that they payoffs may change, and that if they do change, all players will be told what the new payoffs are. With this sort of setup, players quickly find one or the other equilibrium. With three players, two are guaranteed to choose the same color in the first round. Typically, in the next round the odd person out will conform, and a convention emerges.

In the tenth and last round, the payoffs change. One of the three players is given an incentive to break the convention. Now the game looks like Figure 9.2. If the Lucky Player plays differently than the others, he or she will get a larger payoff and the others get nothing. In other words, one player was given an incentive to deviate from the conventional pattern which emerged in their repeated play. In Guala and Mittone's experiment, only 39% of the participants deviated from the convention.

Red/Blue (Initial Rounds)

Other Two Players

		Red	Blue
		Red	Blue
Self	Red	10, 10	0, 0
	Blue	0, 0	10, 10

Figure 9.1 Red/Blue (Initial Rounds)

Red/Blue (Final Round)

Other Two Players

		Red	Blue
		Red	Blue
The Lucky Player	Red	200, 200	300, 0
	Blue	300, 0	200, 200

Figure 9.2 Red/Blue (Final Round)

This result is troubling from Lewis's point of view, since in this new situation, there is no longer a reason to continue following the convention. For some reason, most of the subjects (61%) continued to follow the convention even when they paid a price to do so. Why?

There are two possible explanations for this result. Subjects might be responding to a norm that is external to the game, such as a norm of fairness. On the other hand, the convention created by repeated play might have its own normative force. To separate these two possibilities, Guala and Mittone devised a game-theoretically identical situation which lacked the feature of repeated play. Subjects in this trial played a single game. It had the same payoffs as the tenth round of the repeated game. However, in this game the players played sequentially. The first player might choose randomly, and the rational choice for the second player would be to conform to that choice. The third player was then in the same situation as the tenth round of the repeated game, except that there was no history of coordination in the group—no convention had been allowed to emerge. If norms of fairness external to the game were inclining individuals to cooperate, then one would expect that the behavior in the one-shot game would be the same as the repeated game. Guala and Mittone found that the results of the single-shot game were the opposite of the repeated game: 68% of the subjects defected (chose the higher payoff) in the one-shot game. The repetition alone apparently motivated people to continue cooperating, even when cooperation was costly. Repeated play, they conclude, "generates an intrinsic normative pressure to conform to the group's conventions" (Guala and Mittone 2010).

Guala and Mittone's results seem to both support and challenge Lewis's account of convention. The results support the idea that conventions require regularities of behavior. This contradicts Gilbert's contention that conventions can exist without regularities. If Gilbert's examples of conventions without corresponding behavioral regularities are possible, then, it is because of the special nature of the agreement in her examples. Clubs have a variety of rules already in place (such as bylaws) which make it possible to establish conventions by fiat. At the same time, Guala and Mittone's results run contrary to Lewis's analysis in other ways. For Lewis, self-interest and only self-interest dictates cooperation. The subjects in Guala and Mittone's experiments seem to feel a compulsion to follow a convention even when doing so is no longer in their self-interest. Lewis's account, then, does not capture the motivational force that conventions seem to possess.

Social Norms

Guala and Mittone's experiment highlights a remarkable feature of human cooperation: we will cooperate even when we could individually benefit from defection. These situations invite explanation by norms. Norms of fairness, honesty, or allegiance to a group, for example, would explain why people cooperate when faced with a prisoner's dilemma. What is the force that these norms possess? A normativist might suggest that it is the "unforced force of the better reason." In other words, doing the right thing is sometimes reason enough to do it. When thinking about norms, however, we must be careful not to assume that norms always result in benefits for the group. Many social norms either have no apparent benefit or are positively harmful. Norms prohibiting homosexuality, for example, provide no benefits for the larger group. Norms promoting bribes and other sorts of corruption can make economies inefficient. One of the puzzles about norms, then, is that they not only go against individual interest, but they may also run contrary to the interests of the larger group. In *The Grammar of Society* (2006), Cristina Bicchieri provided an account of social norms which addresses these questions.

Bicchieri's account of social norms relies on two important points. First, games are partly defined by their payoffs. Therefore, whether a pair of players is facing a prisoner's dilemma, a coordination game, or something else depends on what their preferences are. Second, preferences may be conditional. Lewis's account of convention relied on each person having a preference to conform to the regularity *on the condition that others did*. Lewis's insight was that by making preferences depend on what others do, conventions become part of the motivation to conform. Lewis's account is limited, as we have seen, by its reliance on brute regularities and pure self-interest. By contrast, I follow a social norm partly because others expect me to. This arguably distinguishes rule-following from the self-interested desire to reap the benefits of coordination.

The heart of Bicchieri's conception of a social norm is that when the conditions for preferences are satisfied, the new preferences change the strategic situation. Bicchieri's full definition of a social norm is this (Bicchieri 2006, 11):

> Let R be a behavioral rule for situations of type S, where S can be represented as a mixed-motive game. We say that R is a social norm in a population P if there exists a sufficiently large subset $P_{cf} \subseteq P$ such that, for each individual $i \in P_{cf}$:
>
> *Contingency*: i knows that a rule R exists and applies to situations of type S;
> *Conditional preference*: i prefers to conform to R in situations of type S on the condition that:
>
> (a) *Empirical expectations*: i believes that a sufficiently large subset of P conforms to R in situations of type S;
> and either
> (b) *Normative expectations*: i believes that a sufficiently large subset of P expects i to conform to R in situations of type S;

or

(b') *Normative expectations with sanctions*: i believes that a sufficiently large subset of P expects i to conform to R in situations of type S, prefers i to conform, and may sanction behavior.

When the empirical and normative conditions of the agent's preferences are satisfied, we will say that the norm is *activated*. When a norm is activated for an agent, he or she has new preferences. In particular, the agent now prefers to conform to the rule (R).

Consider, for example, the problem of littering. We all know that we should not litter; this is the "behavioral rule R" that applies to the situation. Keeping public areas clean is a public good problem. Since a clean environment is a non-exclusive good, there is an incentive to free ride. As a result, it can be represented as a prisoner's dilemma (Figure 9.3). Suppose that there is some effort involved in throwing my sandwich wrapper in the trash can. And suppose also that all of us like to see a clean park. This means that the highest utility for me is the situation where I drop my sandwich wrapper on the ground while others pick up (because I get the benefit and pay no costs). The second-best situation is where we both pick up (I get the benefit and pay the cost of picking up). The worst situation is where I pick up and nobody else does (I pay the cost and get no benefit). As with any prisoner's dilemma, we seem doomed to end up in a sub-optimal equilibrium. None of us gets the benefit of a clean park, but we don't pay the costs either.

The situation changes when we have a rule like "Don't litter." Suppose, as Bicchieri's definition requires, that we all know this rule applies to the park. Moreover, suppose that I believe most people will follow the "Don't litter" rule and that most people expect me to follow the rule too. This means that the empirical and normative expectations in Bicchieri's definition have been satisfied. The condition of my conditional preference has been satisfied, so now I *prefer to follow the rule*. The change reorders my preferences, and assuming for the moment that the norm has been activated for the others too, we have a new strategic situation (Figure 9.4). Because I prefer to follow the rule, picking up is the best option. As before, if others litter and I pick up, I pay the cost and get no benefit, making it the worst option for me. If others pick up and I litter, then I get the benefits of free riding. Since I already expect others to follow the rule, the rational option is to pick up.

Clean Up the Park

		Others	
		Pick Up	Litter
Self	Pick Up	2, 2	0, 3
	Litter	3, 0	1, 1

Figure 9.3 Clean Up the Park

Follow the Rules to Clean Up the Park

Others

		Pick Up	Litter
Self	Pick Up	3, 3	0, 2
	Litter	2, 0	1, 1

Figure 9.4 Follow the Rules to Clean Up the Park

On Bicchieri's account, then, norms are literally game changers. Notice how the norms are not external forces that override the game. They are built into agents' preferences so that what seems at first look to be a mixed-motive strategic situation is really a self-reinforcing game like the Assurance Game of Figure 7.1.

Of course, not everyone who learned the song "Clean up, clean up, everybody do your share" follows the rule it invokes. One of the interesting features of Bicchieri's account of social norms is that it explains why norms *aren't* followed, even when we know the rules. The key, again, is the empirical and normative expectations. If I do not have the empirical expectation that people follow the rule under the current circumstances, or if I do not have the normative expectation that others expect me to follow the rule, then my conditional preference will not be triggered. The important social scientific question becomes identifying the conditions under which people come to have their empirical and normative expectations fulfilled. The problem of littering recalls the "broken windows theory" from Section 7.3. The presence of litter in the park may make me think that most people do not clean up after themselves in this place or that they do not expect me to do so. And the norms need not be so specific. The presence of trash in the streets and broken windows may lead me to believe that people in this neighborhood do not have much respect for each other. This may keep me from invoking norms and incline me to behave in a self-interested manner. Bicchieri's view can thus explain why the presence of broken windows might lead to the violation of other norms.

But what if I am mistaken about the people in the neighborhood with broken windows? What if they do, in fact, expect me to pick up my own trash? This possibility is consistent with Bicchieri's account as well—the beliefs which constitute the empirical and normative expectations need not be *true*. This permits Bicchieri to explain how unpopular or inefficient norms can arise and persist. Preferences to follow the rule are triggered when the empirical and normative expectations are satisfied, but again, these beliefs might not be true. If I believe that others follow the rule, and believe they expect me to do so, I will prefer to follow the rule even if I think the rule is harmful or inefficient. Bicchieri suggests that this is how norms of corruption are maintained. Everyone may prefer not to pay a bribe, and even prefer that the practice be discontinued. However, if there is a widespread belief that the bribery norm is followed and that others expect me to follow the norm, the norms of bribery will persist. Moreover, since bribery is relatively private, there might be a widespread misconception about whether the rule is followed. In this case, there could be a rule that exists in a society but that is followed very rarely, if at all. Each person would break the rule privately but continue believing that others expected it to be followed.

At the beginning of this chapter, we noted that there are two central questions about norms in the social sciences: what are social norms? And why do people follow them? Bicchieri's account provides answers to both. On her definition, norms are a kind of regularity. They are not a mere regularity of behavior; they are a more complex regularity of belief and conditional preference. Norms exist, on her view, when a "sufficient" number of people within the population have the relevant empirical and normative expectations. This pattern of expectations explains regularities of behavior, but as we have seen, the social norm can exist even if it is followed rarely. Individuals act in accordance with the demands of the rule because doing so is their favored option. Norm-following is instrumentally rational, and the behavioral patterns which emerge are equilibria of strategic interaction.

9.3. Normativity and Practice

Rational choice accounts of conventions and social norms try to construct norms from individual choices and action. The approaches we have been discussing therefore assume that individual action is logically prior to social norms. In other words, it makes sense to think of human beings acting in the absence of any conventions, rules, or norms. Norms arise when we combine individual actions in the right way. Several philosophers and social scientists in the interpretivist tradition have thought this starting point is a mistake. An action is something done for a *reason*, and reasons already have a normative relationship to the action. If the conclusion of Winch's argument in Section 5.1 is accepted, then the social context determines (at least in part) whether an action is appropriate or reasonable under the circumstances. Hence, there could be no fully intentional action at all unless there already were norms. Interpretivists conclude that any approach to normativity based on rational choice theory is circular—it assumes much of what needs explanation.

An alternative approach to normativity favored by many interpretivists looks to the notion of *practice* to articulate social norms. Practice theory has its roots in Ludwig Wittgenstein's discussion of rule-following in the *Philosophical Investigations* (1953). Winch's reading of Wittgenstein has been particularly influential in the philosophy of the social sciences, and we will take Winch as our starting point for discussion. In the social sciences, practice theory is associated with the work of Pierre Bourdieu and Anthony Giddens. These theorists emphasize the active interplay of agents and social norms. To understand how norms are functioning in a particular social setting, one needs to see how the norms are both maintained by ongoing patterns of action and subverted by particular uses of them. Since all these authors take norms to be related to patterns of activity, the problem noticed in Section 9.1 looms immediately: a simple identity of norms with patterns of behavior collapses "ought" to "is." The challenge accepted by practice theorists is to find some way to reconstitute the ought/is distinction from the ongoing activity patterns of a social group.

Norms and Practices

An account of rules or social norms, according to Winch, must satisfy two conditions: (1) norms must be learnable, and (2) mistakes must be possible. The first condition may seem rather trivial, but it has important consequences. Recall Moore's idea that values are non-natural properties which cannot be identified with any physical or psychological property (Section 7.1). One might ask: how do we know whether something is good if goodness cannot be identified with anything we can sense? Unless we postulate special norm-detectors as part of our psychology (which some philosophers have done!), the learnability of norms means that there must be a close relationship between what people do and what the norms are. This is perhaps the idea behind the definition of norms mentioned in Section 7.1: "Social norms are shared ways of thinking, feeling, desiring, deciding, and acting which are observable in regularly repeated behaviors" (Critto 1999, 1). By observing patterns of acting, a child can learn the norms. Winch's second condition entails that Critto's definition is too broad. Some of the regularities that would satisfy Critto's definition are impossible to violate. Citizens of the US walk on the surface of the earth and don't fly like birds. This is a shared and repeated way of acting. According to Winch, it is not a norm because it is impossible—physically impossible—to make a mistake.

There is a more subtle way in which Critto's definition fails to satisfy Winch's second condition. Imagine it is the case that on the streets of Chicago for a period of time, every single person is carrying a handbag, backpack, or briefcase. While it would be possible to deviate from such a regularity of behavior, it is not possible to make a mistake. A person will not be criticized for failing to carry a briefcase on the streets of Chicago. Mistakes are not just deviations from a regular pattern of behavior; they are deviations which others in the community care about. (Notice that this is a point on which Winch and Bicchieri agree.) The character of the response to a deviation marks the boundary between actions which follow the norm and those which do not. Winch therefore conceives of a norm as a pattern of repeated behavior in a community which is maintained through the attitudes and responses of members of the community. Actions which conform to the rule are met by praise, reward, or attitudes of approval, while deviations are met by criticism, punishment, or attitudes of disapproval. These responses must be included as part of the pattern of action which constitutes the practice.

For a practice theorist, following a norm is a practical ability, a point emphasized by Pierre Bourdieu in his development of these ideas (Bourdieu 1977). Norms need not be articulated as explicit rules. Humans pick up on patterns of action without having to say to themselves "When in conditions X, do Y unless Z" or something of the sort. We recognize the pattern and are sensitive to the subtle cues of approval and disapproval from our fellows. Most of the norms which are interesting for social analysis and thick description are implicit in this way. Explicit norms are formulated in language, but their normative content is provided by the underlying practices. The meaning of an explicit norm or rule is thus subject to negotiation in practice. Whether a particular action "fits" the rule as formulated is determined by how members of the community respond to the new variation in behavior. If a variation is taken as following the rule, then the content of the rule includes the new variation. Bourdieu and Giddens pointed out that the gap between the explicit formulation of a rule and the practice often is exploited by agents for their own ends. Acting in new ways may begin to change the character of the rules, and rules can be used in new ways to justify actions which were previously forbidden. As an example, think of the ways that, prior to their legalization, marriage ceremonies and similar displays of commitment between homosexual couples began to change the normative attitudes of the wider community toward gay marriage.

Problems for Practice Theory

On an analysis like Winch's, norms are a particular kind of regularity in a community. This sort of view is open to several objections. First, a regularity can exist only if there is a determinate set of actions from which the instances of the pattern are drawn. After all, if people in a far-away community behave differently than we do, they are not making mistakes. Practice theories of norms thus seem to require that communities have clear and stable boundaries. But we saw in Section 3.3 arguments which have made anthropologists skeptical that communities have clear boundaries. Consider the norms that govern correct use of words. What is the community which establishes the meaning of English words? English words show up in many far-flung places. For example, Bemba is one of the many languages spoken in Zambia, and "Town Bemba" is a dialect used by speakers who want to sound hip and urbane. Debra Spitulnik documented words like *amaguys*, where the English word *guys* is combined with the Bemba plural marker *ama-* (Spitulnik 1999). Presumably, the community who establishes the correct use of this term would be the Bemba speakers. Yet, they use *guys* because it has a particular English meaning. That is, they use it because it follows the norms of another linguistic community. Dialects like Town Bemba or Spanglish exploit the fluid boundaries of linguistic communities. The same point can be made about the permeable boundaries of cultures, ethnicities, and other sorts of social identities. But if there is no clear boundary to "the" community, then it makes no sense to talk about "the" pattern of practice which constitutes a norm.

Even if the practice theorists could develop a suitable conception of "the community," another, deeper problem looms for the regularity conception of norms. The so-called gerrymandering problem was raised by Saul Kripke (1982). Any rule will legislate what ought to happen in cases which have never occurred. For example, consider mathematical rules. No community will have added every pair of numbers. Suppose that no one has ever added 2 to 123,012,112,354. Now we come to it: what is the sum? It depends on what the rule for addition is. Kripke argued that on a regularity view of practice, the rule could be anything which is consistent with what the community has done *so far*. But there is an indefinitely large number of different rules for addition which agree about past cases but disagree about the next one. There might be two rules that agree about past cases but disagree about future cases; while the first says that 2+123,012,112,354=123,012,112,356, the other says 2+123,012,112,354=7. Since the rules agree about the past cases, nothing in our behavior—nothing in the practice—can distinguish between these two rules. Both are equally correct, given a Winchean conception of rules. The conclusion is quite general. Given any set of actions, there are many incompatible, possible rules that would make those actions correct yet disagree about what ought to be done in a new case. Since any response can be correct if the rules are gerrymandered in this way, it is impossible to make a mistake. On Winch's own criteria, one might argue, practices cannot ground norms.

Two further problems arise from the way that rules are learned, given Winch's conception of a rule. First, rules are supposed to be regularities of practice in the whole community (again, supposing we can help ourselves to that notion). But learners never have systematic access to the whole community. The rules of the Czech language are manifested in patterns that are exhibited by ten million people. But even in a small country like the Czech Republic, no learner ever has this kind of database. A person learns from the regularities in their immediate neighborhood. How can the actions and attitudes of others, perhaps far away, determine what is right and wrong for me if I never encounter these patterns?

Second, Winch's model of learning emphasizes cases of training where both the training and the rules are explicit. Learning the rules of a game, or learning how to add, are paradigmatic examples. Here the learner is *told* the rule, and the teacher judges mistakes. Implicit rules are not learned in this way. Consider, for example, norms about conversational distance. In different places, people have norms about how close to stand in a conversation, how much eye contact to make, and so on. If you have travelled, you know that these differences can be striking. By what process were these norms learned? The root of both problems about learning norms is that Winch conceived norms as regularities to be internalized by the learner. It is not obvious how a learner could have access to enough data or the kind of training which would permit them to learn the norms of their community.

Practices Without Regularities

Proponents of practice theory have responded to the problems of community boundaries and gerrymandering by arguing that both are matters *internal* to the community in question. The criticisms treat community boundaries and patterns of practice as if they were objective facts, independent of the judgments of community members. This is a mistake, argue proponents of practice theory. Whether 2+123,012,112,354=7 is a question to be settled by members of the community. They will make this decision by looking at various examples of addition, rules that have been explicitly formulated, and so on. If this new result is raised a possibility, they will have to judge the best fit of the new move in the old game. There is no fact, external to and independent of this decision-making process which makes their decision correct or incorrect. The problem of boundaries is similar.

Boundaries are drawn from the inside: whether speakers of Town Bemba are part of my language community depends on their responses to me and my responses to them. The critic is thus asking for more determinacy than is necessary.

Arguing that boundaries are drawn and new cases adjudicated from the "inside" of practices seems sensible, but it may not resolve the problems for practice theory. The idea that mathematicians just decide whether $2+123,012,112,354=7$ seems capricious. Moreover, it threatens to collapse the difference between being right and seeming right, which is at the heart of the practice theoretic view of norms. Is *any* decision that the community of mathematicians makes the correct decision? If so, then there is no possibility of a mistake, and we no longer have a genuine norm. If not, then we need something else to serve as the standard for correctness. In either case, practice theory seems doomed.

The source of the trouble is, one might argue, the role assigned to fixed patterns or regularities. The patterns of action in a community are taken to be a standard of comparison. My action is right or wrong, depending on whether it is like or unlike the standard. All four of these problems arise out of taking normativity to be a matter of comparison to a community standard. Contemporary practice theorists such as Joseph Rouse (2007a, b) or Robert Brandom (1994) reject the idea that patterns of past practice make current action right or wrong. Following a rule is not a matter of replicating an existing pattern. Instead, we should think of norms as created and maintained by the attitudes of individuals. Brandom calls them "normative attitudes," signaling that this form of practice theory will not try to reduce normativity to something non-normative. The normative attitudes are manifested by responses to another's action, by taking it as being correct or incorrect.

On this version of practice theory, what Rouse calls "normative practice theory" (2007a, b), the emphasis is on the interaction and relationships among individuals. While the attitudes are fundamental, the attitude of taking an action to be permitted (or not) may result in some sort of action. It may result in a complement, for instance. Brandom argued that this response to the action is itself correct or incorrect, and its correctness is constituted by attitudes others take toward the respondent. A practice, then, is not a set of past actions but an interlocking set of future attitudes toward a current action. It is not up to me whether my action follows a rule. It is up to the open-ended set of others who will judge my action and judge those who judge me. Where Winch's view is backward-looking, the practice theory of Rouse and Brandom is future-oriented.

Explicit norms are linguistically formulated rules, regulations, or laws. They arise when participants in the practice express the norms that are already implicit in their practice. For normative practice theory, the content of the explicitly formulated rule is not determined by any regularity of past practice. And for this reason, the problem of gerrymandering does not arise for normative practice theory. Rather, an explicit rule expresses the forward-looking normativity implicit in the responsiveness of individuals toward each other. Once the rule is formulated, it becomes the object of further attitudes. What the rule means is worked out as individuals use it and then criticize those uses. Normative practice theory thus agrees that decisions about how to follow a rule are internal to a community, but the content of the rule is not determined by any particular decision. Moreover, because the underlying practice is constituted by attitudes of individuals toward each other, normative practice theory can treat communities as fluid and permeable. An individual may be a member of many communities, depending on which others are taken as the proper subject of praise and criticism.

9.4. Is Unification Possible?

Two Perspectives: Rules and Equilibria

When we look back over the previous chapters in the light of Sections 9.2 and 9.3, a pattern emerges. There seem to be two perspectives on how to understand the social world. One tradition has its roots in the interpretivist rejection of empiricist theorizing (Section 3.3). Seeking meaning in the social world, it insists on explaining action in terms of reasons (Section 5.1) and explaining reasoning in terms of rules (Section 4.2). This perspective is strongly sympathetic to the qualitative methods we explored in Chapter 4. The practice-theoretic account of normativity discussed in Section 9.3 provides an anti-reductionist account of social norms. From this perspective, then, the key to understanding the structure of the social world is to understand the perspective of the agents, see how their actions are informed by their social and cultural constructions, and how their institutions are supported by rules and implicit norms. From this perspective, the idea of a rule is the master key to understanding the social world: know the rules of a social group, and the rest will follow.

The second perspective takes the notion of an equilibrium to be the master key for understanding societies. Schelling's checkerboard model (Section 6.1) found that a segregated residence pattern was an equilibrium for a modest tolerance threshold. Various equilibria concepts were the key to using game theory in the explanation of revolutions (Section 7.1) and evolutionary game theory in the explanation of cooperation (Section 7.4). In Section 9.2, both Lewis's account of convention and Bicchieri's account of social norms depend on game theoretic equilibria. Methodologically, this perspective draws heavily on the sort of modeling we explored in Chapter 6 and on the sort of game theoretic or decision theoretic analysis we studied in Chapter 5. From this perspective, find the equilibria in the agents' strategic interaction, and the rest will follow.

In this chapter, we have seen each of these approaches stretched to their limits. The rules perspective is committed to normativism and needs to find a convincing way to make sense of the normative force of social rules. So-called normative practice theory arguably escapes from the problems facing a regularity-based account, but it pays a price. The force of norms seems to either dissolve in the shifting winds of contingent, forward-looking practices or solidify into an unreducible normativity that would be anathema to a metaphysical naturalist. Bicchieri's account of social norms, on the other hand, comes at normativity from the equilibrium perspective. The challenge here is to use the resources of rational agents in strategic situations to recover the force of social norms. While it is a powerful account, it too pays a price. It depends on the norms responding to particular kinds of strategic situation (mixed motive games), but a broader account of normativity is necessary if we are to get a full understanding of social phenomena.

Perhaps we have asked too much of these two perspectives. When we see these kinds of intellectual fault lines, it is always tempting to dichotomize them into opposing "paradigms" or "frameworks." This typically turns a couple of good insights into a pair of Total Theories of Everything. Each is pushed beyond its zone of plausibility, and both fail. A possible way forward is to back off the larger ambitions of each perspective and look for the possibility of unification. In *Understanding Institutions* (2016), Francesco Guala proposes a unification: an account of institutions—large-scale social structures like "the church, democracy, the army, the public school system" (Guala 2016, xviii)—in terms of *both* rules *and* equilibria. The rules in question do not require the full resources of either the normativist's or Bicchieri's account of social norms. And the equilibrium on which his view rests, a correlated equilibrium, is a generalization of Lewis's account of convention.

Correlated Equilibria

In Lewis's account, conventions arise as a way of solving coordination problems. We have seen examples of coordination problems in the games Inside/Outside (Figure 5.8), Stag Hunt (Figure 5.9), and Red/Blue (Figure 9.1). Coordination problems are a distinct class of strategic situations because they have more than one Nash equilibrium, so thinking strategically about the payoffs alone will not yield an outcome the players prefer. The problem is for the players to find a way of reliably choosing a strategy that will end up in one of the equilibria. Lewis introduces conventions as a way of resolving this problem. Conventions use past behavioral regularities to set the expectations and preferences of the agents. In the Red/Blue game discussed in Section 9.2, where the play was repeated, the players chose randomly in the first round or two but quickly settled into a pattern. It became a Lewis convention to choose one of the colors.

In Lewis's account, the history of play is external to the strategic situation of the game. A convention is a device that correlates the players' strategies. The idea of a correlated equilibrium adds an additional choice to the game: play what the correlation device says to play. In the case of the repeated Red/Blue game, the correlation device says to continue the pattern. Suppose the players have hit on the "play red" convention. The structure of the game would then be represented as Figure 9.5. The new row and column represent the payoffs for following the convention. To calculate the payoffs in the new row and column, we assume that the other player is choosing a strategy randomly. Hence, the payoff is the expected utility (in this case, the average payoff) over time. So, in the two cells where Player 1 follows the convention and Player 2 does not (the first and second cells of the bottom row),

Red/Blue (Initial Rounds)

Other Two Players

		Red	Blue
		Red	Blue
Self	Red	10, 10	0, 0
	Blue	0, 0	10, 10

Figure 9.5 Red/Blue (Initial Rounds)

The Watering Hole

Farmer 2

		Water	Wait
Farmer 1	Water	0, 0	2, 1
	Wait	1, 2	1, 1

Figure 9.6 The Watering Hole

the payoffs are 1/2. This is the expected utility of the play over time. The cell on the bottom right, where the payoffs are both 1, is a new Nash equilibrium. While this one does not yield a higher payoff, it does reduce uncertainty.

While adding the correlation device does not increase the payoffs in the Red/Blue game, consider a different game. The coordination problems we've been considering so far have symmetrical equilibria, and the players are indifferent between them. The game in Figure 9.6 is different. Here there are two Nash equilibria, and since each player prefers one, any attempt to settle on a symmetrical payoff will be unstable. A simple history of repeated play will not establish a convention. Let us tell a little story to help make sense of the game. Suppose two cattle farmers need to water their cows at the same watering hole. Each has the choice of either waiting or moving the herd in for a drink. If both wait, neither herd gets water, so this is the least valued option. If both move at the same time, the herds mix, and it is all a mess. So, while it is better than not watering the cattle, it is not as good as one herd drinking while the other waits. What they need is a coordination device.

What might the coordination device be? Lewis proposed salience and history as mechanisms that might bump players into coordination. Suppose that after a few trials, one farmer started watering the herd in the morning, while the other watered in the evening. The strategy of the coordination device is conditional. For Farmer 1, the strategy is "Move if and only if it is morning" and for Farmer 2 the strategy is "Move if and only if it is afternoon." In this case, the coordination device yields a Nash equilibrium with a higher payoff than any other symmetrical payoff (Figure 9.7). The payoffs in the lower right cell are "1 1/2, 1 1/2" because, since the day is half morning and half afternoon, in repeated play half the time the farmer is waiting (with payoff of 1) and half the time the farmer is watering the cattle without conflict (payoff of 2).

Watering Hole With a Correlation Equilibrium

Farmer 2

		Water	Wait	Water in Afternoon
	Water	0, 0	2, 1	1, ½
Farmer 1	Wait	1, 2	1, 1	1, 1½
	Water in Morning	½, 1	1½, 1	1½, 1½

Figure 9.7 Watering Hole With a Correlation Equilibrium

Correlated equilibrium is a solution concept that generalizes Lewis's conventions. It is a Nash equilibrium of an expanded game, where a strategy has been added to the original. In the interesting case we have just been considering, the equilibria of the original game were unstable. In the augmented game, the correlated equilibrium is symmetrical and thereby more stable than the alternative Nash equilibria. Notice also that the additional strategies that augment the original game are conditional: if the correlation device says to play the strategy, then do so. Guala sees an opportunity for unification here, since these conditionals can be regarded as rules.

Rules in Equilibria

Guala's unified account of social institutions holds that "The rules are symbolic markers that represent equilibria (or parts of equilibria) and help the players use a particular coordination device." (Guala 2016, 55)

To say that the rules are "symbolic markers" is to say that they are represented by people. Language, of course, is immensely useful for representing rules, but Guala does not hold that the participants in an institution need to communicate with each other. Our two farmers recognize a regularity, but to help solve the coordination problem, that regularity must be transformed into a conditional. The farmers must recognize that whether they take the herd to water is conditional on the time of day. The time of day is the coordination device, and the rules help the two farmers use it to achieve a higher-valued, stable equilibrium. All by themselves, the rules will not create the institution. And all by itself, the strategic situation of Figure 9.6 will not support a convention. The rules and equilibria work together, according to Guala, to constitute the institution. We have thereby unified the rule-based and the equilibrium-based accounts of institutions.

Now, the normativist is unlikely to be happy with this unification. The problem is familiar: Guala's rules are little more than regularities. The rule has the form: when in conditions *X*, do *Y*. Like Lewis's conventions, any normativity they have is inherited from the instrumental rationality of choosing the correlated equilibrium. Guala notes that from the first-person perspective, these conditionals have normative force in the sense that they are regularities I ought to follow (for prudential reasons, to be sure). From Guala's point of view, however, the thin normativity of the rules is an advantage. He does not have to give an account of normativity and answer the harder questions that plagued the normativist in Section 9.3. The thin rules are enough to establish and mark the correlated equilibria, and once established, the participants have reason to follow the rules.

Guala's account has an advantage over Bicchieri insofar as it is not trying to give an account of social norms. Hence, he need not worry about whether the account of norms is sufficiently general. Guala's view can take any account of norms (including the practice theorist's) as its input, if the rules are conditional on some coordination device. Moreover, the equilibrium works to identify a self-reinforcing situation without the more elaborate conditional preferences in Bicchieri's account. To be sure, correlated equilibria solutions will not resolve mixed-motive games like the prisoner's dilemma. So, the two accounts are not truly competitors.

Given Guala's stance with respect to the two perspectives, the unification achieved in his view is less of a grand synthesis than the possibility of an ecumenical pluralism. Guala's rules-in-equilibrium account may give us a satisfying explanation of how some institutions work. But it need not be understood as the only game in town. It is consistent with practice theoretic accounts of some kinds of normativity, it is equivalent to Lewis's conventions in others, and it needs an account like Bicchieri's to handle mixed-motive strategic situations. Returning to the point with which this section began, perhaps there is a valuable lesson here. Rule-based and equilibrium-based perspectives on the social world need not, and perhaps should not, be treated as mutually exclusive alternatives. The social world is complicated, and it may need different accounts in different domains. Yet, ecumenicalism is difficult to maintain, for there *are* ways in which these views conflict. The hard philosophical work lies in identifying and resolving those narrow areas of conflict while recognizing in other areas a productive division of labor.

9.5. Wrap Up

Chapter Summary

How should we understand the appeal to rules and norms in social scientific theories? Normativists who take a strong stance on this question argue that norms cannot be reduced or naturalized without losing their distinctive features. The fact that humans are responsive to what they ought to do, while non-humans are not, shows that there is an important difference between the natural and the social world. Philosophers have long held that "ought" cannot be reduced to "is," which suggests that the difference between the natural and social worlds is an unbridgeable gap. Philosophers in this tradition, which is often aligned with interpretivism, argue that norms force the social sciences to understand social phenomena in very different terms than the natural sciences.

When social scientists articulate conceptions of normativity, the analyses are typically reductionist and naturalistic. Philosophical naturalists have had two kinds of response to the social scientific disenchantment of the world. Turner's "good bad theories" represent the first. Turner treats social scientific theories as replacing talk of norms and rules with non-normative social scientific terminology. Institutions and practices are governed by representations of rules—public statements or private beliefs—but these representations do not refer to real norms. They are practically useful, but representationally empty. The second response treats talk of norms as referring to community-wide patterns of action. Lewis's account of convention treated conventions as salient equilibria of coordination problems. Bicchieri combined the resources of game theory with some cognitive psychology to account for social norms. The practice theorists also made norms depend on the actions and attitudes of individuals, though they eschewed the commitments of rational choice theory. These approaches can be understood as naturalistic insofar as they conceptualize norms and normativity in psychological or evolutionary terms. Norms are not something that stands outside of the causal order. Guala's rules-in-equilibrium account is a suggestive attempt to unify the rule-based and equilibrium-based perspectives.

In the last three chapters, we have assumed that intentions are properties of individuals. There is a class of actions where this assumption seems to fail. In a joint action, two or more agents do something together which neither can do alone. In the next chapter, we will look at examples where a team is trying to win the game, a couple is dancing together, or a parliament is passing a bill. These actions do not resolve neatly into the actions of individuals because the intentions are apparently not individual intentions. *I* cannot intend to win the World Cup, but *we* can. How are such joint intentions to be understood? Do joint intentions provide a new set of resources to analyze and explain social institutions, events, and practices? And do joint intentions provide a different reason for thinking that the social sciences are ontologically or epistemologically unique?

Discussion Questions

1. Find several examples of social phenomena which we would naturally call "conventions." Apply Lewis's definition to them. Do the examples you have found solve coordination problems? Do they require regularities? Are they in the interest of all who participate?

2. Consider the Guala and Mittone experiment in the light of Bicchieri's account of social norms. Can Bicchieri's account explain why people do not act in a thoroughly selfish way?

3. What is the status of the principle of instrumental rationality on Lewis's, Bicchieri's, or Guala's account? Is it a norm, as Winch and Davidson argued? Or is it a law, as Hempel argued? What are the consequences of different answers for the issues of reductionism and naturalism?

4. In Section 9.3, we surveyed four objections to Winch's conception of norms. Can a practice-theoretic account of norms be modified to rebut these objections? Do any of these objections also apply to the views presented in Section 9.2? For example, are Bicchieri's norms subject to the gerrymandering problem?

5. In Section 7.4, we discussed an account of how norms might arise through evolution. How do the two kinds of philosophical account of norms discussed in Sections 9.2 and 9.3 fit with that evolutionary explanation? Is one more amenable to an evolutionary framework than the other? How would a rational choice or a practice theory account of norms need to be modified to be consistent with an evolutionary account like Richerson and Boyd's?

Further Reading

The gap between "is" and "ought" has been extensively discussed in moral philosophy. Some of that literature bears on problems of understanding action, and it thereby overlaps with the philosophy of social science. Some important essays from this literature are Searle, "How to Derive an Ought from an Is" (1964) and von Wright, "Is and Ought" (von Wright 1986).

Lewis's *Convention* (1969) is a classic to be read by anybody interested in the issue of normativity. Cubitt and Sugden (2003) provide an updated reformulation of Lewis's view. Gilbert has argued at length against Lewis's analysis and provided an alternative account in Chapter 7 of *On Social Facts* (Gilbert 1989) and the essays collected in the first part of (Gilbert 1996). See also Marmor's *Social Conventions: From Language to Law* (2009).

Elster argues against the idea that norms are always beneficial, and his account relies on emotion in interesting ways. See Elster, *Explaining Social Behavior: More Nuts and Bolts for the Social Sciences* (2007) and "A Plea for Mechanisms" (1998).

Bicchieri's *The Rules We Live By* (2006) is perhaps the best available account of social norms which relies on the resources of game theory. The sequel, *Norms in the Wild* (Bicchieri 2017), presents the material in a less technical way and considers the more practical questions about how to measure and change norms. Gintis extends Bicchieri's and Lewis's views in interesting ways in "Social Norms as Choreography" (2010). See also Skyrms and Zollman, "Evolutionary Considerations in the Framing of Social Norms" (2010), and Nichols, "Emotions, Norms, and the Genealogy of Fairness" (2010).

Practice theory in the philosophy of social science is indebted to the first two chapters of Winch's *Idea of a Social Science* (1958). Kripke's *Wittgenstein on Rules and Private Language* (1982) contains an important critique of a view like Winch's. Turner's *Social Theory of Practices* (1994) is an extensive critique of both philosophical and social scientific appeals to practice. See also Roth's "Mistakes" (2003) and Henderson's "Norms, Normative Principles, and Explanation: On Not Getting Is from Ought" (2002). Contemporary revival of practice theory in philosophy is largely due to Brandom's *Making it Explicit* (1994), and Rouse's *How Scientific Practices Matter* (2002) is also important. See Schatzki, Knorr Cetina, and von Savigny's (eds.) *The Practice Turn in Contemporary Theory* (2001) for an exploration of the issues and Rouse's "Practice Theory" (2007a) for an overview of the state of the debate. Turner and Rouse debate the issue as well (Rouse 2007b and Turner 2007). Turner's *Explaining the Normative* (2010) argues against normativism more broadly and systematically. Risjord's *Normativity and Naturalism in the Philosophy of the Social Sciences* (2016) has a number of essays that extend the Turner-Rouse debate.

Guala's *Undersanding Institutions* (2016) is an expansion of his earlier collaboration with Hindriks (Guala and Hindriks 2015). Volume 48, issue 6 of *The Philosophy of the Social Sciences* was devoted to a symposium on *Understanding Institutions*, and it includes both a precis of the book and a reply to critics.

10 Intentions, Institutions, and Collective Action

When a football team wins a game, there is a clear sense in which a group has done something that no individual can do. Pelé may have scored the winning goal, but to say that Pelé won the game is a metonym. Even if the great Pelé dribbled past the whole opposing team and scored the game's only goal, Pelé's *team* won the game. Similarly, it is only as a whole that parliaments pass legislation, orchestras perform, nations arrange treaties, and corporations go bankrupt. So far, our discussion of the ontology of the social world has focused on social entities like orchestras and legislatures. We get a different perspective when we shift the focus from social entities to social actions, from orchestras to orchestral performance. Standard accounts of action theory treat individual performances as the primary kind of action. Game theory shows how to aggregate the actions of individuals into stable patterns, but these remain actions of individuals. However, a crowd of people boards a train in a very different sense than congress passes a bill. What is collective, joint, or group action? Is it reducible to individual actions, or is there something more?

There are three broad approaches to the analysis of joint action. The first treats groups as a special kind of agent. When we say that congress passed a bill, on this view, we are speaking literally of a single entity—congress—and attributing an action to it. The members of congress have done something together, and by doing so they have constituted themselves as a collective agent distinct from any individual. In Section 10.1, we will begin by considering the "team reasoning" program proposed by economists Robert Sugden and Michael Bacharach. When a strategic interaction is framed as a team problem, each player chooses what is best for the group. This treats groups as agents in the sense that the group has a utility function which is different from the utility functions of the individuals. In philosophy, Margaret Gilbert and Phillip Pettit have been proponents of treating groups as collective subjects of intention, belief, and value.

The two alternative approaches to joint action reject the idea that groups are a special kind of agent. On these views, only individual humans are agents. The special character of joint action is to be found in the intentions, and the two alternatives to collective agency differ in their analysis of joint intention. In Section 10.2, we will begin by looking at Michael Bratman's analysis. Of the three approaches to joint action, Bratman's is the most thoroughgoing in its individualism. When I

DOI: 10.4324/9781003207795-10

say, "We intend to win the World Cup," it means that *I* intend for *us* to win. The philosophical work is focused on understanding how I can have an intention that reaches out to things that I cannot control (e.g., that *we* win). Philosophers like John Searle and Raimo Tuomela reject Bratman's approach as too individualistic to explain joint action. While Searle and Tuomela agree with Bratman that only individual humans are agents, they think that joint action takes a special kind of mental attitude. When we intend to win the World Cup, each of us has a special sort of intention, a "we-intention." In Section 10.2, we will explore the debate about I-intentions and we-intentions.

Joint actions are those where something is done which cannot be done by a single person. Some joint actions involve small groups and fleeting intentions, such as moving a piano or playing a duet. Others involve institutions, such as winning the World Cup or declaring war. What is the relationship between the joint actions of small, face-to-face groups and social institutions? Could we "build" social institutions out of the joint actions of individuals? At first look, there seems to be an enormous gulf between playing a duet together and a corporation going bankrupt. After all, the first is plausibly something that we intend to do, while the second is probably not something that anyone intended. Social groups seem to "do" things which are not intended by any individuals. In this way, the actions of institutions seem quite different from a joint action like moving a piano. In Section 10.3, we will discuss John Searle's attempt to bridge joint action and large-scale social institutions with we-intentions. His account depends on a particular notion of *function*, and our discussion of Searle's social ontology will thus continue the discussion of functions and functional explanation begun in Section 7.4.

10.1. Agency and Collective Intentionality

Team Reasoning

We saw in Chapters 7 and 9 that humans' remarkable cooperative tendencies are fascinating for social scientists as well as philosophers. Within a rational choice framework, one way to explain cooperation is to argue, as Bicchieri did, that norms change individual preferences. New preferences transform the strategic situation from a prisoner's dilemma (or other mixed-motive game) to one where the cooperative choice is the best for each. It may have seemed to you that this solution is a bait-and-switch: rather than explain why we cooperate despite the cost, Bicchieri's account tells us that cooperation is not costly at all. I may forego the benefits of a free ride, but in my personal utility calculus (as reconstructed by Bicchieri) I really don't want that free ride anyway. On the contrary, one might think that some situations are genuine dilemmas. Sometimes, following a norm or acting with a group requires an individual to sacrifice. The sacrifice is real, even if the social group is better off for it. The hard cases of cooperation to explain are those where my interest conflicts with what is best for the group, yet I choose what is good for the group anyway.

Cases where the good of group trumps individual preference are not difficult to find. Consider Robert Sugden's example:

> When my family discusses how we should spend a summer holiday, we start from certain common understandings about our preferences. We prefer self-catering accommodation to hotels, and hotels to campsites. We prefer walking and looking at scenery and wildlife to big-city sightseeing and shopping. When it comes to walks, we prefer walks of six miles or so to ones that are much shorter or much longer.
>
> (Sugden 2000b, 175)

As Sugden goes on to say, these family preferences are not the same as any individual preferences. *He* prefers longer hikes and less shopping than others in his family. In this sort of case, "We prefer *x* to *y*" may be true, while "Each of us prefers *x* to *y*" is false. The experience of being part of a group and subordinating one's own preferences to the group preferences is quite familiar. Indeed, one of the interesting things about humans is our very strong group orientation. It is well known from experimentation with strategic interactions that when subjects are prompted to think of a mixed-motive game as a problem for a group, cooperation increases. This remains true even when the groups are arbitrary and the subjects *know* that they are arbitrary. There is no honor among thieves, apparently, until the thieves form a union.

In standard rational choice theory, all preferences are individual in the sense that they are reasons for individual action. As we have noted, individual preferences need not be selfish. While I value the health and wellbeing of my family members, this remains *my* value because these values influence my choices. In a strategic interaction, standard game theory treats everyone as having an ordered set of preferences, or utility function. The outcome of each combination of actions is a utility for each player. In normal form representations of games, this means that there are two or more utility values in each cell of the table, one value for each player. By contrast, to think of *the group* as having preferences means that we must define a utility function for the group. Each possible combination of individual actions would have a *single* utility.

Consider, for example, what a prisoner's dilemma might look like if we used group preferences rather than individual preferences. On the standard representation of a prisoner's dilemma (Figure 5.5), the strategy {Defect, Defect} dominates. The reasoning is conditional: *if* my opponent cooperates, then my preferred choice is to defect; *if* my opponent defects, then my preferred choice is still to defect. If we think in terms of team or group preferences, then the question is not "What is best for me?" but "What is best for us?" The game might be represented as Figure 10.1. As before, this is a game between two players. And as before, we are representing ordinal utilities, with higher numbers being better than lower numbers. But now there is only one value in each cell. That number represents the utility for the group composed of Smith and Jones. Represented in this way, the best choice for each

Prisoner's Dilemma (Team Version)

Jones

		Cooperate	Defect
Smith	Cooperate	3	1
	Defect	1	2

Figure 10.1 The Prisoner's Dilemma (Team Version)

player is to cooperate. Notice that this is the best choice only when the player is thinking of him- or herself as a member of the group. The conflict between group and individual preferences is represented by the two ways of framing the problem. Thinking about what to do as an individual, the best option is to defect; thinking about it as a member of the group, the best option is to cooperate. Notice also that the reasoning is no longer conditional in the same way. Because there is only one payoff (the group payoff), each player has the same motivation. I don't need to calculate my best play, given the payoffs for the other player(s). As a member of the team, I choose what is best for the team.

Thinking in terms of group utilities raises at least three interesting issues. First, how are the group utilities to be determined? In this example, you might have wondered why the strategies of {Cooperate, Defect} and {Defect, Cooperate} have lower utility than {Defect, Defect}. Could it be better for the group if one member goes free? Perhaps; it depends on how we tell the story. A full-blown theory of team reasoning will have to specify some way of ranking the group preferences. This raises the second issue. A full-blown theory of team reasoning will have to articulate the relationship between individual preferences and group preferences. This second issue touches on the larger questions of reductionism which we have been exploring in Chapters 7 and 9. Since group and individual preferences may differ, we would not expect any simple and direct connection between them. As a result, theories of group preference are likely to be holist in one sense or another.

The third issue is, perhaps, the fundamental one: what constitutes a group, and what determines whether an individual is a member? Granting the existence of a group, it makes sense to say that a group can go on a hike and get benefits from doing so. And if a group can go on a hike, then it makes sense to say that the group prefers six-mile hikes to ten-mile hikes. Yet, the existence of a group is a lot to grant. It invites us to think of a group mind which somehow determines my preferences and actions. That seems like an implausibly strong form of holism. The problem, then, is to find a way to understand group agency and action.

Joint Commitment

Individualism and holism, especially in their ontological forms, present something of a dilemma. As we saw in Section 7.1, philosophers and social theorists have been reluctant to follow Durkheim and treat social groups as special kinds of objects. And a strictly individualist alternative has often seemed equally unpalatable. The early 20th-century sociologist and philosopher Georg Simmel proposed a middle way. Simmel emphasized the importance of interpersonal relationships and saw social wholes as emerging from more intimate forms of human interaction.

> Societal unification needs no factors outside its own component elements, the individuals. . . . The consciousness of constituting with the other a unity is actually all there is to this unity. This does not mean, of course, that each member of a society is conscious of such an abstract notion of unity. It means that he is absorbed in innumerable, specific relations and in the feeling and the knowledge of determining others and of being determined by them.
>
> (Simmel 1971 [1908], 7)

Simmel was reaching for a kind of unity that does not resolve into a collection of individuals; at the same time, there is no extra thing that is "the group" over and above the individuals. Simmel's view is like non-reductive individualism, which also attempts to split the difference between individualism and holism. The difference between them is that non-reductive individualism does not regard the individuals as changed by the properties which supervene on the aggregate of individuals. The "consciousness" of each other—their attitudes, beliefs, feelings, and behavior toward each other—determines whether individuals form a group. Each "determines" the others and is "determined by them." For Simmel, much more than for the non-reductive individualist, becoming part of a group makes a difference to the agent.

Simmel's suggestion is fascinating, but it needs elaboration and specification. What does "determine" mean? What sort of "consciousness" is required for the formation of a group? No one has done more to develop the ontology of social groups in Simmel's tradition than Margaret Gilbert. In a series of books and essays beginning with *On Social Facts* (1989), Gilbert has articulated criteria for the existence of social groups. On her view, social groups are "plural subjects," analogous in many ways to individual subjects. Like individuals, plural subjects can have beliefs and intentions; they can act. At the heart of Gilbert's view is the notion of a *joint commitment*.

To get a grip on "joint commitment," let us begin with personal commitments. Suppose I tell myself that I am going to start doing an exercise routine every morning. If I'm serious about this intention, we might say that I made a commitment to exercising. This commitment is similar to, but not the same as, a promise. Like a promise, a personal commitment involves some kind of obligation. If I fail to exercise, I will feel like I have let myself down. Unlike a promise, I need not have told anyone about my commitment. It may be entirely private and personal. Also, unlike a promise, I can rescind my personal commitment at any time. A distinctive feature of joint commitment, according to Gilbert, is that a joint commitment cannot be individually rescinded. Suppose we have committed to exercising together every morning. If I wake up one morning and decide not to continue, then I am not merely capricious; I have let you down. It would be appropriate for you to rebuke me. The fact that you have standing to criticize me, Gilbert argues, shows that joint commitments entail obligations to the other parties. In her notion of joint commitment, Gilbert highlights the common experience that working together toward a common goal is more binding than an individual commitment to do so. (And this is why it helps to have an exercise buddy.)

When several people form a joint commitment, they commit to doing the action together, or as Gilbert sometimes says, "acting as a body." This means, at a minimum, that the parties have adopted a goal. Insofar as the parties are jointly committed toward achieving this goal, it is not the goal of any party as an individual. It is, like the team reasoning discussed earlier, the goal of the group. A joint commitment to act may also mean that we have established specific roles that will help us achieve our joint goal. In other contexts, we might be more improvisational about how we will coordinate our individual contributions.

Joint commitments require mutual knowledge. I cannot make a joint commitment alone. Doing so would seem to bind *you* to my decisions without your consent. In a joint commitment, then, other parties must know that the commitment is being undertaken, and each of us must know that the other parties are aware. In the clearest case, joint commitments arise through explicit agreement. For example, suppose we decide to clean the apartment together by saying "Let's clean the apartment." This statement expresses a willingness to adopt the goal of cleaning the apartment. If both parties express such willingness, and each recognizes that the other is doing so (mutual knowledge), then the joint commitment is in place. Of course, as Gilbert realizes, many joint commitments arise without explicit agreement. We may find ourselves working toward a common goal, and the mutual realization may have dawned slowly on us. In such cases, Gilbert contends, we are jointly committed just as if we had explicitly agreed to pursue the goal together.

Implicit joint commitments are the source of a challenge to Gilbert's view. Joint commitment requires mutual knowledge, so what is the role of mutual knowledge in implicit joint commitments? Is the mutual knowledge implicit too, or is it recognized by the parties? If the mutual knowledge is explicit, then the commitment is "implicit" only in the sense of having been formed non-verbally. This makes sense of examples where the plural subject is formed by eye contact or gesture. Yet treating implicit commitments in this way means that all parties to the commitment must be conscious of it. This does not seem to do justice to many of the social groups of which we are part. On the other hand, treating the mutual knowledge as hidden or unconscious robs the notion of mutual knowledge of its point. Mutual knowledge adds an element of consent to joint commitment, and it turns the commitment into a reason for action. It is difficult to accept the idea that I might be bound to obligations flowing from a joint commitment which I do not recognize.

As we have already seen, one of the features of group goals and group actions is that they may run contrary to the goals and interests of an individual. Is it possible, on Gilbert's view, to have a joint commitment which is not consistent with individual preferences? Gilbert's view is strongly anti-reductionist, and she argues that the attitudes, intentions, and actions of a plural subject are not composed from individual attitudes, intentions, or actions. To motivate the idea, she tells the following story:

> The parties are Ned and Olive, and Olive is speaking: "Our plan was to hike to the top of the hill. We arrived at the hill and started up. As he told me later, Ned realized early on that it would be too much for him to go all the way to the top, and decided that he would only go half way. Though he no longer had any intention of hiking to the top of the hill, he had as yet said nothing about this to me, thinking it best to wait until we were at least half way up before doing so. Before then we encountered Pam, who asked me how far we intended to go. I said that our intention was to hike to the top of the hill, as indeed it was."
>
> (Gilbert 2009, 171–172)

Gilbert regards Olive's remark as entirely consistent: we intended to climb the hill, but Ned did not. Indeed, she adds that Olive may have been in the same situation as Ned. Perhaps neither intended to climb the hill individually, but as a plural subject they intended to climb the hill. If so, then Ned and Olive must have formed a joint commitment.

One might wonder whether Gilbert's plural subjects can really support joint intentions that are contrary to individual intentions. In the story about Ned and Olive, it is important that they had not yet spoken about their changing ideas. If they did so, the joint intention might have changed from an intention to reach the top to an intention to just go halfway. But joint commitments need not be explicit. So, did the joint intention change tacitly when Ned and Olive changed their individual intentions? Much depends here on the notion of mutual knowledge, which as we have already seen is problematic in cases where the joint commitment is tacitly formed. Moreover, one might wonder whether the initial joint intention could have been formed at all if neither Ned nor Olive had intended to climb to the top at the beginning. Gilbert remarks that "in the basic case," each party is "personally ready for [the commitment], and that he expresses this readiness" (Gilbert 2009, 180). Willingness on the part of each party seems appropriate for Gilbert's type of account; it would seem irrational to enter a joint commitment that is contrary to a person's interests. But at the same time, this means that group intentions cannot deviate dramatically from individual intentions. Gilbert's plural subjects do not seem to be a good solution to the hard problems of cooperation.

On Gilbert's view, social groups, institutions, and practices are constituted by a web of joint commitments. These will include joint decisions to work toward particular goals, joint intentions to act, joint beliefs about the local environment, and so on. When a group is constituted, it is a genuine agent. Gilbert argues that the "we" in a sentence like "We are exercising" refers to a plural agent, and it is the proper subject of intention, belief, and action. A joint commitment changes each individual; they have new goals, motivations, and obligations as part of the group.

In Simmel's language, each party to a plural subject is determining the others and is determined by them insofar as they have entered joint commitments. On Gilbert's analysis, joint commitments are not individual properties. Therefore, social groups cannot be identified with any set of individuals or individual properties, even if conceptualized in terms of supervenience. At the same time, the analysis does not postulate a new sort of object. When two people jointly commit to an exercise regime, no third object has come into being.

Group Agency

Plural subjects are the agents of joint actions according to Gilbert's view. One might wonder about the notion of "agency" that is being invoked here. Are plural subjects agents in the same sense that an individual human is an agent? If not, then plural subjects "act" only in a metaphorical sense. So, what is an "agent?" How do we distinguish between things that act and things that are only acted upon? Daniel Dennett argued that instrumental rationality informs the simplest and most basic form of the concept of an agent (Dennett 1971). An agent is a system that gathers information about its environment (that is, it has something like beliefs) and has goal-directed actions. The agent's rationality connects the information and goals to the action: an agent acts *because* the action is the best way to achieve the goal in the present environment. Using this conception of agency, we can treat many things as agents: not only other animals, but also chess-playing computers and the GPS system in your car. However, while these beings are pretty sophisticated, it is probably an overstatement to call them all "agents" in the same sense as human beings are agents. In these simple, agent-like systems, the relationship between belief, goal, and action is too simple and mechanical. They have no process for drawing inferences, judging consistency of different goals, or evaluating the evidence for their beliefs. To exclude chess-playing computers and GPS systems, full-blown agency must require processes of inference and evaluation.

Gilbert argues that plural subjects have joint goals and joint beliefs. They thereby must satisfy Dennett's minimal conditions for agency. But one might wonder whether every plural subject formed by joint commitment (even explicit joint commitment) would also satisfy the slightly higher bar that excludes GPS systems. Consider one of Gilbert's favorite examples, walking together. Imagine that John and Sally happen to meet on the street. The two are friends, and it turns out that both are going to the library. Imagine Sally says, "Let's walk together to the library" and John agrees. This explicit statement and its acknowledgement create mutual knowledge. Under this circumstance, it makes sense to think of the pair as having the joint goal of walking together to the library. As they go, they will certainly gather information about their environment. Granting that these are joint beliefs (which would need some more argument to establish), the pair is at least a minimal agent. On the story so far, however, there are no processes in place by which this "agent" can decide among competing goals, respond to new evidence, or draw inferences about different possible means.

The lack of a sufficiently rich decision-making or information-processing capacity is made vivid by Gilbert's claim that failure to continue to walk together is the violation of an obligation created by the joint commitment. She writes:

> Suppose you and I are walking together. . . . You begin to lag behind. Failing some special circumstance, both of us will understand that it is perfectly reasonable for me to rebuke you for this in some way. Thus, I might turn and say in a mildly rebuking tone, "Hey it's hard for me to walk so slowly!"
>
> (Gilbert 1997, 24)

The laggard might object that no agreement had been made as to how fast we were to walk or how to respond to the circumstance that there is a stone in their shoe. Without some sort of process in place for working out joint solutions to these kinds of issues, the obligations entailed by the joint commitment are radically underspecified. When presenting this example, Gilbert typically suggests that the appropriate response to the problem of one person lagging is that the parties talk. Fair enough, but this introduces new requirements for joint action in addition to the simple joint commitment.

To see what group agency requires over and above joint commitment, consider that not just any communication between the walkers will suffice. If one party uses threats and bullying to force the other to act, then it no longer seems to be a case of *joint* action. The parties to a joint commitment to act need some process to reach fair and rational decisions. Christian List and Philip Pettit have argued that no process of individual aggregation of preferences, such as a majority vote, will produce appropriate group decisions (List and Pettit 2011). Where there are multiple issues to be decided, simple majority votes can lead to incoherence. Imagine, for example, that our two walkers are joined by a third, Fred, who is also going to the library but is less pressed for time. They agree to walk together. If they are to get to the library by one o'clock (and thereby have sufficient time to study), they have time for one stop. They might stop for coffee, or they might stop to shop. John wants to shop, Sally wants coffee, and Fred wants to do both (and is willing to forego studying). A majority, then, wants it all—shopping, coffee, and getting to the library on time—but that solution is impossible. John, Sally, and Fred need a different way to decide as a group what to do.

Voting procedures are an important topic of inquiry in philosophy and political science. The details are well beyond our scope here, and fortunately the lesson does not depend on the details. To count as a proper group agent, the group needs processes for reasoning and critically engaging its reasons, goals, and evidence. When such processes are in place, we have a much clearer idea about how to resolve the problems that arise when individual intentions or preferences are different from the group's. The consequence, however, is to raise the bar for what kind of system counts as an agent. List and Pettit argue that properly constructed social systems can count as genuine agents. However, it is equally clear that not every plural subject constituted by joint commitment is a proper agent. In the richer sense of agency appropriate to intentional action, mere joint commitment (and thereby Gilbert's plural subjects) is insufficient. If this conclusion is accepted, then a different approach to joint action is needed to account for those cases of joint action which are simpler and more common.

10.2. Joint Intentionality

Cooperation Again: Ontogeny and Development

We have had several occasions to remark that both common sense and social scientific research confirm that humans cooperate in altruistic ways. Section 6.4 sketched a contemporary evolutionary account of the evolution of cooperation where it was proposed that cooperative tendencies co-evolved with culture. What are the distinctive psychological capacities which make humans so cooperative? One way to approach this question is through comparative studies. Michael Tomasello and his collaborators have conducted a variety of studies which compare the development and cognitive abilities of human children with the development and abilities of chimpanzees.

Tomasello and his colleagues argue that humans and chimpanzees share many social skills. But where chimpanzees and other great apes use these skills individually, humans do so in a way that requires sharing attention and recognizing joint goals. For example, chimpanzees will follow the direction of another's gaze. They use this information in ways that suggest an understanding that the looker is (or is not) seeing an object in the environment: "they pursue contested food only if a dominant [chimpanzee] cannot see it, and they visually conceal their approach to contested food if there is a dominant competitor nearby" (Tomasello and Carpenter 2007, 121). Human children go beyond these capacities to promote joint attention. In joint attention, both parties are experiencing something with the awareness that they are doing so together. Experimentation has clearly established that children as young as one year old actively establish and maintain joint attention with adults. A consequence, Tomasello *et al* argue, is that chimpanzees do not point to objects in the way that human children do. That is, while chimpanzees gesture to communicate, they do not draw another's attention to an object, and they do not understand the communicative value of another's pointing to do so. Tomasello *et al* contend that this is because chimpanzees are not capable of establishing joint attention.

The differences between humans and the great apes extend to social activities. Chimpanzees engage in complex social activities like group hunting. Because they do not establish the common ground of activity with joint attention, however, these group activities remain individualistic. While the interpretation is still controversial, groups of hunting chimpanzees seem to be each pursuing their own best opportunities for catching the prey, while recognizing the other group-members' activities and chances of success. Comparative experiments with very young human children and human-reared chimpanzees show that there are large differences between human collaboration and chimpanzee. Where very young children will try to re-engage another in a joint activity, chimpanzees do not. Human children seem to be recognizing a joint goal of the activity to which all are attending. Tomasello concludes: "Shared intentionality is a small psychological difference that made a huge difference in human evolution in the way that humans conduct their lives" (Tomasello and Carpenter 2007, 124).

The question of this chapter is how we are to understand the shared intentionality which is distinctive of human cooperation, collaboration, and communication. Section 8.1 concluded that understanding joint action in terms of group agency requires processes for gathering information, reasoning, and decision making at the group level. While this account might work for some social groups, particularly institutions which have well defined rules and roles, it excludes many of the more mundane examples of joint action: studying together, playing chess, or performing Beethoven's 5th Symphony. Moreover, Tomasello's research is not strongly supportive of group agency. His argument is that the capacity for shared intention arises early in human development and is a necessary condition for more sophisticated forms of communication and joint action. While pre-linguistic children re-engage the joint attention of adults, it overreaches to think of these children are recognizing a shared commitment in Gilbert's sense. And clearly, infants are not capable of contributing to any sort of sophisticated group decision making. The alternative is to regard only individuals as agents and to treat shared intentions as a special kind of intention. Several philosophers have pursued this line, and the debate has been over the characteristics of the intentions which support and explain joint action.

Before proceeding further, a remark about the use of "reasons" and "intentions" is in order. In our discussion of action explanation so far, we have focused on the agent's *reasons* for acting. In the literature on joint action, the topic shifts to the agent's *intentions*. What is the difference between reasons and intentions? While the issues discussed in this chapter do not hang on there being a deep difference between reasons and intentions, there are several cases where it is more natural to speak of intentions than reasons. Intentions are forward-looking and closely related to plans. For example, suppose I drop my sandwich on the road and a bus runs over it. I might say, "I was intending to eat that for lunch!" Here there is no action to be explained and therefore no reason for acting. The word *intention* signals that I had some kind of plan or was anticipating future actions. In examples of joint action, reasons and intentions can come apart even farther. Suppose you and I intend to have lunch together. We may have different and entirely self-regarding reasons for wanting to have lunch together. There need not be any "joint reasons." Yet it makes sense to say, "We intend to have lunch together," and in this sense there is a joint intention. In the discussion of joint action, then, the questions have turned on the analysis of intentions, rather than the analysis of reasons.

Plans and Joint Intentions

One feature of intention that has seemed obvious to many philosophers is that a person can only intend to do something over which he or she has control. I can intend to eat my sandwich, but I cannot intend that you eat your sandwich. My intentions only cover *my* actions. Let's follow convention and call this the "own-action principle." It suggests an argument for thinking that joint actions must resolve into aggregates of individual actions. If there were true *joint* intentions, one might argue, then when we intend to have lunch together, my intention would somehow extend to your action too. I would be intending for you to eat lunch, and given the own-action principle, that is impossible. Therefore, in an action where a group does something that cannot be done by an individual, the intentions must be a complex of individual intentions. But this raises its own puzzle. Clearly, *I* cannot intend to win the World Cup. So how can "We intend to win the World Cup" be analyzed in terms of individual intentions?

Consider an example somewhat simpler than winning the World Cup. Suppose you and I intend to make dinner together. We will take different roles, and these roles will be coordinated. Someone can't sauté the onions until they have been chopped. And we would just get in each other's way if we tried to stir the sauce at the same time. While we may not have worked out an articulate plan when we agreed to make dinner together, we knew that we each would take on different roles as the proceedings unfolded. This recognition of an interlocking set of responsibilities as we work toward a common goal seems to distinguish the intention to make dinner together from two individual intentions to make dinner. If we are roommates who are both cooking, but aren't cooking together, we may well have to coordinate. But our actions remain independent in the sense that my sequence of actions will depend on my plan. In the individual case, I chop onions so that I can sauté them. In the joint case, I chop onions so that you can sauté them. Seen from this perspective, intending to win the World Cup isn't so different. Members of the team will have different roles and responsibilities, and they will discharge these roles for the sake of the shared goal.

The relationship between intentions and plans has led Michael Bratman to suggest the following analysis of joint intention (Bratman 1993, 106):

We intend to J if and only if

1. (a) I intend that we J and (b) you intend that we J.
2. I intend that we J in accordance with and because of 1a, 1b, and meshing sub-plans of 1a and 1b; you intend that we J in accordance with and because of 1a, 1b, and meshing subplans of 1a and 1b.
3. 1 and 2 are common knowledge between us.

Bratman thus analyzes joint intentions into an interlocking pair of individual intentions, along with common knowledge. The first condition requires that each has an intention that concerns a group activity. This would be already a difference between two people intending to make dinner side-by-side and intending to make dinner *together*. Condition (2) expresses two ways in which the individual intentions interlock to comprise a joint intention. The first is contained in the "in accordance with and because of" clause. This captures the sense in which we intend to do the action together. Two roommates working in the same kitchen to make dinner are not acting jointly if neither cares whether the other is making dinner. If they are making dinner together, each is intending to make dinner partly because the other is intending it too. "Meshing subplans" is the second way in which the intentions interlock. This reflects the sort of coordination between parts of a complex activity where each supports the other. *I* chop onions so that *you* can sauté them so that *I* can mix them into the sauce. Bratman is quite clear that we need not have worked out our sub-plans in advance. It is entirely possible that we improvise as we go along. However, when intending a joint activity, we must intend that our as-yet-unknown subplans will mesh in a way that will ultimately support our joint goal.

While Bratman's analysis only involves individual intentions, one still might argue that it violates the own-action principle. Consider the roommates who are intending to make dinner together. According to Bratman, each must have the intention that "We will make dinner." But neither roommate could bring it about that the group makes dinner together. That would require one person's intentions determining what another would do. Therefore, because it includes plural content (that we *J*) in an individual intention, Bratman's condition violates the own-action principle. One possible solution would be to eliminate the first-person plural form of the intention. Perhaps what each of us intends is that dinner is made. However, when we eliminate the plural content from an individualistic analysis of joint intentions, the conditions can be fulfilled in individualistic ways. Each roommate cooking his or her own dinner would bring it about that dinner was made, but this would presumably not be a joint action. The plural content seems necessary for the analysis, but including it runs afoul of the own-action principle.

In response to objections of this sort, Bratman argues that the own-action principle should not preclude the interdependence of actions (Bratman 1997). In many cases of individual action, success depends on what others do. Intending to buy a loaf of bread at the grocery seems like an unremarkable sort of intention. Yet to do so I will need the cooperation of the cashier. The cashier will have to recognize my intention to buy bread and act in a way that facilitates it. My intention to buy bread thus must include reference to the fact that another independently acting agent will recognize my intention (to buy bread) and form an intention (to sell it) in response. While buying bread is an individual action, it depends on the intentional actions of others in a way very similar to Bratman's analysis of joint action. Yet, buying a loaf of bread does not violate the own-action requirement. Therefore, the interrelated intentions which figure in joint action do not violate the own-action principle either.

We began this section with the empirical research conducted my Tomasello and his colleagues which seemed to show that joint intentionality accounts for our remarkable capacities for cooperation. How does Bratman's individualistic analysis fit Tomasello's developmental framework? Tomasello argues that the capacity for joint intentionality is exhibited by pre-linguistic children. It is hard to imagine a one-year-old child forming an intention in "accordance with and because of" an adult's intention and their meshing subplans. Therefore, one might argue that Bratman's analysis is too demanding to fit Tomasello's data. To be fair, the target of Bratman's analysis is a group of normal adults, and Bratman is quite clear that he presupposes an already existing social context in which such mutual intentions could be formed. While this is a coherent project, it does indicate a shortcoming of Bratman's strategy of making joint action depend on the content of a joint intention. Young children (not to mention adults with limited mental capacities) may not be able to entertain propositions as complex as Bratman's analysis requires. Yet joint action and shared intentions are not limited to normal adults. Bratman's analysis, whatever its other virtues, arguably does not provide an account of the sort of cooperation which is fundamental to human joint action.

We-intentions and the We-mode

We might try to save Bratman's account from the last objection by drawing on Tuomela's analysis of we-attitudes (Tuomela and Miller 1988; Tuomela 2007). For Tuomela, like other philosophers who work in this area, intentions are only one of the attitudes which a group may exhibit. Groups can share beliefs, evaluations, biases, emotions, or perceptions. To distinguish these from their individual counterparts, Tuomela calls them "we-attitudes." He analyzes the general class of we-attitudes this way:

> A person has a we-attitude A (say a goal, intention, or belief) if he has A, believes the others in his collective have A, and believes in addition that there is a mutual belief in the collective that the members have A.
>
> (Tuomela 2002, 10)

According to this analysis, the kind of joint attention discussed by Tomasello counts as a we-attitude. When a mother and child jointly attend to a penguin in the zoo, each is seeing the penguin and there is mutual knowledge that they are seeing the penguin. Indeed, all definitions of joint attention in the psychological literature satisfy something like Tuomela's mutual belief condition. Depending on how we understand "mutual belief," stronger and weaker forms of we-attitudes can be identified. We might treat Bratman's joint intentions as a robust kind of we-attitude where part of the reason that each has the intention is that the other has it too, and an interlocking set of plans is anticipated. In this way, the fully adult version of joint intention can be seen as continuous with a broader set of capacities for we-attitudes which arise early in child development.

Unfortunately, this analysis of we-attitudes will not suffice for joint intentionality. The point can be nicely illustrated by considering the prisoner's dilemma (Figure 5.5). In standard game theory, each player is assumed to have knowledge of the other player's utilities. So, each player knows that the best strategy for the other is to defect. Therefore, each player will intend to defect, each player will believe that the other intends to defect, and there will be a mutual recognition of this intention. Given Tuomela's analysis of we-attitudes, it follows that two players responding to a prisoner's dilemma have a we-intention. But the non-cooperative result of a prisoner's dilemma seems like a paradigm of a non-joint action. By contrast, a joint response to the prisoner's dilemma would be more like the team reasoning approach discussed in Section 8.1. The players would choose the outcome which was best for the group. Based on examples like this, Tuomela argues that we-attitudes can be manifested in more or less collective ways or "modes." Some we-attitudes will arise from the independent actions, beliefs, values, etc., of individuals. Tuomela distinguishes these as I-mode attitudes. In other cases, the participants will approach the situation as a group, collective, or team. There will be goals, intentions, and actions *of the group*. These latter are we-mode attitudes.

Using the distinction between I-mode and we-mode attitudes, Bratman's analysis can be seen as capturing joint intentions, but it does so with intentions in the I-mode. Because the intentions are in the I-mode, defections in a prisoner's dilemma count as joint action. Intentions in the I-mode thus are too weak to capture more robust forms of cooperative joint action. As we will see in the next section, intentions in the we-mode seem necessary to analyze the more complicated cases. Both Tuomela and Searle have developed views of this sort. Their analyses of we-mode joint intentions differ from Bratman's analysis insofar as they require a different kind of intentionality than individual action. Their analyses remain individualistic in the sense that only individual human beings possess intentions. We-mode joint intentions do not postulate supra-individual agents. Tuomela and Searle's analysis therefore differs from the views of Gilbert and Pettit discussed in Section 10.1.

Searle adopts the position that we-mode joint intentionality (what Searle calls "collective intentionality" or "we-intentions") is "a biologically primitive phenomenon" (Searle 1995, 24). By this he means not only that the we-mode does not reduce to the I-mode, but that each we-mode intention is "inside the head" of each participant. It is a distinctive psychological state. Searle invokes the image of a brain in a vat to make this point. A person could be entirely and radically mistaken about the existence of other people, and he or she would still be capable of having we-mode intentions.

You might be wondering how a proponent of we-mode intentions could accommodate the own-action principle. Suppose we have formed a team: the Philosophical Football Club. We intend to win the World Cup. On Searle's analysis, this means that each of us has an intention of the form "We will win the World Cup." Again, since I cannot win as an individual, how can I have the intention that we will win? Searle accepts the idea that any joint action must be carried out by the coordinated actions of individuals. When I have a we-mode intention, I intend that we will do something by means of each of us playing a role. As a member of the Philosophical Football Club, I intend to do my part as a means to the goal of winning the World Cup. Searle builds these "meshing subplans" into the structure of the intention by analogy with other means-ends relationships. When I intend to score a goal, he argues, I intend to do so by kicking the ball. There are not two intentions: the intention to score a goal and the intention to kick. There is just one: the intention to score a goal by means of kicking the ball. The relationship between the individual intentional actions and the we-mode intention is similar: "We intend to win the World Cup by means of me playing forward while you play goalie, etc." I intend for us to win the World Cup, but since the only individual intentions I have concern my own role, Searle's we-mode intentions are consistent with the own-action principle.

Acting as a Group Member

You are probably wondering: what *are* these "we-mode intentions?" The two primary proponents of this view, Tuomela and Searle, have different answers. For Tuomela, we-mode intentions are like team reasoning. To have a we-mode intention is to take the group's goals as one's own. As we saw in the earlier discussion of team reasoning, the plausibility of this view depends on the character of group commitment and decision-making. For Searle, a we-mode intention is a special psychological state. Critics of Searle have found the "solipsistic" character of his conceptualization of we-mode intentionality troubling. On his view, I could have we-mode intentions even if I were the only person in the world. Searle defends his conceptualization by pointing out that there is always a difference between the content of an intention and its satisfaction. Suppose I intend to climb a mountain; when I fail, it does not invalidate my intention. Analogously, I may have the intention that we are climbing a mountain together. If you don't show up because you didn't share the intention, then again, it does not change the character of my we-mode intention.

Searle's critics argue that his analogy between failed individual intentions and failed we-mode intentions does not hold up. Suppose I am sitting in my lounge chair, out of condition and drinking a beer, and I suddenly form the intention to start exercising. Now, this is a genuine intention, even if you think it foolish because you know that I am too lazy to do it. In the same circumstance, for me to form the intention that we will win the World Cup is worse than foolish; it is delusional. "Who will win the World Cup," you might ask me, "you, Pelé, and Beckham? We have to make some calls!" Joint actions take coordination and planning, and forming a legitimate we-mode joint intention includes securing or at least recognizing such agreements. Moreover, as Gilbert emphasized, joint action often involves commitment. It is difficult to see how an intention in my head could commit you to doing something.

Searle assumes that there will be agreements and negotiations in the background. As a matter of normal practice, delusional we-intentions are possible but empty. If I really want us to make dinner together, I need to talk to you. However, these ordinary practices can play no part in his analysis of we-mode intentions because everything relevant to the intention must be "in the head" of the individuals. In this respect, Bratman's analysis is superior to Searle's. It requires the existence of two or more people who, in fact, have intentions which interlace in the right way.

Bratman's version of joint intentions is more genuinely social, even if it remains in the I-mode. Tuomela's analysis of we-mode intentions brings in these social elements.

Tuomela's version of we-mode intentions draws on some of the insights about group action discussed in Section 10.1. The team reasoning theory postulated that when people enter strategic interactions, they sometimes approach the problem as members of a team. When the problem is framed as a group problem, individuals are choosing the best outcome for the group. This commitment to the group or collective is missing from both Bratman's and Searle's analyses. A structure of interrelated intentions and mutual belief like Bratman's is satisfied in the we-mode, Tuomela contends, when an individual intends to act as a member of a group. This means that the individual has accepted whatever goals, values, or beliefs have been collectively accepted by the group and that he or she uses them as reasons for acting. The difference between I-mode and we-mode, then, is the difference between intending to act as an individual and intending to act as a member of a group. The analysis depends on there being a group which has collectively accepted that it will do something or work toward a goal. Unlike Searle's view, on this analysis of we-mode intentions, it is impossible to intend that we will win the World Cup without the cooperation of and coordination with others.

For Tuomela, there is no need to postulate that the we-mode is a special psychological state. The difference between I-mode and we-mode is not hidden in a person's psychology; it is a matter of how the individuals are related to each other. If there is a group which has collectively accepted a goal, then that goal can be part of the reason for each individual's action. Suppose, for example, that a pair of roommates decides to make dinner together on Tuesdays. This now becomes a reason for each to act, and acting for that reason is acting *as* a member of the group. Each would have a we-mode joint intention. As noticed already, I-mode joint intentions are possible too. For Tuomela, the difference depends in part on what sort of agreements or commitments have been accepted and on whether the individual is using these group agreements as part of their reason for acting. Perhaps each roommate intends to make dinner with the other, but there has been no conversation and no commitment. Hence, they are not acting as members of a group, even though they will act jointly. On Tuomela's analysis, then, there is a wide variety of joint actions possible which involve stronger and weaker commitments.

Tuomela's analysis of we-mode intentions permits a more satisfactory approach to the idea of team reasoning than either Searle's or Bratman's analysis. Consider, for example, the problem of revolutions and free riders discussed in Section 7.1. Given the way Searle and Bratman analyze joint intention, it is entirely possible for a person to have the intention "We will overthrow the government" and yet fail to participate in revolutionary activities. Nothing in their analyses requires a person to put group utilities ahead of personal utilities. When a member of a group defects or free rides, that person has stopped, at least temporarily, thinking and acting as a group member. On Tuomela's analysis, the free rider is engaging in joint action in an I-mode way. A proper we-mode intention requires identification with the group. This means that in a strategic situation, one is acting for the good of the group. The utilities are formed by group agreement, and those are the individual's utilities insofar as he or she is acting as a group member. Therefore, when the joint action is in the we-mode, the group utilities are at stake as in Figure 8.1, not the individual utilities of a prisoner's dilemma. On Tuomela's analysis, team reasoning is a direct consequence of we-mode intentions and attitudes.

10.3. Intentions and Institutions

Simmel's vision was that the whole body of social relationships could arise from the particular sort of face-to-face interaction, from "the consciousness of constituting with the other a unity" (Simmel 1971 [1908], 7). The literature on joint intentionality which we have surveyed in Section 10.2 represents one prominent, contemporary attempt to articulate the unity which Simmel envisioned. The question, then, is whether joint intentionality can be amplified into a full account of social institutions. Can we understand banks, churches, or governments as products of joint intentionality? Tuomela and Searle have somewhat different accounts of joint intentionality, but both think that it is the fundamental theoretical concept of social theory. Each has devised an account of how we-mode intentions can explain the creation, maintenance, and dissolution of social institutions. Money is a favorite example of a social institution which, they contend, can be explained in these terms. Let us begin, then, with a discussion of some social scientific thinking about money.

The Strange Tale of the Druid Penny

An enduring theoretical puzzle about money is how objects that are inherently valueless could become valued as money. Theorists standardly distinguish between *commodity money* and *fiat money*. Gold is commodity money. It is already valued in itself and can serve as a standard measure for exchange and debt. On the other hand, paper money is fiat money, as are the symbols encrypted in your bank's computer. They count as money because we treat them as money. This latter property is a striking, even spooky, social creation. There is a common story about how both commodity money and fiat money evolved from a barter economy. Barter is limited because it requires a match between those who have surplus with those who have need. In a market where not enough people want my eggs, the rational choice is for me to trade them for something that I can be sure that everyone wants. Commonly consumed and durable items are a good candidate. Rare and useful metals like gold and silver fit this requirement. In many places, cigarettes have served as commodity money. Objects which are marks of status, or which have religious significance, are also good choices as commodity money. A coin made of a precious metal, where the value of the coin is at least the value of the metal, remains commodity money.

Fiat money is not valuable in itself, and the difficult question is how and why fiat money emerges. One pathway is through the issuance of paper certificates representing commodities. It is hard to carry around a substantial amount of gold, so it is stored in a safe place. The banker issues a promissory note or certificate that can be exchanged for the gold. The certificate comes to have the exchange value of the gold, but only if people continue to trust the certificate system. Note that the certificates are not yet fiat money, since they simply represent gold. Contemporary currencies cannot be exchanged for precious metals. According to one of the major theories of money, the further step to fiat money is facilitated by the state. By issuing coins that are worth less as a commodity than their face value (or paper money with no intrinsic value at all), the state can create currency to pay its civil servants and soldiers. But the currency will only have value if there is demand for it. So, the state must also demand the currency back in payment, as taxes. As long as the state is stable, the currency will function as money.

The problem with this standard story is that it is largely speculative. What evidence we have points to a more complicated process, at the very least. The story of the Druid penny, however, is an historical event which follows something of the same trajectory, though with interesting deviations.

In late 18th-century England, there was a shortage of small change. English money was based on the pound sterling, defined as 1,719 grains of sterling silver. The Royal Mint issued shillings, where 20 shillings equaled one pound of silver. Merchants who obtained silver through trade could take it to the Royal Mint and have it turned into shillings at this rate. Pennies, minted in copper, were defined as being worth 1/20th of a shilling, so that there were 240 pennies to the pound. The stipulated value of the penny was well above the actual value of the copper in the coin. So, while the shilling was commodity money, the penny was fiat money. The difference in value between the copper and the coin meant that counterfeiting was profitable. There were so many counterfeits that pennies were only reluctantly exchanged for shillings. As a result, pennies collected in merchant's tills, out of circulation. To fight this, the Royal Mint periodically stopped making pennies in the 18th century.

The 1790s were the dawn of the industrial revolution, and the working classes were expanding dramatically in England. Work was available in mills and mines, and this meant a dramatic increase in the number of people who were dependent on wages, rather than on the land. The larger mills employed hundreds of workers. At this time, a male industrial worker would earn between one and two shillings (between \$4.50 and \$9.00) for a day's work (Selgin 2008, 9). This meant that the everyday transactions required coins valued at less than a shilling. Half-pennies and farthings (one quarter of a penny) were an absolute necessity for the working classes. When selling their goods in bulk, companies would take in high-value coins (or promissory notes based on bank holdings). But they couldn't pay the workers with these, and so as the 18th century came to a close, there was an ever-increasing demand for copper coinage.

In 1787, industrialist Thomas Williams devised a solution to the problem. Williams controlled the Parys Mine Company, which ran the world's largest copper mine. They employed thousands of miners and smelters. To satisfy the need for small change, he produced an exquisitely engraved coin which bore the slogan "We promise to pay the bearer one penny." On the other side was the image of a rustic priest (hence, the name Druid). The promise of exchange was backed by Parys Mine Company. The idea was that workers could exchange the coins for small payments at pubs and stores. Merchants would exchange the promissory pennies for shillings and guineas. Williams established exchange offices in Anglesey, where the mine was located on the west coast of England, as well as Liverpool and far-away London.

As it turned out, very few of the copper coins were exchanged for silver or gold. The demand for small change reached across England, and the coins quickly began to circulate independently of the Parys Mine Company payroll. The quality of the engraving made them hard to counterfeit, and for some merchants they became the preferred copper coinage. Other employers had been experimenting with several solutions to the same problem. They adopted Williams's solution of issuing pennies backed by their own companies, and private mints quickly sprang up to fill the need for pennies. By the turn of the century, there were 200 or more private mints creating coins backed by the promises of industrialists. By some estimates, they produced 40 million commercial pennies, minting more pennies in a decade than the Royal Mint had produced in the previous half-century.

Function and Rules in Institutions

The story of the Druid penny is an interesting example of the creation and maintenance of a social institution. How can it be explained in terms of joint intentions? Four features of the story are relevant to Searle's and Tuomela's account of institutions. (For the sake of exegetic clarity, we will focus on Searle's account in the remainder of this section.) First, while the Druid penny was officially backed by a promise to exchange the tokens for silver or gold, they quickly took on the character of fiat money. They were money because people treated them as money. Second, the Druid penny is an object with a function. However, unlike biological functions, the ability of the Druid penny to function as a unit of exchange does not seem to depend on the physical properties of the coin. Third, there seems to be a normative dimension to the function. In the case of the Druid penny, this is most apparent in the promise printed on the coin. Should the exchange office fail to trade the copper coins for silver, they would be criticized by merchants. Notice that in this case, the promise was backed by neither laws nor a king. The normativity is somehow intrinsic to the practice of accepting the Druid penny as money. Finally, these characteristics of institution of the Druid penny are maintained in some way by the activity of accepting and using the pennies. If the workers had refused to take the Druid pennies as salary, or if merchants had refused to take the pennies in payment, the Druid pennies could not have functioned as money. Searle's theory of institutions is designed to explain these four features of the creation and maintenance of an institution.

Let us begin with Searle's conception of function. He argues that the functions of artifacts depend on the purposes to which we put them. Searle calls such functions "agentive functions." Agentive functions are independent of both the causal powers of the object and its history. Independent of human intentionality, there is nothing intrinsic to an object which makes it a hammer. The agent's purpose provides its function. Of course, given our purposes, some objects will be better suited than others. One would have to be in a pretty special circumstance to use a banana as a hammer, for instance. The crucial role of intentions screens off the causal history. When I pick up a banana and use it as a hammer, it thereby acquires the agentive function of a hammer even if no banana has even been used that way before. Purposes make all agentive functions normative because there is something that the object *ought* to do, given the agent's purpose. If I want to drive a nail, the banana will fail as a hammer. On the other hand, if I want to gently crimp the soft raw crust of a pie, the banana will be an excellent hammer.

Status functions are a particularly important kind of agentive function. A status function is imposed on an object when we treat the object as having a status, and as having a particular purpose or use in virtue of that status. The Druid penny, on Searle's account, took on the status of "money" or "unit of commercial exchange." The mine workers treated the coins as if they had the same status as coins issued by the Royal Mint. Once they were given this status, they could be used to serve the same purposes as those coins. According to Searle, the logical form of a status function is:

X counts as Y in conditions C.

The X-term names a type of object which will have the status, and the Y-term names the status. Because the function is to be imposed by agents, the X and Y terms must be independent. As Searle points out, "objects that are designed and used to be sat on by one person count as chairs" does not constitute a status function, since satisfying the X-term is sufficient for satisfying the Y-term (Searle 1995, 44). In a status function, the Y-term will go beyond any properties entailed by the X-term. The C-term indicates the crucial difference between status functions and other agentive functions. Whether a banana functions as a hammer for me depends only on my intentions. But whether a piece of paper counts as the Queen of Hearts depends on whether we are playing cards.

A playing card like the Queen of Hearts has its powers only within the context of a particular game. In Section 3.3, we encountered the idea of a "rule-constituted activity," and games were a central example. Searle regards all institutions as rule-constituted, and he suggests that all the rules which constitute social institutions have the form of status functions. Very often, social institutions give *people* status functions. In football, the rules give the person with the status of "goalie" a number of abilities (functions) which are not provided to the other players. One sort of status function is the capacity to declare new status functions. A person with the status function of "king" can declare that a new coin will be struck. That is, this fellow, George, counts as king in the context of the nation of England. One of the functions of a king is to issue currency. To do so, George issues the declaration that coins made of gold struck with the insignia of the Royal Mint count as guineas. In this way, status functions can form a hierarchy; some status functions are made possible by the existence of others.

While agentive functions can be imposed individualistically—perhaps only I use a banana hammer—the status functions which form the rules constitutive of social institutions cannot. Thomas Williams's declaration that "these coins are worth one penny" would have meant nothing unless it had been accepted by the workers and merchants. For Searle (and Tuomela), this acceptance must involve we-mode intentionality. *We* count the disc of copper as a coin. One argument for the necessity of we-mode intentionality is that without it, the status functions do not confer the right sort of normativity. When I impose the function of a hammer on my banana, the only appropriate criticism is that the banana will not serve my purposes. That is, I am right or wrong to use the banana that way only in the light of my own goals. By contrast, when a merchant fails to take legal tender in exchange for goods, a deeper sort of criticism is appropriate. The shopkeeper's individual goals and preferences are irrelevant. *We* treat the coins as money, and failure to do so runs afoul of a rule *we* have imposed on ourselves. We-mode acceptance thus turns a status function into a constitutive rule.

Explaining Social Institutions

Searle's account of status functions and constitutive rules gives him the resources he thinks he needs to explain the emergence of fiat money, like the Druid penny. It is important that the Druid pennies bore the slogan "We promise to pay the bearer one penny." Promises are speech acts, and in making a promise one imposes obligations on oneself. The declarations which impose status functions are also speech acts, on Searle's account. By issuing a coin with this promise, the Pays Mine Company imposed a status on the coin and created a specific obligation. Recall that the company kept exchange offices where the Druid pennies could be exchanged for currencies of the Royal Mint. The plural subject of the slogan, "*We* promise to pay," makes it clear that this is not the promise of an individual but of a corporation. Companies were taken to be entitled to issue such promises, and on Searle's account this exhibits a status function imposed on a company that underlies the ability to issue a promissory coin.

Once the coins were in wider circulation, their promissory aspect diminished in importance. The workers and merchants treated them as real pennies in places far from the Pays Mine exchange offices. Hence, they did not function just as tokens to be exchanged for proper money. On Searle's account, this must be a new status function. The canonical form of a status function is "*X* counts as *Y* in conditions *C*." The *X* term describes the physical object, in this case, the copper disc. It counts as worth one penny (Y) under the conditions that it was minted by the Pays Mine company (C). For this to be a constitutive rule of the practice of exchange, the rule that the Druid coin counts as a penny must have been collectively accepted—a joint action—by the workers and merchants. Notice that no king or authority declared that the new coin would have the status of money. And the Pays Mine Company certainly did not do so, since such a declaration would have amounted to creating a counterfeit penny. So, the Druid penny seems to be a case where a status function was created through a collective acceptance of the Druid penny as having the same status function as a Royal Mint penny.

One might object at this point that the workers and merchants didn't understand what they were doing in anything like Searle's terms. Surely no 18th-century miner thought, "We intend to take this Druid penny as a penny in the context of our economic transactions." In response to this kind of problem, both Searle (and Tuomela) are quick to point out that while explicit agreement is the simplest case, agreement is not necessary. The action of accepting the Druid penny, giving it back in change, treating it as interchangeable with the Royal Mint penny, and so on constitute a collective acceptance of its function. And the workers and merchants did these actions deliberately. "In the course of consciously buying, selling, exchanging, etc.," Searle writes, "they may simply evolve institutional facts" (Searle 1995, 47).

It has been argued that collective acceptance is a dubious notion. In some cases, status functions exist in a context where most of the community does *not* accept the function. For example, not all such payment schemes like the Druid penny were greeted with acceptance. In the same period, other employers responded to the lack of small change by issuing credits, called "scrip," to their employees. Unlike the Druid pennies, scrip had to be redeemed in the company store. And since the company owned both the factory or mine *and* the company store, the system was ripe for abuse. Under this sort of system, the workers often felt cheated and resentful because the scrip was redeemed for less than they thought their labor was worth. The workers were trapped because they needed to feed their families and had no opportunity to find other work. Scrip was regarded as illegitimate by its users but used as currency anyway. The mere taking of the promissory coins in payment thus does not imply that the workers accepted the status function of the scrip.

In his later work, Searle has recognized the force of this objection. His reply is to distinguish between cooperation and collective recognition (Searle 2010, 57–58). Cooperative action requires we-mode intentions. Collective recognition is merely the I-mode recognition of a status function with mutual knowledge. In the case of scrip, the lack of collective acceptance means that the workers only collectively recognized the scrip. The workers recognized that the scrip tokens had the status function of money, but they did not engage in a we-mode intention. They individually recognized the existence of the scrip system knowing that others individually recognized it too. They accepted the tokens as payment and used them simply because others did so; there were no we-mode intentions in this case. However, it is not clear that this solution fully resolves the difficulty with scrip; two problems remain. First, Searle writes that "the particular transactions within the institution require *cooperation*" (Searle 2010, 57, emphasis in original). So, while the workers did not collectively accept the status function of scrip, they still had to cooperate in individual transactions, which requires joint intentions to recognize the status function. That is, in individual transactions, both parties still had to take the scrip as currency. Second, if the workers did not collectively accept the scrip and impose the status function of money on it, then who did? Presumably the officers of the mine company did so. But if the workers did not collectively accept the scrip, then it is not clear why they would collectively accept the authority of the company to issue it. Overall, the distinction between collective acceptance and collective recognition does not seem to help distinguish the successful Druid penny from scrip, which was regarded as illegitimate but used nonetheless.

While the business of collective-acceptance-that-is-not-accepted is puzzling, there is a deeper problem with Searle's account. The transition from commodity money to fiat money requires that a coordination problem be solved. Fiat money like the Druid penny is convenient, and there are several advantages to using it instead of the commodity money of sterling silver shillings. However, the Druid penny is valuable only if others will take it in exchange. If I lose my confidence that others will accept it, I am better off using the silver shilling. The strategic situation can be modeled as a Stag Hunt game (Figure 5.9). If we both use Druid pennies (hunt stag), we both get the higher payoff. But there is a second equilibrium with a lower pay off (hunting rabbits, using silver) into which we will fall if our coordination is not successful. Searle's joint-intention account does not recognize that there is a coordination problem underlying fiat money. In virtue of what do rules help resolve the coordination problem? When we pose the question this way, a very different answer emerges.

In Section 9.4, we briefly explored Guala's rules-in-equilibrium account of institutions. On his view, rules provide coordination devices that create new, correlated equilibria for the original strategic situation. On first look, Searle's account seems to be able to use the same device. The transition from commodity money to fiat money *is* a coordination problem. The constitutive rule "This copper disk counts as money in the condition that it is issued by the Pays Mine Company" is a coordination device, just as Guala suggested, and there is now a new equilibrium in the game. However, this solution is less successful than it seems for two reasons.

First, Searle's status functions and constitutive rules are not necessary to resolve the coordination problem. Much simpler rules, accepted only in the I-mode will do. Suppose the rule is simply "Accept the coin if and only if it is issued by Pays Mine Company." An individual can accept this rule, and by doing so, that individual can adopt the strategy of following it. The success of a coordination equilibrium depends on the coordination device being public. In the case of the Druid penny, the device was the promise to pay made by the operator of the largest copper mine in the world. This is a very public signal that creates common knowledge of the strategy. No collective acceptance, and hence no status functions or constitutive rules, are necessary.

Second, without the collective acceptance, the problem of accounting for the difference between the accepted Druid penny and the resented scrip system becomes clear. In the scrip system, the company followed the same strategy as a state follows when it issues fiat money and demands it back in the form of taxes. By demanding the fiat money back in the company store, the company was guaranteeing that there would be demand for the fiat money. The rule "Accept the scrip if and only if it is issued by X company" is also a strategy in the coordination game, and the fact that the company issued the scrip is a public coordination device. So, the scrip functions in the same way as the Druid penny, which is what we would expect since both function as fiat money. The difference is that the scrip system was limited to the company wages and the store. Outside of that environment, no one had any incentive to take the scrip. The Druid penny was not involved in such a mandatory buy-back scheme to maintain its value; hence it could circulate more widely.

While joint action is an important phenomenon, and it is doubtless an important dimension of the social world, it is less clear that it can be leveraged in to a full "structure of human civilization" as Searle proposes. At the very least, competitors like Guala's rules-in-equilibrium account can cover the same territory. And arguably, they do so with less metaphysical baggage. Defenders of Searle, as well as the die-hard normativists, will no doubt reject Guala's solution, but that debate must be left for another forum.

10.4. Wrap Up

Chapter Summary

The philosophers whose work we have surveyed in this chapter take joint action to be the foundation of sociality. Their work represents three approaches to understanding the intentions which stand behind joint action. First, joint intentionality might be a property of a special kind of collective agent. This view highlights the importance of collective acceptance and mutual recognition, but it faces difficulty with groups that don't have procedures for gathering information and making decisions. The other two approaches reject the idea that there are collective agents. They look to the characteristics of the intentions to distinguish joint from individual action. The second approach tries to find the joint character of action in the content of individual intentions: I intend that *we* make dinner. This sort of view is reductionist while preserving a distinction between individual and joint action. However, the second approach struggles to account for the sort of cooperation which would solve the difficult cases of joint action, such as the prisoner's dilemma. If joint action is to be the foundation of sociality, then presumably the barriers to cooperation must be surmounted. The third view proposes to explain cooperation in terms of a special sort of attitude—intentions in the "we-mode." These accounts are arguably the most successful in accounting for cases of joint action. If joint intentionality is to be the foundation of sociality, however, we need an account of how social-level phenomena can be explained in terms of joint action and intention. Searle and Tuomela have provided elaborate conceptual analyses of social institutions. Whether they are acceptable, however, is ultimately a matter of whether they provide better explanations than some of the other approaches we have surveyed in this book.

The views discussed in this chapter take important positions in the reductionism and naturalism debates. The views of collective agency discussed in Section 10.1 are strongly anti-reductionistic. The alternatives all treat individual agents as a privileged level of analysis. Only Bratman's view, however, is strongly reductionist. Both Searle and Tuomela, for slightly different reasons, treat we-mode joint intentions as irreducible to I-mode joint intentions. They therefore think that the social level cannot be reduced to the individual level. Nonetheless, there are no purely social properties for these theorists insofar as all social institutions can be analyzed into we-mode joint intentions which are held by individuals.

With respect to the naturalism debates, all the positions surveyed in this chapter are strongly anti-naturalist in the sense that they see a large divide between the social and the natural sciences. All are concerned with explanations which appeal to intention, and they assume that appeal to intentions cannot be replaced by explanations which look to causal relationships between social-level properties, by evolutionary explanations, or by explanations which look to sub-personal cognitive or neurological states. In the next chapter, we will turn to the possibilities of such causal explanations for the social sciences. What forms does causality take in the social world? Do social entities have causal powers? How are causes identified in the social sciences?

Discussion Questions

1. Find some other examples which are like Sugden's family vacation plans in the sense that it is true to say, "We prefer x to y" but false to say, "Each of us prefers x to y." In your examples, what role does group identity play? Is there a joint commitment in Gilbert's sense? Was this commitment explicit or implicit?
2. Consider again the experiment by Guala and Mittone, discussed in Section 7.2. Is it plausible to think that the subjects have formed an implicit joint commitment? If not, what are the consequences for Gilbert's view of plural subjects?
3. Is it true that a person can intend to do only things that he or she can control? What about these examples: a sergeant ordering a private to do 50 pushups; a parent intending for a child to go to college; a pharaoh beginning the construction of a pyramid which will be completed long after his death. How plausible is the own-action principle?
4. Analyses of joint intention emphasize the cooperative character of joint actions. Can any of the analyses be extended to joint actions where the participants are competing? Consider a game of tennis, a bar fight, or a bicycle

race. Are there non-cooperative joint actions? Are these best understood as we-intentions or I-intentions?

5.   Are social institutions always normative? If so, what is the best way to account for this normativity? Does it, as Searle, Tuomela, and Gilbert argue, arise from the characteristics of joint action? Or can it be accounted for by the theorists discussed in Chapter 9?

Further Reading

On the use of team reasoning to account for joint action, see Bacharach, *Beyond Individual Choice: Teams and Frames in Game Theory* (2006) and Sugden, "Team Preferences" (2000b). In "Collective Intentions and Team Agency" (2007), Gold and Sugden relate this phenomenon to views of collective intentionality.

The history of the Druid penny is discussed in Selgin, *Good Money* (2008). The transition from commodity money to fiat money is complicated. Phenomena like the Druid penny are found throughout the world; see Helleiner, *The Making of National Money* (2003).

Schweikard and Schmid's "Collective Intentionality" entry in the *Stanford Encyclopedia of Philosophy* (2021) is a concise overview of the collective intentionality debate. Jankovic and Ludwig's (eds.) *Routledge Handbook of Collective Intentionality* (2017) is a comprehenive treatment of issues.

Gilbert's contributions begin with *On Social Facts* (1989) and are further developed and elaborated in *Living Together* (1996) and *Joint Commitment* (2014). Pettit's *The Common Mind* (1993) is an important argument for a holistic view; see also Pettit and Schweikard, "Joint Actions and Group Agents" (2006); Pettit, "The Reality of Group Agents" (Pettit 2009); as well as List and Pettit, *Group Agency: The Possibility, Design, and Status of Corporate Agents (2011)*. For critique, see Tollefsen, "Collective Intentionality and the Social Sciences" (2002) and Miller, "Against Collective Agency" (2002).

Bratman articulated his view in a series of essays. These are now collected in *Intention, Plans, and Practical Reason* (1987) and *Faces of Intention (1999)*. A good exchange between Bratman and Gilbert is contained in Bratman (2009) and Gilbert (2009).

Tuomela has been developing his view since "We Intentions" (1988), written with Miller. Subsequent elaborations are found in *The Philosophy of Social Practices* (2002) and *The Philosophy of Sociality: The Shared Point of View* (2007). While intricate and complex, these works repay careful study. See Hakli *et al,* "Two Kinds of We-Reasoning" (2010) for an application to team reasoning experiments.

Searle's main arguments for joint intentionality are contained in the essay "Collective Intentions and Actions" (1990), but it needs to be understood against the background provided in *Intentionality* (1983). He subsequently applied his analysis to questions of social ontology in *The Construction of Social Reality* (1995) and *Making the Social World: The Structure of Human Civilization* (2010). Collections of commentary include Tsohatzidis (ed.), *Intentional Acts and Institutional*

Facts (2007) and Koepsell and Moss, *John Searle's Ideas about Social Reality: Extensions, Criticisms, and Reconstructions* (Koepsell and Moss 2003). Other useful critical responses to Searle's view are found in Schmid, "Can Brains in Vats Think as a Team?" (2003); Viskovatoff, "Searle, Rationality, and Social Reality" (2003); Turner, "Searle's Social Reality" (2002 [1999]); and Tiffenbach, "Searle and Menger on Money" (2010). Guala's critique is found in *Understanding Institutions* (2016), and Mäkelä et al (2018) reply to his critique.

Tomasello and his colleagues make explicit appeal to philosophical views in "Understanding and Sharing Intentions: The Origins of Cultural Cognition" (2005). See also Tomasello *et al*, *Why We Cooperate* (2009). The way in which joint intentionality might fit into a naturalized, psychological framework has been explored in Vromen, "Collective Intentionality, Evolutionary Biology, and Social Reality" (2003); Tollefsen, "Let's Pretend" (2004); and Tollefsen and Dale, "Naturalizing Joint Action: a process-Based Approach," (2011).

11 Causality and Law in the Social World

Science aims to uncover hidden causes. Reading about how the Higgs field is responsible for mass or how DNA molecules replicate engenders a sense of awe. Here, science seems capable of understanding the ultimate structure of nature. When we turn to the social sciences, awe is replaced by an uncanny feeling. Surely, I am free to act as I choose. It is hard to believe that hidden clockwork generates my actions, or that natural laws explain the events within my family, church, or college. And yet at the same time, we love to complain about busses that don't run on schedule and companies that can't deliver their goods. Another arrangement would be better, we complain, precisely because it would be more *effective*. Social reorganization would *cause* a different result. Our social systems seem to be at once the products of free human action and causal mechanisms that run behind our backs.

One might wonder whether seeking causes and laws in the social sciences is a fool's errand. We have already seen some of the grounds for this point of view. If, as the interpretivists do, we insist that the object of the social sciences must be to uncover the meanings, intentions, and values which animate the social world, the search for impersonal and general causal laws misses the point. In Chapter 5 we saw this objection in the discussion of whether intentional actions should be explained by subsuming actions under laws. These ideas will surface again in Section 11.2 as we turn our attention to laws of the social world. Are there features of the social world that make it unsuitable for description by general laws? Does the complexity, context-sensitivity, or unpredictability of human social interaction limit the possibility of broad generalizations? And does it mean that our knowledge of social regularities must have a different character than our knowledge of nature?

If we grant that it is appropriate to try to understand social phenomena in terms of causes or laws, two further philosophical problems emerge: the metaphysics and epistemology of causality. Hume's analysis of causation in terms of regularities was the dominant view in the social sciences (as well as philosophy) for most of the 20th century. In the last several decades, several new conceptualizations of causality and causal explanation have become popular. These views recover alternatives to Hume's analysis of causality from philosophers like Aristotle, Reid, and Mill. This is a metaphysical debate in the sense that it seeks an account of what causality *is*. Section 11.3 will discuss the relative merits of these different ways of thinking about causality in the social sciences. These new ways of thinking about

DOI: 10.4324/9781003207795-11

causality separate causes from laws. Insofar as we can understand causes without assuming that they conform to universal regularities, our theories in the social sciences do not need to be formulated in terms of laws. As a result, these new conceptualizations have contributed to the demise of the empiricist view of theory. In its place, many social scientists prefer to think of theorizing in terms of modeling, which we explored in Chapter 9.

11.1. The Democratic Peace Hypothesis

To understand the search for causes, correlations, and laws in the social sciences, let us begin by considering an example of research which has focused on them: the democratic peace hypothesis. Immanuel Kant argued that rational people would not vote "to bring down the miseries of war upon their country" (Kant 1903 [1795], 122). As we know too well, however, nationalism or racism can overwhelm the calm reflections of a philosophical mood. Kant's theoretical arguments, then, raise the empirical question of whether democracies are more peaceful than other forms of government. Perhaps the first explicit scientific investigation was an essay by Dean Babst (1964), who used World Wars I and II as test cases. In these conflicts, many countries went to war with each other, and they exhibited a variety of forms of government. In these two wars, democracies went to war with non-democracies, but no democracies went to war with each other. Could this have been just a matter of chance? By Babst's count, 33 independent nations were at war in WWI. Of the countries who went to war, 10 had elective governments. There are 528 possible conflicts between pairs of nations which went to war in WWI. There were, in fact, 72 actual declarations of war, which means that 14% of the pairs of countries which could have gone to war did so. If the form of government had nothing to do with whether a pair of countries went to war, we would expect the proportion of democracies which went to war with each other to be about the same as the proportion of non-democracies. Interestingly, this is *not* what happened in either WWI or WWII. Out of the 45 different possible conflicts among the 10 democracies involved in WWI, none went to war with each other. The pattern for WWII was the same. In WWI and WWII, democracies did not go to war against each other. All declarations of war involved at least one non-democratic nation.

Babst concluded his paper by saying: "This study suggests that the existence of independent nations with elective governments greatly increases the chances for the maintenance of peace" (Babst 1964, 14). Notice two things about this remark. First, the conclusion is couched in probabilistic language—the presence of a democracy "greatly increases the chances" of peace. One wonders whether Babst is asserting a causal relationship here or merely noticing the correlation. We will return to this question in Section 11.3. Second, Babst's conclusion echoes Kant's thesis that democracies are more peaceful than non-democracies. However, his data shows that conflict *between democracies* is less likely than between democracies and states with other forms of government. The more limited thesis that democracies do not tend to go to war with each other is sometimes called the "democratic peace," to distinguish it from Kant's broader thesis that democracies are more peaceful.

By calculating the proportion of possible conflicts which were actual, Babst demonstrated a *correlation*. As you know if you've had a course in statistics, a correlation is a dependence relationship between two properties or variables. When a pair of variables is correlated, the presence (or value) of one changes the probability that the other will be present (or take a particular value). The height of children is thus correlated with the height of their parents: tall children are more likely to have tall parents. In the philosophical and methodological literature, correlations are typically expressed in terms of conditional probabilities. The probability that a normal die will roll a two is 1/6; there are six faces, and one has a "2." This is normally represented as:

$$Pr(\text{Two}) = 1/6 = 16.6\%$$

Similarly, we can calculate the probability that a die will roll an even number:

$$Pr(\text{Even}) = 1/2 = 50\%$$

A conditional probability expresses a relationship between two variables. If you know that I have rolled an even number, then the chance that it is a two is no longer 1/6. Since there are three even numbers on the die, the chances are now 1/3. In other words, *given that* the roll is even, there is a 1/3 chance that it will be a two. This is standardly represented as:

$$Pr(\text{Two given Even}) = 1/3 = 33.3\%$$

When two binary variables, X and Y, are correlated, the probability that Y will occur given X is either greater or less than the probability that Y will occur in the absence of X. (The absence of X is represented as $\sim X$.) Formally:

$Pr(Y \text{ given } X) > Pr(Y \text{ given } \sim X)$ Positive correlation between Y and X
$Pr(Y \text{ given } X) < Pr(Y \text{ given } \sim X)$ Negative correlation between Y and X
$Pr(Y \text{ given } X) = Pr(Y \text{ given } \sim X)$ No correlation between Y and X

In Babst's study, the variables were whether a pair of countries went to war (W) and whether both members of the pair were democracies (D). In WWI and WWII, no democracies went to war with each other. This is obviously much less than the proportion of the possible conflicts which occurred between either mixed pairs or pairs of non-democracies ($\sim D$). Hence:

$$Pr(W \text{ given } D) < Pr(W \text{ given } \sim D)$$

Since the difference in probability is large, this is a very strong negative correlation. Indeed, because $Pr(W \text{ given } D)$ is zero, it is a *perfect correlation*.

Babst analyzed data only from WWI and WWII, but his conclusion is general: pairs of democracies are less likely to go to war with each other than are other mixes of government type. The next step, then, is to see whether the correlation holds up in a larger data set. Scholars immediately ran into the problem of defining "war" and "democracy." The issues are related to those discussed in Chapter 3: how are concepts of the social sciences developed? As so often happens in the social sciences, we begin with common notions. And like most colloquial terms for social phenomena, *war* and *democracy* are vague and evaluatively loaded. Many countries want to call themselves democracies, and few want to admit that their conflicts are wars. This is a case, then, where self-identification is not useful. As we saw in Section 3.1, refining a concept is a substantial endeavor. Political scientists must develop a broader theory which gives substance to the concepts and justifies their operationalization. Babst defined democracies as having legislation controlled by an elected body, a separately elected executive, and "some" freedom of the press. Subsequent refinements have included scalar variables which represent institutions as more and less democratic. With respect to the conceptualization of "war," one commonly used body of data comes from the *Correlates of War* project. This data set defines war as requiring 1,000 battle deaths per year of conflict (among other criteria), and its current version lists 95 inter-state wars between 1816 and 2007. Using data sets like the *Correlates of War*, scholars have found that the negative correlation between democratic conflict and war holds, though the question of whether democracies are more peaceful in general is much less clear.

As we have noted already, Babst concluded that the presence of a democracy "greatly increases the chances" of peace. Most scholars have not limited themselves to the observation that the variables of democracy and war are correlated. They have gone on to draw the causal conclusion. Something about democratic institutions reduces the risk of war with another democracy. Now, one will often hear social scientists balk at talk of causality. Correlation is not causality, they will remind us, and this true maxim is taken as a blanket prohibition on making causal statements based on correlational evidence. While caution is a good epistemic attitude, it is arguably too strong to refuse to countenance causal inference in statistics. The social scientist who eschews talk of causality when describing their results often does not hesitate to make policy recommendations when describing the results' significance. Policy recommendations presumably rely on causal relationships. The reason we are interested in many social phenomena is that we want to control them; we want to decrease poverty and war, and to increase education and happiness. For this we need something more than mere correlations. Therefore, a blanket prohibition on inferring causes from correlational data will not serve the social sciences.

11.2. Are There Social Scientific Laws?

The correlation between democracy and peace is very strong. In this way, it seems like the laws discovered in the natural sciences. Should we regard the democratic peace hypothesis, if true, as a *law*? This question strikes to the heart of what it means to be a social science. The discovery of laws is usually regarded as the mark of a genuine science. We have already seen how laws were made prominent by the empiricist conception of theory (*cf.* Sections 3.2 and 5.1). But one need not be committed to empiricism to think that laws have a special relation to scientific activity. The power and generality of theory makes science distinctive, and theories can be general only insofar as they identify the laws underlying phenomena. The question of whether the social sciences could discover laws is thus one of the pivots of the debate over (epistemic) naturalism—whether the social sciences are distinct from the natural sciences. Depending on one's perspective on this debate, the apparent lack of laws in the social sciences can be either treated as an indication of their failure to be genuine sciences, or as a mark of their distinctive character.

Characteristics of Natural Laws

Before one could decide whether the democratic peace is a social scientific law, one would need criteria for identifying a law of any domain. Two conditions are generally agreed upon which distinguish laws from mere correlations:

1. Laws must be general, making no reference to particular objects, times, or places.
2. Laws must support counterfactual statements.

To see why these conditions are necessary, consider this true generalization: all the books on my desk on May 23, 2013, are written in English. It is obviously not a law of nature. The reference to particulars keeps it from having the appropriate level of generality. Second, it does not let us infer what *would* happen *if* an object satisfied the generalization. If Descartes's *Méditations Métaphysiques* were to fall from the bookshelf onto my desk, it would not be miraculously translated into English. By contrast, Newton's laws of motion tell me that *if it were* dropped from a height of 150 meters above the surface of the moon, *it would be* traveling at roughly 16 meters per second on impact. Now, my copy of Descartes's *Méditations* has never been to the moon, nor will it likely be, and in this sense the statement about its velocity is "counterfactual." The generalization about my desk provides no similar grounds for counterfactuals.

If laws are general regularities which support counterfactuals, then the democratic peace is a law. It is a strong correlation that makes no mention of particular objects, places, or times. And it seems to support counterfactuals. American foreign policy in the latter 20th century has often aimed to reduce war by spreading democracy. This policy is supported by the idea that if a country becomes a democracy, it is less likely to declare war; if North Korea *were* a democracy, it *would be* less hostile to South Korea. In this sense, then, the democratic peace supports counterfactuals and is entitled to *prima facie* status as a law.

Some philosophers have suggested a further condition for a generalization to qualify as a law. Proper laws must be exceptionless, universal generalizations. They say something about what happens to all objects under certain conditions. Newton's Law of Universal Gravitation, for example, says that for *any* two masses m_1 and m_2, the force between them is a function of the distance between them.

On this view of laws, any qualification of a law either reflects the intrusion of external factors or shows that the purported law is not genuine. So, if we found an example where the force between two masses did not satisfy Newton's Law of Universal Gravitation, we would either conclude that there was another force involved (say, a magnetic field) or we would revise the law. In the social sciences, the proposed laws are typically qualified with a clause that isolates the regularity from disturbing forces: the law holds *ceteris paribus*, or all things being equal. While proposed laws in the social sciences are typically qualified with *ceteris paribus* clauses, contemporary philosophers of social science do not take this as a knock-down argument against social scientific laws. The reason is that the laws of biology are similarly qualified, and perhaps even the laws of physics as well. The interesting questions are whether laws qualified by *ceteris paribus* clauses can be explanatory, and what such limited regularities might tell us about causality. We will return to these issues in Section 9.3.

Creativity and Complexity

The unpredictability of human behavior seems incompatible with the existence of social scientific laws. Since a law must be general, it is true of events past, present, and future. This means that where there is a genuine law, there must be predictability. Therefore, if human behavior is unpredictable, then there are no laws of the social world. People can be creative, and the very nature of creativity precludes prediction. Moreover, human societies are much more complex than natural phenomena. The creativity and complexity of human behavior seems to make it unpredictable. Therefore, one might argue, it is misguided to think of the social sciences as analogous to the natural sciences.

One might argue that that creativity is not merely difficult to anticipate; it is logically impossible. The creation of something truly novel requires new concepts, new technologies, or new social relationships. To predict an innovation would require the social scientist to use the very concepts, or to describe the very technologies or social relationships, which are supposed to be invented later. In making the prediction, then, the social scientist would be the inventor. The invention would then exist at the time the prediction was made, not at the predicted time. Any attempt to predict invention, therefore, is self-defeating. To illustrate the point, Peter Winch quotes jazz musician Humphrey Lyttelton who, when asked where jazz was going, replied "If I knew where jazz was going, I'd be there already" (Winch 1958, 94).

The argument from creativity seems subject to immediate counterexample. Jules Verne imagined a flight to the moon before heavier-than-air travel was possible. This shows that the argument must be carefully formulated. In his version of the argument, Alasdair MacIntyre makes two refinements (MacIntyre 1981, 94). First, the innovations must be "radically new" in the sense that they are not simply new assemblages of existing materials. This means that predictions like "Next generation computers will be faster than current computers" don't count against the argument. Second, the predictions need to be based on principle, not simply imagined possibilities. The Greek legend of Icarus therefore does not count as a prediction of the Wright brothers' airplane. The inherent or systematic unpredictability of human events shows that there is a kind of historical asymmetry to the study of human behavior. Looking backward, we can explain why a conceptual innovation caught on or how a technological change made a social change possible. But the unpredictability of human events means that we cannot look into the future in the same way as we look into the past. The social sciences are thus historical in a way that the natural scientific study of laws is not.

A critic might respond by granting the logical point about predicting radically new inventions but argue that the conclusion that human events are *inherently* or *systematically* unpredictable is a bit of a stretch. When one looks at the fine details of conceptual, technological, or social invention, the changes are often incremental. The required limitation to "radically new" innovations thus shrinks the scope of the argument to moments of true genius. And even if there are such moments of genius, the vast breadth of human history and social life is quite ordinary. The argument only shows that the search for social laws will fail in some cases. Notice that there is a parallel with the natural sciences on this point. Quantum mechanical events are sometimes interpreted as being indeterministic. They can at best be represented with statistical generalizations. The lack of exceptionless laws in this domain is not grounds for saying that there are no natural laws at all. Thus, even acknowledging human creativity, one might conclude that the social sciences are rather like the natural sciences.

A second argument for the inherent unpredictability of social events is based on the complexity of human behavior. The powerful generalizations of the natural sciences can be identified because it is possible to exclude external influences from our experiments, thereby isolating simple systems and repeatable phenomena. In the social sciences, we are interested in phenomena that cannot be isolated or described in simple terms. For example, while it may be possible to isolate people in a lab and study their choice behavior, we are not just interested in how people respond to prisoner's dilemmas. We are interested in phenomena like democracy and war, and their explanations require many more variables. Humans are remarkable in their capacity to engage with this complexity. The simplest and most fundamental human social interactions require sensitivity to a mass of subtle signals and cues. Conversations are fundamental parts of human life, but consider the conversations among diplomats in an international crisis. In his formulation of the argument, Michael Scriven emphasized that the conclusion is not that laws are *a priori* impossible in the social sciences. Rather, the "multiplicity of critical variables in the simplest interesting cases" suggests that "simple laws will very rarely be found" (Scriven 1956, 335).

In response to this argument, Lee McIntyre has pointed out that it privileges our existing descriptions of social phenomena (McIntyre 1993). In the natural sciences, new laws typically require us to reconceptualize the underlying phenomena, and theoretical advances often provide a new language. Boyle's law, for example, relates temperature, pressure, and volume of a gas. These three values are observable and retain their ordinary meaning in Boyle's law. The kinetic theory of heat and the molecular conceptualization of gas, however, introduced a radical conceptual change. Temperature became mean kinetic energy, and pressure became the transfer of energy from the gas molecules to the walls of the container. Twentieth-century science has similarly transformed our conceptions of disease, space, and species. Using ordinary concepts for social phenomena, it may be true that there are no tractable generalizations to be found. It does not follow that there are no laws which could be formulated in another vocabulary.

Neither of the arguments discussed in this section succeeds in showing that laws in the social world are impossible. At best, they show that there may be limits to what can be described and explained by social laws. The arguments also suggest that it might be helpful to separate the notion of law from the notion of predictability. Human behavior may be unpredictable in certain respects, but it does not follow that there are no underlying laws (or causes) to be discovered. John Stuart Mill pointed out that many physical phenomena arise from complex interactions of underlying laws. His example was the study of tides, where variations in local conditions (depth, wind, current, etc.) made generalizations impossible (Mill 1987 [1872]). The mathematics of chaos theory has reinforced this point. In chaotic systems, each event is fully determined by laws. However, their interaction is such that no matter how precisely the initial values of the variables are specified, any predictions after some future point in time will be impossible. Whether human social interaction is chaotic in this sense is an empirical question. It can only be answered by trying to discover the underlying laws and understanding their interactions. And, one might argue, this may entail development of new vocabularies for describing ourselves. If it turns out that significant aspects of human life cannot be described using laws, then an anti-naturalist conclusion will hold for those domains: they must be understood in terms other than explanation by fundamental laws.

11.3. Causation and Law

Constant Conjunction

Perhaps the most famous definition of causality is Hume's succinct analysis:

> an object followed by another, and where all the objects, similar to the first, are followed by objects similar to the second. Or, in other words, where, if the first object had not been, the second never had existed.
>
> (Hume 1955 [1777], 87)

Without trying to do justice to the vast scholarship on this passage, a couple of interpretive remarks are in order. First, Hume uses the word *object* where contemporary philosophers who follow him would use *event* or perhaps *property*. The white billiard ball considered only as an object sits inert, causing nothing. The *event* of the white ball striking the red ball, on the other hand, causes the red ball to move.

Second, the two quoted sentences give strikingly different definitions. The first iden-tifies causality with an empirical regularity. The second sentence identifies it with a counterfactual: if the cause *were not* to occur, then effect would not occur either. We will return to this feature of Hume's definition. Finally, Hume requires a regular co-occurrence of cause and effect: "all the objects, similar to the first, are followed by objects similar to the second." This means that whenever we assert a causal rela-tionship between two events, x and y, there must be two kinds (or *types*) of event, X and Y, and there must be a true generalization of the form "Whenever X occurs, Y occurs." It also means that when we explain an event by reference to its cause, we are implicitly invoking a causal law. (And here you see the deeper rationale behind Hempel's Deductive-Nomological form of explanation discussed in Section 5.1.)

The notorious problem with a regularity conception of causation is that regularities are too easy to find. For example, I was told as a child that the cows lie down in the field when it is about to rain. Clearly however, even if the association was absolutely reliable (which it isn't), no one in their right mind would suggest that the prostration of the cows causes rain. Or again, suppose I have the habit of snapping my fingers. Then it will be true that *whenever I snap my fingers on November 1 of an election year, someone is elected President of the United States on November 2*. So, have I acquired the power of creating US Presidents? Obviously not. On a regularity analysis of cau-sation, ruling out these cases requires specifying the right sort of regularity. We might begin by requiring that the regularities which constitute causation are laws of nature. This means that the metaphysics of causality will be tightly tied to the metaphysics of natural laws. The two features of natural laws discussed in Section 9.2 help exclude spurious regularities. The finger-snap generalization fails to be a law because it men-tions specific objects and times. And presumably, these generalizations do not support counterfactuals. We can't make it rain by encouraging the cows to lie down.

The prostrating cows illustrate a further issue about the sort of regularities which constitute causal relationships. The real reason that we deny causal powers to the cows is that we believe the behavior of the cows and the rain to be products of a single, underlying process. The cows sense the change in the meteorological condi-tions that also produce rain. In this case there is a *common cause* which explains the observed regularity. The regularity observed between cow behavior and rain is trumped by a further pair of regularities: a regular association between changes in the wind, pressure, or temperature and the prostration of the cows, and another association between those same events and rainstorms. This raises both metaphysi-cal and epistemological problems. Metaphysically, the regularity theorist needs to specify that the observed regularities are not the product of a common cause. But then the difficulty becomes epistemological; identifying common causes is a deep challenge for any view of causation.

Linear Equation Modeling and Causal Regularities

The democratic peace hypothesis is remarkable because the correlation is so strong, perhaps even perfect. Most regularities of interest to the social sciences are shot through with exceptions. The dominant approach in the social sciences has been to represent the regularities in terms of probabilities. We encountered the fundamental notion of a probabilistic dependence, or correlation, in Section 9.1. Where two event types are correlated, the presence of X either raises or lowers the probability of Y. In symbols:

$$\Pr(Y \text{ given } X) \neq \Pr(Y \text{ given } \sim X)$$

Since we expect causal relations to exhibit probabilistic dependence, it is natural to extend the sort of regularities which constitute causality to probabilistic regularities.

In the discussion so far, our event types have been "binary variables," which means that they are either true or false. In other words, a government is either democratic or non-democratic; a war either occurs or it does not. Many of the relationships we are interested in, however, are not all-or-nothing. For example, do extra years of school raise a person's income later in life? If you imagine a graph that plots the number of years of school against income at, say, age 35, it will probably be a cloud of data points. Whether the two variables are correlated depends on the shape of that cloud. If the points in the cloud are randomly scattered and don't cluster in any way, then we would say that there is no connection between schooling and income. The variables are uncorrelated. At the other extreme, the values might fall perfectly along a line. Each additional year of schooling would be worth, let's imagine, exactly another $5,000 in income. This would be a perfect correlation. Chances are, however, that the data points would be a kind of an oblong cloud that sloped up to the right. The narrower that oblong cloud—the more like a line—the higher the degree of correlation. For a very strong correlation, knowing the years of schooling will allow a fairly precise prediction of income at age 35. A weak correlation corresponds to a fatter cloud and a correspondingly vague prediction about income based on years of schooling.

In a question about the relationship between school and income, we are not just interested in whether the variables are correlated; we want to know *how much* one factor contributes to another. This corresponds to the slope of the oblong cloud of data points. The more schooling raises income, the steeper the line will rise. A linear regression model estimates this slope and represents it in a formula of this form:

$$Y = a + bX + U$$

Here, the coefficient b represents the slope. Intuitively, this represents the amount or strength of the effect. If b is large, more schooling raises income a lot. The final term, U, is the "error term." You can think of this as capturing the effect of other variables besides X or perhaps representing the error of the measurement. U is not a known or measured factor. It is a distribution of probabilities which will give us the probability for a particular value of Y, given a particular value of X. In general, we do not expect events to have unique causes. Events come about because several factors came together in the right way. Income is affected not only by schooling, but perhaps by the prestige of the school, the subjects you study, the region in which you live, and so on. Additional factors can be added into the simple model:

$$Y = a + b_1X_1 + b_2X_2 + \ldots + b_nX_n + U$$

Each of the various independent variables (X_n) is associated with its own coefficient, representing the different contributions made by the variable.

Once we have the power of statistical measures of correlation in hand, it is very tempting to identify causes and correlations. That is, we might just say that:

X causes Y if and only if $\Pr(Y \text{ given } X) \neq \Pr(Y \text{ given } {\sim}X)$

But if you've had a statistics course, you are probably throwing up your hands and crying foul. "Correlation is not causation!" you say. To confuse the two is the classic fallacy of statistical methodology. But wait, Hume's point was precisely that correlation *is* causation. There is nothing to causality but constant conjunction, and all this math is nothing more than a fancy way of expressing conjunction. What's going on? Contrary to first appearances, a regularity theorist like Hume would agree with your statistics teacher. The mere fact that X is correlated with Y is not enough to constitute causality. At the very least there must be no other variables Z which are common causes of X and Y. Moreover, to say that X causes Y is to say that if X were to occur, then Y would too. So, the identification of causes with correlations is too strong. More plausibly, the existence of a correlation is a necessary, but not sufficient, condition for a regularity to be causal regularity (or law).

11.4. Interventions, Capacities, and Mechanisms

Dissatisfaction with regularity views of causation has prompted a broader exploration of alternatives. In this section, we discuss two: interventionism and the capacity account. Both accounts encourage social scientists to think in terms of causal mechanisms, which we will explore at the end of the section.

Interventionism

The regularity conception of causality suggests that we can identify causal relations by simply looking at a pattern of occurrence. On the contrary, one might say, the sciences depend on experimental interventions. The investigator manipulates the purported cause, showing that Y can be changed by making changes in X. An alternative to Hume's regularity conception of causality, one which can be traced back to Thomas Reid in the 18th century, is to think of causes in terms of manipulation, intervention, and experiment. As a first pass, one might explain causality this way: X causes Y if and only if a person can bring about changes in Y by changing X. In recent work, James Woodward has refined this *interventionist* conception of causality (Woodward 2003). The notion of an intervention has also been useful in understanding causal inference, though we will postpone discussion of the epistemic consequences until Section 12.1.

An obvious challenge to any account of causality which depends on intervention is that it is anthropocentric. If causality depends on the possibility of intervention, we cannot make causal claims about history. Since it is impossible to travel back in time and change whether Archduke Ferdinand would be killed by an assassin, we cannot claim that his assassination was among the causes of World War I. To address this problem, Woodward removes reference to what a person could do in his definition:

> A necessary and sufficient condition for X to be a direct cause of Y with respect to some variable set V is that there be a possible intervention on X that will change Y (or the probability distribution of Y) when all other variables in V besides X and Y are held fixed at some value by interventions.
>
> (Woodward 2003, 55)

The point of the analysis, it should be emphasized, is not to show how causes are demonstrated. It is to articulate the content of a causal claim. An intervention which stopped Gavrilo Princip from assassinating Archduke Ferdinand is possible in the sense that someone could have stopped him at the time. Of course, it did not actually happen, and we could not bring it about now. When we say that the assassination of Ferdinand caused WWI, then, we are saying that if a different event had occurred, such as Princip's gun misfiring, it would have changed whether WWI began.

Two features of Woodward's conditions for X to be a direct cause of Y deserve comment. First, note that all variables except for X and Y are held fixed. The analysis presupposes that it is possible to isolate X and "surgically" intervene on it. In the literature, this is called the modularity assumption. In real causal systems, this may be impossible. Socialist countries, for example, often have had planned economies. The transition to democracy in Eastern Europe was thus accompanied by substantial social and economic change. One might argue that it is impossible for the form of government of a country to change from a non-democracy to a democracy without also changing at least some of its social and economic systems. If so, then modularity fails for the democratic peace hypothesis because we cannot intervene on the hypothesized cause alone. We will return to this point in the next section.

Second, the analysis invokes a set of causal variables, V. As Woodward points out, this means that there can be direct causes at different levels of analysis. If our set of variables includes only country-level properties like form of government, economic institutions, and so on, then form of government might be a direct cause of peace. On the other hand, we might have a lower-level analysis where the beliefs and attitudes of the leaders are variables. There might also be direct causal relations at this level. For any event, a variety of causal accounts are possible, and these are often at different levels of analysis. This has consequences for the issue of reductionism discussed in Chapter 6. On Woodward's version of an interventionist account of causality, it is possible to have causal relationships at the social level. If we succeed at generating powerful causal theories which make no reference to individual-level properties, then an anti-reductionist position will be supported.

An interventionist account of causality has at least two advantages over a regularity account. First, on an interventionist account, causal explanations can be given in the absence of laws. There is no law-like regularity associating assassinations with the outbreak of war. A regularity account must look elsewhere for the underlying laws which substantiate the causal claim about the beginning of WWI. On an interventionist analysis, the causal claim is about how things would have been different if the assassin's shots had not been fired. Hence, the causal explanation can be given directly: WWI began because of the shots fired in Sarajevo.

The second advantage that the interventionist view has over the regularity view concerns the distinction between genuine and spurious generalizations. As we saw in the previous section, the regularity conception of causality has a special need to get this distinction right. Without a clear distinction between genuine laws and spurious correlations, the regularity conception of causality collapses. However, the distinction is independently important. If the correlation between democracy and peace were spurious, then trying to promote peace by spreading democracy would be pointless. Woodward argues that the notion of an intervention can be recruited to do this work. Proper causal relationships are *invariant*:

> A generalization G (relating, say, changes in the value of X to changes in the value of Y) is invariant if G would continue to hold under some intervention that changes the value of X in such a way that, according to G, the value of Y would change— "continue to hold" in the sense that G correctly describes how the value of Y would change under this intervention.

> (Woodward 2003, 15)

The generalization about the cows and the rain is not invariant. When we intervene on the cows by making them lie down on a sunny day, no rain is forthcoming. The generalization about democracy and peace is a better candidate for an invariant generalization. If the democratic peace hypothesis is true, we would expect nations to be more or less likely to engage in armed conflict as their form of government changed. Woodward points out that thinking of causal generalizations in terms of invariance provides a very natural way to interpret linear equations:

$$Y = a + b_1 X_1 + b_2 X_2 + \ldots + b_n X_n + U$$

In this kind of causal model, the coefficients (b_n) appear to say something about the strength or magnitude of the causal factor (X_n). On a regularity view, it is hard to understand what "strength" could mean, since the equation is interpreted as reporting only a correlation. On the interventionist view, if the generalization is invariant, then b_n is reporting *how much* a change in Y will be brought about by a change in X_n.

A further, practical virtue of the interventionist analysis is that it helps disambiguate causal claims. It is not unusual in the social sciences to see claims like this:

Being female causes one to receive a lower salary.

An interventionist view invites us to consider what sort of interventions on the cause would change the effect. Once we do this, the statement is a bit misleading. It suggests that if a woman wants to change her salary, she should have a sex-change operation. This is probably not the causal relationship the social scientist had in mind. Rather, the point is about discrimination by those who hire and fix salaries. A relevant experimental manipulation would be something which affected the beliefs of the boss. And this is what actual research tends to do. For instance, the researcher might send out resumes which are identical except for the gender-specific names to see if there is a difference in salary offer. Alternatively, one might claim that discrimination is independent of the beliefs of the management. The discrimination might arise from institutional rules or informal practices that have the unintended consequence of depressing the salaries of female employees. Again, this causal relationship suggests an entirely different sort of intervention. Thinking of causal relationships in terms of how changing one variable brings about changes in another can thus make our causal explanations more precise.

Capacities and Nomological Engines

A second alternative to a Humean conception of causality invokes the idea of causal capacities or tendencies. Both the Humean and the interventionist accounts of causality agree that a correlation is a necessary, but not sufficient, condition of causality:

If X causes Y, then $\Pr(Y \text{ given } X) \neq \Pr(Y \text{ given } {\sim}X)$.

In other words, where there is a genuine causal relationship, there is a correlation. Importantly, this entails that where there is no correlation, there is no causation. (This latter point plays an important role in the epistemology of causal inference, and we will discuss it further in Section 10.1.) By contrast, the capacity views of causality reject correlations as a necessary condition of causes. On the capacity view, the correlations we observe arise from underlying causal relationships. Those causal powers exist even if the causes cancel each other out or are masked by other causal forces. The capacity view thereby stands opposed to both Humean and interventionist views. Because it treats causes as powers or properties which stand behind and explains observed regularities, this view is often called a "realist" view of causation.

Like the interventionist view, a capacity view downplays the role of laws in the conception of causality. In our earlier discussion of laws (Section 9.2), we noted that the laws found in the natural science typically require *ceteris paribus* clauses.

Kepler's first law of planetary motion, for example, says that a planet will travel in an ellipse with the sun at one of the two foci. This is true only if we ignore the influence of the planet's moons and the other planets in the solar system. Laws also have limited ranges of application. Boyle's law, which relates gas pressure to volume, breaks down when the pressures are too high. The important point is not that the laws have exceptions, but that science progresses as we come to understand *why* the laws fail. The objects have causal properties: because massive bodies attract each other gravitationally, they move in ways that approximate Kepler's laws. When a system is simple and isolated, the causal properties will be manifest. Since the other large planets are so far from, say, Mars, the orbit of Mars closely approximates Kepler's first law. When Kepler's law fails, as it does for the orbit of Uranus, it is explained by the gravitational pull of another planet (Neptune). The causal capacities of the objects thus explain the observed law and its exceptions, and therefore causes cannot be identified with law-like regularities.

Do social properties have causal powers analogous to gravitation, magnetism, or charge? We certainly speak colloquially of social roles and institutions as having causal powers. Police officers can do things that no citizen can do, and this is not because of any special powers of the individual who happens to be an officer, but because of the social status. And on a capacity conception of cause, it seems natural to interpret the democratic peace hypothesis as claiming that democracy has the power to bring about peace. Proponents of the capacity view are divided on this issue. Some have seemed tempted to attribute causal power to social entities. Doing so, however, suggests that social entities would act "on their own" if isolated. Even to an anti-reductionist, there is something odd about the claim that, say, a social role could *by itself* bring about a pattern of behavior. Social entities arguably have their effects manifested by the actions of the people who occupy the roles. For this reason, some proponents of a capacity theory locate the causal powers of social things in individual agency. This means that the causal efficacy of police forces or schools must be understood in terms of underlying mechanisms. The ultimate elements of these mechanisms are people who make decisions based on both their individual preferences and on their understanding of their environment (natural and social). Other philosophers are more skeptical. While the best social science can articulate the working of some social systems, they have not yet done so in terms of fundamental capacities. On a more skeptical view of social capacities, all social phenomena (even agents) are systems constructed from more fundamental causal properties. This dispute is clearly important for the issue of reductionism, for if institutions, social roles, and so on, have irreducible causal powers, then one can argue that they are ontologically irreducible.

Whether or not there are irreducible social capacities, capacity theorists agree that most social phenomena gain their causal efficacy from the fact that they are parts of, or rely on, larger causal systems. As an analogy, notice that an automobile has no causal powers of its own. Left alone as an isolated system, an automobile would do nothing. Therefore, it is not appropriate to attribute causal powers to it. An automobile is a system engineered to produce particular kinds of regularities: it accelerates when I press the gas pedal; it decelerates when I press the brake; and so on. There is a causal relationship between pressing the pedal and the acceleration of the vehicle, and that relationship is mediated by the whole system. Nancy Cartwright called such systems "nomological engines." The fact that causal relationships often depend on larger causal systems (nomological engines) also explains why *ceteris paribus* clauses are necessary in many causal generalizations. Pressing the gas pedal accelerates the car only if the engine is running, the tank is full of gas, the wheels are touching the ground, etc. These qualifications are neither eliminable nor fully specifiable. After all, there is no end to the possible ways in which the system may fail. Thinking of social phenomena as causal systems, rather than entities with causal powers of their own, therefore explains the pervasiveness of *ceteris paribus* clauses in causal generalizations.

The idea that social phenomena have causal powers because they are parts of causal systems has several important consequences for the social sciences. Some are epistemic, and we will discuss them in the next chapter. Here we will focus on points which help differentiate the capacity view of causation from the regularity and interventionist conceptions. First, both the regularity and the interventionist conceptions of causality tend to view causes as independent and isolatable. This commitment is sometimes called "modularity." While proponents of the regularity and interventionist recognize that real-world causal relationships take place against a complicated background, they treat this background as something from which the social scientists can abstract. In the interventionist definition of cause, this emerged as the requirement that all other variables in the system be held "fixed" while the one variable is manipulated. Cartwright has argued, to the contrary, that "Modularity is not a universal feature of deterministic causal systems" (Cartwright 2007, 96). Very often, a system is set up so that one causal variable cannot be manipulated without changing the values of several others. As discussed earlier, it is probably impossible to change a country's form of government without making substantial changes in its economy, educational institutions, military, and so on. If so, one might argue, the democratic peace hypothesis cannot be a causal generalization according to the interventionist view. A capacity theory emphasizes the systematic character of causality, but it does not insist on modularity. The tangled character of causal systems is thus no problem from the capacity point of view.

The interventionist may respond that the objection confuses a practical difficulty with an in-principle impossibility. The interventionist conception of cause explicitly does not require that humans be able to make the interventions that define causes. The conception requires only that *if* (counterfactually) we were to isolate the form of government and intervene on it, then there would be peace with other democracies. While the interventionist can accept the fragility of actual systems, especially in the social world, admitting too much undermines one of the motivations for interventionism. The interventionist view is attractive because it identifies causes that are relevant for our practical interaction with social institutions. When modularity fails, Cartwright argues, then "*the right way* of jiggling *A* to test if it causes *R* is almost never the way we would expect to do it to produce *R*"

(Cartwright 2009, 11). Indeed, there may be cases where the correlation is known to be the result of an underlying common cause. For example, both sexist remarks and inequitable treatment result from a person's underlying beliefs and attitudes. However, the causal system which includes the feedback between belief, behavior, and social sanction might be such that restricting sexist remarks *also* changes inequitable treatment. In such a case we would manipulate one effect of a common cause (the speech) to change the other effect of a common cause (the behavior). By attending to the causal system, we see what interventions might be effective.

One objection to a capacity view of causation brings us full circle and back to Hume. Hume criticized the notion of natural necessities because they were mysterious. In this vein, one might argue that conceptualizing causality as a power, tendency, or capacity is not very informative. It simply gives a new name to the concept to be analyzed. Furthermore, if we do not know whether there are social capacities, what relevance does the capacity analysis have for the practice of social scientific inquiry? There are two possible responses a capacity theorist might suggest. First, like the interventionist view, the capacity view rids the social scientist of the fixation on laws and generalizations. Social scientific theory should search for the underlying mechanisms which produce those generalizations. Second, the capacity theory highlights the importance of causal systems, with their limits and fragility. In contrast to the interventionist view, the capacity analysis does not require modularity, and it can treat causal relationships which depend on unknown and complex mechanisms as genuine.

Secret Springs and Principles: Causes and Mechanisms

"The historian," wrote Hume in the *Inquiry*, "traces the series of actions according to their natural order, remounts to their secret springs and principles, and delineates their most remote consequences" (Hume 1955 [1777], 34). Thus, even Hume found it natural to think of causes in terms of mechanisms. Superficial correlations are supported by "secret springs and principles" which must be uncovered and brought to light if history is to be properly understood. Many social scientists have become dissatisfied with the kind of correlational research which results from the search for laws. On a deductive-nomological account of explanation (recall Section 5.1), the law-like generalization relating democracy and peace explains why Britain and France, for example, have not gone to war since the Napoleonic era. Some have objected that this "explanation" does nothing more than summarize the correlation. We want to understand *why* democracy is correlated with peace, and for that we need to unwind the secret springs and principles of social phenomena.

Consider, for example, Karen Rasler and William Thompson's study of democratic peace. They propose that democracy and peace are mediated by a mechanism with two parts: the presence of neighboring countries which are perceived to be hostile, and the degree to which the politicians of a country hold concentrated power. Their diagram of the model is in Figure 11.1 (Rasler and Thompson 2004, 885).

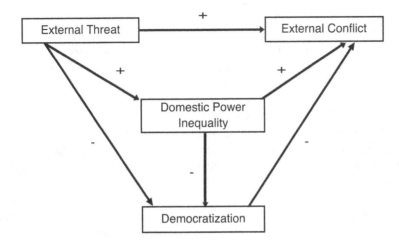

Figure 11.1 Rasler and Thompson Model of Democratic Peace

In Figure 11.1, the boxes represent the variables, and the arrows represent the causal relations. The "+" and "—" signs indicate causes that increase the effect and causes that suppress it. Conflict is thus modeled as the product of three causal factors. Perceived external threat and domestic power inequality increase the likelihood of conflict, while democratization lowers it. The precise character of these causal relationships is formulated in terms of linear equations, such as (Rasler and Thompson 2004, 897):

$$\log(\text{Dispute})t = \alpha + \beta 1(\text{Threat})t + \beta 2(\text{Democracy})t + \beta 3(\text{Peace Years})t + \beta 4(\text{War})t + \beta 5(\text{Disputes})t - 1 + \text{error}$$

The difference between Rasler and Thompson's causal model and Babst's correlation is twofold. First, the causal model tries to represent the process by which the form of government creates peace. In so doing, it can present a more nuanced account. Democratization tends to increase the chances of peace, but its effect may be overwhelmed by the other factors. Second, the variables are more naturally interpreted as causal factors. At the level of Babst's correlation, one is left wondering how democracy could influence war. Rasler and Thompson's variables are things like perceived external threat and power inequalities. These are the kinds of factors that influence human action.

Proponents of mechanistic understanding contend that discovering correlations is important, but it is only the beginning of social scientific inquiry. Correlations by themselves explain nothing, even when we have a robust generalization like the Democratic peace. To explain or fully understand a phenomenon, we must show *why* the observed regularity exists. Throughout the history of science, progress has been made by searching out the underlying mechanisms which explain the surface-level phenomena. Mechanistic explanation is therefore necessary to "open the black box" and explain the observed regularities. To do so, we build a causal model that accounts for the observed regularity. Like all models, these abstract away from some aspects of the real systems, and they will idealize causal factors. Since we explored some of the challenges of making inferences from such models in Chapter 6, it is important to note here that the models in question are very empirical. Rasler and Thompson devised the model by examining empirical studies of democracies in conflict and tested the linear equations expressing the causal relationships. As a result, a proponent of causal modeling will argue, mechanistic models are not subject to problems that afflict highly idealized, theoretical models.

Proponents of mechanistic explanation believe it is a distinct and superior approach to the causal explanations commonly found in the social sciences. As we saw in Chapter 6, models are typically autonomous from theories and do not depend on law-like regularities. Presenting mechanistic explanation as something different from other causal explanations, however, creates a tension between two features of mechanistic explanation. Pierre Demeulenaere has pointed out that:

> On the one hand, [appeal to mechanism] clearly implies some kind of regularity, causality and predictability; in the absence of such features it would seem an abuse of language to speak of a mechanism. . . . On the other hand, it has to be linked to the historical aspect of social life, and to the necessity of taking into account the uniqueness of events, the very frequent difficulty of making predictions, and the apparent difficulty of using the notion of a "law" in the social sciences.
>
> (Demeulenaere 2011, 176)

Those who hold mechanism to be a distinct approach to the social world emphasize the second feature. In Rasler and Thompson's model, the links to "the historical aspect of life" are constituted by the relationship and the data sets on which it was based. For example, in developing the model, they used data from nine "major powers" of the 19th and 20th centuries: Austria-Hungary, Britain, China, France, Germany, Italy, Japan, Russia, and the United States (Rasler and Thompson 2004, 891). Putting values into the variables for Germany, say, will yield a different pattern than Britain. The model is thus closely tied to a historical context.

At the same time, the model itself is characterized by three linear equations, one of which was illustrated earlier. These are versions of the standard correlational formulae we discussed in Section 11.3. And this is not surprising: if there were no casual regularities in play, it is hard to see how the model could really be characterizing causal mechanisms. In response to the arguments for mechanistic explanation, then, one might conclude that the call for mechanistic foundations is nothing more than an insistence on reductionism. The model is a set of ordinary causal explanations at a "lower" level.

The tension between the generalizing and localizing impulses of mechanistic explanation is created, at least in part, by different conceptions of causality. If one adopts a regularity standpoint, then mechanistic explanation is nothing more than explanation by laws governing the micro-level phenomena. Combined with an empiricist standpoint on theories, this conception of causality entails that mechanistic explanation is just the ordinary use of laws in the social sciences to create models of a specific phenomenon. This means that if mechanistic understanding is to be distinct, it must adopt either an interventionist or a capacity view of causality. For the interventionist, appeal to causal laws is replaced by appeal to invariant generalizations. These will be dependent on the causal systems under study. The capacity theorist can take a similar approach. This means that while mechanistic explanations will require some generalizations, their gambit may not reach very far beyond the systems under investigation. The appeal to mechanisms is causal, but the explanation does not rely on general laws in the way that the deductive-nomological view of explanation suggested. Hence for the interventionist and capacity views of causation, mechanistic explanation is distinct from the attempt to use laws to explain broad swaths of human behavior.

Causal models express the mechanisms that underly observed regularities. By doing so, they are valuable whether we understand them as closely associated with causal generalizations and theory or whether we regard models as autonomous. But how do we know what the causes are? This is the question for our next chapter.

11.5. Wrap Up

Chapter Summary

Are there laws of the social world? In Section 11.2 we saw the objection that the unpredictability of human action precludes social scientific laws. We saw that that these arguments do not show that laws are impossible. It may be that finding laws will force us to deeply reconceptualize human action. Such reconceptualization has struck some as impossible. Thinking of ourselves in terms of intentionality, meaning, and value is central to our ability to act at all. The resistance to such change is being gradually undermined by the success of cognitive psychology, neuroscience, and behavioral economics. These fields seem to be finding behavioral regularities of which we are not aware, and these are arguably changing the way we think about ourselves.

In Sections 11.3 and 11.4, we contrasted three different ways of conceptualizing causality. The regularity view treats causes as instances of general laws. This view has been an important presupposition of much social science which searches for correlations and causes, including the use of linear equation modeling. The regularity view faces substantial philosophical challenges, and many philosophers today prefer either an interventionist view or a capacity view of causality. According to the interventionist, causality is closely related to our ability to change one property by changing another. Wiggle the cause, and the effect will wiggle. The interventionist view can interpret linear equations as showing how much change will occur in the effect, given a change in the cause. Interventionism, however, presupposes that such changes are "modular" in the sense that causes can be wiggled without disrupting the whole system. The capacity view treats causes as real, underlying properties of objects. Both regularities and their exceptions are the product of deeper casual capacities. Most regularities in the social world, the capacity theorists point out, are limited to arrangements that are often quite fragile. On a capacity view, the regularities we observe are the product of the underlying capacities of objects arranged into specific kinds of systems.

Discussion Questions

1. Consider a domain of creative, artistic endeavor. What sorts of activities in this domain are predictable? What sorts are not? What does that tell us about the possibility of finding laws in the social sciences?
2. It was argued in Section 9.2 that finding laws in the social sciences might require developing vocabularies which are very different from those we ordinarily use to describe ourselves. Is it self-defeating or otherwise impossible for us to think about our own action in such terms?
3. People who occupy particular social positions have the power to *do* things that others cannot. This is a causal claim. Is it best understood in regularity, interventionist, or capacity terms?
4. The interventionist and capacity views of causation do not rely on the idea of a law, at least not in the way that the regularity view does. Consider the interventionist and capacity views of causation in light of the arguments against social laws in Section 9.2. Do those arguments show that there is something misconceived about searching for social causes?
5. Social science needs causal knowledge to support social policy. When we are thinking about interventions to reduce crime, increase educational achievement, and so on, does it matter whether we think about the causes in regularity, interventionist, or capacity terms? Why?

Further Reading

The democratic peace hypothesis has been the subject of a large literature. See Bremer, "Dangerous Dyads: Conditions Affecting the Likelihood of Interstate War, 1816–1965" (1992) and Rousseau, "Assessing the Nature of the Democratic Peace, 1918–88" (1996) for overviews. The *Correlates of War* database is available at www.correlatesofwar.org.

Arguments that the creativity of human action makes laws of the social world impossible can be found in Chapter 3 of Winch's *The Idea of a Social Science* (1958), MacIntyre's "The Character of Generalizations in Social Science and their Lack of Predictive Power" (1981), and Fay's "General Laws and Explaining Human Behavior" (1983). The argument based on complexity can be found in Scriven, "A Possible Distinction between the Traditional Scientific Disciplines and the Study of Human Behavior" (1956), and in Popper, "Prediction and Prophecy in Social Science" (1965). McIntyre replies to these arguments in "Complexity and Social Scientific Laws" (1993); see also *Laws and Explanation in the Social*

Sciences (McIntyre 1996). Henderson defends a role for social scientific laws in *Interpretation and Explanation in the Human Sciences (1991)*. Kincaid discusses the problem of *certeris paribus* clauses in *Philosophical Foundations of the Social Sciences* (1996).

Hume's conception of causality has been subject to an enormous critical and historical literature. Von Wright's analysis and critique in *Explanation and Understanding* (von Wright 1971) remains important, and Groff's "Getting Past Hume in the Philosophy of Social Science" is a more contemporary treatment (2011).

Woodward's *Making Things Happen* (2003) is a very important argument for the interventionist account of causality. His "Causal Models in the Social Sciences" (2007) surveys the issues and also argues for interventionism. In "Methodological Individualism, Explanation, and Invariance" (2006), Steel draws out consequences of interventionist causal explanation for methodological individualism. Steel's *Across the Boundaries: Extrapolation in Biology and Social Science* (2008) includes a critical discussion of both interventionism and capacity theories of causation, as well as the problems associated with *ceteris paribus* clauses and mechanistic explanation. The issue of extrapolation is discussed by Steel (2008) and Runhardt (2016).

Capacity theories have been articulated and defended by Kincaid, *Philosophical Foundations of the Social Sciences* (1996); Varela and Harre, "Conflicting Varieties of Realism: Causal Powers and the Problems of Social Structure" (1996); Little, *Microfoundations, Method, and Causation* (1998); and Bhaskar, *A Realist Theory of Science* (2008 [1975]). Cartwright has developed an important body of work around the concept; see *How the Laws of Physics Lie* (1983), *Nature's Capacities and their Measurement* (1989), *Hunting Causes and Using Them (2007)*, and *The Dappled World* (2008). See Lewis (2000) and Reiss (2008) for discussions of whether and how to attribute causal powers to social entities.

Arguments in favor of mechanistic explanation include Elster, "A Plea for Mechanisms" (1998); Machamer, Darden, and Craver, "Thinking about Mechanisms" (2000); and Mayntz, "Mechanisms in the Analysis of Social Macro-Phenomena" (2003). Hedström and Ylikoski's "Causal Mechanisms in the Social Sciences" (2010) is a careful appraisal of the current debate. For specific applications of mechanistic explanation, see Steel, "Mechanisms and Functional Hypotheses in Social Science" (2005); Kuorikoski and Pöyhönen, "Looping Kinds and Social Mechanisms" (2012); Weber, "Social Mechanisms, Causal Inference, and the Policy Relevance of Social Science" (2007); and Pozzoni and Kaidesoja (2021). Critical responses to the call for mechanistic explanation can be found in Reiss, "Do We Need Mechanisms in the Social Sciences?" (2007), and in Kincaid (1996).

12 Methodologies of Causal Inference

The discussion of causation up to this point has aimed to evaluate the idea that the social sciences should search for causal explanations. Our questions have been, in this sense, metaphysical. While metaphysical questions often arise in methodological discussion, students of the social sciences are more likely to encounter questions like: Is it possible to infer causal relationships based on correlational data? and What methods permit us to discover and test causal hypotheses? These are questions about the epistemology of causation, that is, questions about how we can know about causal relationships in the social world. There are a wide variety of methods which purport to identify and test causal hypotheses. In this chapter, we will discuss three of the most prominent: causal modeling, case studies, and experimentation.

The metaphysical and epistemological questions about causality are intertwined. A regularity analysis, for example, ties the metaphysics and the epistemology of causation into a tidy package. Since causes *are* regularities (of a certain sort), when we have discovered the regularities, we have discovered the causes. Both the interventionist and capacity approaches to causality conceptually separate the surface regularities from the underlying causes. These alternatives to Hume treat causes as something hidden which need to be brought to the surface by scientific inquiry. An interventionist view has a natural affinity for experimental manipulations, while a capacity view highlights the importance of knowledge of the whole system. We have also seen in Chapter 11 how the alternatives to Hume have shifted the discussion from general laws of society to mechanisms underlying specific social phenomena. A parallel change has occurred in social scientific methodology. All three of the methods we will be discussing are arguably ways of testing hypotheses about causal mechanisms.

Statistical methods remain one of the most common ways to develop and test social scientific theories. Any elementary statistics course will emphasize that correlation is not causation, and in Section 11.3, we saw some of the reasons why. It would be a mistake, however, to suppose that regression analysis and similar methods could not provide *evidence* for causation. The fundamental question, then, is to determine the criteria for a reliable inference

DOI: 10.4324/9781003207795-12

from correlation to causation. In the last decades of the 20th century, important progress was made on this issue. The "Bayesian Network" approach to causal modeling uses insights from the interventionist account of causality to exclude spurious correlations and narrow down the range of causal hypotheses. In Section 12.1 we will look at some of the details of this kind of approach and explore its philosophical consequences.

Advocates of case studies argue that by looking at the details of a particular social event (or place and time), we can understand the causal processes that underlie large-scale social phenomena. It is interesting that case studies typically use the qualitative methods discussed in Chapter 3. Yet, in contrast to the defenders of interpretation, proponents of case studies argue that interviews, archival research, and other qualitative methods can uncover causal processes. We will thus engage the debate over interpretation and explanation from a new perspective.

Experimentation also has clear virtues as a method for teasing apart complex causal systems. Traditionally its use in the social sciences has been limited. The complexity, reflexivity, and context-sensitivity of social phenomena have often been thought to be barriers to the use of experiments. The concern is that the artificial context of the experiment prevents the social scientist from making meaningful generalizations outside of the experimental context. Whether this is true depends, at least in part, on the background understanding of causality and mechanism in the social world. It also depends on the details of the experiment, and in Section 12.3 we will examine some of the ways that social scientists have tried to make their experiments more reliable.

Causal knowledge is taken to be useful because it is general and thereby can be applied to new situations. If democracy really were a cause of peace, then it is a cause always and everywhere (other things being equal). Therefore, we reason, creating new democracies will reduce war. Our *evidence* for causal hypotheses, by contrast, is always limited. Only a small number of democratic governments have existed, and they have only existed for a couple of centuries. Moreover, as we saw in the last chapter, causal relationships in the social sciences are often dependent on underlying causal systems, or as Cartwright called them, nomological engines. This means that even if we can identify the causal relationship between a pair of variables in one situation, there is an open question about whether we can generalize to other cases. This epistemological challenge is sometimes called the problem of "external validity." It is especially acute for methodologies of experimentation and case study because both of these methods focus on an isolated system. How can we determine whether the causal relationships we find will also be manifested elsewhere? And since one of the reasons we want causal knowledge of the social world is to intervene in social processes, the question of external validity goes to the heart of whether the social sciences can provide useful knowledge. These will be the issues discussed in Section 12.4.

12.1. Bayesian Networks and Causal Modeling

Confounds and Common Causes

The existence of *confounds* or *common causes* is an enormous challenge for any account of causal inference. Consider, for example, the challenge to the democratic peace hypothesis known as "the McDonald's peace hypothesis:" no pair of countries goes to war after both get a McDonald's restaurant. In less frivolous terms, perhaps the reason that democracies do not go to war with each other has nothing to do with democracy and everything to do with economics. Advanced economies with free-market institutions tend to be democratic, and advanced economies have too much to lose by going to war with each other, or so one might argue. If the McDonald's peace hypothesis is true, then the correlation between democracy and peace is spurious. There is a third factor—an advanced economy—which is responsible for the observed correlation between democracy and peace. The problem for inferring causes from probabilities is that there is always more than one causal model which fits the probabilities. How can we determine which is correct?

It has become common to use a certain kind of diagram to represent possible causal relationships. More precisely, these graphs are directed acyclic graphs (DAGs). We encountered a similar diagram in Figure 11.1, which presented the Rasler and Thompson model of the democratic peace. In these diagrams, an arrow stands for a direct causal relationship. Rasler and Thompson used "+" and "—" to indicate that the cause was contributing or inhibitory. Current philosophical presentations are a little more abstract and dispense with this specification. Just as with the Rasler and Thompson diagram, a DAG represents a causal model. It is a hypothesis about the real causal relationships that obtain in the system. Any correlational evidence we may have is generated by this underlying causal structure.

Using a directed graph, Figure 12.1 represents the hypothesis that democracy is the direct cause of peace. The McDonald's peace hypothesis supposes that there is a third property of a nation—advanced economic institutions—in play. Figure 12.1 is silent on the role of the economy in producing peace. If we take the economy into account, we must add this variable to our diagram. There are (at least!) three possible causal models. First, Figure 12.2a represents the idea that democracy is a direct cause of peace and that the economy is a direct cause as well. Each variable contributes independently to the effect. Figure 12.2b represents the hypothesis that advanced economic institutions are caused by a democratic form of government and that they, in turn, bring about peace. Economy is an intervening variable between democracy and peace; the economy is the direct cause of peace, while democracy is indirect. Alternatively, democracies might arise when economic conditions have

Figure 12.1 Democracy as a Direct Cause of Peace

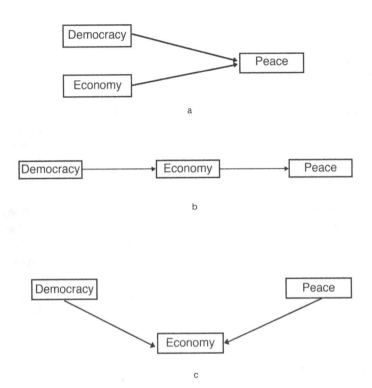

Figure 12.2 Three Causal Models

developed in a certain way, and those economic conditions might make war less likely too. This case is represented in Figure 12.2c, where the advanced economy is the common cause of both democracy and peace.

In our discussion of the democratic peace, we noted that the evidence could be expressed this way:

$$\Pr(W \text{ given } D) < \Pr(W \text{ given } {\sim}D)$$

In other words, the probability of a pair of countries going to war (W) given that both are democracies (D) is lower than the probability of them going to war when both are not democracies. This very same data could have been generated by any of the three causal structures represented in Figure 10.2. Therefore, our data cannot distinguish between these causal hypotheses. This point is of fundamental importance. Any study which identifies correlations among variables has a profound problem with causal inference. The mantra "Correlation is not causation" is correct in the sense that there is always more than one possible underlying causal structure which would give rise to an observed correlation. We have presented some obvious alternatives, but innumerable other possible causal structures could produce the same correlation. Perhaps the causal arrow goes the other way, and peace causes democracy. Or perhaps there are a dozen hidden mechanisms which mediate the relationship. The problem of causal inference, then, is to find a reason to eliminate possible alternative causal hypotheses.

Many philosophers have thought that the problem of confounds was unsolvable using the resources of probability and statistics alone. Since confounds are possible for *every* correlation, adding new variables and correlations will not eliminate confounds. Causal inference, then, must look beyond statistical evidence to something more. The most common proposals suggested either interventions or looking to other theories for support. The Koch postulates, which arose from Robert Koch's investigation of tuberculosis in the 19th century, required that potential pathogens be isolated, cultured, and introduced into healthy animals. The correlational evidence was thus supplemented by experimentation before a causal conclusion could be drawn. The Hill criteria (Hill 1965), which were proposed in the context of epidemiology, drew from a wider range of supplementary evidence. Importantly, Hill required consistency with existing theory. Theories of the causal pathways at the micro-level have been taken to be particularly important. Investigation into mechanisms, in other words, ruled out spurious correlations and helped identify the genuine causal relationships.

Bayesian Inference

In the last decades of the 20th century, progress in the foundations of statistics has provided grounds for some optimism about the justification of causal inferences based on statistical data alone. Recent work by Judea Pearl (2000) and by Peter Spirtes et al (2000) begins by turning the problem of causal inference on its head. Up to this point in the discussion, we have been focused on probabilistic dependencies. We have supposed that the correlation between two variables hints, unreliably, at causal relationships. Perhaps the opposite is a more reliable guide:

If $\Pr(Y \text{ given } X) = \Pr(Y \text{ given } \sim X)$, then X is **NOT** the cause of Y.

Clearly, where there is no probabilistic dependence, knowing that X occurred would provide no information about whether Y is going to occur. If we created a graph which plotted the values of X against Y, the result would be nothing more than a randomly scattered cloud. While this does mean that X is not the cause of Y, it may strike you as irrelevant to the problem. But recall that the problem of causal inference is to rule out possible causal hypotheses that are consistent with a given correlation. So, perhaps we can use the idea of independence to *exclude* possibilities and thereby settle on the right one.

To see how this might work, consider what happens in an experiment. Imagine an omnipotent (but not omniscient!) social scientist who could experimentally investigate the democratic peace hypothesis. Suppose she is concerned with the hypotheses diagrammed in Figure 12.2. In an experiment, we seek to isolate a

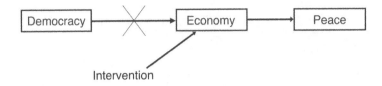

Figure 12.3 Intervening on the Economy

causal system and manipulate just one factor. So, she creates a possible world with several nations that go to war now and again. If she wants to discriminate among the possibilities in Figure 12.2, she will have to manipulate either the form of government or the economy. Ideally, when an experiment manipulates the independent variable, it is isolated from any other causes. When our omnipotent social scientist intervenes on the economy, *she* will decide how to change it—the form of government is no longer determinative of the economic institutions. This means that she has made the economy and form of government probabilistically *independent*, so there could not be a causal relationship between democracy and economy. This situation is represented in Figure 12.3. If manipulating the economy alone changed whether counties went to war, we would seem justified in concluding that the economy was the direct cause of peace, not democracy.

The central insight is that interventions make one variable independent of all its prior causes. Once the economy is independent, any change in the economy which is correlated with peace must be due (at least in part) to the economy. Since probabilistic independence is doing the work, we do not need the fanciful omnipotent experimenter anymore. Correlations and non-correlations can be identified in non-experimental data. To distinguish between the three hypotheses of Figure 12.2, all we need is the descriptive statistics from a database like *Correlates of War*. Considered alone, democracy and peace are correlated. What happens when we add consideration of the economy? If, given the kind of economy, democracy and peace become *independent*, then democracy could not be a direct cause of peace. The hypothesis diagrammed in Figure 12.2a would be falsified, leaving the other two. And notice that the second and third agree on a crucial point: that the economy is a direct cause of peace. In general, if variables X and Y are independent given consideration of a third variable Z, then there is no direct causal relationship between X and Y. In the contemporary literature, you may see the claim that X and Y are independent, given Z written as $X \perp Y$ given Z.

Bayesian Network analysis (or more simply "Bayes Nets") synthesizes these ideas into a theory of causal modeling. This approach makes several assumptions about the underlying causal structures and their relationship to the observed probabilities. The underlying structures are represented by the DAGs we have been using, and statistical analysis will give us probabilities (or better, probability

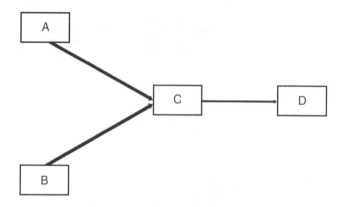

Figure 12.4 Illustration of the Causal Markov Condition

distributions) for the variables. The central assumption which links the two is the Causal Markov Condition:

> In any probability distribution P generated by a given causal graph G, each variable X is probabilistically independent of the set Y consisting of variables that are not effects of X, conditional on the direct causes of X. That is $\forall\, X \in$ G, $X \perp$ Non-effects of X, given the direct causes of X in P.
>
> (based on Scheines 2005, 929)

Unpacking this, it says that, when we take the direct causes of a variable into account, it is independent of every variable which is *not* one of its effects. Consider, for example, the graphical representation of a causal structure in Figure 12.4. In this graph, A and B are independent causes of C. That means that A is a non-effect of B, and vice versa. Hence, if this graph satisfies the Causal Markov Condition, then when we measure variables A and B, we find that they are independent (symbolically, $A \perp B$). Since lack of causation means no correlation, this is exactly what one would expect. More interestingly, when we take C into account, the Causal Markov Condition requires that D become independent of A and B (that is, $D \perp \{A, B\}$ given C). In other words, C "screens off" the earlier causes. Again, this is what we would expect. Once C happens, D will happen; it does not matter how C was brought about. And, of course, there is a correlation between C and D, since C is the direct cause of D. The Causal Markov Condition stipulates when we take the direct cause of a variable node into account, all variables which are *not* its effects become independent. The variables which remain dependent, then, are effects of the variables in question.

Bayes nets are a surprisingly powerful tool for making causal inferences. Just as an experimental intervention identifies a cause by screening off all other variables (and thereby rendering the effect independent of them), Bayes nets screen off variables by identifying independencies which are in the data. Formalizing this idea has facilitated search algorithms which narrow down the space of possible hypotheses. The algorithms are not magical of course. The algorithms rely on the variables that are in the data set. If there are variables which we didn't think to measure, the algorithms will not identify them for us. This point not only reminds us that science is fallible, but that inferring causal structure from observational data is not the whole of science. It takes background knowledge to guess what needs to be measured, and it takes imagination to theorize possible causal structures.

Challenges to Causal Modeling

While Bayes Network causal modeling has become very sophisticated, there are some lingering concerns, both practical and philosophical. The central assumption of a Bayes Network approach is that when two variables are probabilistically independent, neither is the direct cause of the other. The Causal Markov Condition embodies this intuition and uses it to guarantee a relationship between the observed probabilities and the underlying causal structure. Critics point out that the social sciences provide many examples where this assumption is violated. For example, Jon Elster has argued that when we look at the deeper mechanisms which lie behind social phenomena, we sometimes find processes which oppose each other:

> Theories of voting behavior, for instance, have identified both an underdog mechanism and a bandwagon mechanism. . . . Those subject to the former tend to vote for the candidate who is behind in preelection polls, whereas those subject to the latter vote for the front-runner. With many voting for the underdog, the frontrunner might lose, and vice versa. If the two types are more evenly mixed, there might be no noticeable net effect, so that the polls would be good predictors of the actual vote.
>
> (Elster 1998, 70–71)

A causal model of Elster's example would look like Figure 12.5. The bandwagon and underdog effects are both direct causes of the poll results. Earlier polling

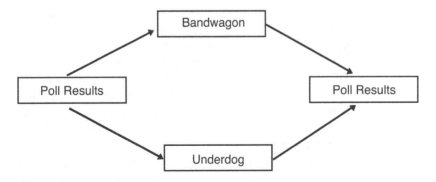

Figure 12.5 Offsetting Causal Processes

showing that candidate A is ahead of B will increase A's support through the band-wagon effect and increase B's support through the underdog effect. Because they have opposite effects on the later poll, they cancel out. Under the right conditions, the polls will be independent of voters' propensity to vote for or against the front-runner. There will be no correlation in our data between these two causes (the bandwagon and underdog effects) and their joint consequence. But this means that there are causal relationships which are probabilistically independent, contrary to the assumptions of a Bayesian Network approach.

Examples like Elster's have motivated some critics to argue that there is a deep difference between correlational studies and mechanistic explanation. To deter-mine whether a given correlation is a genuine causal relationship or a spurious association, we need to investigate the mechanisms which support the observed correlations. The mechanisms rule out (or confirm) the possible confounds or com-mon causes. Moreover, as in Elster's example, the mechanisms show what is hap-pening even when the surface-level correlations are not present.

A defender of Bayes Nets might argue that the problem of opposed mechanisms does not show an inherent limitation to the Bayesian logic of causal inference. Rather, it shows the need to build better causal models of the underlying variables. Elster's puzzle arises because the polling results are aggregated. If we separated the polling responses of those who voted for the underdog from those who jumped on the bandwagon, the correlations would reappear, and the causes would be dis-entangled. A casual model does not have to use only superficial or macro-level variables. A causal model can use any measurable variable. Causal models can therefore represent micro-level and macro-level causal relationships. Of course, the Bayes Net algorithms alone will not tell us which variables to choose for our explanations. Again, social science takes imagination and background knowledge to determine which variables might be relevant and how to measure them.

Causal inference is also difficult to represent in Bayes Network terms when the causes and effects are mediated by complex processes. Cartwright has sug-gested the example of a bank transaction (Cartwright 2007, 65–66). Imagine that I speak with the banker near my home, and later in some far-flung part of the world, my daughter withdraws cash from an ATM. The causal relationship between bank transactions and money shooting out of an ATM can be mediated by an indefinite range of processes. Perhaps the whole transaction occurs within a single commer-cial bank, or perhaps there are several intermediaries. And—believe it or not—there are still places in the world where the banks rely on paper records; these processes will be different from electronic ones. Banking regulations vary around the globe, creating still more possible variations in the causal pathway. The infor-mation may be transmitted by the internet, voice telephone, carrier pigeon, and so on. In each individual bank transaction, there will be a specific chain of events running from cause to effect. But considering the event types, not the tokens, there is no variable we can put between cause and effect in the graph. This means that we have a causal relationship (the call to my banker causes the money to appear elsewhere), but it cannot be represented by a Bayes Net approach.

In cases like the bank transaction, the relationship between cause and effect depends on an underlying causal system. The cause (e.g., the initiation of the transfer) does not bring that system into existence. The cause-effect relationship rides along on top, so to speak. In complex cases, there may be a number of distinct, even incompatible, systems on which the causal relationship can piggyback. Hence, there is a causal relationship (and a probabilistic dependency) without the variables being related by "direct causation," as this is conceived in a Bayesian Network approach. While this shows a limitation of the representational capacities of directed graphs, a defender of Bayesian Networks might argue that it is not a deep problem with the method. Unless we are studying the ultimate interactions of elementary particles, *all* causal relationships are mediated by underlying mechanisms. Any causal hypothesis abstracts away from the whole system and isolates a small number of causes. The bank transaction example reminds us that some of these causes may be at a lower level.

Both objections to Bayes Nets surveyed in this section serve as reminders that the hypotheses tested in any causal study isolate only a small part of a larger system. We can use the measured probabilities of our variables to infer causation, but we must bear in mind that other processes may be necessary for the causal relationships to hold. Our hypothesis that a causal relationship holds might be undermined by consideration of other parts of the system (as in the bandwagon/underdog example) or made possible by them (as in the bank transaction example). Since knowledge of this larger system will always be necessary to support a causal inference, probabilistic dependencies alone are never sufficient to justify a causal inference, no matter how sophisticated the mathematics.

12.2. Case Studies and Causal Structure

The Apparent Value of Case Studies

We have seen that our ability to identify causal relationships depends on which variables we have thought to measure. Spurious correlations are distinguished from genuine causes by adding more variables to the regression. We add economic development, for example, and see whether it eliminates the effects of democracy. Proponents of mechanism contend that such refinements do not answer the deeper question: why do these correlations occur? What feature of democracies makes them less likely to declare war on each other? Case studies are often put forward as ways of answering such questions about the processes by which broad social regularities are produced.

As an example, consider Bernard Finel and Kristin Lord's study of transparency and the democratic peace (Finel and Lord 1999). One suggested mechanism for the democratic peace has to do with the relative transparency of democratic societies. Democracies are more peaceful, not because leaders are elected, but because they typically contain processes like a free press, public disputes about policy, disclosure of government procedures, and so on. Such transparency makes it more difficult for leaders to hide their intentions and thereby makes it difficult to bluff. Threats by transparent governments are more credible, and peaceful entities are more trustworthy. In their case study, Finel and Lord suggest that the "positive logic of transparency" (that transparency helps democratic leaders transmit their intentions) is opposed by a "negative logic of transparency." Transparency of one nation also can overwhelm the leaders of another nation. They might miss the true intentions of the government amid the noise of the opposition parties. Or they might over-emphasize the importance of some voices in the cacophony of press reports. Transparency can therefore both help diffuse a crisis (the positive logic) or exacerbate it (the negative logic). Both are mechanisms in the process by which states manage their crises.

To test whether the positive and negative mechanisms of transparency are, in fact, responsible for the democratic peace, Finel and Lord conducted a case study in which they looked closely at six conflicts. To choose the cases, they first identified a typology of seven relevant kinds of conflict. These seven vary on (1) whether the parties to the conflict are both transparent, both non-transparent, or mixed; (2) whether the conflict escalated to war; and (3) which kind of party (transparent or non-transparent) escalated the conflict. They then chose conflicts which satisfied all different combinations of these criteria and investigated the processes which led to the escalation or de-escalation of the conflict. They paid careful attention to the press coverage of the conflict, as well as to the public statements of government officials, members of the opposition party, and non-governmental interest groups. They also examined diplomatic correspondence and after-the-fact reflections by the leaders about how they interpreted the intentions of the other side. They found that, more often than not, transparency exacerbated conflicts, either helping escalate them to war or postponing the resolution. Finel and Lord conclude:

> It is possible that both very high transparency, because it accurately signals intentions, and very low transparency, because it prevents the "noise" of domestic politics from overwhelming diplomatic signals, allow states to defuse crises. If accurate, only moderate transparency would exacerbate crises because it would allow enough information to confuse the opponent, but not enough to clarify peaceful intentions.
>
> (Finel and Lord 1999, 335–336)

They go on to suggest that:

> Transparent states, which are often democratic, do not seem particularly adept at managing crises. However, our difficulty in even identifying plausible cases of potentially militarized crises between transparent states is suggestive. Democracies rarely get into militarized crises with one another, suggesting some mechanism or set of norms that usually keeps them out of crisis-producing scenarios in the first place.
>
> (Finel and Lord 1999, 336)

Finel and Lord's case study thus (arguably) succeeded in identifying a mechanism relevant to the escalation of conflict among states, but the details of how this mechanism works *undermine* its ability to explain the democratic peace correlation! As they note, further mechanisms need to be identified.

Finel and Lord's study of transparency illustrates several of the purported strengths of the case study method. By looking at the process by which decisions were made, the case study can identify the micro-level processes which produce the macro-level correlation. But, as the example of transparency shows, social phenomena can be the product of mechanisms that are in conflict. Social systems are thus unlike artifacts in this sense: while the cuckoo clock is created so that its parts work in harmony to produce a specific result, the various processes within a social system might counteract each other. Case studies, arguably, let social scientists identify the multiple processes that together produce the broader patterns and correlations. By looking at the range of variation—in Finel and Lord's study, this was the range of possible conflict types—we can begin to determine the conditions under which one or another process will come to predominate.

Epistemological Challenges of Case Studies

Case studies characteristically concern a very small number of examples. Unlike correlational studies, there is no attempt to collect enough numbers to be statistically significant. Lack of statistical power alone is no criticism. As defenders of case study methods often point out, it is an empty criticism to point out that a non-statistical study fails to conform to statistical practice. The more interesting challenge for case study methodology is to understand how a small number of cases can constitute robust evidence for causal claims. There are two philosophical problems here. First, can we really identify the causes without comparing the cases with a larger sample? Second, supposing that we can identify the causal structures at play a small number of cases, what is our basis for drawing general conclusions, if any? Roughly, these questions concern the internal and external validity of case study methods.

Small samples raise the concerns of internal validity. For example, once I was sitting and talking with some friends at a mountain lodge. A large stone fireplace held a gas log. Oddly, the fire would come on for a few minutes and then go off. Someone suggested that perhaps it was sensitive to the noise we were making, like those lights that turn on and off at the sound of a clap. She playfully clapped her hands, and to our delight, the fire lit. Was this causality or just lucky coincidence? The obvious test was to clap again. (Sadly, it didn't work.) Case studies seem to suffer from the same problem as the hand clap. A single case is no pattern at all, and a small number of cases might be a lucky accident. This leads some scholars to be suspicious of causal claims based on case studies. More deeply, it casts doubt on the claim that case studies can go beyond correlational studies by "opening the black box" and establishing the mechanisms which underlie the larger pattern.

Without another larger pattern of which the proposed mechanism is an example, one might argue, case studies cannot identify causes at all.

In the Finel and Lord study, transparency had its effects through the medium of human psychology. Their analysis showed how the decision making of leaders was influenced (for better or worse) by the information available about the intentions of the opposing leaders. Their study thus relied on broader causal claims about how information affects decision making and how leaders' decisions cause the actions of a state. So, the beginning of an answer to the internal validity challenge is that, while case studies do rely on causes that are established more broadly, they do not do so in a circular or otherwise problematic way. The Finel and Lord study assumes a causal account of decision making, but this is not what they set out to discover. Their question was how the amount and character of information provided by transparent and non-transparent states affected the leaders' decisions to escalate or de-escalate. A case study cannot occur in an epistemic vacuum, nor can any empirical method. All methods are supported by scientific knowledge drawn from other domains. The lesson to be highlighted is that case study researchers need to carefully consider what sort of causal knowledge they are using in their explanations. Correspondingly, consumers of case study research need to carefully inspect the causal assumptions used to help support the conclusions.

The foregoing response might quiet doubts that case studies are somehow circular, but other doubts may linger. If case studies must rely on other scientific knowledge of causes (such as the relationship between information and belief), then are case studies valuable at all? One might think that to determine whether moderate transparency really does prolong a crisis, Finel and Lord's examples would need to be supplemented by a larger sample. One might argue in this way: case study methodology is not a sound way to discover causal mechanisms because causes are regularities, and the sample sizes of cases studies are too small to establish robust causal conclusions. Insofar as case studies seem to discover causes, they are implicitly relying on knowledge of causality imported from other domains. Put in these terms, the argument presupposes a regularity conception of causality. If causes are understood as correlations which meet a special set of conditions, then any conclusions based on a small sample will be suspicious. As we saw in Chapter 11, however, the regularity conception of causality is not the only conception on offer. Do case studies fare any better if we adopt either an interventionist or a capacities account of causality?

The interventionist account, you will recall, did not require the social scientist to make actual, experimental interventions into a social system. The account depended, rather, on what *would* happen if certain factors *were* varied. It presupposes that the system in question is relatively modular and that the interventions are invariant. As discussed in Section 11.4, interventions are invariant (roughly) when the relationship between the intervention variable and the outcome variable is stable and reliable across a range of changes. Clearly, a single case cannot establish stability and reliability: recall the fire and the hand clap. Under suitable circumstances, however, an interventionist account might be more sanguine about small samples than a regularity account of causality. Finel and Lord's study arranged the combinations of transparency and escalation of conflict into seven possibilities. Their study does, therefore, examine a range of "interventions," and their results are apparently stable across the possibilities.

The capacity conception of causality has a similar consequence, and it shares an important feature with the interventionist perspective on case studies. On the capacity view, you will recall from Section 11.4, it is important to understand the limits of the "nomological engine" which is assembled from the underlying capacities. If we know that we are working with a relatively stable system, it is possible to determine causal relationships in a very small number of trials. It doesn't take repeated trials to show that the red button on my new phone causes it to end a call. Moreover, such knowledge generalizes to other systems of this type (such as other phones made by the same company). This last remark is the crucial point: the systems must be similar. The interventionist would agree that if I know that I am working with a stable and relatively autonomous system, invariant interventions can be established from examining a small number of cases. The real problem is to know whether the system we are studying *is* stable and autonomous.

By itself, a case study will not establish the limits of the social system on which it depends. Once again, we see ways in which the methodology of causal inference relies crucially on (causal) background knowledge. In Finel and Lord's study, the relevant systems were state bureaucracies. They presupposed that these social systems could produce and process information in predictable ways, and they presupposed that the people within these systems had a typical set of decision-making abilities. Notice that the case study did not discover the positive and negative logics of transparency. These mechanisms were already plausible as general features of the information processing of a bureaucracy. Against this background, Finel and Lord were able to establish a range of variation and determine the causal relationships among specific features of the social systems. What is drawn from the outside (or presupposed) are the general features of the social system. The case study establishes how those causal processes work in the specific system under study.

Justification and Discovery

Case studies tend to rely heavily on interviews, archival research, and other "qualitative" methods. As we saw in Chapters 3 and 4, the need for interpretation is often used as an argument against the search for causes and laws in the social sciences. Thick description does not seem like a good basis for hypotheses about causes. There is, then, a tension between the actual practice of case study research and the call for case studies to discover causal mechanisms. This tension has motivated some methodologists to exclude case studies from research which discovers correlations and makes causal inferences. For example, the first edition of the *Penguin Dictionary of Sociology* defined a case study in this way:

> *Case Study.* The detailed examination of a single example of a class of phenomena, a case study cannot provide reliable information about the broader class, but it may be useful in the preliminary stages of an investigation since it provides hypotheses, which may be tested systematically with a larger number of cases.
>
> (Abercrombie et al 1984, 14)

While this strong view is not universally acknowledged, even sympathetic treatments of case studies use them as devices for discovery. For example, Alexander George and Andrew Bennett's *Case Studies and Theory Development in the Social Sciences* (2005) is a recent defense of case study methods. It is telling that in their enumeration of the "Strengths of Case Study Methods," their descriptions rely heavily on verbs of discovery: "*deriving new* hypotheses," "*exploring* causal mechanisms," and "*identify* relevant variables" (George and Bennett 2005, 19–21).

Relegating case studies to the domain of discovery solves some of the epistemic difficulties which case studies seem to face. Causal claims aren't really tested by case studies, on this view. Case studies only suggest causal hypotheses to be tested by larger inquiries. Therefore, the questions discussed earlier do not arise. In addition, social scientists worry about bias in the selection of case studies. A case study might select (by design or by accident) only the examples which support a causal generalization. While the literature on case studies has extensive discussions of this problem, it is moot if case studies are only used for discovery. Issues of bias don't come up for processes of discovery, because any bias in the initial case will presumably be discovered as the causal claims are tested by a larger sample.

What is the difference between scientific "discovery" and "justification"? This issue has a history in 20th-century philosophy of science. A slogan of empiricist philosophy of science was "no logic of discovery." As we have seen (Chapter 3), the empiricist view of theory took the epistemology of science to be a matter of testing theories against observation. Confirmation required hypotheses to be derived from the theory, so that the test of the hypothesis against observation would be a test of the theory. The epistemology of theory testing, then, required theories to already exist. Where do theories come from? One might suppose that there is an epistemology of theory development too, that is, a logic of discovery. This would require the scientist to justify the invention of a new theory based on observation. The empiricists argued that this is incoherent. To determine that a new theory is epistemically respectable is to test it, and this requires the deduction of hypotheses from the theory. *Discovery*, then, has no epistemology; any source of inspiration will do (daydreams, poetry, drum-circle trances, drug-induced hallucinations, whatever). The good theories will be sorted from the bad ones by systematic empirical testing. It would make no sense to think of the process of discovery as biased or unbiased, or so the empiricists argued.

With a strong distinction between justification and discovery in the background, it is easy to see how assigning case studies to discovery (and not to justification) helped overcome the challenges they faced. Interpretive research was kept distinct from causal theorizing, and questions of generalization, bias, and small sample did not arise. It is obvious that case studies *can* be used to discover new phenomena. The interesting epistemological question is whether case study methods *must only* be used for theory discovery and development, not for direct support of causal claims. This strong thesis has some important consequences. If true, it would reinforce a distinction between those parts of the social sciences which are interpretive and those that are explanatory or causal. It would also undermine one of the advertised strengths of case studies—their ability to uncover mechanisms of the social world.

There are at least two objections to the strict separation of case studies as a form of discovery. The first is simple and telling. Bent Flyvbjerg has pointed out that the logical empiricists themselves recognized that a single case could falsify a theory (Flyvbjerg 2001). As a matter of logic, it takes only one black swan to contradict "all swans are white." The Finel and Lord study of transparency shows that the "positive logic" of transparency did not defuse conflict, and it therefore falsifies (at least a simple version of) the transparency explanation of the democratic peace. This quick argument shows that it would be a mistake to deny case studies any role in theory testing. Flyvbjerg's argument has limited significance, however, because it only gives case studies a role in falsification. If this were the only way that case studies functioned in theory development, then they would not be useful for finding social mechanisms.

The second objection begins by noticing that the "discovery" processes of case studies require loads of justification. The social scientist needs to be confident that the claims of a case study are accurate. The processes must be properly traced, the types must be identified correctly, the interviews must be well interpreted, and so on. A case study, in other words, is already a significant piece of "theory" which must be supported (justified) by the available evidence. This means that the epistemological questions around bias and case selection cannot be sidestepped by calling case studies "exploratory."

If we do not treat case studies as mere devices for discovery and thereby segregate them from other kinds of research, we must come to terms with the relationship between causal theories and interpretations. Case studies are typically "multimethod" in the sense that they draw on a range of qualitative and quantitative methods. When a case study is used to test causal hypotheses, it is easy to see why a variety of methods would be necessary. The Finel and Lord study, for example, required knowledge of the leaders' beliefs about each other's intentions. Any reading of the content of beliefs, attitudes, goals, norms, or laws will be an interpretation. At the same time, Finel and Lord set out to test whether the positive and negative logics of transparency influenced whether a conflict escalated. As we have already noted, knowledge of meaning does not support claims about causality, at least not all by itself. This is the idea that keeps interpretation and causal theorizing apart. To try to bring them into contact, we might consider two points.

The causal claims in Finel and Lord's study concern the items with the content: beliefs, goals, norms, or laws. For example, the belief that the other side is about to attack (along with the goal of avoiding such an attack) causes the leader to order a preemptive strike. Without the ability to understand what a leader's beliefs were about, Finel and Lord would have been unable to identify any causal processes related to transparency. Interpretation thus supports the causal analysis in an indirect way. It provides the content and thereby identifies the beliefs (etc.) which are used in the casual account. Similar points might be made if the causation were at either lower or higher levels than intentional states like beliefs and goals. Cognitive-level explanations like those proposed by Atran (discussed in Section 4.3) or Sperber (Section 7.3) require "representations." Like beliefs, these are distinguished by their content and require an interpretation for their identification. And if the causal mechanism concerns social entities like roles, norms, or laws, an interpretation will again be necessary to know what these are. The first point, then, is that interpretation supports causal theorizing by providing the necessary content.

The second point is that causal theorizing helps support interpretation. All psychological or social entities which are said to have meaning—beliefs, goals, norms, social roles—also have causal powers. And, one might argue, their content cannot be separated from their effects. Having the belief that it will rain, for instance, makes it likely that the person will carry an umbrella; say, "Tut, tut, it looks like rain;" and cancel plans for the barbeque. Occupying the social role of a police officer entails a variety of dispositions to react to cries for help. A central part of the evidence for an interpretation must be what people say and do, and this, one might argue, presupposes a causal relationship between the content of the belief, norm, or social role and the behavior. If this argument is correct, then any interpretation depends on a constellation of background beliefs about psychological and (perhaps) social causality. This is exactly the background against which the causal claims of a case study are made, and in the light of which the causal conclusions of a case study might become plausible.

The interpretive and causal aspects of case studies, arguably, require each other for epistemic support. If this is right, then it is a mistake to pigeon-hole case studies as either qualitative or quantitative. Case studies also show that it is a mistake to insist that qualitative and quantitative research must be strictly separated, as some methodologists do. Rather, case studies are a form of research which exemplifies Lawson and McCauley's interactionism (*cf.* Section 4.3).

12.3. Experimentation

What Can We Learn From Social Scientific Experimentation?

Experimentation is one of the iconic practices of science. So much so that Galileo dropping stones off the leaning tower of Pisa is the veritable origin myth of modern science. Given its centrality in our image of science, it is surprising that experimentation has been largely shunned by the social sciences. The traditional exceptions have been psychology and those parts of sociology which draw on psychology. Experimentation seems to be an exemplary way of identifying causal mechanisms, and as social scientists have shifted their focus toward causal mechanisms, experimentation has taken a more prominent role in disciplines like economics and anthropology. These developments of the last few decades have pushed the philosophical questions about experimentation to the fore. Is the lack of experimentation an indication of the methodological weakness of the social sciences relative to the natural sciences? Or is there something about the social sciences which makes experimentation difficult, or even inappropriate?

Standard accounts of the epistemology of experimentation identify two roles for experiments in scientific inquiry. The first is theory testing. This view fits neatly with an empiricist conception of theory, confirmation, and causality. On this sort of view, causal relations can only be identified through regularities. These are expressed by the generalizations or laws of a theory. An experiment lets us create an observation corresponding to a prediction of the theory. If the observation fails to correspond, the theory is falsified and must be revised. The second view emphasizes the controlled character of experiment. The idea of experimental control fits with the interventionist conception of causality. On this view, the goal of an experiment is to isolate and manipulate a purported cause. To experimentally determine whether a substance is toxic to a strain of bacteria, for example, populations of the bacteria would be divided into experimental and control groups. The design ensures that the two groups are treated exactly the same way to keep any other possible causes of bacterial growth or death constant. The experimental group is treated with the substance in question, and we observe the difference between the test bacteria and the controls. A successful experiment thus identifies a causal relationship between two factors, X and Y by showing that changes in X are correlated with changes in Y.

Needless to say, we can't treat humans the way we treat bacteria. Setting aside the moral questions, some philosophers and social scientists have thought that experimental methods are not useful (or of limited use) in the social sciences. John Stuart Mill famously argued against them in his *System of Logic* (Mill 1987 [1872], 70–71). Mill held that social phenomena were entirely determined by the actions of individuals, and he thought that there were laws (and thereby causes) of individual behavior. As we saw in Chapter 7, Mill was both an ontological and explanatory individualist. Nonetheless, he was skeptical about our capacity to isolate the causes of social phenomena. The root of the problem, he argued, was in the way that the causal factors combine and influence one another. The interactions are so complex that it is impossible to isolate a possible causal factor in the way demanded by experiment.

Mill's concern applies to experiments conceived either as theory tests or as manipulation of causes. A test of a theory requires deriving a hypothesis. Our social theories have not developed to the point where we can derive predictions precise enough for meaningful experiments. Economics has the most precise theories, but economic predictions are notoriously fallible. When the predictions fail, we chalk it up to complexities of the interaction that are not captured by the theory. Considered as manipulations, on the other hand, experiments require the scientist to set up a situation where all other factors are fixed. For large-scale social phenomena, it is impossible to find controls that are exactly the same as the experimental group. Cultural, occupational, educational, and other kinds of differences will guarantee that any pair of real human groups will be different from each other in more than one way. Short of morally impermissible isolation and control of people, it is impossible to shield the subjects from interference.

The foregoing argument has its strongest force when we are contemplating experimental manipulation of large-scale social phenomena. The experimental test of something like the democratic peace theory does indeed seem hopeless unless the experimenter was omnipotent. Of course, experimentation on humans need not be so ambitious. Experimental programs in behavioral economics and social psychology have brought small numbers of people into laboratory settings. By screening subjects and then randomly assigning them to control and experimental groups, we can be somewhat confident that the experimental and control groups have similar backgrounds. And by carefully constructing the tests, we try to isolate different causal factors from possible confounds. These programs seem to have been successful, but laboratory work with humans has then been criticized on the opposite grounds: by isolating the system one is unable to identify the real causes of social events. Social phenomena arise because of the complex interactions among agents. The different causal capacities of agents, the mechanisms which have causal force, and so on, both cancel out and interfere with each other. Even if we could shield lab subjects from outside social influences, doing so we would only guarantee that our experiments were irrelevant to theorizing about the social world.

We can remove some of the sting of these objections to experimentation by rethinking the epistemology of experiments and their relationship to theory. Looking at examples in the natural sciences, Ian Hacking argued that the relationship between theory and experiment had been misunderstood by philosophers of science (Hacking 1983). Experiments rarely test hypotheses derived from theory, nor do they typically confirm the causal mechanisms predicted by theory. Experimentation is often dedicated to the production of "effects" or "phenomena." Philosophers should note that the word *phenomenon* is not used as a synonym for *experience* in this literature. Phenomena or effects are events that experimenters learn to reliably reproduce. The shielding of the experiment from outside influences lets the experimenter expose one of the causal tendencies of the natural world. While experiments never occur without any prior theory, Hacking argued that the theories which influenced the experimenters were often wrong. Experimental production of phenomena requires as much engineering and ad-hoc tinkering as it does theoretical understanding. Much of the difficult and creative work in experimental science is oriented toward making the phenomenon more robust and reliable, as well as finding out what sorts of variation are relevant.

Hacking's conception of experiments as the reliable production of phenomena has been adopted by some proponents of experimentation in the social sciences.

There is a remarkable similarity between the production of effects in physical experiments and the experimental use of the prisoner's dilemma, the trust game, or the ultimatum game. As we discussed in Chapter 5, when game theoretical predictions were tested in the lab, real people did not conform to the demands of game theory. While these were initially treated as anomalies, experimenters soon turned to tinkering with the experimental designs. They found that the same results could be obtained under a range of conditions, and they figured out which variations influenced the outcome. Like the effects of physics, the phenomena discovered by behavioral economics become the subject of social scientific theories. Bicchieri's theory of norms, discussed in Chapter 9, is a good example. In her work, we saw that the experimental results of behavioral economics were part of what the theory needed to explain. The capacities thought to underlie the experimental phenomena (such as pro-social attitudes) played an important role in Bicchieri's account. Indeed, many—if not all—of the results of cognitive psychology which we have discussed in this book can be interpreted as the creation of laboratory effects, which then become either something to explain or something to appeal to in explanation.

Quasi-Experiments and Randomized Controlled Trials

Whatever the virtues of isolating a system for study, laboratories cannot be created for many of the social phenomena we would like to understand. Consider, for example, the question of whether classroom size influences education achievement. This question has been debated since the early 20th century. The first large and systematic study, *The Coleman Report*, used surveys to canvass over a half-million students and 60,000 teachers (Coleman et al 1966). Analyzed by linear regression models, the data showed that lower teacher-student ratios slightly raised student achievement. The effect of class size, however, was very small compared to the effects of socio-economic factors. Since the economic background of an individual student does not cause their classroom to have a large or small number of students, the model for this causal relationship should be diagrammed as in Figure 12.6. Inferring that this is the causal structure which underlies the correlations, however, is difficult because the independent variables are intertwined. Schools which had lower teacher-student ratios tended to be in districts where the students had more wealthy families. Therefore, socio-economic status and student-teacher ratio variables will be correlated in the data. This means that the Casual Markov Axiom is violated, and the logic of Bayes Nets will not apply.

If we consider this problem from the point of view of an interventionist conception of causality, Figure 12.6 is telling us that *if* we were to change the teacher-student ratio in a student's classroom, and *if* that were the only change, then the student's achievement would change. We could demonstrate the causal relationship by intervening on the teacher-student ratio (and on *only* that variable). The problem is that we cannot intervene directly on an individual. A particular 8-year-old student goes through the third grade only once. If we made him do it again, he would be a year older than the typical third grader, and he would be repeating

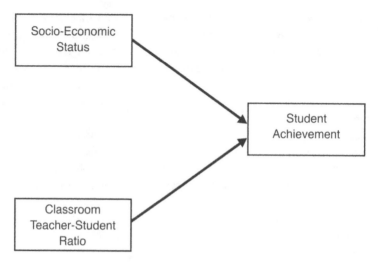

Figure 12.6 Causes of Student Achievement

material. We therefore cannot vary the teacher-student ratio for a given student. To solve this problem, we turn our attention from the individual student to a population of students. We divide students into two groups, and we provide each group with different teacher-student ratios. If this is to count as a legitimate intervention, then all other variables (except for the two we are investigating, class size and achievement) must be "held fixed." To satisfy this requirement, we need to make sure that there are no systematic differences between our two groups. We would, perhaps, make sure that the two groups are evenly matched for socio-economic factors. Any difference in performance would be attributed only to the difference in class size. And notice that when we have controlled for the other variables in this way, we make class size probabilistically independent of any other possible causes. Therefore, the Causal Markov Axiom is satisfied, and we *can* use a Bayesian justification for causal inferences.

The common practice of dividing experimental subjects into two groups which differ only with respect to the intervention variable is thus justified by an interventionist account of causality (and the closely related Bayes Net logic of causal inference). This underlying rationale for causal inference is experimental, but it does not require the isolation of a laboratory. The trick is to mimic the logic of laboratory experiments in the social environment. One of the most famous experimental studies of class size took place in Tennessee during the 1980s. Project STAR (Student-Teacher Achievement Ratio) involved more than 6,000 school children in classes from kindergarten to third grade. It divided children into two groups: classes of 13 to 17, and classes of 22 to 25. In this case, "dividing" the children did not involve moving them around. In each participating school, the classrooms were assigned so that some children went to small classes and others went to large classes. The experiment thus took place in a setting which was in every way a normal elementary school. The intervention tried to create a condition in which the only difference between the groups of students was the size of their classroom. The study found that smaller classes had a significant, positive effect on educational outcomes, and later phases of the study showed that it lasted beyond the early elementary school years.

The method of identifying two groups which differ on just one variable does not require that the experimenters introduce the division or the intervention themselves. The interventionist conception of causality will be satisfied when there is no human intervention at all. Suppose there are two naturally occurring populations which are identical in all respects except two: the purported cause, X, and the outcome variable, Y. The difference on X is the "intervention," directly analogous to a change introduced by an experimenter. Nature is wiggling the X variable in the sense that the two groups exhibit a difference only with respect to X. And just as with a laboratory experiment, the fact that the two groups are otherwise identical means that X will be probabilistically independent of any variables which are not effects of X. This means that if X is correlated with Y, we may infer that X is a cause of Y. Methods which try to discover causes in this way are known as "natural" or "quasi-" experiments.

Just as a laboratory experiment is reliable only to the extent that the system can be isolated from interference, a quasi-experiment is reliable only to the extent that the independent variable (X) is the only difference between the two groups. Obviously, no two groups of people will be *identical*. And fortunately, strict identity is not necessary anyway. Nonetheless, in both laboratory and quasi-experiments, there are two kinds of situations with which the social scientists must be concerned, represented in Figure 12.7.

In either of the causal models in Figure 12.7, intervention could produce observed correlations between the X and Y variables; yet in neither is X the cause of Y. A situation like Figure 12.7a would arise if the intervention not only changed the independent variable but also modified a third variable (Z). In Project STAR, this problem might have come about if the smaller classes also had better teachers (Z). Figure 12.7b illustrates the problem of sample bias. The outcome variable is

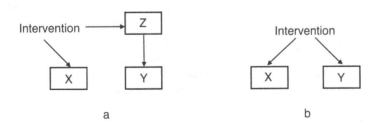

Figure 12.7 Confounded Interventions

influencing the intervention in some way. In Project STAR, it might have arisen if a student's test scores influenced the group into which they were placed. While that would be a rather blatant error in study design, similar situations arise which are more difficult to detect. For example, if students were allowed to volunteer for small or large classes, or if teachers of the small classes were permitted to pick students, the small and large classes might start to differ with respect to student aptitude. More highly motivated students might end up in smaller classes, and motivation would be closely tied to the outcome being investigated. Once again, class size and achievement would have been correlated even in the absence of a causal relationship between them.

Project STAR protected against both problems mentioned earlier with randomization. Within a given school, both students and teachers were randomly assigned to large or small classes. The idea of randomization is that differences in teaching ability, scholastic aptitude, and any other potential cause will be evenly distributed. They thereby become probabilistically independent of the effect we are investigating (scholastic achievement, in the STAR case). The beauty of randomization is that we don't need to guess about possible confounds or unintended biases. The method of a randomized controlled trial (RCT) implements randomization in a thoroughgoing way. In an RCT, the two groups—usually called "treatment" and "control" in this context—are entirely determined by random selection. RCTs have been widely used in tests of drugs and other medical treatments. When the intervention is as simple as taking a pill, complete randomization of the study population is easy to achieve. Perhaps we just flip a coin for each subject to determine whether he or she is in the treatment or control groups. The coin flip makes the variable on which we are intervening (say, taking the pill) independent of all variables which might also influence the outcome. For this reason, RCTs are regarded as a particularly powerful way of identifying causes.

Experimentation in the laboratory, quasi-experiments, and RCTs use the same rationale for supporting causal inference. The differences among the methods have to do with the way in which they try to guarantee that the independent variable is truly independent. Randomization is one method for doing so, but it need not be applied as thoroughly as is done in an RCT. In the STAR study, the randomization occurred within schools, not within the entire population of elementary school students in Tennessee. Scrambling students from around the state into entirely new schools would not only have been impractical, but it would have disrupted many of the things which already make education effective. In this case, the epistemically more robust choice was to maintain some of the differences among students (such as which school they attend) and randomize others. The lesson for social science methodologists, then, is that internal validity is not guaranteed by insisting on particular techniques (like randomization) but by attending carefully to features of the context which disrupt the independence of a hypothesized causal variable.

12.4. Extrapolation and Social Engineering

Evidence-Based Policy

The questions about possible confounds and biases which we have been discussing so far in this chapter concern the *internal* validity of a study. A study has internal validity if it supports a robust causal inference about the experimental subjects, study population, or case. The questions of external validity concern whether the same causal mechanisms operate in other contexts. Why should we believe that the findings of a case study will generalize to other cases? Why should we suppose that the knowledge gained about the artificial social system in a laboratory can be transferred to a real social system? The STAR project found that smaller class sizes increased scholastic achievement *in Tennessee*, but will they do so in New York?

In the last decade of the 20th century, there was a new movement to improve the quality of the evidence on which governmental agencies or other institutions made decisions. "Evidence-based policy" became a buzzword, and several guides to evidence quality were published. These guides rated RCT studies as the most reliable, with quasi-experimental and case studies falling second and third. If interpretive studies were included at all in these guides, their evidence is regarded as the weakest. Consider, for example, the advice given by the US Department of Education about evidence for educational policy. Educators are advised to adopt policies for which the evidence is strong in both "quality" and "quantity." Strong quality is defined as "randomized controlled trials that are well-designed and implemented," and strong quantity is defined as two or more RCTs in "typical school settings" that include "a setting similar to that of your schools/classrooms" (Coalition for Evidence-Based Policy 2003, v). Quasi-experimental designs are taken to show that the effectiveness of the intervention is possible but needs to be confirmed by an RCT. If neither RCTs nor quasi-experiments have been done, then "one may conclude that the intervention is not supported by meaningful evidence" (Coalition for Evidence-Based Policy 2003, v).

The Department of Education's guide assumes that a well-conducted RCT has external validity. This assumption is not unreasonable. After all, the authors of the guide argue, if the RCT is well-designed, it will have discovered a real causal relationship between the intervention and the outcome variables. If the relationship is causal, then presumably it is general. And that means that it will apply to similar cases. The catch, however, lies in the judgment of similarity. Systems similar in some ways will be different in others. If the new situation is different in the wrong ways, then the cause will not be operative in the situation where we want to implement the new policy. The right sort of similarity, of course, is the one where *the same causes* are operative. So, we come back to the question: how do we know that the situation in which we want to make policy is subject to the same causes as our test case?

We can get a bit of purchase on this question by considering the notion that certain causal relationships depend on a local causal system, or nomological machine.

Just as the causal relationship in a bank transaction (*cf.* Section 12.1) depends on an underlying system, the relationship between classroom size and achievement depends on a particular institutional arrangement. For example, students are in classes five days a week with the same teacher, schooling is mandatory, classes are separated by age, and so on. Nancy Cartwright has argued that because of the way that causal relationships depend on underlying systems, causal relationships discovered in the social sciences are both *local* and *fragile*. They are local in the sense that they hold only when the system is in place to support the causal relationship. And the causal relationship is fragile in the sense that trying to make a change in the causal relationship often makes many other changes. Policy changes and interventions may thus disrupt the very thing they set out to promote. Given this background, the earlier question of similarity can be made more precise as two questions: does the context in which we want to implement the result of an RCT share the same underlying causal system? And can we make the policy change without disrupting the system that supports the causal relationship we want to promote?

There is some reason to think that RCTs are particularly *poor* resources when we need to decide whether to implement a new policy. The epistemological strength of the RCT—randomization—is the practical weakness. Randomization of the study population into control and treatment groups insulates the study variables from all other causes, known and unknown. Possible confounds or biases which might produce a correlation in the absence of causation are thus screened off. By the very study design, then, we know nothing about the system which makes the causal relationship possible. Nor do we know anything about the ways in which the policy we intend to implement might interfere with other aspects of the system. For example, in 1996 the State of California tried to implement the results of Project STAR on a massive scale. To do so, they had to increase the number of teachers in kindergarten through third grade by 46%. The high demand meant that many of the new teachers were not fully qualified. After the program was implemented, there was no clear effect of reduced class size. It is likely that the lowered instructional quality offset the gains of small classrooms (Bohrnstedt and Stecher 2002). Project STAR used only fully qualified teachers, and then randomized classroom assignment. The study design screened off possible confounds, but they also screened off aspects of the underlying system relevant to policy implementation.

One might argue, then, that contrary to the advice of the evidence-based policy guides, quasi-experiments and case studies are *superior* to RCTs as evidence for policy implementation. In quasi-experiments and case studies, the investigators must make careful determinations about what kinds of confounds and biases might be present. This requires, as we have seen, some understanding of the larger social system under study. We therefore know which aspects of the underlying system have been controlled for, and we can use this as a basis for judging whether the target system is relevantly like the study population. Once again, however, the strength of quasi-experiments and case studies hides a weakness. We are beholden to the imagination and knowledge of the social scientists who designed the study. If they failed to foresee a possible confound or bias, the correlations will not reflect the underlying causal relationship. We return, then, to the point which has recurred throughout our discussions of methodology. The reliability of an inference based on evidence depends on the adequacy of the wider understanding of the social system under study. In the case of causal inference, the importance of mechanism is foregrounded. The external validity of RCTs, case studies, and quasi-experiments all depend on knowing the limits of the underlying causal system. Knowledge of this underlying system is precisely what proponents of mechanism were emphasizing.

The FCC Auction

The technological world of the 21st century is ample testimony to our ability to transfer experimental knowledge of natural causes to the messy and complex world outside the lab. Our record of success with social engineering, by contrast, is dismal. One might suppose that this confirms Mill's conclusion that social phenomena are just too complicated to be approached mechanistically. Even if we could identify the underlying causal capacities of the social world, their interactions are just too complex to yield to experimental knowledge. An apparent counterexample to this narrative of despair is the design and implementation of a process for auctioning the radio spectrum by the United States Federal Communications Commission (or FCC). In this case, economists were able to use a combination of theoretical modeling and laboratory experiment to design a functioning social institution. Because of its success in the face of overwhelming real-world complexity, the FCC auction has been much discussed by philosophers of the social sciences. It appears to be a case where economists were able to successfully extrapolate from laboratory results to the real world, thus demonstrating—*pace* Mill—that knowledge of large-scale social phenomena can be based on a mechanistic knowledge of the parts.

The challenge facing the US Congress and the FCC in the late 1980s and early 1990s was to design an auction for licenses to segments of the radio spectrum. The growth in popularity of cell phones and similar devices had increased demand by telecommunications companies. Among other desiderata, the designers wanted a market that was efficient in the sense that the products were sold to the companies who most valued them at the highest price those companies would be willing to pay. Markets at equilibrium are efficient in this sense, but this situation was not a normal market. In the terminology of economics, the licenses exhibited "complementarity." Owning the licenses to two contiguous regions, for example, might be more valuable than the sum of the two individual licenses owned separately. In economic models, markets with strong complementarities tend to be unstable and to lack a unique equilibrium. Complementarity is just the kind of complexity that was worrying Mill. Knowledge of the parts (the value of individual licenses to the telecommunications companies) is insufficient for knowledge of the whole (the value at auction).

In designing the spectrum auction, the theorists were presented with a problem which had no known theoretical solution. Because of the complementarities and other complexities of the telecommunications license environment, there was no way to derive the structure of an efficient auction system from theoretical principles. As a result, they took a piecemeal approach which relied on both theory and experimentation. Theoretically, they used game theory to model specific parts of proposed systems. These models were the basis for arguments that some possible auction systems would give rise to strategic interactions with inefficient equilibria. For example, as modeled by game theory, it appeared that some auction systems permitted free riders. Game theory was thus being used not as a set of axioms from which a single best solution could be derived, but as a toolkit for modeling local parts of a larger system.

Experiments aided the development of the spectrum auction rules in different ways at various phases of the project. Early on, experimental "test beds" were created to exemplify simplified models of different model auction systems. By running laboratory versions of the auctions, the experimental economists were able to determine the basic properties of their mechanisms. They were also able to determine the relative advantages and limitations of the different auction models. Once a specific auction system was under development, experiments on this system identified several problems that had not (and perhaps could not have) been anticipated by the theorists. The participants interpreted and used the rules in creative ways. Moreover, the rules would interact unexpectedly. Experiments with trial versions of the auction rules revealed several implementation issues that had to be resolved by the final auction system. Once the spectrum auction was underway in 1994, the experimenters continued to monitor the results. By comparing their experimental trials of the full system with the actual results, they could evaluate the performance of the real auction.

Breaking the Extrapolator's Circle

The 1994 FCC spectrum auction was hailed as a success for both game theory and experimental economics. It appears to be a case where social scientists solved the problem of extrapolation (or external validity): they successfully exported knowledge from the lab to the "real world." The problem of external validity has several proposed solutions. What is the best way to understand the success of the FCC spectrum auction? In this section and the next, we will consider three possible accounts of how experimental knowledge (and causal modeling in general) can be transferred to real-world contexts. As we will see, much depends on how one thinks about the topics we have been discussing through the last two chapters: causality, mechanisms, modeling, and experimentation. (And note that while we will be focused on experiments in this section, very similar arguments could be given to justify or challenge extrapolation from any case study or causal model.)

First, suppose one accepts the arguments of Section 12.3 that a laboratory experiment creates a reliable experimental phenomenon. Experimental phenomena are supposed to expose the elements of social mechanisms. On this sort of view, the challenge is to predict how these mechanisms will behave in less-sheltered, natural environments. One plausible account of the inference from experiment to real social systems relies on analogy. The form of the argument is something like this: in the laboratory, mechanism X is responsible for the system-level phenomenon Y; in the social world, we observe the system-level phenomenon Y; therefore, mechanism X is responsible for Y in the social world. The strength of the analogy depends on whether there are factors that make the social system different from the laboratory system. In the social world, are there factors other than X which might be responsible for Y? Is there anything that would suppress or block the effects of X? These questions ask about the similarity between lab and social world, and insofar as the two are similar, the argument is strengthened.

An important challenge to this first account of how we can extrapolate from experiment to the social world is what Daniel Steel called the "extrapolator's circle" (Steel 2008). The strength of the analogy depends on the similarity between the laboratory phenomenon and the social system. Hence, the analogy could be known to be strong only if we knew the properties of both the laboratory phenomenon and the social system. But, of course, we *don't* know the properties of the social system. That's why we do social science. So, we could use analogy to extrapolate only if we already know what we are trying to discover. Proponents of analogy recognize this and emphasize that any inference from experiment to social system is an empirical hypothesis which needs to be tested. Moreover, social scientists are not completely ignorant of the properties of social systems, and therefore they can have some justification for the initial analogy. It is a program of social scientific research to determine what sort of additional factors might be present in the social system that would disrupt the analogy.

Proponents of the second view of extrapolation are unconvinced by the idea that experimentation can identify the specific causal mechanisms of the social world. For instance, one might hold a capacity view of causation, and think that all the real causal capacities are natural, not social. In other words, there are no social capacities, only natural capacities. Social systems might be nomological machines built from only natural parts. On this second view of extrapolation, experimentation shows how to manipulate particular social mechanisms, and our ability to manipulate them does not depend on an accurate understanding of their internal composition. In defense of this idea, one might point out that the FCC auction ultimately ran simulations of the complete auction system. What made the auction successful was not an analogy between lab phenomenon and a social system but the creation of a social system. The experiments showed that a whole system would function in a particular way, not that it worked via a particular mechanism. Against this interpretation, one might point out that the early experiments were different from the later simulations. The FCC design built upon stable phenomena that were well established by experiment. Also, since the mechanism in this case was a set of rules (the rules that defined the auction), the FCC did know that the mechanism in the lab (both earlier and later) was the same as the mechanism of the real auction.

Performativity and Social Engineering

It is remarkable that in the FCC spectrum auction, economists created a whole institution. In this way, social experimentation might appear different from natural experimentation. Creating an effect or phenomenon in a physical experiment is very different from engineering a device that works. The Monroe effect, for example, is a reliable experimental phenomenon that concerns the shape of shockwaves from an explosion. A solid explosive with a depression or dent in its surface will propagate a shockwave in the direction of the dent. This effect is fundamental for designing armor-piercing shells. But by demonstrating the Monroe effect in the lab one has not thereby made a torpedo. On the other hand, by demonstrating the spectrum auction in the lab, the FCC did make an auction. Insofar as experimentation and theoretical modeling are used for social engineering, one might think, they are phases in the direct creation of social institutions. The notion of "external validity" is thus the wrong way to frame the issue. External validity presupposes that we possess laboratory knowledge and wonder whether it truly describes the real world. On the contrary, perhaps the process of applying social scientific knowledge is less like comparing theory to observation and more like tinkering with the shape of a torpedo so that it will sink a battleship. This thought is the basis for a third, more radical approach to the relationship between experiments and social systems, sometimes called the "performativity thesis."

According to the performativity thesis, social scientists act to make the social world more like their models. They are not describing an independent reality; they are creating the reality they describe. In Chapter 8 we discussed the ways in which people adopt social categories and make them real. This is the "looping" character of humankind. As we noticed in the earlier discussion, many categories are derived from social scientific theory—the way in which the anthropological concept of culture has been adopted by indigenous peoples is a prominent example. The project of designing an economic system like the spectrum auction is an especially clear example of the design and implementation of a social mechanism. The FCC intentionally created a system of rules to be taken up and applied. There are also many in-between examples, for instance in criminology, educational studies, or political science, where the social sciences create models that become norms or rules for behavior. The adoption of any category or norm will require social decision-making (either explicit or implicit), and therefore there will be aspects of the uptake which will be political. The performativity of the social sciences, then, is another way in which they are value-laden (*cf.* Chapter 2).

In its strong form, performativity is rather controversial. Insofar as it would deny that social scientific theories are descriptive, it denies that they are true or false. Like promises, social scientific theories create what they describe. Promises are successful or unsuccessful, not literally true or false. In response, a performativity theorist can point out that not just any social scientific model can be successfully taken up. When the goal is explicitly social engineering, models, computer simulations, case studies, and experiments are used to find designs that are likely to work.

Whether they work is not just a matter of the power or prestige of the scientists. Theoretical modeling and the related empirical methods are thus, one might argue, getting at something. And the fact that they "get at something" needs to be part of our picture of the social sciences. If arguments like these are used to soften the more strident claims about social scientific performativity, then there may be a possible *rapprochement* among the three different views we have been discussing. We might admit that performativity is an important dimension of the social sciences, especially those which lie close to issues of policy. At the same time, it is important that the models built by the social sciences be based on evidence. This latter point means that we cannot ignore the epistemic questions of how models are developed and tested by methods like case study and experimentation.

12.5. Wrap Up

Chapter Summary

This chapter considered three different social scientific approaches to the epistemology of causal inference: causal modeling, case studies, and experimentation. The Bayesian Network approach is a very powerful way to use probabilistic relationships to narrow the range of possible causal models which might explain an observed correlation. In ideal cases, only one possible causal model is possible, given the data. Real evidence is messy, however, and Bayes Nets can run into trouble when causes are unanticipated by the social scientist. Also, as Cartwright argued, the causal relationships discovered by Bayes Network analysis often depend on the existence of a larger causal system. This is an important reminder that causes in one domain may not transfer to another.

One of the limitations of Bayes Networks is that they require a pre-determined set of variables. Before the logic of inference can begin, the social scientist must already have determined what the possible causes might be. If we do not already know the causes, how do we know that we are measuring the right variables? Case study methods respond to this problem by taking an intensive look at a small number of events, social structures, or institutions. Proponents argue that by carefully tracing the chain of events, the relevant causes can be identified. Moreover, case studies make it possible to discover mechanisms that are invisible to the surface correlations because they cancel out in the aggregate. The uniqueness of the case study creates its own epistemological challenges. How can causal generalizations be based on the study of one case? Here, we found that the interventionist and capacity theories were a helpful way to think about the causes discovered in a case study. If the boundaries of the underlying causal system are known, causal relationships can be discovered without many instances. Of course, this means that the case study will always rely heavily on knowledge external to the case. But in this way, arguably, case studies are like all other scientific inquiries.

Experimentation is a well-known way to identify causes, and in recent years experimentation has become a more prominent method in the social sciences. However, the way that social phenomena mutually influence each other, creating phenomena like economic complementarities, has been used as an argument against experimentation in the social sciences. Any causes isolated in the laboratory are unlikely to be found in the social world. In Section 12.3 we saw that this objection can be met, at least in part, by rethinking the epistemology of experimentation. Rather than tests of theory, experiments aim to reliably produce "effects." The question is then whether and how knowledge of such effects can be used to understand the mechanisms of the social world. Quasi-experiments and randomized controlled trials rely on an epistemology similar to experiments, but they use different ways to isolate potential causes. In general, we have found that these experimental methods are better conceptualized in terms of an interventionist or capacity view of causality than in empiricist terms.

All methods of identifying causal relationships in the social sciences face the problem of extrapolation (or external validity). Once we have identified a causal relationship in a particular case, or in a laboratory setting, what gives us confidence that the cause is operative in other contexts? Extrapolation depends on the new context being similar in the relevant way, but determining whether the context is similar seems to require that we already know the relevant causal features of the context. In Section 12.4 we saw three ways to break out of the extrapolator's circle: reasoning by analogy, limiting inference to the same underlying causal system, and performativity. The last, performativity, is less a way of breaking out of the circle than dissolving the problem entirely. It makes the radical suggestion that at least some social scientific research is the direct creation of social reality, rather than its representation. This thought brings us full circle, back to the questions of how social science and social policy are related.

Discussion Questions

1. Consider the following correlations. Imagine as many possible causal models as you can to explain the observations. Use DAGs to diagram the models. What variable would you measure or intervene upon to rule out one of the possible models? Why would the model be ruled out?

    a. In all elementary schools, there is a positive correlation between height and reading ability. Taller children read better.

    b. Famine is very rare in democracies. There is a negative correlation between famine and democracy.

    c. Consider the correlations between violent media and aggression described in Section 3.1.

2. Is there an important difference between the *discovery* of social scientific theories and their *justification*? Should case studies be treated as only means of discovering possible variables to measure in a later correlational study?

3. Evaluate Mill's claim that human society is too complex for experimental methods to be useful.
4. In what ways are quasi-experiments *unlike* laboratory experiments? Does this make quasi-experiments stronger or weaker, epistemologically speaking?
5. Compare laboratory experiments, quasi-experiments, and RCTs with respect to internal and external validity. What similar challenges do they all face? Where are some designs stronger or weaker?
6. Is performativity restricted to economics, or could the results of other social scientific disciplines also be made true by our undertaking the descriptions? How is this related to Hacking's looping effects (discussed in Section 3.4)?

Further Reading

Pearl, *Causality: Models, Reasoning, and Inference* (2000) and Sprites, Glymour, and Scheines, *Causation, Prediction, and Search* (2000) are important advances in our understanding of the epistemology of causal inference. Good introductory explanations or surveys include Scheines, "The Similarity of Causal Inference in Experimental and Non-Experimental Studies (2005); Woodward, "Causal Models in the Social Sciences" (2007); and Steel, "Causality, Causal Models, and Social Mechanisms" (2011). For a different take on these issues, see Cartwright "How to Get Causes From Probabilities" (Cartwright 1989) and "How to Do Things With Causes" (Cartwright 2009).

Steel's "Social Mechanisms and Causal Inference" (2004) assimilates the process-tracing methodology of case studies to the Bayes Net approach. Arguments that case study methods can justify causal hypotheses are also found in Flyvbjerg, "The Power of Example" (2001); Flyvbjerg, "Five Misunderstandings about Case-Study Research" (2006); Ruzzene, "Drawing Lessons from Case Studies by Enhancing Comparability" (2012); Crasnow, "The Role of Case Study Research in Political Science: Evidence for Causal Chains" (2011); and Crasnow, "Evidence for Use: Causal Pluralism and the Role of Case Study Research" (2012).

Hogarth, "The Challenge of Representative Design in Psychology and Economics" (2005) is a good discussion of Mill's problem of complexity and its relationship to external validity. The argument that social systems are open, while experiments necessarily involve closed systems, can be traced to Bhaskar, *The Possibility of Naturalism* (1979); see also Kemp and Holmwood, "Realism, regularity and social explanation" (2003).

Experimentation in economics has been a hot topic in recent years. Guala's *The Methodology of Experimental Economics* (2005) is a comprehensive philosophical study. See also Urbach, "Randomization and the Design of Experiments" (1985); Smith, "Economics in the laboratory" (1994); Smith, "Method in Experiment: Rhetoric and Reality" (2002); Guala, "Paradigmatic Experiments: The Ultimatum Game from Testing to Measurement Device" (2006); Sugden, "The Changing Relationship between Theory and Experiment in Economics" (2006); and Mayo, "Some Methodological Issues in Experimental Economics" (2008).

Cartwright has been sharply critical of the external validity of RCTs; see "What are Randomized Controlled Trials Good For?" (2010) and Cartwright, Goldfinch, and Howick, "Evidence-Based Policy: Where is Our Theory of Evidence?" (2009). Reiss's "Against External Validity" (2019) moves in the same direction. Steel's *Across the Boundaries: Extrapolation in Biology and the Social Sciences* (2008) is a thorough discussion of the issues. The FCC Auctions have been a widely discussed case study in extrapolation. See Guala, "Building Economic Machines: the FCC Auctions" (2001) and Alexandrova and Northcott, "Progress in Economics: Lessons from the Spectrum Auctions" (2009).

For discussion of the performativity thesis, see Callon, "What Does It Mean to Say that Economics is Performative?" (2007); Mackenzie, Muniesa, and Siu, "Do Economists Make Markets? On The Performativity of Economics" (2007); Mirowski and Nik-Khah, "Markets Made Flesh: Performativity, and a Problem in Science Studies, Augmented with Consideration of the FCC Auctions" (2007); and Nik-Khah "A Tale of Two Auctions" (2006).

References

Abercrombie, Nicholas, Stephen Hill, Bryan S. Turner, and S. A. Erofeev. 1984. *The Penguin Dictionary of Sociology*. Harmondsworth: Penguin.

Ahern, Kathryn J. 1999. Ten Tips for Reflexive Bracketing. *Qualitative Health Research* 9 (3):407–411.

Ajzen, Icek. 1991. The Theory of Planned Behavior. *Organizational Behavior and Human Decision Processes* 50:179–211.

Alexander, Jason, and Brian Skyrms. 1999. Bargaining with Neighbors: Is Justice Contagious? *Journal of Philosophy* 99 (11):588–598.

Alexandrova, Anna. 2008. Making Models Count. *Philosophy of Science* 75 (3):383–404

Alexandrova, Anna, and Robert Northcott. 2009. Progress in Economics: Lessons from the Spectrum Auctions. In *The Oxford Handbook of Philosophy of Economics*, edited by D. Ross and H. Kincaid. Oxford: Oxford University Press.

American Academy of Pediatrics. 2000. *Joint Statement on the Impact of Entertainment Violence on Children* [cited November 19, 2011]. Available from www.aap.org/advocacy/releases/jst-mtevc.htm.

Anderson, Craig A., and Brad J. Bushman. 2002. Human Aggression. *Annual Review of Psychology* 53:27–51.

Anderson, Elizabeth. 1995. Knowledge, Human Interests, and Objectivity in Feminist Epistemology. *Philosophical Topics* 23 (2):27–58.

Anderson, Elizabeth. 2004. Uses of Value Judgments in Science: A General Argument, with Lessons from a Case Study of Feminist Research on Divorce. *Hypatia* 19 (1):1–24.

Anscombe, G. E. M. 1963. *Intention*, 2nd edition. Ithaca: Cornell University Press.

Appiah, Kwame Anthony. 2006. How to Decide If Races Exist. *Proceedings of the Aristotelian Society* 106:365–382.

Ardestani, Babak Mahdavi, David O'Sullivan, and Peter Davis. 2018. A Multi-Scaled Agent-Based Model of Residential Segregation Applied to a Real Metropolitan Area. *Computers, Environment and Urban Systems* 69:1–16.

Aronovitch, Hilliard. 2011. Interpreting Weber's Ideal Types. *Philosophy of the Social Sciences* 41 (3):1–14.

Asad, Talal (ed.). 1973. *Anthropology and the Colonial Encounter*. London: Ithaca Press.

Atkinson, Paul, and David Silverman. 1997. Kundera's Immortality: The Interview Society and the Invention of the Self. *Qualitative Inquiry* 3 (3):304–325.

Atran, Scott. 2002. *In Gods We Trust: The Evolutionary Landscape of Religion*. Oxford: Oxford University Press.

Axelrod, Robert. 1984. *The Evolution of Cooperation*. New York: Basic Books.

Axelrod, Robert. 1997. *The Complexity of Cooperation: Agent-Based Models of Competition and Collaboration*. Princeton: Princeton University Press.

Babst, Dean V. 1964. Elective Governments: A Force for Peace. *Wisconsin Sociologist* 3 (1):9–14.

Bacharach, Michael. 2006. *Beyond Individual Choice: Teams and Frames in Game Theory.* Princeton: Princeton University Press.

Bermudez, Jose Louis. 2005. *Philosophy of Psychology: A Contemporary Introduction.* London: Routledge.

Bevir, Mark, and Jason Blakely. 2018. *Interpretive Social Science: An Anti-Naturalist Approach.* Oxford: Oxford University Press.

Bhaskar, Roy. 1979. *The Possibility of Naturalism.* London Routledge.

Bhaskar, Roy. 2008. *'A' Realist Theory of Science*, 2nd edition. London: Taylor and Frances. Original edition, 1975.

Bicchieri, Cristina. 2006. *The Grammar of Society: The nature and Dynamics of Social Norms.* Cambridge: Cambridge University Press.

Bicchieri, Cristina. 2017. *Norms in the Wild.* Oxford: Oxford University Press.

Boas, Franz. 1911. *The Mind of Primitive Man.* New York: The MacMillan Co.

Bohman, James. 1991. *New Philosophy of Social Science.* Cambridge, MA: MIT Press.

Bohman, James. 1999. Theories, Practices, and Pluralism: A Pragmatic Interpretation of Critical Social Science. *Philosophy of the Social Sciences* 29 (4):459–480.

Bohman, James. 2021. Critical Theory. In *The Stanford Encyclopedia of Philosophy*, edited by E. N. Zalta. Spring 2021 Edition. URL <https://plato.stanford.edu/archives/spr2021/entries/critical-theory/>

Bohrnstedt, George W., and Brian M. Stecher (eds.). 2002. *What We Have Learned about Class Size Reduction in California.* Palo Alto, CA: CSR Research Consortium.

Bourdieu, Pierre. 1977. *Outline of a Theory of Practice.* Cambridge: Cambridge University Press.

Bouvier, Alban. 2011. Invidiualism, Collective Agency, and the 'Micro-Macro Relation'. In *The SAGE Handbook of the Philosophy of the Social Sciences*, edited by I. C. Jarvie and J. Zamora-Bonilla. Los Angeles: SAGE Publications.

Boyd, Robert, and Peter Richerson. 2009. Culture and the Evolution of Human Cooperation. *Philosophical Transactions of the Royal Society Biological Sciences* 364 (1533):3281–3288.

Brandom, Robert. 1994. *Making It Explicit.* Cambridge, MA: Harvard University Press.

Bratman, Michael E. 1987. *Intention, Plans, and Practical Reason.* Cambridge, MA: Harvard University Press.

Bratman, Michael E. 1993. Shared Intention. *Ethics* 104 (1):97–113.

Bratman, Michael E. 1997. I Intend that We J. In *Contemporary Action Theory Volume 2: Social Action*, edited by R. Tuomela and Holmstrom-Hintikka. Dordrecht: Kluwer.

Bratman, Michael E. 1999. *Faces of Intention.* Cambridge: Cambridge University Press.

Bratman, Michael E. 2009. Modest Sociality and the Distinctiveness of Intention. *Philosophical Studies* 144 (1):149–165.

Bremer, Stuart A. 1992. Dangerous Dyads: Conditions Affecting the Liklihood of Interstate War, 1816–1965. *The Journal of Conflict Resolution* 36 (2):309–341.

Briggs, Charles L. 1986. *Learning How to Ask: A Sociolinguistic Appraisal of the Role of the Interview in Social Science Research.* Cambridge: Cambridge University Press.

Bushman, Brad J., and Craig A. Anderson. 2015. Understanding Causality in the Effects of Media Violence. *American Behavioral Scientist* 59 (14):1807–1821.

Buss, Arnold H., and Mark Perry. 1992. The Aggression Questionnaire. *Journal of Personality and Social Psychology* 63 (3):452–459.

Callon, Michel. 2007. What Does It Mean to Say that Economics Is Performative? In *Do Economists Make Markets? On the Performativity of Economics*, edited by D. A. Mackenzie, F. Muniesa and L. Siu. Princeton: Princeton University Press.

Camerer, Colin F. 2003. *Behavioral Game Theory: Experiments in Strategic Interaction.* Princeton: Princeton University Press.

Cartwright, Nancy. 1983. *How the Laws of Physics Lie*. Oxford: Clarendon Press.

Cartwright, Nancy. 1989. *Nature's Capacities and Their Measurement*. Oxford: Oxford University Press.

Cartwright, Nancy. 2007. *Hunting Causes and Using Them*. Cambridge: Cambridge University Press.

Cartwright, Nancy. 2008. *The Dappled World: A Study of the Boundaries of Science*. Cambridge: Cambridge University Press.

Cartwright, Nancy. 2009. How to Do Things with Causes. *APA Proceedings and Addresses* 83 (2).

Cartwright, Nancy. 2010. What Are Randomized Controlled Trials Good For? *Philosophical Studies* 147 (1):59–70.

Cartwright, Nancy, Andrew Goldfinch, and Jeremy Howick. 2009. Evidence-Based Policy: Where Is Our Theory of Evidence? *Journal of Children's Services* 4 (4):6–14.

Cartwright, Nancy and Eleanora Montuschi (eds.). 2016. *Philosophy of Social Science: A New Introduction*. Oxford: Oxford University Press.

Charness, Gary, and Matthew Rabin. 2002. Understanding Social Preferences with Simple Tests. *The Quarterly Journal of Economics* 117 (3):817–869.

Clark, Kenneth, and Martin Sefton. 2001. The Sequential Prisoner's Dilemma: Evidence on Reciprocation. *The Economic Journal* 111 (468):51–68.

Clark, William A.V. 1986. Residential Segregation in American Cities: A Review and Interpretation. *Population Research and Policy Review* 5:95–127

Clarke, Kevin A., and David M. Primo. 2012. *A Model Discipline: Political Science and the Logic of Representations*. Cambridge: Oxford University Press.

Clifford, James. 1983. On Ethnographic Authority. *Representations* 1 (2):118–146.

Clifford, James, and George Marcus (eds.). 1986. *Writing Culture: The Poetics and Politics of Ethnography*. Berkeley: University of California Press.

Coalition for Evidence-Based Policy. 2003. *Identifying and Implementing Educational Practices Supported By Rigorous Evidence: A User Friendly Guide*. Washington DC: National Center for Education Evaluation and Regional Assistance.

Coleman, James S. 1990. *Foundations of Social Theory*. Cambridge, MA: Harvard University Press.

Coleman, James S. et al. 1966. *Equality of Educational Opportunity*, edited by E. Department of Health, and Welfare. Washington, DC: US Government Printing Office.

Collingwood, R. G. 1946. *The Idea of History*. Oxford: Oxford University Press.

Cosmides, Leda. 1989. The Logic of Social Exchange: Has Natural Selection Shaped How Humans Reason? Studies with the Wason Selection Task. *Cognition* 31 (3):187–276.

Cox, Gary W. 1999. The Empirical Content of Rational Choice Theory: A Reply to Green and Shapiro. *Journal of Theoretical Politics* 11 (2):147–169.

Crasnow, Sharon. 2006. Feminist Contributions to Anthropology and Sociology. In *Philosophy of Anthropology and Sociology*, edited by S. Turner and M. Risjord. Amsterdam: Elsevier.

Crasnow, Sharon. 2011. Evidence for Use: Causal Pluralism and the Role of Case Studies in Political Science Research. *Philosophy of the Social Sciences* 41 (1):26–49.

Crasnow, Sharon. 2012. The Role of Case Study Research in Political Science: Evidence for Causal Chains. *Philosophy of Science* 79 (5):655–666.

Critto, Adolfo. 1999. *Choosing Models of Society and Social Norms: Improving Choices and Quality of Life*. Lanham, MD: University Press of America.

Cronbach, Lee J., and Paul E Meehl. 1955. Construct Validity in Psychological Tests. *Psychological Bulletin* 52 (4):281–302.

Cubitt, Robin P., and Robert Sugden. 2003. Common Knowledge, Slaience, and Convention: A Reconstruction of Lewis' Game Theory. *Economics and Philosophy* 19 (2):175–210.

Davidson, Donald. 1963. Actions, Reasons and Causes. *Journal of Philosophy* 60:685–700.

Davidson, Donald. 1980. *Essays on Action and Events*. Oxford: Clarendon Press.

Davidson, Donald. 1984. *Inquiries in to Truth and Interpretation*. Oxford: Clarendon Press.

Davies, James C. 1962. Toward a Theory of Revolution. *American Sociological Review* 27 (1):5–19.

Demeulenaere, Pierre (ed.). 2011. *Analytic Sociology and Social Mechanisms*. Cambridge: Cambridge University Press.

Demeulenaere, Pierre. 2011. Causal Regularities, Action, and Explanation. In *Analytical Sociology and Social Mechanisms*, edited by P. Demeulenaere. Cambridge: Cambridge University Press.

Dennett, Daniel. 1971. Intentional Systems. *Journal of Philosophy* 68 (4):87–106.

DiMarco, Marina, and Kareem Khalifa. 2019. Inquiry Tickets: Values, Pursuit, and Underdetermination. *Philosophy of Science* 86 (5):1016–1028.

Douglas, Heather E. 2000. Inductive Risk and Values in Science. *Philosophy of Science* 67 (4):559–579.

Douglas, Heather E. 2009. *Science, Policy, and the Value-Free Ideal*. Pittsburgh: University of Pittsburgh Press.

Dray, William H. 1957. *Laws and Explanation in History*. Oxford: Oxford University Press.

Dray, William H. 1963. The Historical Explanation of Actions Reconsidered. In *Philosophy and History: A Symposium*, edited by S. Hook. New York: New York University Press.

Dray, William H. 1995. *History as Re-Enactment*. Oxford: Oxford University Press.

Du Bois, W. E. B. 1996. *The Philadelphia Negro*. Philadelphia, PA: University of Pennsylvania Press. Orignal edition, 1899.

Dupré, John. 2004. Human Kinds and Biological Kinds: Some Similarities and Differences. *Philosophy of Science* 71 (5):892–900.

Durkheim, Emile. 1938. *The Rules of the Sociological Method*. Translated by S. Solovay and J. Mueller. New York: Free Press. Original edition, 1895.

Elder-Vass, Dave. 2010. *The Causal Power of Social Structures: Emergence, Structure and Agency*. Cambridge: Cambridge University Press.

Eley, Thalia C., Paul Lichtenstein, and Terrie E. Moffitt. 2003. A Longitudinal Behavioral Genetic Analysis of the Etiology of Aggressive and Nonaggressive Antisocial Behavior. *Development and Psychopathology* 15:383–402.

Elliott, Kevin C. and Ted Richards (eds.). 2017. *Exploring Inductive Risk*. Oxford: Oxford Univeristy Press.

Elster, Jon. 1998. A Plea for Mechanisms. In *Social Mechanisms: An Analytical Approach to Social Theory*, edited by P. Hedstrom and R. Swedberg. Cambridge: Cambridge University Press.

Elster, Jon. 2007. *Explaining Social Behavior: More Nuts and Bolts for the Social Sciences*. Cambridge: Cambridge University Press.

Epstein, Brian. 2008. When Local Models Fail. *Philosophy of the Social Sciences* 38 (1):3–24.

Epstein, Brian. 2009. Ontological Individualism Reconsidered. *Synthese* 166 (1):187–213.

Epstein, Brian. 2015. *The Ant Trap: Rebuilding the Foundation of the Social Sciences*. Oxford: Oxford University Press.

Evans-Pritchard, E. E. 1937. *Witchcraft, Oracles and Magic Among the Azande*. Oxford: Clarendon Press.

Farley, Reynolds, Howard Schuman, Suzanne Bianchi, Diane Colasanto, and Shirley Hatchett. 1978. 'Chocolate City, Vanilla Suburbs:' Will the Trend Toward Racially Separate Communities Continue? *Social Science Research* 7 (4):319–344.

Fay, Brian. 1983. General Laws and Explaining Human Behavior. In *Changing Social Science: Critical Theory and Other Critical Perspectives*, edited by D. R. J. Sabia and J. Wallulis. Albany: State University of New York Press.

Feleppa, Robert. 1988. *Convention, Translation, and Understanding*. Albany, NY: State University of New York Press.

Feleppa, Robert. Forthcoming. Rationality Assumptions and Their Limits. *Philosophy of the Social Sciences* 51 (6).

Ferguson, Christopher J., and John Kilburn. 2009. The Public Health Risks of Media Violence: A Meta-Analytic Review. *The Journal of Pediatrics* 154 (5):759–763.

Fessler, Daniel M., and Edouard Machery. 2012. Culture and Cognition. In *The Oxford Handbook of Philosophy of Cognitive Science*, edited by E. Margolis, R. Samuels and S. P. Stich. Oxford: Oxford University Press.

Finel, Bernard I., and Kristin M. Lord. 1999. The Surprising Logic of Transparency. *International Studies Quarterly* 43 (2):315–339.

Flyvbjerg, Bent. 2001. *Making Social Science Matter: Why Inquiry Fails and How It Can Succeed Again*. Cambridge: Cambridge University Press.

Flyvbjerg, Bent. 2006. Five Misunderstandings about Case-Study Research. *Qualitative Inquiry* 12 (2):219–245.

Føllesdal, Dagfinn. 1973. Indeterminacy of Translation and Underdetermination of the Theory of Nature. *Dialectica* 27:289–301.

Fossett, Mark. 2006. Ethnic Preferences, Social Distance Dynamics, and Residential Segregation: Theoretical Explorations Using Simulation Analysis. *The Journal of Mathematical Sociology* 30 (3–4):185–273.

Freedman, David A., and Kenneth W. Wachter. 2007. Methods for Census 2000 and Statistical Adjustments. In *The SAGE Handbook of Social Science Methodology*, edited by W. Outhwaite and S. Turner. Thousand Oaks, CA: SAGE Publications.

Fricker, Miranda. 2007. *Epistemic Injustice: Power and the Ethics of Knowing*. Oxford: Oxford University Press.

Frigg, Roman and James Nguyen. 2020. *Modeling Nature: An Opinionated Introduction to Scientific Representation*. Dordrecht: Springer.

Fumagalli, Roberto. 2016. Why We Cannot Learn from Minimal Models. *Erkenntnis* 81 (3):433–455

Gallagher, Shaun. 2020. *Action and Interaction*. Oxford: Oxford University Press.

Galster, George. 1988. Residential Segregation in American cities: A Contrary Review, *Population Research and Policy Review* 7:93–112.

Gau, Jacinta M., and Travis C. Pratt. 2010. Revisiting Broken Windows Theory: Examining the Sources of the Discriminant Validity of Perceived Disorder and Crime. *Jounal of Criminal Justice* 38 (4):748–766.

Geertz, Clifford. 1973a. *The Interpretation of Cultures*. New York: Basic Books.

Geertz, Clifford. 1973b. Thick Description: Toward an Interpretive Theory of Culture. In *The Interpretation of Cultures*. New York: Basic Books.

George, Alexander L., and Andrew Bennett. 2005. *Case Studies and Theory Development in the Social Sciences*. Cambridge, MA: MIT Press.

Giddens, Anthony. 1979. *Central Problems in Social Theory: Action, Structure, and Contradiction in Social Analysis*. Cambridge: Cambridge University Press.

Giddens, Anthony. 1984. *Constitution of Society: Outline of the Theory of Structuration*. Cambridge: Polity Press.

Gigerenzer, Gerd. 1991. How to Make Cognitive Illusions Dissapear: Beyond 'Heuristics and Biases.' *European Review of Social Psychology* 2 (1):83–115.

Gigerenzer, Gerd. 2008. *Rationality for Mortals: How People Cope with Uncertainty*. Oxford: Oxford University Press.

Gilbert, Margaret. 1989. *On Social Facts*. Princeton: Princeton University Press.

Gilbert, Margaret. 1996. *Living Together: Rationality, Sociality, and Obligation*. Lanham, MD: Rowman and Littlefield.

Gilbert, Margaret. 1997. Concerning Sociality: The Plural Subject as Paradigm. In *The Mark of the Social: Discovery of Invention?*, edited by J. D. Greenwood. Lanham, MD: Rowman & Littlefield Publishers.

Gilbert, Margaret. 2008. Social Convention Revisited. *Topoi* 27 (1–2):5–16.

Gilbert, Margaret. 2009. Shared Intention and Personal Intentions. *Philosophical Studies* 144 (1):167–187.

Gilbert, Margaret. 2014. *Joint Commitment: How We Make the Social World*. Oxford: Oxford University Press.

Gintis, Herbert. 2009. *The Bounds of Reason: Game Theory and the Unification of the Behavioral Sciences*. Princeton: Princeton University Press.

Gintis, Herbert. 2010. Social Norms as Choreography. *Politics, Philosophy and Economics* 9 (3):251–264.

Goering, John. 2006. Shelling Redux: How Sociology Fails to Make Progress in Building and Empirically Testing Complex Causal Models Regarding Race 1 and Residence. *The Journal of Mathematical Sociology* 30 (3–4):299–317.

Gold, Natalie, and Robert Sugden. 2007. Collective Intentions and Team Agency. *Journal of Philosophy* 104 (3):109–137.

Goldman, Alvin. 1970. *A Theory of Human Action*. Englewood Cliffs: Prentice-Hall.

Goldman, Alvin. 1989. Interpretation Psychologized. *Mind and Language* 4 (3):161–185.

Goldstone, Jack A. 1994. Is Revolution Individually Rational?: Groups and Individuals in Revolutionary Collective Action. *Rationality and Society* 6 (1):139–166.

Gouldner, Alvin W. 1968. The Sociologist as Partisan: Sociology and the Welfare State. *The American Sociologist* 3 (2):103–116.

Green, Donald, and Ian Shapiro. 1995. *Pathologies of Rational Choice Theory*. New Haven, CT: Yale University Press.

Greve, Jens. 2010. Emergence in Sociology: A Critique of Nonreductive Individualism. *Philosophy of the Social Sciences* 42 (2):188–223.

Groff, Ruth. 2011. Getting Past Hume in the Philosophy of Social Science. In *Causality in the Sciences*, edited by P. M. Illari, F. Russo and J. Williamson. Oxford: Oxford University Press.

Grüne-Yanoff, Till. 2013. Appraising Models Nonrepresentationally. *Philosophy of Science* 80 (5):850–861.

Grüne-Yanoff, Till, and Philippe Verreault-Julien. 2021. How-Possibly Explanations in Economics: Anything Goes? *Journal of Economic Methodology* 28 (1):114–123.

Guala, Francesco, and Hindriks, Frank. 2015. A Unified Social Ontology. *The Philosophical Quarterly* 65 (259):177–201.

Guala, Francesco. 2001. Building Economc Machines: The FCC Auctions. *Studies in History and Philosophy of Science* 32 (3):453–477.

Guala, Francesco. 2005. *The Methodology of Experimental Economics*. Cambridge: Cambridge University Press.

Guala, Francesco. 2006. Has Game Theory Been Refuted? *The Journal of Philosophy* 103 (5):239–263.

Guala, Francesco. 2006. Paradigmatic Experiments: The Ultimatum Game from Testing to Measurement Device. *Philosophy of Science* 75 (5):658–669.

Guala, Francesco. 2013. The Normativity of Lewis Conventions. *Synthese* 190 (9):3107–3122.

Guala, Francesco. 2016. *Understanding Institutions: The Philosophy and Science of Living Together*. Princeton: Princeton University Press.

Guala, Francesco, and Luigi Mittone. 2010. How History and Convention Create Norms: An Experimental Study. *Journal of Economic Psychology* 31:749–756.

Hacking, Ian. 1983. *Representing and Intervening*. Cambridge: Cambridge University Press.

Hacking, Ian. 1995. The Looping Effects of Human Kinds. In *Causal Cognition: A Multi-Disciplinary Debate*, edited by D. Sperber, D. Premack and A. J. Premack. New York: Oxford University Press.

Hacking, Ian. 1999. *The Social Construction of What?* Cambridge, MA: Harvard University Press.

Hage, Jerald. 1972. *Techniques and Problems of Theory Construction in Sociology*. New York: Wiley Interscience.

Hage, Jerald. 2007. The Intersection of Philosophy and Theory Construction: The Problem of the Origin of Elements in a Theory. In *Philosophy of Anthropology and Sociology*, edited by S. Turner and M. Risjord. Dordrecht: Elsevier.

Hakli, Raul, Kaarlo Miller, and Raimo Tuomela. 2010. Two Kinds of We-Reasoning. *Economics and Philosophy* 26 (3):291–320.

Hammersley, Martyn. 1992. *What's Wrong with Ethnography?* London: Routledge.

Hannaford, Ivan. 1996. *Race: The History of an Idea in the West*. Baltimore: Johns Hopkins University Press.

Harcourt, Bernard E. 1998. Reflecting on the Subject: A Critique of the Social Influence Conception of Deterrence, the Broken Windows Theory, and Order-Maintenance Policing New York Style. *Michigan Law Review* 97 (2):291–389.

Harding, Sandra. 1987a. The Method Question. *Hypatia* 2 (3):19–35.

Harding, Sandra (ed.). 1987b. *Feminism and Methodology: Social Science Issues*. Bloomington: Indiana University Press.

Harding, Sandra. 1993. Rethinking Standpoint Epistemology: What Is 'Strong Objectivity'? In *Feminist Epistemologies*, edited by L. Alcoff and E. Potter. London: Routledge.

Hausman, Daniel. 1992. *The Inexact and Separate Science of Economics*. Cambridge: Cambridge University Press.

Haywood, O. G. Jr. 1954. Military Decision and Game Theory. *Journal of the Operations Research Society of America* 2 (4):365–385.

Hechter, Michael, and Satoshi Kanazawa. 1997. Sociological Rational Choice Theory. *Annual Review of Sociology* 23:191–214.

Hedstrom, Peter. 2005. *Dissecting the Social*. Cambridge: Cambridge University Press.

Hedstrom, Peter, and Petri Ylikoski. 2010. Causal Mechanisms in the Social Sciences. *Annual Review of Sociology* 36 (49–67).

Hedstrom, Peter, and Richard Swedberg (eds.). 1998. *Social Mechanisms*. Cambridge: Cambridge University Press.

Heidl, Stefan. 2016. *Philosophical Problems of Behavioural Economics*. London: Routledge.

Helleiner, Eric. 2003. *The Making of National Money: Territorial Currencies in Historical Perspective*. Ithaca: Cornell University Press.

Hempel, Carl. 1942. The Function of General Laws in History. *Journal of Philosophy* 39:35–48.

Hempel, Carl. 1963. Reasons and Covering Laws in Historical Explanation. In *Philosophy and History: A Symposium*, edited by S. Hook. New York: New York University Press.

Hempel, Carl. 1966. *Philosophy of Natural Science*. Englewood Cliffs, NJ: Prentice Hall.

Hempel, Carl. 1983. Valuation and Objectivity in Science. In *Physics, Philosophy, and Psychoanalysis*, edited by R. Cohen and L. Lauden. Dordrecht: Ridel.

Henderson, David K. 1993. *Interpretation and Explanation in the Human Sciences*. Albany, NY: State University of New York Press.

Henderson, David. 1987. The Principle of Charity and the Problem of Irrationality. *Synthese* 73:225–252.

Henderson, David. 1991. On the Testability of Psychological Generalizations. *Philosophy of Science* 58:586–606.

Henderson, David. 2002. Norms, Normative Principles, and Explanation: On Not Getting Is from Ought. *Philosophy of the Social Sciences* 32 (3):329–364.

Henrich, Joseph, and Robert Boyd. 2001. Why People Punish Defectors: Weak Conformist Transmission can Stabilize Costly Enforcement of Norms in Cooperative Dilemmas. *Journal of Theoretical Biology* 2008 (1):79–89.

Henrich, Joseph et al. 2005. 'Economic Man' in Cross-Cultural Perspective: Behavioral Experiments in 15 Small-Scale Societies. *Behavioral and Brain Sciences* 28:795–855.

Hill, A. B. 1965. The Environment and Disease: Association or Causation? *Proceedings of the Royal Society of Medicine* 58:295–300.

Hogarth, Robin M. 2005. The Challenge of Representative Design in Psychology and Economics. *Journal of Economic Methodology* 12 (2):253–263.

Holland, Paul W. 2008. Causation and Race. In *White Logic, White Methods: Racism and Methodology*, edited by T. Zuberi and E. Bonilla-Silvapp. Lanham, MD: Rowman & Littlefield Publishers.

Hollis, Martin, and Steven Lukes (eds.). 1982. *Rationality and Relativism*. Cambridge, MA: MIT Press.

Hollis, Martin. 1967. Reason and Ritual. *Philosophy* 43:231–247.

Horkheimer, Max. 2002. *Critical Theory: Selected Essays*, translated by M. O'Connell. New York: Continuum Press. Original edition, 1968.

Hough, Richard. 1959. *Admirals in Collision*. London: Hamish Hamilton.

Hume, David. 1955. *An Inquiry Concerning Human Understanding*. New York: Bobbs-Merrill. Original edition, 1777.

Hume, David. 1978. *A Treatise of Human Nature*, edited by L. A. Selby-Bigge and P. H. Nidditch, 2nd edition. Oxford: Oxford University Press. Original edition, 1740.

Huxley, Julian, and A. C. Haddon. 1936. *We Europeans: A Survey of 'Racial' Problems*. New York: Harper & Brothers.

Iris Young. 1988. Five Faces of Oppression. *The Philosophical Forum* 19 (4):270–290.

Jankovic, Marija, and Kirk Ludwig (eds.). 2017. *The Routledge Handbook of Collective Intentionality*. London: Routledge.

Jarvie, Ian Charles, and Jesus Zamora-Bonilla (eds.). 2011. *The SAGE Handbook of the Philosophy of Social Sciences*. Los Angeles: SAGE Publications.

Jarvie, Ian Charles. 1972. *Concepts and Society*. London: Routledge and Kegan Paul.

John, Stephen. 2021. *Objecitvity in Science*. Cambridge: Cambridge University Press.

Johnson, Charles. 1943. *Patterns of Negro Segregation*. New York: Harper & Brothers.

Johnson, James. 2021. Models-as-Fables: An Alternative to the Standard Rationale for Using Formal Models in Political Science. *Perspectives on Politics* 19 (3):874–889.

Kahneman, Daniel. 2002. *Maps of Bounded Rationalty*. Nobel Media. Available from www.nobelprize.org/nobel_prizes/economic-sciences/laureates/2002/kahneman-lecture.html.

Kaldis, Byron (ed.). 2013. *The Encyclopedia of Philosophy and the Social Sciences*. Los Angeles: SAGE Publications.

Kant, Immanuel. 1903. *Perpetual Peace: A Philosophical Essay*, translated by M. C. Smith. London: George Allen & Unwin LTD. Original edition, 1795.

Karp, Ivan, and Martha B. Kendall. 1982. Reflexivity in Field Work. In *Explaining Social Behavior: Consciousness, Human Action, and Social Structure*, edited by P. F. Secord. Beverly Hills, California: Sage.

Kastenbaum, David. 1998. Census 2000: Where Science and Politics Count Equally. *Science: New Series* 279 (5352):798–799.

Kemp, Stephen, and John Holmwood. 2003. Realism, Regularity and Social Explanation. *Journal for the Theory of Social Behaviour* 33 (2):165–187.

Khalifa, Kareem. 2019. Is Verstehen Scientific Understanding? *Philosophy of the Social Sciences* 49 (4):282–306.

Khalifa, Kareem, and Richard Lauer. 2021. Do the Social Sciences Vindicate Race's Reality? *Philosophers Impriint* 21 (21).

Kidd, Ian James, José Medina, and Gaile Pohlhaus. 2017. *Routledge Handbook of Epistemic Injustice*. London: Routledge.

Kincaid, Harold. 1986. Reduction, Explanation, and Individualism. *Philosophy of Science* 53 (4):492–513.

Kincaid, Harold. 1996. *Philosophical Foundations of the Social Sciences: Analyzing Controversies in Social Research*. Cambridge: Cambridge University Press.

Kincaid, Harold. 2007. Functional Explanation and Evolutionary Social Science. In *Philosophy of Sociology and Anthropology*, edited by S. Turner and M. Risjord. Dordrecht: Elsevier.

Kincaid, Harold (ed.). 2012. *The Oxford Handbook of Philosophy of Social Science*. Oxford: Oxford University Press.

Kincaid, Harold. 2015. Open Empirical and Methodological Issues in the Individualism-Holism Debate. *Philosophy of Science* 82 (5):1127–1138.

Kincaid, Harold. 2018. Debating the Reality of Race, Caste, and Ethnicity. *Philosophy of the Social Sciences* 48 (2):139–167.

Koepsell, David, and Laurence S. Moss (eds.). 2003. *John Searle's Ideas about Social Reality: Extensions, Criticisms, and Reconstructions*. Oxford: Blackwell Publishing.

Kögler, Hand Kerbert, and Karsten Stueber (eds.). 2000. *Empathy and Agency: The Problem of Understanding in the Human Sciences*. Boulder Colorado: Westview Press.

Kratz, Corrine A. 2010. In and Out of Focus. *American Ethnologist* 37 (4):805–826.

Kripke, Saul A. 1982. *Wittgenstein on Rules and Private Langauge*. Cambridge, MA: Harvard University Press.

Kuhn, Thomas. 1977. Objectivity, Value Judgment, and Theory Choice. In *The Essential Tension*. Chicago: University of Chicago Press.

Kuorikoski, Jaakko, and Aki Lehtinen. 2009. Economics Imperialism and Solution Concepts in Political Science. *Philosophy of the Social Sciences* 40 (3):347–374.

Kuorikoski, Jaakko, and Samuli Poyhonen. 2012. Looping Kinds and Social Mechanisms. *Sociological Theory* 30 (3):187–205.

Lacey, Hugh. 1999. *Is Science Value Free?* London: Routledge.

Lawson, Thomas E., and Robert N. McCauley. 1990. *Rethinking Religion*. Cambridge: Cambridge University Press.

Lehtinen, Aki, and Jaakko Kuorikoski. 2007. Unrealistic Assumptions in Rational Choice Theory. *Philosophy of the Social Sciences* 37 (2):115–138.

Lewis, D. 1969. *Convention*. Cambridge, MA: Harvard University Press.

Lewis, Paul. 2000. Realism, Causality, and the Problem of Social Structure. *Journal for the Theory of Social Behavior* 30 (3):249–268.

Linne, C. V. 1964. *Systema Naturae*. New York: Stechert-Hafner Service Agency. Original edition, 1758.

List, Christian, and Philip Pettit. 2011. *Group Agency: The Possibility, Design, and Status of Corporate Agents*. Oxford: Oxford University Press.

List, Christian, and Kai Spiekermann. 2013. Methodological Individualism and Holism in Political Science: A Reconciliation. *American Political Science Review* 107 (4):629–643.

Little, Daniel. 1991. *Varieties of Social Explanation*. Boulder: Westview Press.

Little, Daniel. 1998. *Microfoundations, Method, and Causation: On the Philosophy of the Social Sciences*. London: Transaction Publishers.

Little, Daniel. 2007. Levels of the Social. In *Philosophy of Anthropology and Sociology*, edited by S. P. Turner and M. W. Risjord. Amsterdam: Elsevier.

Little, Daniel. 2009. The Heterogenous Social: New Thinking about the Foundations of the Social Sciences. In *Philosophy of the Social Sciences: Philosophical Theory and Scientific Practice*, edited by C. Mantzvainos. Cambridge: Cambridge University Press.

Longino, Helen. 1990. *Science as Social Knowledge: Values and Objectivity in Scientific Inquiry*. Princeton: Princeton University Press.

Longino, Helen E. 2013. *Studying Human Behavior: How Scientists Investigate Aggression and Sexuality*. Chicago: University of Chicago Press.

Lukes, Steven. 1968. Methodological Individualism Reconsidered. *British Journal of Sociology* 19:119–129.

Machamer, Peter, Lindley Darden, and Carl F. Craver. 2000. Thinking about Mechanisms. *Philosophy of Science* 67 (1):1–25.

MacIntyre, Alasdair. 1981. *After Virtue*. Notre Dame: University of Notre Dame Press.

Mackenzie, Donald A., Fabian Muniesa, and Lucia Siu (eds.). 2007. *Do Economists Make Markets? On The Performativity of Economics*. Princeton: Princeton University Press.

Mäkelä, Pekka, Raul Hakli, and S. M. Amadae. 2018. Understanding Institutions without Collective Acceptance? *Philosophy of the Social Sciences* 48:608–629.

Mäki, Uskali. 2005. Models Are Experiments, Experiments Are Models. *Journal of Economic Methodology* 12 (2):303–315.

Mäki, Uskali. 2009. MISSing the World: Models as Isolations and Credible Surrogate Systems. *Erkenntnis* 70 (1):29–43.

Makkreel, Rudolph. 1975. *Dilthey: Philosopher of the Human Studies*. Princeton: Princeton University Press.

Malinowski, Bronislaw. 1922. *Argonauts of the Western Pacific*. New York: E. P. Dutton & Co.

Mallon, Ron. 2016. *The Construction of Human Kinds*. Oxford: Oxford University Press.

Mallon, Ron. 2018. Constructing Race: Racialization, Causal Effects, or Both? *Philosophical Studies* 175 (5):1039–1056.

Mallon, Ron, and Daniel Kelly. 2012. Making Race out of Nothing: Psychologically Constrained Social Roles. In *The Oxford Handbook of the Philosophy of Social Science*, edited by H. Kincaid. Oxford: Oxford University Press.

Mandelbaum, Maurice. 1955. Societal Facts. *British Journal of Sociology* 6:305–317.

Marchionni, Caterina, and Petri Ylikoski. 2013. Generative Explanation and Individualism in Agent-Based Simulation. *Philosophy of the Social Sciences* 43 (3):323–340.

Marmor, Andrei. 1996. On Convention. *Synthese* 107:349–371.

Marmor, Andrei. 2009. *Social Conventions: From Language to Law*. Princeton: Princeton University Press.

Martin, Michael. 2000. *Verstehen: The Uses of Understanding in Social Science*. New Brunswick: Transaction Publishers.

Massey, Douglas, and Nancy A. Denton. 1993. *American Apartheid: Segregation and the Making of the Underclass*. Cambridge, MA: Harvard University Press.

Mauss, Marcel. 2000. *The Gift: The Form and Reason for Exchange in Archaic Societies*, translated by W. D. Halls: W. W. Norton and Company. Original edition, 1925.

Mayntz, Renate. 2003. Mechanisms in Teh Analysis of Social Macro-Phenomena. *Philosophy of the Social Sciences* 34 (2):237–259.

Mayo, Deborah. 2008. Some Methodological Issues in Experimental Economics. *Philosophy of Science* 75 (5):633–645.

McIntyre, Lee. 1993. Complexity and Social Scientific Laws. *Synthese* 97:209–227.

McIntyre, Lee. 1996. *Laws and Explanation in the Social Sciences: Defending a Science of Human Behavior*. Boulder CO: Westview Press.

Mercier, Hugo, and Dan Sperber. 2017. *The Enigma of Reason*. Cambridge: Harvard University Press.

Merton, Robert K. 1957. *Social Theory and Social Structure*, revised edition. Glencoe, IL: Free Press.

Michell, Joel. 2007. Measurement. In *Philosophy of Anthropology and Sociology*, edited by S. Turner and M. Risjord. Dordrecht: Elsevier.

Mill, John Stuart. 1987. *On the Logic of the Moral Sciences*. Peru, Illinois: Open Court. Original edition, 1872.

Miller, Seumas. 2002. Against Collective Agency. In *Social Facts and Collective Intentionality*, edited by G. Meggie. Ontos: Verlag.

Mirowski, Philip, and Edward Nik-Khah. 2007. Markets Made Flesh: Performativity, and a Problem in Science Studies, Augmented with Consideration of the FCC Auctions. In *Do Economists Make Markets?: On the Performativity of Economics*, edited by D. A. Mackenzie, F. Muniesa and L. Siu. Princeton: Princeton University Press.

Monson, Ingrid. 1996. *Saying Something: Jazz Improvisation and Interaction*. Chicago: University of Chicago Press.

Moore, George Edward. 1993. *Principia Ethica*, edited by T. Baldwin. Cambridge: Cambridge University Press. Original edition, 1903.

Morgan, Mary S. 2005. Experiments Versus Models: New Phenomena, Inference, and Surprise. *Journal of Economic Methodology* 12 (2):317–329.

Morgan, Mary S. 2012. *The World in the Model: How Economists Work and Think*. Cambridge: Cambridge University Press.

Morgan, Mary S. and Morrison, Margaret. 1999. *Models as Mediators: Perspectives on Natural and Social Science*. Cambridge: Cambridge University Press.

Nagel, Ernest. 1961. *The Structure of Science*. New York: Harcort, Brace & World.

Nichols, Shaun. 2010. Emotions, Norms, and the Genealogy of Fairness. *Politics, Philosophy and Economics* 9 (3):275–296.

Nik-Khah, Edward. 2006. What the FCC Auctions Can Tell Us about the Performativity Thesis. *Economic Sociology-European Electronic Newsletter* (2):15–21.

Outhwaite, William. 2007. Phenomenological and Hermeneutic Aproaches. In *Philosophy of Anthropology and Sociology*, edited by S. Turner and M. Risjord. Amsterdam: Elsevier.

Outhwaite, William, and Stephen P. Turner (eds.). 2007. *The SAGE Handbook of Social Science Methodology*. Los Angeles: SAGE Publications.

Palecek, Martin. 2020. The Evolution of 'Culture': Juggling a Concept. *Anthropological Theory* 20 (1):53–76.

Paternotte, Cedric. 2011. Rational Choice Theory. In *The SAGE Handbook of the Philosophy of the Social Sciences*, edited by I. C. Jarvie and J. Zamora-Bonilla. Los Angeles, CA: SAGE Publications.

Patton, Michael Quinn. 2002. *Qualitative Research and Evaluation Methods*, 3rd edition. Thousand Oaks, California: Sage Publications.

Pearl, Judea. 2000. *Causality: Models, Reasoning, and Inference*. Cambridge: Cambridge University Press.

Pettit, Philip. 1993. *The Common Mind: An Essay on Psychology, Society, and Politics*. Oxford: Oxford University Press.

Pettit, Philip. 1996. Functional Explanation and Virtual Selection. *British Journal for the Philosophy of Science* 47 (2):291–302.

Pettit, Philip. 1998. Defining and Defending Social Holism. *Philosophical Explorations: An International Journal for the Philosophy of Mind and Action* 1 (3):169–184.

Pettit, Philip. 2009. The Reality of Group Agents. In *Philosophy of the Social Sciences: Philosophical Theory and Scientific Practice*, edited by C. Mantzvainos. Cambridge: Cambridge University Press.

Pettit, Philip, and David P. Schweikard. 2006. Joint Actions and Group Agents. *Philosophy of the Social Sciences* 36 (1):18–39.

Pizzorno, Allesandro. 2007. Rational Choice and Collective Action. In *Philosophy of Sociology and Anthropology*, edited by S. Turner and M. Risjord. Dordrecht: Elsevier.

Polonioli, Andrea. 2014. Blame It on the Norm: The Challenge from 'Adaptive Rationality.' *Philosophy of the Social Sciences* 44 (2):131–150.

Popper, Karl. 1957. *The Poverty of Historicism*. London: Routledge and Kegan Paul.

Popper, Karl. 1965. Prediction and Prophecy in the Social Sciences. In *Conjectures and Refutations: The Growth of Scientific Knowledge*. New York: Harper Torchbooks.

Porter, Theodore. 2006. Speaking Precision to Power: The Modern Political Role of Social Science. *Social Research* 73 (4):1273–1294.

Pozzoni, Gianluca, and Tuukka Kaidesoja. 2021. Context in Mechanism-Based Explanation. In *Philosophy of the Social Sciences*. Published onlind. DOI:10.1177/0048393121991657.

Rasler, Karen, and William R. Thompson. 2004. The Democratic Peace and a Sequential, Reciprocal, Causal Arrow Hypothesis. *Comparative Political Studies* 37 (8):879–908.

Rasmusen, Eric. 2007. *Games and Information: An Introduction to Game Theory*. Oxford: Blackwell Publishing.

Reiss, Julian. 2007. Do We Need Mechanisms in the Social Sciences? *Philosophy of the Social Sciences* 37 (2):163–184.

Reiss, Julian. 2008. Social Capacities. In *Nancy Cartwright's Philosophy of Science*, edited by S. Hartmann, C. Hoefer and L. Bovens. London: Routledge.

Reiss, Julian. 2012a. The Explanation Paradox. *Journal of Economic Methodology* 19 (1):43–62.

Reiss, Julian. 2012b. Idealization and the Aims of Economics: Three Cheers for Instrumentalism. *Economics & Philosophy* 28 (3):363–383.

Reiss, Julian. 2013a. The Explanation Paradox Redux. *Journal of Economic Methodology* 20 (3):280–292.

Reiss, Julian. 2013b. *Philosophy of Economics: A Contemporary Introduction*. London: Routledge.

Reiss, Julian. 2019. Against External Validity. *Synthese* 196 (8):3103–3121.

Richerson, Peter, and Robert Boyd. 2005. *Not by Genes Alone: How Culture Transformed Human Evolution*. Chicago: University of Chicago Press.

Ringer, Fritz. 1997. *Max Weber's Methodology: The Unification of the Cultural and Social Sciences*. Cambridge: Harvard University Press.

Risjord, Mark. 2000. *Woodcutters and Witchcraft: Rationality and Interpretive Change in the Social Sciences*. Albany, NY: SUNY Press.

Risjord, Mark. 2004. The Limits of Cognitive Theory in Anthropology. *Philosophical Explorations* 7 (3):281–297.

Risjord, Mark. 2007. Scientific Change as Political Action: Franz Boaz and the Anthropology of Race. *Philosophy of the Social Sciences* 37 (1):24–45.

Risjord, Mark. 2012. Models of Culture. In *The Oxford Handbook of Philosophy of Science*, edited by H. Kincaid. Oxford: Oxford University Press.

Risjord, Mark. (ed.). 2016. *Normativity and Naturalism in the Philosophy of the Social Sciences*. London: Routledge.

Risjord, Mark. 2021. Rationality and Interpretive Methodology: Transformations in the Apparent Irrationality Debate. In *Stephen Turner and the Philosophy of the Social: Essays in Honor of His 70th Birthday*, edited by C. Adair-Toteff. Leiden: Brill.

Root, Michael. 1986. Davidson and Social Science. In *Truth and Interpretation*, edited by E. LePore. Oxford: Basil Blackwell.

Root, Michael. 1993. *Philosophy of Social Science*. Oxford: Basil Blackwell.

Root, Michael. 2000. How We Divide the World. *Philosophy of Science* 67 (Supplement):S68–S639.

Rosaldo, Renato. 1989. *Culture and Truth: The Remaking of Social Analysis*. Boston: Beacon Press.

Rosenberg, Alex. 2005. Lessons from Biology for Philosophy of the Human Sciences. *Philosophy of the Social Sciences* 35 (1):3–19.

Ross, Don. 2011. Game Theory. In *The Stanford Encyclopedia of Philosophy*, edited by E. N. Zalta. Winter 2012 edition. URL <http://plato.stanford.edu/archives/win2012/entries/game-theory/>.

Ross, Don. 2011. Naturalism: The Place of Society in Nature. In *The SAGE Handbook of the Philosophy of Social Sciences*, edited by I. C. Jarvie and J. Zamora-Bonilla. London: SAGE Publications.

Roth, Paul. 1987. *Meaning and Method in the Social Sciences*. Ithaca: Cornell University Press.

Roth, Paul. 1989. Ethnography without Tears. *Current Anthropology* 30 (5):555–569.

Roth, Paul. 2003. Mistakes. *Synthese* 136 (3):389–408.

Rouse, Joseph. 2002. *How Scientific Practices Matter*. Chicago: University of Chicago Press.

Rouse, Joseph. 2007a. Practice Theory. In *The Philosophy of Anthropology and Sociology*, edited by S. Turner and M. Risjord. Amsterdam: Elsevier.

Rouse, Joseph. 2007b. Social Practices and Normativity. *Philosophy of the Social Sciences* 37 (1):46–56.

Rousseu, David L., Christopher Gelpi, Dan Reiter, and Paul K. Huth. 1996. Assessing the Nature of the Democratic Peace, 1918–88. *The American Political Science Review* 90 (3):512–533.

Rubinstein, Ariel. 2006. Dilemmas of an Economic Theorist. *Econometrica* 74 (4):865–883.

Rudner, Richard S. 1953. The Scientist *Qua* Scientist Makes Value Judgments. *Philosophy of Science* 20 (1):1–6.

Rudner, Richard S. 1966. *Philosophy of Social Science*. Englewood Cliffs, NJ: Prentice-Hall.

Runhardt, Rosa. 2016. Causal Comparability, Causal Generalizations, and Epistemic Homogeneity. *Philosophy of the Social Sciences* 47 (3):183–208.

Ruzzene, Attilia. 2012. Drawing Lessons from Case Studies by Enhancing Comparability. *Philosophy of the Social Sciences* 42 (1):99–120.

Salzman, Philip Carl. 2002. On Reflexivity. *American Anthropologist* 104 (3):805–813.

Sanchez-Cuenca, Ignacio. 2008. A Preference for Selfish Preferences: The Problem of Motivationsin Rational Choice Political Science. *Philosophy of the Social Sciences* 38 (3):361–378.

Sangren, Steven. 1988. Rhetoric and the Authority of Ethnography: 'Postmodernism' and the Social Reproduction of Texts. *Current Anthropology* 29 (3):405–435.

Satz, Debra, and John Ferejohn. 1994. Rational Choice and Social Theory. *Journal of Philosophy* 91 (2):71–87.

Sawyer, Keith. 2002. Nonreductive Individualism: Part I—Supervenience and Wild Disjunction. *Philosophy of the Social Sciences* 32 (4):537–559.

Schatzki, Theodore, Karin Knorr Cetina, and Eike Von Savigny (eds.). 2001. *The Practice Turn in Contemporary Theory*. London: Routledge.

Scheines, Richard. 2005. Similarity of Causal Inference in Experimental and Non-Experimental Studies. *Philosophy of Science* 72 (5):927–940.

Schelling, Thomas C. 1960. *The Strategy of Conflict*. Cambridge: Harvard University Press.

Schelling, Thomas C. 1969. Models of Segregation. *American Economic Review* 59 (2):488–493.

Schmid, Hans Bernhard. 2003. Can Brains in Vats Think as a Team? *Philosophical Explorations: An International Journal for the Philosophy of Mind and Action* 6 (3):201–217.

Schroeder, S.Andrew. 2019. Which Values Should Be Built Into Economic Measures? *Economics & Philosophy* 35 (3):521–536.

Schutz, Alfred. 1953. Common-Sense and Scientific Interpretation of Human Action. *Philosophy and Phenomenological Research* 14 (1):1–38.

Schutz, Alfred. 1954. Concept and Theory Formation in the Social Sciences. *Journal of Philosophy* 51 (9):257–253.

Schweikard, David P. and Hans Bernhard Schmid. 2021. Collective Intentionality. In *The Stanford Encyclopedia of Philosophy*, edited by E. N. Zalta. URL <https://plato.stanford.edu/archives/fall2021/entries/collective-intentionality/>.

Scriven, Michael. 1956. A Possible Distinction between Traditional Scientific Disciplines and the Study of Human Behavior. *Minnesota Studies in the Philosophy of Science* 1:330–339, edited by H. Feigl and M. Scriven. Minneapolis: University of Minnesota Press.

Searle, John. 1964. How to Derive 'Ought' from 'Is'. *The Philosophical Review* 73 (1):43–58.

Searle, John. 1983. *Intentionality: An Essay in the Philosophy of Mind*. New York: Cambridge University Press.

Searle, John. 1990. Collective Intentions and Actions. In *Intentions in Communication*, edited by P. R. Cohen and J. L. Morgan. Cambridge: MIT Press.

Searle, John. 1995. *The Construction of Social Reality*. New York: Free Press.

Searle, John. 2010. *Making the Social World: The Structure of Human Civilization*. Oxford: Oxford University Press.

Selgin, George. 2008. *Good Money: Birmingham, Button Makers, The Royal Mint and the Beginnings of Modern Coinage 1775–1821*. Ann Arbor: The University of Michigan Press.

Sen, Amartya K. 1977. Rational Fools: A Critique of the Behavioral Foundations of Economic Theory. *Philosophy and Public Affairs* 6 (4):317–344.

Simmel, Georg. 1971. How Is Society Possible? In *On Individuality and Social Forms*, edited by D. N. Levine. Chicago: University of Chicago Press. Original edition, 1908.

Skyrms, Brian. 2000. Game Theory, Rationality, and Evolution of the Social Contract. *Journal of Consciousness Studies* 7 (1–2):269–284.

Skyrms, Brian, and Kevin J. S. Zollman. 2010. Evolutionary Considerations in the Framing of Social Norms. *Politics, Philosophy and Economics* 9 (3):265–273.

Smith, Adam. 1937. *An Inquiry into the Nature and Causes of the Wealth of Nations*. New York: Modern Library. Original edition, 1776.

Smith, Dorothy E. 1974. Women's Perspective as a Radical Critique of Sociology. *Sociological Inquiry* 44 (1):7–13.

Smith, Vernon L. 1994. Economics in the Laboratory. *Journal of Economic Perspectives* 8 (1):113–131.

Smith, Vernon L. 2002. Method in Experiment: Rhetoric and Reality. *Experimental Economics* 5 (2):91–110.

Spencer, Quayshawn. 2012. What 'Biological Racial Realism' Should Mean. *Philosophical Studies* 159 (2):181–204.

Spencer, Quayshawn. 2014. A Radical Solution to the Race Problem. *Philosophy of Science* 8 (5):1025–1038.

Spencer, Quayshawn. 2019. A More Radical Solution to the Race Problem. *Proceedings of the Aristotelian Society* 93 (1):25–48.

Sperber, Daniel. 1996. *Explaining Culture*. Oxford: Blackwell.

Sperber, Daniel. 2011. A Naturalistic Ontology for Mechanistic Explanations in the Social Sciences. In *Analytical Sociology and Social Mechanisms*, edited by P. Demeulenaere. Cambridge: Cambridge University Press.

Spirtes, Peter, Clark Glymour, and Richard Scheines. 2000. *Causation, Prediction, and Search*, 2nd edition. Cambridge MA: MIT Press.

Spitulnik, Debra. 1999. The Language of the City: Town Bemba as Urban Hybridity. *Journal of Linguistic Anthropology* 8 (1):30–59.

Steel, Daniel. 2004. Social Mechanisms and Causal Inference. *Philosophy of the Social Sciences* 34 (1):55–78.

Steel, Daniel. 2005. Mechanisms and Functional Hypotheses in Social Science. *Philosophy of Science* 72 (5):941–952.

Steel, Daniel. 2006. Methodological Individualism, Explanation, and Invariance. *Philosophy of the Social Sciences* 36 (4):440–463.

Steel, Daniel 2008. *Across the Boundaries: Extrapolation in Biology and Social Science*. Oxford: Oxford University Press.

Steel, Daniel. 2011. Causality, Causal Models, and Social Mechanisms. In *The SAGE Handbook of the Philosophy of the Social Sciences*, edited by I. C. Jarvie and J. Zamora-Bonilla. Los Angeles: SAGE Publications.

Stueber, Karsten. 2002. The Psychological Basis of Historical Explanation: Reenactment, Simulation, and the Fusion of Horizons. *History and Theory* 41 (1):25–42.

Stueber, Karsten. 2006. *Rediscovering Empathy: Agency, Folk Psychology, and the Human Sciences*. Cambridge: MIT Press.

Stueber, Karsten. 2013. The Causal Autonomy of Reason Explanations and How Not to Worry About Causal Deviance. *Philosophy of the Social Sciences* 43 (1):24–45.

Sugden, Robert. 2000a. Credible Worlds: The Status of Theoretical Models in Economics. *Journal of Economic Methodology* 7 (1):1–31.

Sugden, Robert. 2000b. Team Preferences. *Economics and Philosophy* 16:175–204.

Sugden, Robert. 2006. The Changing Relationship between Theory and Experiment in Economics. *Philosophy of Science* 75 (5):621–632.

Sundstrom, Ronald. 2002a. Race as a Human Kind. *Philosophy and Social Criticism* 28:91–115.

Sundstrom, Ronald. 2002b. 'Racial' Nominalism. *Journal of Social Philosophy* 33 (2):193–210.

Sundstrom, Ronald. 2003. Race and Place: Social Space in the Production of Human Kinds. *Philosophy and Geography* 6 (1):83–95.

Tanney, Julia. 1998. Investigating Cultures: A Critique of Cognitive Anthropology. *The Journal of the Royal Anthropological Institute* 4 (4):669–688.

Tanter, Raymond, and Manus Midlarsky. 1967. A Theory of Revolution. *The Journal of Conflict Resolution* 11 (3):264–280.

Taylor, Charles. 1971. Interpretation and the Sciences of Man. *Review of Metaphysics* 25:1–51.

Taylor, Charles. 1973. Neutrality in Political Science. In *The Philosophy of Social Explanation*, edited by A. Ryan. Oxford: Oxford University Press. Original edition, 1967.

Taylor, M. Clare. 2005. Interviewing. In *Qualitative Research in Health Care*, edited by I. Holloway. New York: Open University Press.

Tedlock, Barbara. 1991. From Participant Observation to the Observation of Participation. *Journal of Anthropological Research* 47 (1):69–94.

Tieffenbach, Emma. 2010. Searle and Menger on Money. *Philosophy of the Social Sciences* 40 (2):191–212.

Tocqueville, Alexis de. 1955. *The Old Regime and the French Revolution*, translated by S. Gilbert. New York: Anchor. Original edition, 1856.

Tollefsen, Deborah Perron. 2002. Collective Intentionality and the Social Sciences. *Philosophy of the Social Sciences* 32 (1):25–50.

Tollefsen, Deborah Perron. 2004. Lets Pretend. *Philosophy of the Social Sciences* 35 (1):75–97.

Tollefsen, Deborah Perron, and Rick Dale. 2011. Naturalizing Joint Action: A Process-Based Approach. *Philosophical Psychology* 25 (3):385–407.

Tomasello, Michael. 2009. *Why We Cooperate*. Cambridge: MIT Press.

Tomasello, Michael, and Malinda Carpenter. 2007. Shared Intentionality. *Developmental Science* 10 (1):121–125.

Tomasello, Michael, Malinda Carpenter, Josep Call, Tanya Behne, and Henrike Moll. 2005. Understanding and Sharing Intentions: The Origins of Cultural Cognition. *Behavioral and Brain Sciences* 28 (5):675–690.

Tooby, John, and Leda Cosmides. 1992. The Psychological Foundations of Culture. In *The Adapted Mind: Evolutionary Psychology and the Generation of Culture*, edited by J. Barkow, L. Cosmides and J. Tooby. Oxford: Oxford University Press.

Trout, J. D. 1998. *Measuring the Intentional World*. Oxford: Oxford University Press.

Tsohatzidis, Savas L. 2007. *Intentional Acts and Institutional Facts*. Dordrecht: Springer.

Tsou, Jonathan Y. 2020. Social construction, HPC Kinds, and the Projectability of Human Categories. *Philosophy of the Social Sciences* 50 (2):115–137.

Tuomela, Raimo. 2002. *The Philosophy of Social Practices*. Cambridge: Cambridge University Press.

Tuomela, Raimo. 2007. *The Philosophy of Sociality: The Shared Point of View*. Oxford: Oxford University Press.

Tuomela, Raimo, and Kaarlo Miller. 1988. We-Intentions. *Philosophical Studies* 53 (3):367–389.

Turner, Stephen. 1994. *The Social Theory of Practices*. Chicago: University of Chicago Press.

Turner, Stephen. 2002. Searle's Social Reality. In *Brains/Practices/Relativism*. Chicago: University of Chicago Press. Original edition, 1999.

Turner, Stephen. 2007. Explaining Normativity. *Philosophy of the Social Sciences* 37 (1):57–73.

Turner, Stephen. 2010. *Explaining the Normative*. Cambridge: Polity Press.

Turner, Stephen, and Mark Risjord (eds.). 2006. Philosophy of Anthropology and Sociology. In *Handbook of Philosophy of Science*, edited by D. Gabbay, J. Woods and P. Thagard. Vol. 15. Amsterdam: Elsevier.

Turner, Stephen, and Paul Roth (eds.). 2003. *The Blackwell Guide to the Philosophy of the Social Sciences*. Malden MA: Blackwell Publications.

Tversky, Amos, and Daniel Kahneman. 1974. Judgment Under Uncertainty: Heuristics and Biases. *Science* 185 (4157):1124–1131.

Urbach, Peter. 1985. Randomization and the Design of Experiments. *Philosophy of Science* 52 (2):256–273.

US Department of Commerce. 2013 [cited August 17, 2013]. Available from www.census.gov/dmd/www/pdf/underus.pdf.

Valsiner, Jaan, ed. 2019. *Social Philosophy of Science for the Social Sciences*. Dordrecht: Springer.

Van Bouwel, Jeroen, ed. 2009. *The Social Sciences and Democracy*. New York: Palgrave Macmillan.

Van Bouwel, Jeroen. 2004. Individualism and Holism, Reduction and Pluralism: A Comment on Kieth Sawyer and Julie Zahle. *Philosophy of the Social Sciences* 34 (4):527–535.

Varela, Charles R., and Rom Harré. 1996. Conflicting Varieties of Realism: Causal Powers and the Problems of Social Structure. *Journal for The Theory of Social Behavior* 26 (3):313–325.

Veit, Walter. 2019. Model Pluralism. *Philosophy of the Social Sciences* 50 (2):91–114.

Viskovatoff, Alex. 2003. Searle, Rationality, and Social Reality. *American Journal of Economics and Sociology* 62 (1):7–44.

von Wright, George Henrik. 1971. *Explanation and Understanding*. Ithaca: Cornell University Press.

von Wright, George Henrik. 1986. Is and Ought. In *Facts and Values*, edited by M. C. Doeser and J. N. Kraay. Dordrecht: Martinus Nijhoff.

Vromen, Jack. 2003. Collective Intentionality, Evolutionary Biology, and Social Realtiy. *Philosophical Explorations: An International Journal for the Philosophy of Mind and Action* 6 (3):251–265.

Watkins, J. W. N. 1953. Ideal Types and Historical Explanation. In *Readings in the Philosophy of Science*, edited by H. Feigl and M. Brodbeck. New York: Appleton Century Crofts.

Watkins, J. W. N. 1970. Imperfect Rationality. In *Explanation in the Behavioral Sciences*, edited by R. Borger and F. Cioffi. Cambridge: Cambridge University Press.

Weber, Eric. 2007. Social Mechanisms, Causal Inference, and the Policy Relevance of Social Science. *Philosophy of the Social Sciences* 37 (3):348–359.

Weber, Max. 1949. 'Objectivity' in Social Science and Social Policy. In *The Methodology of the Social Sciences*. New York: Free Press. Original edition, 1904.

Williams, Bernard. 1985. *Ethics and the Limits of Philosophy*. London: Fontana Press.

Wilson, Bryan R. (ed.). 1970. *Rationality*. Oxford: Basil Blackwell.

Winch, Peter. 1958. *The Idea of a Social Science*. London: Routledge and Kegan Paul.

Winch, Peter. 1964. Understanding a Primitive Society. *American Philosophical Quarterly* 1:307–324.

Wittgenstein, Ludwig. 1953. *Philosophical Investigations*, translated by G. E. M. Anscombe. New York: Macmillan Publishing Company.

Woodward, James. 2003. *Making Things Happen: A Theory of Causal Explanation*. Oxford: Oxford University Press.

Woodward, James. 2007. Causal Models in the Social Sciences. In *Philosophy of Anthropology and Sociology*, edited by S. Turner and M. Risjord. Amsterdam: Elsevier.

Woodward, James. 2009. Experimental Investigations of Social Prefernces. In *Oxford Handbook of Philosophy of Economics*, edited by D. Ross and H. Kincaid. Oxford: Oxford University Press.

Wright, Tommy. 1998. Sampling and Census 2000: The Concepts. *American Scientist* 83 (3):245–253.

Wright, Tommy. 1999. A One-Number Census: Some Related History. *Science, New Series* 283 (5401):491–492.

Wylie, Alison. 1992. The Interplay of Evidential Constraints and Political Interests: Recent Archeological Research on Gender. *American Antiquity* 57 (1):15–35.

Wylie, Alison. 2000. Rethinking Objectivity: Nozick's Neglected Third Option. *International Studies in Philosophy of Science* 41 (1):5–10.

Wylie, Alison. 2006. The Feminism Question in Science: What Does It Mean to 'Do Social Science as a Feminist'? In *Handbook of Feminist Research*, edited by S. Hesse-Bieber. London: Sage Press.

Wylie, Alison, and Lynn Hankinson Nelson. 2007. Coming to Terms with the Values of Science: Insights from Feminist Science Scholarship. In *Value Free Science: Ideal or Illusion?*, edited by H. Kincaid, J. Dupre and A. Wylie. Oxford: Oxford University Press.

Zack, Naomi. 2002. *Philosophy of Science and Race*. London: Routledge.

Zahle, Julie. 2003. The Individualism-Holism Debate on Intertheoretic Reduction and the Argument from Multiple Realization. *Philosophy of the Social Sciences* 33 (1):77–99.

Zahle, Julie. 2007. Holism and Supervenience. In *Philosophy of Anthropology and Sociology*, edited by S. P. Turner and M. W. Risjord. Amsterdam: Elsevier.

Zahle, Julie. 2012. Practical Knowledge and Participant Observation. *Inquiry* 55 (1):50–65.

Zahle, Julie. 2013. Participant Observation and Objectivity in Anthropology. In *New Challenges to Philosophy of Science*, edited by H. Anderson, D. Dieks, W. Gonzalez, T. Uebel and G. Wheeler. Dordrecht: Springer.

Zahle, Julie, and Finn Collin (eds.). 2014. *Rethinking the Individualism-Holism Debate*. Dordrecht: Springer.

Zahle, Julie, and Harold Kincaid. 2019. Why Be a Methodological Individualist? *Synthese* 196 (2):655–675.

Zamora-Bonilla, Jesus. 2012. Why the Social Sciences Are Natural, and Why They Can't. *EMPIRIA: Revista de Metodología de Ciencias Sociales* 23:101–116.

Zuberi, Tukufu. and Bonilla-Silva, Eeduardo (eds.). 2008. *White Logic, White Methods: Racism and Methodology*. Lanham, MD: Rowman & Littlefield Publishers.

Index

9 781032 075877